To

JOHN PHILIP ENGLISH

THE STORY
OF THE
SALEM WITCH TRIALS

"We Walked In Clouds and Could Not See Our Way."

Bryan F. Le Beau

Creighton University

 Prentice Hall, Upper Saddle River, New Jersey, 07458

Library of Congress Cataloging-in-Publication Data

Le Beau, Bryan F.
    The story of the Salem witch trials : "We walked in clouds and
could not see our way." / Bryan F. Le Beau.
        p.   cm.
    Includes bibliographical references and index.
    ISBN 0-13-442542-1
    1. Trials (Witchcraft)—Massachusetts—Salem. 2. Salem
    (Massachusetts)—History—Sources.   I. Title.
KFM2478.8.W5L43 1998
345.744′50288—dc21   97-5456
                                           CIP

Editor-in-Chief: Charlyce Jones Owen
Production Editor: Jean Lapidus
Prepress and Manufacturing Buyer: Lynn Pearlman
Copy Editor: Michele Lansing
Photo Research: Rona Tuccillo
Cover Design: Rosemarie Votta
Cover Image: A painting by T. H. Matteson, titled *Examination of a Witch, 1855.*
Photographer: Mark Sexton. From the Peabody Essex Museum, neg. #17292.
Sub-title: from John Hale, *A Modest Inquiry into the Nature of Witchcraft* (1702). (See
Bibliography)

This book was set in 10.5/12.5 Century Schoolbook by BookMasters, Inc.
and was printed and bound by Courier Companies, Inc.
The cover was printed by Phoenix Color Corp.

 © 1998 by Prentice-Hall, Inc.
Simon & Schuster/A Viacom Company
Upper Saddle River, New Jersey 07458

Printed in the United States of America
10 9 8 7 6 5 4 3 2 1

ISBN 0-13-442542-1

PRENTICE-HALL INTERNATIONAL (UK) LIMITED, *London*
PRENTICE-HALL OF AUSTRALIA PTY. LIMITED, *Sydney*
PRENTICE-HALL CANADA INC., *Toronto*
PRENTICE-HALL HISPANOAMERICANA, S.A., *Mexico*
PRENTICE-HALL OF INDIA PRIVATE LIMITED, *New Delhi*
PRENTICE-HALL OF JAPAN, INC., *Tokyo*
SIMON & SCHUSTER ASIA PTE. LTD., *Singapore*
EDITORA PRENTICE-HALL DO BRASIL, LTDA., *Rio de Janeiro*

Contents

Preface

Between June 10 and September 22, 1692, nineteen people were hanged for witchcraft in Salem, Massachusetts. One man was pressed to death, and over 150 others from twenty-four towns and villages went to jail, where four adults and one infant died and some remained until the following May. Compared to other witch-hunts in the Western world, it was a minor affair, or as one historian has put it, "a small incident in the history of a great superstition."[1] It was the largest of its kind in the British colonies of North America, however, and it has never lost its grip on either the popular or scholarly imagination.

Historians often protest that too much time has been spent and too many pages have been written on the Salem witch trials, but they nevertheless continue to fill library shelves with books on the subject and to engage in sometimes heated debate over its causes. And there is no indication that any of this is likely to end soon. Nor should it, as the Salem witch trials remain one of the most interesting, indeed dramatic, as well as meaningful, episodes in history. Still, we wonder how such a tragic event could have ever occurred.

It would be impossible to review all of the answers historians have offered to this question. The most persuasive have pointed to the economic, political, social, and religious turmoil into which New England was plunged at the end of the seventeenth century; to New Englanders' beliefs that the turmoil from which they suffered had resulted from their fall from grace as God's chosen people, thereby making them vulnerable to a "conspiracy of witches and the Devil;" to the mistreatment of the Salem village youngsters who first fell victim to some form of psychic, if not spiritual, affliction, promoting uncontrollable fear on the part of some and fraud on the part of others; to the Court's inappropriate use of evidence in hearings for the accused against which there was hardly any defense; to inordinate pressure brought to bear upon the accused to confess and name their accomplices in order to escape almost certain execution; and, finally, to the failure of authorities to act earlier and more decisively when serious questions were raised regarding the conduct of the Court. These explanations are central to this book.

As far as it is possible in any single volume, this book provides a synthesis of the major schools of thought on the Salem witch trials. It goes to considerable length to place the events of 1692 into a historical context, both of seventeenth-century New England and of the Great European Witch-hunt, which lasted some three centuries. Without such context, when viewed in isolation, the events of 1692 are impossible to understand. It employs a narrative format that was once popular among historians but that has fallen out of favor. Such an approach is intended to make the subject more accessible to the reader, to recapture some of the drama that has held people spellbound for so long, and to suggest yet another way of looking at the event. As Larry Gragg has reminded us, to fully appreciate what happened in 1692, we must "explore the particular decisions made by the individuals involved and their consequences."[2] When all other avenues of interpretation have been exhausted, we are left with the fact that individuals and individual decisions matter.

The first chapter of this book provides a brief history of European witchcraft. It seeks its origins in pagan antiquity and in the perspective Christians developed about the Devil during the first centuries of its formation. It shows that European witchcraft was mostly a creation of the Early Modern Period, or from the fifteenth through the seventeenth centuries, and that it was in this period that the practice of witchcraft came to be seen not only as dangerous but also heretical and threatening to church and state. The concluding pages of chapter one focus on witch-hunts in England, in reference to which the most direct comparisons can be made to developments in New England.

Chapter two narrows our focus to seventeenth-century America. After some brief allusions to the fate of supposed witches in the Spanish, French, and Dutch, as well as other British colonies, it discusses the treatment of witches in New England. Two points are made. First, that what was commonly believed to be witchcraft was practiced in seventeenth-century New England, as it was elsewhere in the Western world. Second, although what happened in 1692 far exceeded anything that occurred before in New England, there were precedents for the Salem witch trials. The chapter concludes with some discussion of those precedents, as well as of the state of affairs in the second half of the seventeenth century that led colonists to conclude that they were the victims of diabolical assault.

Chapter three discusses the origins of the Salem witch trials. It begins by exploring the difficulties Salem village faced in the closing decades of the seventeenth century. It explains the problems the Reverend Samuel Parris had with his congregation and community, and the goings-on in his home during the winter of 1691–1692 that sparked the flames that consumed Salem village. It concludes with an account of the initial terrors of the young women of Salem village and the first charges of witchcraft they brought against the most likely suspects.

Chapters four through six provide an overview of the principal arrests and preliminary examinations of those taken into custody before the Salem town magistrates. They show how what might have been just another local and limited scare, similar to the dozens that had preceded it in seventeenth-century New England, became the region's only true witch-hunt. Emphasized are key hearings, major developments, decisive decisions, and important turning points. Shown is how those charged by the young girls who led the prosecution came increasingly from higher rungs on the social ladder. And, included for comparative purposes, chapter six contains an account of developments in Andover, Massachusetts, the site of the single largest witch-hunt outside of Salem.

Chapters seven through nine cover what were actually the Salem witch trials. It is at this juncture in the story that, although the preliminary hearings continued, the Court of Oyer and Terminer took center stage. Chapter seven shows how William Phips, the recently appointed Royal Governor of Massachusetts, established the Court of Oyer and Terminer and charged it with hearing those cases that had been brought against suspected witches by the Salem magistrates. A substantial sampling of those trials follows, concluding in chapter nine with an explanation of the Court's demise in October 1692. It shows how a newly appointed court, although constituted almost entirely by the same judges, was led by different rules of procedure from an unrelenting record of conviction to an equally impressive string of acquittals. It concludes with some discussion of the steps Governor Phips took to end the trials altogether and to release those awaiting trial or execution from jail.

Chapter ten describes the aftermath of the Salem witch trials, the wreckage strewn in their wake, and the attempts taken to make amends. It considers the fate of Salem village and its struggle to heal itself; the confessions that were offered by many, but not all, of those responsible for what had happened; and the attempts made by the convicted and their families to settle outstanding legal and financial matters. As this chapter suggests, Salem's ordeal did not end with the adjourning of the Court; it lingered for decades.

Finally, a brief epilogue provides some perspective on witch-hunts after the Salem witch trials. It attempts to explain the rapid decline in the number of trials in Europe and New England after 1692, as well as reasons for the growing disbelief in witches. It concludes with some remarks about the continued popularity among Americans of the Salem witch trials and the parallels drawn by some between the Salem witch trials and what appear to be regularly occurring witch-hunts in the United States ever since.

Three final points should be made concerning documentation and the use of language in the text. First, Paul Boyer and Stephen Nissenbaum have gathered, in *The Salem Witchcraft Papers* (1977), the verbatim transcripts of nearly all of the surviving legal documents of the Salem witch trials. It is an invaluable collection, certainly far more accessible to the reader than the various archives in which the records are located. Therefore, nearly all references in this study to legal docu-ments are made to the Boyer and Nissenbaum collection.

Second, the author has made a concerted effort to let the actors in this drama speak for themselves. Wherever possible, he has either quoted directly from the record or carefully paraphrased it to retain the flavor of their remarks. He has occasionally made slight adjustments in spelling and punctuation in order to render the remarks more accessible to the modern reader, as well as provide a consistency where it is generally lacking. The records of the Salem witch trials are typically, for their time, inconsistent in both.

Third, the author has chosen to use the words "possession" and "affliction" to describe different forms of the phenomenon of witchcraft. Various historians have reminded us that currently popular mixed usage confuses the point that, for people in the seventeenth century, the two were not the same.[3] In simplest terms, seventeenth-century believers identified the victims of witchcraft as being either possessed or afflicted (alternately bewitched or obsessed). The possessed's thoughts and actions, it was believed, were directly controlled by the Devil. In the case of the afflicted, demonic power was mediated by a witch. The possessed, it was assumed, had brought about their possession, or opened themselves up to it, by certain wicked deeds. The afflicted were innocent victims. And if the possessed could be cured, it would be by prayer, whereas the afflicted could be healed only by identifying and eliminating the offending witch or witches.

During the Great European Witch-hunt, there were comparatively few cases of possession, but where such diagnoses were reached the search for cause ended. Much more common, no doubt supported by those closest to the victims, were cases of affliction. Suspicions of affliction usually elicited two responses on the part of civil and clerical leaders: identification and elimination of the one or more witches responsible for the affliction; and, especially in large-scale witch-hunts, soul searching as to why God had allowed the Devil to afflict, or assault, the innocent party or parties, or even the community. As David Harley has pointed out, if the first people who exhibited signs of diabolical influence in Salem village in the early months of 1692 had been diagnosed as possessed, the course of events would have been quite different. But, that was not the case.[4].

ACKNOWLEDGEMENTS

Any writer on the Salem witch trials is deeply indebted to the large number of historians who have contributed so much to our understanding of the event. They are too numerous to list, but I thank them nonetheless.

In the writing of this history of the Salem witch trials, I am particularly indebted to the helpful suggestions of David Katzman, Professor and Chair of American Studies at the University of Kansas; Steven Watts, Associate Professor of History at the University of Missouri; Joyce Goodfriend, Professor of History at the University of Denver; Ronald Johnson, Professor of History and Chair of American Studies at Georgetown University; James Farrell, Patricia Boldt Distinguished Teaching Professor of Humanities at St. Olaf College; Sheila Skemp, Associate Professor of History at the University of Mississippi; Maurice Crouse, Professor of History at the University of Memphis; and Glenn Linden, Associate Professor of History at Southern Methodist University.

I am also indebted to the librarians at the James Duncan Phillips Library of the Peabody and Essex Museum and at Creighton University's Reinert/Alumni Library for their valuable research assistance; to the editorial staff at Prentice Hall for its work in preparing this volume for publication; and to Maryellen Read, Secretary for Creighton University's Center for the Study of Religion and Society for her capable assistance in preparing the manuscript.

Bryan F. Le Beau
Omaha, Nebraska

1

"A Biography of a Terrible But Perfectly Normal Superstition"

The people of Salem believed in witches. It is a simple proposition, sometimes difficult for the modern mind to accept, but it is essential for our understanding of what happened in 1692. What they believed was part of a complex tradition, commonly referred to as European witchcraft, which had been formulated two centuries earlier. As George Lyman Kittredge said, what happened in Salem in 1692 was neither an aberration nor an isolated event; it was "a mere incident, [a] brief and transitory episode in the biography of a terrible, but perfectly normal superstition."[1]

Today, the term "witchcraft" encompasses a wide variety of phenomena. In the seventeenth-century West, however, it meant something quite specific. The word witchcraft was derived from the Old English verb *wiccian,* which referred to the art of bewitching, casting spells, or manipulating the forces of nature in any supernatural way. By the fifteenth century, however, religious and civil leaders came to insist that such activities were not possible without the assistance of the Devil. When that association was made, the stage was set for the massive witch-hunts that shook the Western world for nearly three centuries.[2]

THE ORIGINS OF EUROPEAN WITCHCRAFT

The people of seventeenth-century Europe pictured witches, mostly women, as rising from their beds in the dark of the night to attend their Sabbat, the witches' version of the Christian Sabbath ceremony, presided over by the Devil. Those who lived nearby went on foot; others flew on animals, brooms, or stools to cellars, caves, or isolated fields. If neophytes were present, they began with an initiation ceremony, wherein the Devil obliged initiates to keep the secrets of the cult, sign his book, and renounce their Christian faith, sealing their apostasy by stamping or excreting on a crucifix and expressing their adoration for their new master by kissing his buttocks!

Following the initiation, all of those assembled enacted a parody of the eucharistic feast—eating, drinking, and offering to the Devil the bodies of infants, usually provided by those recently initiated into the cult of the Devil. When the ceremony ended, the torches were extinguished and all engaged in a promiscuous orgy, at the completion of which the witches took ritual leave of their master and returned home to their unsuspecting families, friends, and neighbors.

It took fifteen hundred years to construct this image, or what is referred to as the "cumulative concept of witchcraft," drawing upon several different sources. The first images came from the ancient world where, for example, the most terrible of Sumerian, Hebrew, and Graeco-Roman demons were described as frigid, barren female spirits with wings and taloned hands and feet. Often accompanied by serpents, such creatures swept shrieking through the night, seducing sleeping men or drinking their blood, attacking sleeping children and their mothers or nurses.[3]

Greco-Roman sorcerers, mostly women it was believed, met at night in isolated places, in caves or deserted fields, where they tore apart and devoured black lambs and clawed the ground with their taloned fingers, evoking spirits of the underworld. Usually they were led by a male priest and the image of a dark, shaggy, and horned goat, the symbol of fertility, in rituals that included wine-drinking, ecstatic dancing, and animal sacrifice. And although at first they were seen as sources of either good or evil, in time they became almost exclusively associated with the powers of darkness.[4]

Belief in Satan (from the Hebrew) or the Devil (from the Greek) as the sole source of evil on earth, however, is largely a Christian phenomenon. The Hebrew Bible took for granted the existence of malevolent supernatural beings. It identified them as "the satan," meaning opponent or adversary, but they were nonetheless angelic members of God's council to whom God assigned the task of afflicting or test-ing man's loyalty, as in the case of Job in the Old Testament. More-over, the satan was not an independent being; he merely served God's purpose.[5]

This classical view of evil changed at the start of the Common Era (CE), when dissident Jews redefined Satan and his connection to the world. They began to portray him as a more independent creature, as well as the leader of their enemies. They identified themselves as God's chosen people, separate from other nations that they often considered their enemies. In the second century before the Common Era, however, dissidents found an enemy within their own ranks, among their fellow Jews. Those Jews who had assumed the ways of their foreign rulers be-came the intimate enemy, as opposed to the alien enemy. They were la-beled apostates and charged with having been seduced by the power of evil, the Prince of Darkness, or Satan.[6]

This redefinition of Satan and his identification with the intimate enemy was adopted by those dissident Jews of the first century CE who chose to follow the teachings of Jesus. Satan stood at the center of the New Testament, wherein the kingdom of God is continually at war with the kingdom of Satan, and Satan rules over a kingdom of dark-ness and gathers to him all God's opposition, including infidels, heretics, and sorcerers. When the early Christians adopted that binary world and saw themselves as the children of God, they labeled those who had rejected Christ's teachings as the children of the Devil.[7]

Two points should be made at this stage. First, it is important to note that prior to the Great European Witch-hunt, fear of the Devil and his minions was kept in check by confidence in the power of the Church to control them. Early Christians believed that the Devil's power over men, although great, was limited; unlike God, he was not an independ-ent being or eternal principle. He could not act contrary to God's will, and perhaps more important for our purposes, he could not force men and women to sin against their will. Those crucial limitations were badly shaken, if not lost, by the fifteenth century.

Second, although the foregoing points to what could be seen as two patterns of belief in witches, the witch as outsider and the witch as insider, this book focuses almost exclusively on the second. That is not to say that both were not present in the Great European Witch-hunt—Europeans hunted Jews and New Englanders hunted Native Americans—but that the second dominated the first. Indeed, the Great European Witch-hunt can best be explained as an attack on insiders, or the intimate enemy. In the great majority of cases, Christians found witches among their Christian neighbors.[8]

THE DEVELOPMENT OF EUROPEAN WITCHCRAFT

If European witchcraft employed ancient images that were largely universal, Christianity infused those images with unique and potentially devastating elements. Those elements were widespread in the Western world by the end of the fourth century, but they were not fully developed until the fifteenth. Moreover, contrary to what is popularly believed, European witchcraft was not the product solely of that ignorance or superstition usually associated with the common people. Rather, it was the province as well of the literate of both the ecclesiastical and secular worlds, of theologians and lay scholars. As Brian Levack said, "the Great European Witch-hunt could not have taken place until the members of the ruling elites of European countries, especially those men who controlled the operation of the judicial machinery, subscribed to the various beliefs regarding the diabolical activities of witches."[9]

The people of medieval Europe believed in sorcery or magic and accused their neighbors of doing them harm if they believed those neighbors had employed such powers to hurt them. They needed no further explanation. Nevertheless, churchmen and other scholars convinced them not only that such practices were pagan, but also that they were the result of a compact with the Devil. Augustine, among the most influential of early Christian theologians, as early as the fourth century argued that pagan religion and sorcery had been invented by the Devil for the purpose of luring humanity from Christian truth. He allowed that some of the supposed effects of sorcery were illusions, but that others were real and both were works of the Devil. Taking a page from the Greco-Roman world, he insisted that to be effective, sorcerers summoned pagan spirits or demons, all of whom served the Devil. Pagan religion, then, as well as sorcerers, Augustine and subsequent Church fathers insisted, must be eradicated; they served the Devil by frustrating Christ's plan for the salvation of the world.[10]

The Church not only opposed all non-Christian faiths it encountered in Europe, it also condemned all pagan beliefs and rituals retained by its converts, a not uncommon phenomenon. In 743 the Synod of Rome outlawed offerings to pagan deities, and in 744 the Council of Leptinnes drew up an extensive "List of Superstitions," which it prohibited. The council approved a baptismal formula wherein the catechumen renounced all "works of the demon, and all his words," to wit it mentioned Thor, Odin, and other northern European pagan deities. In 829 the Synod of Paris reasoned that since the Bible (see Exodus 22:18) decreed that they should not be permitted to live, kings should have the right to punish sorcerers severely. And, indeed, kings did assume such powers, even executing sorcerers where their incantations resulted in death.[11]

The most important and revealing of the early documents on witchcraft was the Canon *Episcopi*. The Canon *Episcopi*, written by Regino of Prüm of France in about 900, condemned "wicked women . . . who believe that they ride out at night on beasts with Diana, the pagan goddess." Much as Augustine had once reasoned, Regino explained that such visions were more imagined than real, likely a remnant of pre-Christian folk beliefs, but that they were nonetheless the doings of the Devil, thrust by him into the minds of the faithless. It read:

> Some wicked women are perverted by the Devil and led astray by illusions and fantasies induced by demons. . . . Such fantasies are thrust into the minds of faithless people, not by God, but by the Devil. . . . In this form he captures and enslaves the mind of a miserable woman and transforms himself into the shapes of various different people. He shows her deluded mind strange things and unknown people, and leads it on weird journeys. It is only the mind that does this, but faithless people believe that these things happen to the body as well.

The Canon *Episcopi* rejected the reality of people's perception of witches, but it nevertheless presented the first written detailed description of that perception, which by the fifteenth century was assumed to be real.[12]

Two points in the Canon *Episcopi* will be of particular importance in our discussion of the Salem witch trials. First, it assumed that the Devil could possess only faithless people. Second, it insisted that witches could only serve the Devil of their own free will, giving rise to the idea of a pact that was the central tenet of European witchcraft. The belief that human beings could sell their souls to the Devil became widespread in the ninth century, when various legends regarding pacts were circulated. In some legends, the person was saved from such a pact through the realization of his or her error, confession, and divine intervention. But by the fifteenth century, that element of the story was largely lost; a pact with the Devil sealed a person's fate once and for all.[13]

The first trials resembling those of witches yet to come occurred in central and southern France and northern Italy in the eleventh and twelfth centuries. Defendants were charged with a form of heresy known as Dualism; that is, they proclaimed the forces of good and evil equal and eternal. They taught that the Spirit of Evil, the Devil, had created the material world to entrap the spirit, which was God's creation. What is more important, however, is that the accused were believed to have been enticed into their heretical beliefs by the Devil. They were charged with having participated in nocturnal rituals presided over by the Devil, wherein they engaged in orgies, renounced Christ, desecrated the crucifix, and paid homage to the Devil. They called up evil spirits, it was believed, and killed and cremated children conceived at previous orgies, using their ashes to blaspheme the eucharist. The Church deemed them heretics, silenced them through the Albigensian Crusade and a Court of Inquisition, and burned many at the stake.[14]

Such trials became more frequent over the course of the next few centuries, but once again two points need to be clarified. First, although precedent-setting trials occurred as early as the eleventh century, the Great European Witch-hunt did not begin for another 400 years. It did not take place during the Middle Ages, or the so-called Dark Ages, but during the more enlightened Renaissance. In fact, Renaissance culture contributed to the Great European Witch-hunt.

It is true that the Renaissance was characterized by both a more mechanized view of the universe and a contempt for medieval learning, including its view of the Devil, but Renaissance thinkers did not deny the Devil's existence. They rejected the idea that magical occurrences were necessarily the work of the Devil, but they continued to allow that some people could control the powers of the universe. And, finally, many learned Renaissance humanists practiced magic, thereby lending it a measure of respectability. Renaissance intellectuals may have been talking about a learned magic, rather than witchcraft, but such fine points of distinction were understandably lost on the less well-educated and comparatively more superstitious masses.[15]

Second, the earlier-noted Inquisition, though important, did not play as large a role in the Great European Witch-hunt as is often assumed. The Inquisition was established by the Church in a series of papal decrees between 1227 and 1235 to deal with the crime of heresy. In persecuting witches, courts of inquisition not only confirmed the connection between sorcery and heresy, but they also provided the means, or mechanism, by which witches could be more efficiently prosecuted. In 1198, Pope Innocent III ordered the execution of those who persisted in heresy after having been convicted and excommunicated. In 1231, Pope Gregory IX mandated that heretics, after condemnation, be delivered to secular authorities to be burned at the stake, and, in 1252, Innocent IV authorized the use of torture by the Inquisition. In 1275, at Toulouse, France, the first witch was burned, and in time the Inquisition provided what might be termed the inquisitors' manual for the examination of witches. But by the fifteenth century, during the Great European Witch-hunt, most cases were tried in secular courts of law.[16]

The Great European Witch-hunt

The Great European Witch-hunt consisted of hundreds of separate hunts involving anywhere from one to thousands of individuals. The hunts occurred at different places and different times, peaking in the years from 1580 to 1630. Each hunt has its own history and should be studied separately for a more complete understanding of the larger phenomenon. All that can be offered here is a brief summary of what happened.

The Great European Witch-hunt began in France. In 1428, secular judges at Valais tried over 100 individuals for worshipping the Devil and employing sorcery to various nefarious ends, from causing hailstones to ruining crops to murdering people. From 1428 to 1447, 110 women and 57 men were executed for witchcraft in Dauphiné.[17] The most commonly agreed upon starting point, however, was in the French city of Arras, where, between 1459 and 1462, thirty-four people were accused of witchcraft and twelve were executed. All were charged with devil worship, with only one prosecuted for doing harm, or maleficia. All cases resulted from accusations lodged against one man who was tortured into confessing and naming others. They in turn were tortured, confessed, and implicated still others. The trials ended only when local merchants, upset with the chaos the trials had created (which was no doubt bad for business), appealed to the Duke of Burgundy.

The Duke solicited the opinion of the theology faculty at the University of Louvain, but the faculty could not agree on the reality of Sabbats, central to the Arras trials. The Duke sent an observer to the court, and his mere presence was sufficient to cause a halt to the arrests. Four more of the previously accused were tried and convicted, but only one was executed before the Parlement of Paris, on the appeal of one of the convicted, which put an end to the trials and ordered most of those jailed released. The Bishop of Arras, who had been in Rome but returned to his diocese at that point, freed the rest. In 1491, the Parlement investigated the Arras trials, declared all of the accused innocent, pardoned the convicted, and ordered the erection of a large cross at the place of execution, paid for by fines placed on local prosecutors.[18]

Three witches burned alive from a German Broadside, circa 1555. In Europe, convicted witches were often burned alive. This 1555 woodcut shows the execution of three people, with a demon withdrawing backwards from the mouth of one of the victims. Stock Montage, Inc./Historical Pictures Collection.

The surge in witch trials precipitated the appearance of a prominent group of witch-hunters, the best known of which was the German Dominican Heinrich Kramer, or Institoris (his Latin name). In 1474, the Vatican appointed him inquisitor in southern Germany, and he presided over nearly fifty executions for witchcraft in the diocese of Constance alone, between 1481 and 1486. When faced with resistance from local ecclesiastical and secular authorities, he persuaded Pope Innocent VIII to issue the bull *Summis Desiderantes Affectibus (Wishing with Greatest Concern,* 1484) in which the pope offered his full support for Kramer's work and called on German officials to cooperate with him in the hunt.[19]

In 1486, Kramer and fellow Dominican Jacob Sprenger, inquisitor for the Rhineland, used Innocent VIII's bull as the preface to their *Malleus Maleficarum (The Hammer of Witches),* the major treatise in the West on witchcraft.[20] Described as "a case-book manual for inquisitors," the *Malleus* was essentially a synthesis of arguments for, and examples of, European witchcraft as it had developed thus far. It was reprinted in twenty-nine separate editions in Italy, France, and Germany between 1489 and 1669, and it was read by Protestants and Catholics alike.

The *Malleus* established the reality of witchcraft by defining and explaining its nature. It outlined its effects, showed it to be a corporate rather than a solitary activity, and identified its practitioners as being mostly female. It described what witches did, and it set out the procedures to be used against them, whether in an ecclesiastical or a secular court. And through its influence and that of other similar manuals, the list of questions asked of suspected witches throughout Europe became uniform: Who seduced you into signing a pact with the Devil? Why did you give in? What did the Devil promise you? When did you make a pact with the Devil? What was the Devil like? What was it like to have sexual relations with him?[21]

Kramer and Sprenger identified the four essential points of witchcraft: renunciation of Christianity, devotion to the Devil, offering unbaptized children to the Devil, and engaging in orgies that included intercourse with the Devil. They described witches as typically shifting their shapes, flying through the air, and abusing Christian sacraments. But just as important, Kramer and Sprenger pictured a secret society of Devil-worshiping witches, directed by the Devil in a cosmic plot against Christian society. To be sure, the Devil could operate without human assistance, but he preferred not to, as it proved to be more effective. Therefore, the authors concluded, all witches were to be found and executed.[22]

As important as inquisitors such as Kramer and Sprenger were, most of the trials that occurred in the Great European Witch-hunt took place in secular courts. By the fifteenth century, witchcraft had become a civil, even a capital, crime. The result was a more effective and efficient witch-hunt than would have transpired if left to the Church. Witchcraft continued to be a crime punishable by death (burning at the stake on the Continent, hanging in England and New England), and on the Continent, civil courts continued to use torture to obtain confessions, but procedural matters were more clearly defined and regulated by law.[23]

The courts designed tests by which guilt or innocence could be established. They commonly employed the ordeal, whereby, for example, the accused would hold a hot iron for a period of time. Her hand was then properly bandaged and if the skin healed within a few days, it was seen as God's sign that she was innocent. They also used the "swimming test," wherein the accused, after being bound hand and foot, was thrown into the water. If she sank, God's creature water had accepted her, and she was deemed innocent and hauled ashore. If she floated, it had rejected her, and she was condemned. And, strip searches were ordered in search of the Devil's mark, a sign of the pact, and of "witches' teats," used to nurture familiars.[24]

Also important for the better prosecution of witches, a new court system evolved in Europe quite independent of the witch trials. An inquisitorial system of criminal procedure replaced the older accusatorial system. Under the accusatorial system, private parties both initiated charges against and prosecuted individuals. The judge's job was to weigh the evidence and pass judgment. If those who brought charges failed to make their case, however, they were subject to criminal prosecution. Under the inquisitorial system, which was in place throughout most of Europe by the sixteenth century (England being the notable exception), charges could be brought by civil officials. Upon receipt of complaints, or even without formal charges having been brought, they could order investigations and arrests, and they were immune to the threat of countersuit.[25]

The inquisitorial system facilitated the prosecution of witches from the top down and enhanced the power of judges, who assumed nearly complete control of the witch-hunting process. They could decide which cases to prosecute and which to ignore. They controlled the use of torture, determined guilt or innocence, and passed sentences. That is not to say that protective measures for defendants did not exist; in fact, they were considerable. The testimony of two eyewitnesses, for example, was usually required for conviction, but those who could give eyewitness accounts of diabolism were often suspected of being the witch's accomplice. Therefore, they were not likely to testify, unless they had been charged as well.

The use of torture was regulated. Generally, judges could not order torture unless there was sufficient evidence to merit a presumption of guilt, in which case its purpose was to ascertain the facts of the crime and the names of other conspirators. The severity of torture was to be limited only to what was necessary to achieve its desired ends, from sleep deprivation to thumb screws to use of the rack, and it was not to cause death. To guard against forced confessions, testimony taken in the torture chamber was not admissible. Defendants had to confess "freely" outside of the chamber and within twenty-four hours, and those who recanted their confessions were not to be repeatedly tortured.[26]

The results of torture, however, were predictable. In one study of witch trials in Lorraine, 90 percent of the accused confessed. In Baden-Baden and Ellsangen, the percentage was even higher, leading in the latter case to the implication of as many as twenty-nine others.[27] Some confessed without torture or inordinate pressure, convinced they were in fact witches and in need of saving their souls through confession. And there were those who confessed and/or implicated others to escape the stake, but that tactic was seldom successful. There were only a few cases, largely in the Inquisition in southern Europe, where confession was seen as a reconciliation with God, thereby meriting a pardon.

Protective measures were of limited value when emotions ran high, which was often the case. At the height of the Great European Witch-hunt, regulations concerning torture and other matters were often ignored. Witchcraft was regarded as an exceptional crime, posing a threat to church and state, and many judges felt little compunction in ignoring the law. This was especially true in local courts, wherein the majority of cases were heard, and which operated with a large measure of independence from what central authority existed at the time.[28]

Belief in the diabolical conspiracies of witches was a prerequisite for the Great European Witch-hunt, but social forces provided the impetus. As numerous as they were, only certain areas of Europe experienced witch-hunts, and those areas were commonly characterized by the high anxiety that accompanies political, social, economic, and religious problems. In fact, although it is difficult to measure, historians have argued persuasively that witch-hunts were the product of the intense anxiety such problems commonly evoked, including plagues, famines, and wars. In particular, they have pointed to the repercussions of religious strife in the sixteenth and seventeenth centuries, as well as to dislocations that accompanied Europe's passage into the Early Modern Period.[29]

In brief, although the Protestant Reformation rejected much Church doctrine, Protestants did not distance themselves immediately from the Roman Church's teachings on witchcraft. In time, the Protestant emphasis on God's sovereignty made its adherents more skeptical of aspects of witchcraft, but at least at the start they were equally zealous. As Richard Weisman has written about the early years of Protestantism, "the more Protestants elevated divine will beyond the range of human manipulation, the more desperate and urgent their struggle against any resurgence of interest in magical practices became." The more they enhanced the powers of the Devil, the more they left the people defenseless. Not surprisingly, then, historians have found the same pragmatic attitudes toward the use of charms and incantations after the Reformation as before. And, although irreversibly divided and hostile to one another in most other ways, Protestant and Catholic leaders collaborated, albeit unofficially, in hunting witches.[30]

Catholics and Protestants alike interpreted the Reformation—a great civil war for Christians—as another example of the Devil's presence in the world, and they responded with even greater emphasis on eradicating remaining superstitious beliefs and pagan practices. Luther called for the burning of witches as heretics who had made pacts with the Devil, whether or not they had actually harmed anyone, and although Calvin seemed to have been less concerned with witches than his followers, Calvinists were as zealous as any in hunting witches. The most extensive witchcraft prosecutions in Catholic French-and Catholic and Protestant German-speaking regions occurred between 1550 and 1650, after the Reformation, but still in the wake of the turmoil it created. Moreover, witch-hunting was most intense in Germany, Switzerland, Poland, Scotland, and along the borders of France, all of which were religiously heterogeneous. Religiously homogeneous and more secure states, like Spain and Italy, experienced far lower levels of activity.[31]

Historians have also suggested that some of the economic, social, and demographic developments that accompanied Europe's move into the Early Modern Period added to the tensions that provoked witchcraft accusations. The transition from a dominantly rural agrarian to an increasingly urban commercial, capitalist economy bred inflation, increased poverty by providing for a rapidly growing population that taxed a less rapidly expanding supply of resources, and instigated changes in the structure of the family, including a larger number of un-attached females.[32]

When combined with the religious and political struggles of the period, such social and economic changes created a mood of anxiety in all segments of society that made people more sensitive to the supposed dangers of witchcraft. As Brian Levack said, the Early Modern Period was one of the "most psychically disturbed periods in human history," and that anxiety created a mood both among the elite and the common people that greatly encouraged witch-hunts. Among the elite, it encouraged a tendency to attribute the turmoil, instability, and confusion they saw in the world to the Devil and to the activities of his witches. Among the common people, attacks on witches helped relieve their pain and anxiety. In sum, witches became scapegoats for the entire community.[33]

The reader may well object that many historical periods experience substantial change and consequent anxiety, but that they do not all resort to witch-hunts. Historians have offered no definitive response to this objection, except to say that change in the Early Modern Period was truly exceptional, unleashing a number of highly destructive civil rebellions and international conflicts, and that perhaps those communities that did resort to witch-hunts were less capable of coping with that change. Why some communities were less able to cope requires an investigation of local conditions beyond the scope of this brief account, but it will be undertaken in the case of Salem village.[34]

In the meantime, it should be noted that witch-hunts in the Early Modern Period tended to follow three patterns. Although less dramatic and well-known, the most common involved the prosecution of fewer than three people. Medium-sized hunts, involving five to ten witches, occurred less frequently. These small panics were most common in French-speaking Switzerland, but they could be found in Germany and Scotland as well. Torture was a major factor in such cases, resulting in the naming of names, but in the case of medium hunts the list of the accused did not go beyond the names of those previously suspected of such activity.[35]

Finally, there were the infamous, though far less common, full-blown hunts that occurred mostly in the sixteenth and seventeenth centuries. They claimed anywhere from dozens to hundreds of victims and were characterized by panic or hysteria. They were most common in Germany, but nearly every country experienced at least one, and regardless of where they occurred, they tended to follow what has become known as the "classic" pattern. They were chain reactions, wherein successive victims, perhaps in a desperate attempt to escape execution, named others, including many never before suspected of any such activity. In Trier, for example, during the 1580s and 1590s, 306 accused witches named about 1,500 others, while at Rouen, in 1670, nine individuals alone initiated 525 indictments.[36]

The absence of complete records makes it difficult to establish the exact number of cases or executions during the Great European Witch-hunt. Historians have verified over 10,000 cases for the 250-year period beginning in the mid-fifteenth century, but estimates of actual total prosecutions vary greatly, venturing even into the millions. Such figures, of course, are exaggerated; a more responsible reading of the record suggests that the number of prosecutions was between 110,000 and 180,000, with perhaps 60,000 to 100,000 executions.[37]

Prosecution and execution rates varied from place to place. Perhaps as many as 75 percent of witchcraft prosecutions occurred in Germany, France, Switzerland, and the Low Countries, an area encompassing roughly 50 percent of the entire population of Europe. During the early years of the Great European Witch-hunt, most prosecutions took place in France, especially along its borders, but by the late sixteenth century, Germany took the lead. In the end, perhaps half of all of those prosecuted in the Great European Witch-hunt lived in German-speaking lands, with the next heaviest concentrations occurring nearby in Poland, Switzerland, and the borderlands of France. Similarly, execution rates were highest in those areas, reaching and even exceeding 90 percent of those tried in parts of France, Germany, and Poland at the peak of their witch-hunting activity.[38]

Witch-hunting in Spain and Italy lagged much further behind. In Spain, from 1580 to 1650, about 3,500 witches were tried. In Italy, the numbers were higher, but, excluding the Italian-speaking Alpine regions along the Swiss border, it is difficult to find evidence for more than 500 executions, a percentage far lower than other regions.[39]

It is difficult to explain the comparative reluctance in Italy and Spain to execute witches during the Great European Witch-hunt, but some points are clear and important to note. First, the cumulative concept of witchcraft described earlier as common in northern Europe did not take hold in the south. The *Malleus Maleficarum,* for example, was not well-received, perhaps, at least in the case of Italy, because of the strength of Humanism within intellectual circles. Second, in all their severity and cruelty, the Spanish and Roman Inquisitions were rigorous in following trial procedures. Unlike most civil courts of the time, the Church made provision for legal counsel; it furnished defendants with copies of charges and evidence used against them; and it placed little value on the testimony of condemned witches, or the naming of names, which was so devastating elsewhere. And, as noted earlier, the use of torture was carefully regulated, generally being ordered only where the evidence was considerable, if still circumstantial.[40]

Third, the flames of witch-hunting in Spain may have been contained by the comparatively strong central control of its judiciary. As noted above, virile witch-hunts tended to occur in local courts, those subject to more personal and even intimate knowledge and prejudices against the accused, and beyond central control. And, fourth, the Spanish may have been less ardent in their execution of witches because of their much stronger concern with Jews and Muslims. In Spain, much more so than in other countries in Europe, witch-hunting had as much to do with the demonizing of outsiders and intruders—Muslims who occupied Spanish territory, Jews, and conversos (those who had converted to Christianity)—as insiders or Christians.[41]

Although the previously cited figures on prosecution and execution rates are lower than those noted in some other studies, they nevertheless point to the grim reality of the Great European Witch-hunt. This is especially true if the following points are considered. First, the figures do not take into account the number of individuals, likely quite large, who were never officially charged but who nevertheless lived under a cloud of suspicion. And, second, prosecutions and executions were not evenly distributed, but rather concentrated in certain areas, thereby magnifying their destructiveness on the social fabric of those locales. We can only imagine what resulted in Bamberg, Germany, for example, when between 1623 and 1633, 600 witches were burned; in the Prince Bishopric of Eichstatt, when in the course of one year, 274 people were executed; or in the lands of the Convent of Quedlinburg, when in 1589, 133 witches were put to death in one day![42]

Further, certain types of people were disproportionately represented among the accused. Various reasons have been offered for this, but most historians agree that some were more likely to be charged than others because their being singled out allowed members of early modern European communities to resolve conflicts between themselves and their neighbors and to explain misfortunes that befell them in their daily lives. In brief, witches were scapegoats. When witch-hunts were initiated from above (i.e., by inquisitors or magistrates), when torture was used, when charges of diabolism took precedence over charges of maleficia, the principal pattern was upper-class officials condemning lower-class witches. When charges were brought from below (i.e., neighbor versus neighbor), where protection from maleficia was paramount, witch-hunts commonly pitted members of the lower classes against each other, members of the elite serving as arbiters, or at times supporters of the accusers.

The reasons for the disproportionate number of accusations against the poor are obvious. They were the weakest and most vulnerable members of society, and therefore they were easy targets. Further, more so than today, the poor were dependent on those better off than they (as opposed to government programs) for their well-being, and that aroused feelings of resentment and even guilt. The number of poor increased in the Early Modern Period, and the economic situation of others became precarious. Therefore, historians have argued, accusations may well have been used by those only marginally better off to break off long-standing, but now intolerable, relations with their poorer neighbors.[43]

More difficult to explain is why about 80 percent of those accused of being witches were female. Some have argued that witchcraft is universally specific to women, but others have shown that such gender identification has been more pronounced in patriarchal societies like those in the West. Moreover, given the history of Western Christendom's attitudes toward them, it is clear that early modern European women were suspect, at least in part, because they were believed to be morally weaker than men and therefore more likely to succumb to diabolical temptation.[44] Kramer and Sprenger, in the *Malleus Maleficarum,* described those women who had not renounced their bodies in the image of the Virgin Mary as particularly susceptible because they were not only intellectually inferior and superstitious, but also subject to a greater extent than men to an insatiable carnal lust—insatiable, that is, unless quenched by the Devil:

> All witchcraft comes from carnal lust, which in women is insatiable. . . . Wherefore for the sake of fulfilling their lusts they consort with devils. . . . [So] it is sufficiently clear that it is no matter for wonder that there are more women than men found infested with the heresy of witchcraft . . . . [45]

At the height of the Great European Witch-hunt, especially on the Continent, witches were said to be not only Devil worshippers, but the Devil's sexual slaves, leading some historians to conclude that the witch trials were symptomatic of a dramatic rise in fear of women's sexuality. But there were also less theoretical reasons for the charging of women. Those women who served as healers and midwives, for example, were particularly vulnerable. They employed a variety of folk remedies often deemed magical, and such remedies were welcome when employed successfully. When things went wrong, however, as in the case of about 20 percent of all births, they could easily be charged with employing "black magic" or using the same arts for evil purposes.[46]

Finally, it has been argued that women, especially poor women, may have been disproportionately charged with witchcraft because, in the minds of their accusers, their physical, economic, and political weaknesses made them more likely to seek diabolical power as an instrument of protection or revenge. That is to say, ironically, that the most vulnerable people of the Great European Witch-hunt may have become victims because they were feared by their neighbors as potentially powerful and threatening.[47]

Other factors characteristic of accused witches involved age and marital status. The accused in the Great European Witch-hunt were largely over fifty years old, and, more often than should have been the case, given their numbers in the general population, they were widowed or never married. In Geneva, 75 percent of the accused were over fifty, for example, while 56 percent were not married at the time they were charged.[48] The factor of age might simply reflect the tendency of the accused to accumulate suspicion over time, as well as criminal records and histories of antisocial behavior, but that they were also disproportionately single begs further explanation.

In the Early Modern Period, because of the plague and warfare, both of which killed more men than women, the percentage of widows among all women increased from 10 percent to as high as 30 percent in some areas. The percentage of never-married women increased from about 5 percent to nearly 20 percent, as the age of first marriages increased and the population of convents declined. Widows and never-married women were vulnerable because, unless they were committed to chastity, having been denied the usual outlets, they were seen as more likely to seek sexual satisfaction through extraordinary means—with the Devil, for example. Moreover, their growing numbers were seen as a threat to the male-dominated society, in general, and to the institution of marriage, in particular.[49]

Finally contributing to the profile of most suspects was the witch's personality. As personalities, they exhibited considerable diversity, but there were certain characteristics common to the accused. They were often pictured as sharp-tongued, bad-tempered, and quarrelsome, often engaged in numerous disputes with neighbors and incurring ever-increasing resentment toward them within the community. They were known for their scolding and cursing, which was easily confused with casting spells. And they often had court records for violations such as non-attendance at church, Sabbath-breaking, cursing, fornication, prostitution, abortion, adultery, and homosexuality. At the least, the accused were commonly guilty of what was seen as inappropriate behavior for their sex. They did not adhere to traditional behavioral standards. They defied contemporary standards of docility and domesticity and inverted the ideal of the good Christian wife and mother."[50]

A Summary View of Witch–hunts in England

England had lower rates of prosecution and execution of witches than did most other countries in Europe, including Scotland. During the Great European Witch-hunt, England indicted approximately 2,000 individuals, executing only about 500, or about 25 percent, and even its major witch-hunt of the 1640s paled in comparison to those of various locales on the Continent. Historians have credited the lower rates to the English judicial system, which did not follow the Continent's lead into the inquisitorial system. Judges did not initiate cases, neighbors did. The courts were not allowed to use torture to secure confessions, and verdicts were rendered by juries, who were comparatively lenient in their verdicts. But they have also been attributed to a different concern with the true dangers of witchcraft. Whereas authorities on the Continent were most concerned with heresy, those who brought charges in England feared maleficia.[51]

In England, most cases of witchcraft were brought by neighbor against neighbor. Judges were less concerned with ferreting out an organized witch society or cult of Satan than they were with dealing with the harm caused to others. Suggestively, the *Malleus Maleficarum,* which was so influential on the Continent and emphasized the diabolical rather than the malefic aspect of witchcraft, did not appear in an English translation until 1584, the same year Reginald Scot criticized that work in *Discoverie of Witchcraft.*[52]

Nevertheless, England participated in the Great European Witchhunt, and there were many similarities between what happened in England and on the Continent. Witches were just as likely to be women. Alan Macfarlane has estimated that in Essex County, for example, 85 percent of the accused were women and a disproportionate number of them were widows; 87 percent of the accused were between fifty and seventy years old, and those of low social status were overrepresented. As on the Continent, women who engaged in midwifery and other healing arts were likely targets, but only if they had been suspect for years before they were actually charged with witchcraft.[53]

The English were more likely than Continental Europeans to make reference to witches' familiars (perhaps as the result of the British fondness in folklore for the "little people"), and those familiars had intercourse with witches and sucked at witches' teats, but there was significantly less emphasis on sex, especially between witches and the Devil. Moreover, because greater emphasis was placed on the power of witches to engage in maleficium than on their worshipping the Devil, it was almost entirely a civil matter, and not a religious one; and, in most cases, those convicted were jailed or banished, and even in the extreme, hanged not burned.[54]

Finally, Macfarlane found that almost all bewitching occurred within villages, or even neighborhoods. He did not find any meaningful correlation between the frequency of accusations and religious grouping, or church attendance. Neither could he establish any relationship between witchcraft accusations and previous criminal records (e.g., theft, murder, breaking the Sabbath, quarreling, scolding, or sexual offenses), but he did find that witches were often thought of as quarrelsome and unpleasant. Thus, in England, more so than on the Continent, witch trials were often an outgrowth of community conflict. They arose out of quarreling between neighbors, often over loans and gifts, and followed oral outbursts and subsequent unexpected misfortune suffered by one of the parties.[55]

As on the Continent, there is a long history of sorcery in England, and of course there were evil sorcerers, but for centuries they were dealt with locally. As early as 747, the Council of Clovesho directed bishops to speak out against sorcerers, and several secular, or civil, laws were passed threatening those who participated in such activities with imprisonment, banishment, and even execution. Nevertheless, sorcery, at least insofar as it involved fortune-telling, the casting of spells, and the use of charms to heal or ward off disease, continued to be very popular—that is, until the English Reformation.[56]

The first statute specifically concerned with witchcraft was enacted in 1542, just after the English Reformation but still during the reign of Henry VIII. Its passage indicates a more aggressive policy toward witchcraft under the Church of England, while its wording reflects the greater emphasis the English placed on maleficium, rather than heresy. The statute made witchcraft a felony "without benefit of clergy," punishable by death. It defined witchcraft as using invocation, conjuration, or sorcery to find money or to waste, consume, or destroy any person "in his body, members, or goods," or to provoke anyone to unlawful love or for any other unlawful intent or purpose.[57]

Few cases resulted from the statute of 1542, and it was revoked under Edward VI five years later, as were other felony laws passed by Parliament under Edward's father. In 1563, however, Parliament acted again, this time passing a more complex piece of legislation. The

Elizabethan statute retained the death penalty for invoking evil spirits for any purpose and for committing murder by witchcraft, but it reduced the penalty for those found guilty of using "witchcraft, enchantment, charm, or sorcery" to cause bodily harm short of death or to steal or destroy property. Such lesser offenses were punishable by as little as one year's imprisonment, in the case of first offenses.[58]

The first major trial for witchcraft in England occurred in 1566 at Chelmsford in Essex County. Charged were Elizabeth Francis, Agnes Waterhouse, and Agnes's daughter Joan. Elizabeth was charged with bewitching a child and committing other evil deeds. In her confession, she explained that she had learned witchcraft from her grandmother when she was twelve years old. Her grandmother had led Elizabeth to renounce God, and she had given her a cat named Sathan, who was the Devil in animal form. The cat, whom Elizabeth was to suckle with her own blood and with whom Elizabeth could speak, promised her riches and a husband, and indeed Sathan brought her livestock and one Andrew Byles. Byles, however, after enjoying her favors, refused Elizabeth's hand in marriage, whereupon Sathan caused his death and taught Elizabeth how to abort his child. Elizabeth later married and had a daughter, but the infant so annoyed her that she had Sathan murder it as well.[59]

After having him some sixteen years in her possession, Elizabeth gave Sathan to her daughter Agnes. Agnes, wanting the wool that lined the cat's box, changed Sathan into a toad, and together they carried out many evil deeds (e.g., drowning cows, killing geese, spoiling butter) until both Elizabeth and Agnes were arrested. Agnes was hanged in 1566. Elizabeth, perhaps because of her helpful testimony, was spared the death penalty, but she was hanged for a second conviction thirteen years later. Her granddaughter Joan, who was also charged, was found not guilty.[60]

In 1579, once again in Essex County, several more women were tried for witchcraft, and in 1582 another notorious case occurred, wherein thirteen witches were convicted in St. Osyth's, near Colchester. The latter case made such a "great noise," George Lyman Kittredge has written, that it incurred a response by Reginald Scot. Scot's response, however, which appeared in 1584, titled *Discoverie of Witchcraft*, was as well a critique of the *Malleus Maleficarum*, which, as previously noted, had only recently been published in English in England. In brief, while allowing that evil spirits existed, Scot insisted that the evil acts with which witches had been charged were illusions, a point made centuries earlier in the Canon *Episcopi*.[61] Scot's reasoning did not prevail, however, and the number of witchcraft trials steadily increased during the 1580s and 1590s, before a momentary lull in activity greeted the new century.

Particularly critical of Reginald Scot was King James VI of Scotland, with whom, along with publication of the *Malleus Maleficarum,* continental ideas on witchcraft arrived in England. Scotland was a hotbed of witch-hunting, and although James did not initiate it or even became instrumental to it, he was a believer and an active participant. He had been converted to the cause during the North Berwick witch trials of 1590–1592, which involved a young girl named Gilly Duncan. Duncan, who had the reputation of being able to cure the sick, was charged with practicing witchcraft, whereupon she confessed and named several other women and men in and around Edinburgh. James examined one of the accused, Agnes Sampson, himself. When she refused to confess, Sampson was stripped, shaved, and searched for the Devil's mark. Upon its being found, she was tortured until she confessed, named still others, and told of a group of men and women who had sailed in sieves to North Berwick on Halloween, entered a church illuminated by black candles, paid homage to the Devil in the form of a man, and plotted to raise a storm to sink the King's ship when he sailed to Denmark.[62]

By 1597, James was convinced that the hunting of witches had gone too far, that fraud had been involved in many cases, and that innocent people had been condemned, and he used his influence to end it. He nevertheless published his *Daemonologie,* a direct attack on the moderate voices of critics such as Reginald Scot. James insisted that witches did exist, explaining that although man had been made in God's image, he had lost that image through original sin. God had restored that image to the elect, James continued, but the rest of mankind was relegated to the Devil, whereupon they bore his image. They became his followers, and some even chose to become witches in order to do harm to those whom God had elected and the Devil opposed. They needed to be searched out, James concluded, and eradicated for the good of mankind.[63]

Daemonologie was reissued in England upon James's ascension to the throne in 1603, and in 1604 he encouraged Parliament to adopt a statute that made penalties more severe. Death was prescribed for those guilty of an even greater list of witchcraft-related crimes, including those who would "consult, covenant with, entertain, employ, feed, or reward any evil or wicked spirit to or for any intent or purpose, whether it be a first or subsequent offense."[64] Further, James commissioned an English translation of the Bible (the "Authorized" or "King James Version") in which a certain ambiguous Hebrew word in

Exodus 22:18 was translated and thereby rendered more explicitly "witch"—as in "Thou shalt not suffer a witch to live."

In fairness, it should be noted that James's actions did not signal a full-blown witch-hunt in England; that occurred some four decades later during the English Civil War. Much as had been the case on the Continent, the English witch-hunt was clearly tied to the anxiety the Civil War produced. It was centered in Essex County, and leading the charge was Matthew Hopkins, the most notorious English witch-hunter. In two years under his charge, more Englishmen were hanged for witchcraft than in the previous century.[65]

Unlike continental inquisitors such as Jacob Sprenger, who were men of the cloth, Hopkins was a lawyer. The Witch-Finder General, as he was known, was a Puritan, and he operated during a period in which Puritans came to dominate Parliament. Nevertheless, English witch-hunting was not exclusively, or even mostly, a Puritan affair. First, the mid-seventeenth-century Essex County hunt was the only one in which Puritans dominated. Second, even in that hunt, Hopkins was both opposed by his fellow Puritans and supported by non-Puritans, some of whom led the charge after Hopkins's reign ended. And, third, once again in reference to the Essex County affair, once the Puritan leader Oliver Cromwell secured power, the witch trials languished. In sum, the Hopkins's outbreak, like others, is best seen as the result of the disturbed condition of the country during the English Civil War, rather than as the product of Puritan theology.[66]

Operating through a Special Commission of Oyer and Terminer, granted in 1645, Hopkins's methods were unusually cruel by English standards. Although the evidence that he used torture is inconclusive, he did at least deprive the accused of food and sleep, and thereby elicited a sufficient number of confessions to lend credibility to his actions. In contrast to other English witches, Hopkins's victims confessed to behavior more commonly admitted to by those on the Continent, including sexual intercourse with the Devil and attendance at the Sabbat, and he placed greater emphasis on the naming of names. Hopkins, however, moved too quickly, and by 1646 the flames he had ignited consumed him. He was forced to retire, and the following year he died in disgrace.[67]

The number of witch trials in England declined rapidly after Hopkins's resignation. Belief in witches continued, and learned treatises on the subject were published. In 1666, for example, John Glanville published *Some Philosophical Considerations Touching Witches and Witchcraft*, in which he defended belief in witches on the basis of Christian theology and argued that disbelief proceeded from atheism. To reject the Devil, he explained, is to deny the entire spirit world, including God. Further, some notable cases no doubt influential in New England occurred in the remaining decades of the seventeenth century. In Bury St. Edmunds, for example, a group of women was convicted of witchcraft in large part on the testimony of children. In 1664 at Somerset, several women were charged with attending covens led by a man in black clothing, and in Exeter in 1682 a group of "very old, decrepit, and impotent" women, as one eyewitness described them, was condemned.[68] By the end of the seventeenth century, however, the scene of English witch-hunts had shifted to New England.

2

Having "Familiarity With the Devil"

The purpose of chapter one was to provide a brief overview of the Great European Witch-hunt, so we might better see the roots of the Salem witch trials in the European experience and understand that, although somewhat late in that experience, the Salem trials were neither historically out of place nor greatly different. For much the same reason, in this chapter we will explore the history of witch-hunts in seventeenth-century New England.

WITCH-HUNTS IN SEVENTEENTH-CENTURY AMERICA

As might be expected, belief in witchcraft in the European colonies of America was widespread, the specific nature of that belief and the response of the authorities in each group of colonies paralleling that of the mother country. In Dutch territory, there was only one case of an individual being charged with being a witch, and that occurred in the town of Easthampton, which was populated by Englishmen who had migrated south out of New England.[1] Perhaps as many as forty-three individuals were charged in New France, but they were seldom convicted, and then only mildly punished.[2] The single notable exception involved Daniel Vuil. Vuil, a Huguenot, was accused of casting a spell on a fourteen-year-old girl with whom he had fallen in love, after he had been rejected by her parents. He was executed.[3]

In New Spain, the Holy Office of the Inquisition set out to destroy witchcraft, but, much as in Spain where the Holy Office dealt mostly with conversos, in the colonies it tended to focus on Native Americans and blacks. It was incorporated into the larger drive to evangelize Native Americans and to eradicate pagan religion in the process. Witchhunts appeared irregularly, but they were pursued with fervor. Sentences were sometimes harsh, but as a whole the courts were lenient and the executions few, as they were in Spain. For example, in Mexico between 1536 and 1543, the Holy Office charged twenty people with witchcraft, including fifteen women, of whom at least five were lower-class blacks or "mixed bloods." All were punished, some by public whipping, but none were executed. In 1675, authorities hanged four Indians in what is now New Mexico for practicing sorcery, but they were accused as well of killing seven missionaries. The uncommonly harsh penalty helped trigger the Pueblo Revolt of 1680.[4]

Following England's example, the number of witch trials in the English colonies was low. There were several cases in the Bermudas during the second half of the seventeenth century, beginning, according to the principal historian of the event, with the arrival of Scottish servants with their "superstitions" into a dominantly Puritan environment, ruled by a governor sympathetic to attempts to ferret out witches. Fifteen individuals, twelve women and three men, were initially charged with witchcraft, the records of nearly all of their cases making mention of various forms of maleficia rather than heresy. Five were executed, including four women. By the end of the century, when the Bermuda trials all but ended (there was one incompletely recorded case during the early years of the eighteenth century), the number of accused reached twenty-one, including sixteen women. One more woman was executed, but most of the rest of the cases ended in dismissal. There is little in the records by which to draw a profile of the accused. All we have is the previously noted historian's comment that the trials involved "harmless old women and half-crazy men."[5]

There were occasional trials in various British colonies of mainland North America, including Virginia, New York, New Jersey, Pennsylvania, and Maryland. In Virginia, between 1627 and 1705, nine cases of accused witches made it to court; ten defamation cases involving witchcraft accusations were heard as well, most of them after 1668. Only one of the accused, however, William Harding of Northumberland

County, in 1665, was convicted, and he was whipped and banished. Unique to Virginia were three shipboard executions of women accused of witchcraft, but little is known of their cases.[6]

Aside from Virginia's shipboard executions, Maryland has the distinction of being the only British colony of mainland North America outside of New England wherein an execution for witchcraft took place. Rebecca Fowler was hanged in 1685, but the details of her case have not survived. Otherwise, historian Francis Neal Parke has found only five cases in colonial Maryland, four occurring between 1665 and 1686, the last in 1712. Four of the five involved women, and although the records are incomplete, no more than two (including the man) were convicted.[7] All other cases in British America, numbering well over 200, occurred in New England, over half during the Salem witch trials.

WITCH-HUNTS IN SEVENTEENTH-CENTURY NEW ENGLAND

As was the case in the Spanish, French, and Dutch colonies of the Americas, the British colonists assigned Native Americans to Satan almost from the start. They too believed that prior to their arrival, New England had belonged to the Devil, and that the Devil had a grip on its native inhabitants—that the Devil "visibly and palpably reigne[d] there," as the Reverend William Crashaw of Virginia put it. As David Lovejoy has suggested, given their religious intensity, New England Puritans may have exaggerated the Devil's role, thereby providing themselves with an explanation for their minimal success in evangelizing the "heathen," as well as a rationale for the bloody Pequot (1637) and King Philip's (1675) Wars. But in British America, Native Americans were seldom actually charged with witchcraft; that crime was reserved almost exclusively for Christians.[8]

It is not entirely clear why the overwhelming number of witch-hunts in British America occurred in New England. Once again, as was the case in our discussion of Matthew Hopkins's activity in England, the reader might be tempted to blame it on the Puritans. As Karen Armstrong has recently concluded:

> [A]s Salem shows, they [the Puritans] brought their phobias and frustrations with them. They also brought from Europe an inadequate conception of religion. Instead of seeing compassion as the primary religious virtue, the Puritans of New England—latter-day crusaders—cultivated a harsh, unyielding righteousness that was quick to judge and condemn. Instead of seeing God as all-powerful and all-forgiving, the Puritans saw Satan everywhere.[9]

Further, although their authority was beginning to wane by the 1690s, Puritans dominated seventeenth-century New England and, as some have argued, the ministry may have been anxious to use any pretext to reestablish their influence. There is no evidence, however, that levels of activity in New England followed lines of heightened religiosity.

In their sermons, especially at executions for witchcraft, ministers linked maleficia and diabolism. They occasionally interrogated the accused and provided advice for public officials and the courts. But over the course of the century, Puritan ministers were not disproportionately numbered among the proponents of the trials. The records show that many were opposed and even instrumental in controlling them. Perhaps, then, without exonerating the Puritan ministry from any culpability, George Lyman Kittredge was right in warning that to tie witch trials in New England to religious opinions alone would be a serious error; the people of seventeenth-century New England believed in witchcraft not because they were Puritan, but because they were men of their time. To quote John Demos, witchcraft "belonged to the regular business of life in premodern times; or at least it belonged to the belief system, the value structure, the predominant psychology of those times," but then that still leaves us with the problem of explaining the large number of cases in New England.[10]

As we have seen, European witch-hunts were most common in areas of great turmoil, whether it be political, social, economic, or religious, and of such turmoil the people of New England at the end of the seventeenth century had more than their fair share. That, combined with their unique sense of having been chosen by God to establish a New Jerusalem and their fear that they had failed in their mission, led Puritan New Englanders to establish blame for that failure. Upon their arrival in the wilderness, John Winthrop had warned them that if they failed, God's wrath would be turned against them, and there was evidence by 1692 that indeed that was happening.[11] What they needed to do was find out who was responsible, punish them, and thereby return to God's path and merit His favor once again.

New Englanders, as typical Englishmen, were steeped in the lore of witchcraft. As Richard Godbeer has found, "alongside Protestant Christianity, there co-existed a tangled skein of magical beliefs and practices that the colonists brought with them from England." To use the anthropological term, they were *magico-religious,* and it is that with which Puritan ministers were particularly concerned—not with those who had rejected Puritanism, for they were few. Puritan ministers emphasized God's absolute sovereignty, insisting that everything in the world was determined by God, and they urged people to submit to His sovereignty without exception. They made great strides in persuading their flocks to that point of view, but their victory over pagan practices was not absolute, largely because so many of the laity did not see any conflict between the two.[12]

While Puritan ministers condemned any form of magic as blasphemous and diabolical, most of their flock continued to believe in astrology, fortune-telling, divining, and the use of charms and potions to ward off evil or attract good fortune, love, and wealth. Because such practices were informal and not part of any coherent doctrinal system or organized institutional structure, they were so elusive as to defy any counterattack. As long as they did not elicit any significant opposition, which was most of the time, the practices were a nearly indistinguishable part of everyday life.[13]

New Englanders, then, added little to the concept of witchcraft they inherited from England. For ministers, witchcraft may have been about repudiating Christ and worshipping the Devil, but for the common people it was primarily about doing harm. Thus, although the laws of seventeenth-century New England embodied the theological views of witchcraft and demanded proof of direct contact between the accused and the Devil, lay folk tended to focus on the suspect's malevolence. They were more concerned with a witch's use of occult skills to do harm. And as Richard Godbeer has speculated, this "disjuncture between legal conceptions of witchcraft and popular testimony about witchcraft made conviction extremely difficult."[14]

As was the case in England, most cases in New England were initiated by people charging their neighbors with using witchcraft to harm members of their family or to destroy their livestock and personal possessions. Charges were essentially face-to-face interactions within communities where relationships—familial, spatial, gendered, and economic—became charged with suspicion, anger, and revenge.[15]

Moreover, the history of witch trials in seventeenth-century New England reveals a similar tendency on the part of accusers to project guilt upon, and expel, certain members of the community. Much as Keith Thomas and Alan D. Macfarlane have found in England, charges in New England followed lines of intrinsic tension and hostility. In England, such tension was especially common in the Early Modern Period, when the sense of community of the traditional English village was disintegrating. Change was hardest on dependent members of the community—the poor and widowed, for example—whose subsistence depended on the generosity of their neighbors. They were often the first to be charged with witchcraft, and their accusers were likely to be those who had denied the accused's request for assistance, thereby failing to conform to the traditional code of community behavior. In the process, they not only felt guilty about their moral lapse but also, when some misfortune befell them, they projected that guilt onto the accused by holding them morally culpable for the incident. Not surprisingly, the marginally better-off were particularly well-represented among the accusers.[16]

There may have been fewer truly needy in seventeenth-century New England, but the same thesis applies. When the traditional mutuality or communal pattern of which we have spoken began to unravel, as it did in the late-seventeenth century, the same feelings emerged. In fact, it may have been even more pronounced in New England because of its emphasis on the covenanted community. John Winthrop had told the Puritans upon their arrival in Massachusetts that God required their harmony if His mission for them was to succeed, but as the century wore on in the face of the new social and cultural values and attitudes that accompanied New England's transformation from a traditional rural, agricultural society to a more cosmopolitan, urban, and commercial world, that harmony was lost. Whatever sense of responsibility and charity had characterized New England at its founding was declining.[17]

Given all of this, John Demos has gathered the following statistics concerning those accused of witchcraft in seventeenth-century New England. Of all suspects for whom he could determine social class, 73 percent were below the midpoint on his social scale. Those with declining fortunes, though not necessarily poor, were also disproportionately represented among the accused, and both were much more likely to be aggressively prosecuted and convicted.[18]

As was true in England, 80 percent of those charged with witchcraft in New England were women, and at least half of those men who were charged were the husbands, sons, or close associates of women cried out against first. Men among those charged were less likely to be tried and convicted, and if convicted, their sentences were usually less severe. The only partial exceptions to this rule, and it was a matter of degree in both instances, were the two large-scale witch-hunts of Hartford and Salem. In the former case, the portion of females was 64 percent, in the latter, 73 percent, suggesting that, as in Europe, when fear of witchcraft was particularly strong, stereotypes tended to crumble but not to collapse.[19]

As was the case in England, the accused of New England were largely older women, but still middle-aged. At a time when sixty was considered the beginning of old age, 67 percent of those prosecuted for witchcraft were between the ages of forty and sixty. At the time they were first suspected, 82 percent fell into that age bracket. As John Demos has explained, women in their forties and fifties had reached their peak in terms of authority or power in the Puritan community; they had fully realized their role in society and had presided over a household of several children, servants, and apprentices. The accused, however, generally were not so accomplished. Never-marrieds were not disproportionately represented among the accused in New England, but being a widow was clearly a liability, and even more vulnerable were those with fewer children than average. Twice the proportion of the accused as that of the general population were childless, and the percentage of those who bore fewer children was higher as well.[20]

Carol Karlsen has argued that women over age forty were singled out because they lived in a society in which men exercised substantial legal, political, ideological, and economic authority over women. Witch-hunting, therefore, was a means of reaffirming this authority at a time when some women were testing those constraints. Especially vulnerable, Karlsen notes, were women without brothers and widows who remained single or remarried but who had no sons by their previous marriage. Both stood to inherit property, and they stood in the way of the orderly transmission of property from one generation of males to another and were resented for it.[21]

Of particular importance in New England was the accused's relationship to the community and to his or her family. To use Demos's words, "a peaceful household was seen as the foundation of all social order." Thus, any suspicion that a man, or especially a woman, caused domestic disharmony invited unfavorable notice from neighbors, and if it persisted, suspicion of witchcraft. Not surprisingly, men and women who had criminal records were disproportionately represented among the accused witches of seventeenth-century New England. Demos set the rate at a minimum of 36 percent, but allowed that the figure could be as high as 63 percent. Either level is significant when it is compared to a crime rate for the general population of from 10 to 20 percent, and, among women, of only 5 percent.[22]

Just as interesting, however, is the type of crime with which witches were charged. When Demos organized the specific charges brought against those included in his study, he found that the single largest group by far (41 percent) had been charged with assaultive speech, and the rest with theft, lying, sex offenses, physical assault, resisting authority, arson, and fraud. Assaultive speech included slander and defamation, mostly, but it also referred to "filthy" and "scandalous" speech, and as historian Jane Kamensky has found, "disorderly speech," when employed by women, was seen as especially disruptive of the social order and particularly damaging for seventeenth-century New England women on a number of different counts, including their being more likely to be charged with being a witch.[23]

In sum, historians have drawn a composite image of witches in seventeenth-century New England as being comparatively poor, female, middle-aged, and married or widowed; having fewer than the average number of children; often being in trouble with the law or in conflict with friends and family; having practiced some form of medical healing; and appearing abrasive in style and contentious in character.[24] Few suspects conformed to all of these specifications, but the better someone fit this description, the more likely she or he would be accused of witchcraft. A similar portrait can be drawn of the supposed victims of witchcraft.

Those individuals in seventeenth-century New England best known for being the victims of witches were the teenagers of Salem village in 1692. When we look beyond 1692 to the century as a whole, however, and include all of the victims, not just the psychically or spiritually afflicted, a more complicated picture emerges. To begin with, 55 percent of all victims of witchcraft were men, with young men from the ages of twenty to thirty-nine accounting for over half of that number. And, among women, the single largest group of victims was between the ages of twenty and thirty-nine. They accounted for 14 percent of all cases, 13 percent being women from the age of forty to fifty-nine and only 9 percent falling between the ages of ten and nineteen.[25]

Why these groups were particularly prone to becoming victims is unclear. John Demos has suggested that for men in their twenties and thirties it might have resulted from the frustration they felt at not being able to realize what was expected of them, and what they no doubt wanted, namely their acquiring property and marrying. As the century drew to an end, there was less and less land available to them. Menopausal women, he has offered, seem to have been more preoccupied with body states, illness and injury, and morbidity and child mortality, while young women in their teens found their place in society awkward at best.[26]

In the seventeenth century, much like today, adolescence was a period of transition from childhood to adulthood, of the trying on of roles and of the anticipation and anxiety that produces. In the seventeenth century, however, the choices were fewer for young women, and "elements of identity came to them almost ready-made." Quite likely, adolescent charges of witchcraft were a reaction to, or a protest against, conventional standards and received authority. In their attacks, they struck out against middle-aged women, women about their mothers' ages, or those who had the greatest control over their lives.[27]

Richard Weisman has added to this portrait of victims. He too found that most victims of witchcraft in seventeenth-century New England were men, but he then divided charges of witchcraft into two categories: ordinary witchcraft, or those that involved injury to the person or his or her property; and affliction or possession, wherein the victim's thoughts and actions were altered or controlled. Over 90 percent of the cases prior to 1692 were of the former type, the latter being prevalent only during the Salem trials.[28]

In the former, the victim commonly traced the source of the malefic, or harmful, action to someone with whom he or she had had a transaction and who had been dissatisfied with the results of that transaction. Thus, both the suspect and motive were apparent. In the latter, no such preexisting contact was evident, and therefore no simple identification was possible. A third party, a family member or friend, often stepped forward to provide an acceptable interpretation of the victim's words and deeds. Moreover, as Weisman has suggested, the afflicted or possessed displayed "greater vulnerability to mystical harm" and seemed particularly helpless to defend themselves. Thus, not surprisingly, he found that although the overwhelming majority of victims of ordinary witchcraft were men, women comprised nearly 88 percent of the afflicted or possessed, and 79 percent of those women were single and twenty-one years of age or younger![29]

This information indicates that whatever might be said of women's inferiority to men in Puritan society as a whole, the role of unmarried younger women was even more problematic. Married women, especially those with several children, had at least some authority and legal rights in seventeenth-century New England, perhaps even more than elsewhere in the West. They often worked side by side with their husbands on the farm or in the family business; they had some protection under the law from abuse, and upon the death of their husbands, they retained certain property rights not provided elsewhere. Unmarried women under age twenty-one, in contrast, had no such rights. Further, they were often removed from the family home to serve as maidservants to neighbors, thereby eliminating even that level of protection. Not surprisingly then, Weisman has found, among the victims of witchcraft in seventeenth-century New England, there was a "close affinity between social subordination and this expression [affliction or possession] of victimization."[30]

As in England, suspicions of witchcraft in New England were usually handled extralegally at the local level through intermediaries like ministers, physicians, or magistrates. Formal charges were usually avoided, as many no doubt feared the countersuit of slander any failed charges of witchcraft would likely, and commonly did, evoke. Often, as has been noted, counter-magic was employed and, occasionally, retaliatory physical violence. But when formal charges were brought, usually by one neighbor against another, court procedures closely paralleled those used in England.

Laws on witchcraft in New England followed the English statute of 1604, but their wording was more closely drawn from the Old Testament. By 1647, all of the New England colonies had incorporated the death penalty for conviction into their legal codes. That of Massachusetts Bay Colony of 1641 (modified only slightly in its wording in 1648) was typical: "If any man or woman be a witch (that is hath or consulteth with a familiar spirit), they shall be put to death. Exodus 22:18; Leviticus 20:27; Deuteronomy 18:10." Elsewhere in New England, it might be described as a "solemn compaction with the Devil," or simply as "giving entertainment to Satan," but it was always deemed punishable by hanging. The statutes made no reference to maleficia, or the use of diabolical powers to do harm, but in practice that was the source of nearly all complaints.[31]

Cases of witchcraft in seventeenth-century New England passed through a judicial system that paralleled England's. There were three levels of courts in Massachusetts. The lowest level consisted of local magistrates who were empowered by colonial legislatures to hear and decide certain minor cases. County courts, manned by three to five magistrates, constituted the second level. The filing of depositions against putative witches could occur at either level, but given witchcraft's status as a capital offense, neither had jurisdiction. They simply decided whether sufficient evidence existed to merit trial, whereupon they referred the case and the evidence they had gathered to the upper house of the Massachusetts legislature, the Court of Assistants. If that body found the evidence credible, it summoned a grand jury, and if the grand jury issued an indictment, trial by jury in a superior court of law followed.[32]

Witchcraft was a capital crime requiring two witnesses. Moreover, in order to convict, witnesses had to give evidence of a diabolical pact as well as maleficia. Given the private nature of a pact, such evidence was difficult to obtain. Confession was the surest route to conviction, but prior to 1692 only 7 percent of the accused confessed. As in England, the easiest evidence to gather was signs of witches' teats, with which witches nourished their familiars. But ministers and magistrates urged that precautions be taken to assure that the validity of any such finding meet with the "approbation of some able physicians."[33]

Testimony by those who believed they had seen a witch's familiar was allowed, but it was difficult to ascertain or prove, as was spectral evidence. Spectral evidence was based on the belief that demons could assume the identity of—and only of—the person who had signed a pact with the Devil. Where the assumption held, it was irrefutable evidence, but the assumption generally did not hold. Theologians in England and New England simply refused to state unequivocally that the Devil could not employ the specter of an innocent person, and therefore prior to 1692 courts could not rely on such testimony for conviction.[34]

In sum, the laws of seventeenth-century New England, when properly applied, made conviction for witchcraft difficult, and the record shows that most of the time they were properly applied. Prior to 1692, approximately 100 people were formally indicted for witchcraft in New England. Only twenty were convicted and sixteen executed, and as the century progressed, the frequency of both declined. In fact, there were no executions for witchcraft in the twenty-five years after 1663.[35]

At first glance, then, witch-hunting in seventeenth-century New England seems to have been a minor disturbance, even by British standards. That, however, was not the case. To begin with, in order to contrast what had happened in 1692 to what had occurred during the past century, the numbers for the Salem witch trials have been omitted from the preceding figures. When we add them, we are forced to draw quite different conclusions.

First of all, the overall record shows that the 250 cases were not uniformly distributed. Indeed, they were as geographically concentrated and, therefore, locally as devastating as in England and in many parts of the European continent. Prior to 1692, in Massachusetts, for example, the counties of Essex and Norfolk in the northeast, and Hampshire in the west accounted for approximately two-thirds of the known legal complaints brought against witches. The Salem witch trials added at least 135 of the 150 legal actions taken in 1692 to Essex County alone![36]

Second, if we take into account New England's much smaller population and shorter history, its rate of indictments and executions for witchcraft was several times larger than England's. It may have fallen short of areas such as Germany, Switzerland, France, and even Scotland, but it was large enough to suggest that witch-hunting in New England was not such a minor affair after all.[37]

SOME NOTABLE WITCH TRIALS
IN SEVENTEENTH-CENTURY NEW ENGLAND

Although she was never formally charged, the first recorded case of suspected witchcraft in seventeenth-century New England was that of Jane Hawkins of Boston. Hawkins was banished from Massachusetts to Rhode Island in the aftermath of the Antinomian controversy of 1636–1637, which also involved the better-known Anne Hutchinson and Mary Dyer. Apparently, Hawkins returned to Massachusetts, because she was banished a second time in 1641. In both instances, in his journal, Governor John Winthrop made it clear that he suspected witchcraft. In April 1638, he wrote that Hawkins, a midwife who had been present at the birth of Mary Dyer's "monster" (a badly deformed fetus), had left the colony, and that her leaving was appropriate "for it was known, that she used to give young women oil of mandrakes and other stuff to cause conception." She was suspected of being a witch, he continued, because "it was credibly reported that when she gave any medicines (for she practiced physic) she would ask the party, if she did believe, she could help her, etc." In 1640, Winthrop added that even before she came to Massachusetts, while Hawkins lived in England, "divers ministers and others" suspected her of having "familiarity with the Devil."[38]

Alice Young was the first to be executed in New England for witchcraft. Little is known of the case except for a brief note in Winthrop's journal, that she lived in Windsor, Connecticut, and that she was executed at Hartford in 1647. It was quite likely her grandson who, in 1677, sued a man for saying that his mother was a witch and that he looked like one—a charge not as easily dismissed then as now![39]

Margaret Jones of Charlestown was the first person to be charged and executed for being a witch about whom we know much at all. Not surprisingly, she was a healer, or what was known as a cunning woman, and, like Jane Hawkins, a midwife. Margaret was married to Thomas Jones, who also was suspected of witchcraft, but he was never prosecuted. Margaret was tried in May and executed in June 1648.[40]

John Winthrop explained that the evidence used against Margaret Jones made essentially six points: that she was "found to have such a malignant touch" that it caused her patients to go deaf, vomit, or experience other types of pain and sickness; that she employed medicines that "had extraordinary violent effects"; that she told those who would not accept her treatment that they would continue to suffer, and they had; that she had foretold future events that had actually come to pass; and that she had two witch's teats "in her secret parts." When the first was discovered, it seemed "as fresh as if it had been newly sucked," but soon thereafter it withered and the other developed elsewhere. While Jones was in prison, Winthrop continued, she had been seen with a child in her arms. That child, however, vanished when a prison official approached, only to reappear twice more, in one case before another woman who fell ill, only to be cured by Jones. And, finally, Winthrop noted that at her trial Margaret Jones was "very intemperate, lying notoriously and railing upon the jury and witnesses." She died "in the like distemper," he added, and on the same day and at the same hour that she was executed "there was a very great tempest at Connecticut, which blew down many trees."[41]

Mary Johnson, of Wethersfield, Connecticut, was the first to confess to having entered into a pact with the Devil. She was apparently a servant, and she had been convicted of thievery in 1646. The record of her indictment dated December 7, 1648, simply reports that a jury had found that "by her own confession" she was guilty of "familiarity with devil." Cotton Mather, in his *Memorable Providences, Relating to Witchcrafts and Possessions* (Boston, 1689), wrote that she reported that the Devil had tempted her with many "services"; that when her master blamed her for not carrying out the ashes, the Devil had cleared the hearth for her; and that when her master had sent her into the field to drive out the hogs, the Devil helped her and made her laugh in the process! Johnson admitted, Mather continued, that her first familiarity with the Devil had come about as a result of her discontent and complaints; that she was guilty of the murder of a child; and that she had been guilty of "uncleaness with men and devils." In the end, Mather added, Mary Johnson repented and "went out of this world with many hopes of mercy through the merit of Jesus Christ."[42]

Sometimes cases of witchcraft took years, escalating from suspicions to indictments. One of the first such cases in New England was that of Jane Walford of Portsmouth, New Hampshire. Between 1648 and 1669, Walford was charged with being a witch at least three times. She was never convicted, but neither she nor her children ever escaped the onus of the charge.[43] Other examples include John Godfrey, of Essex County, Massachusetts, who was charged with witchcraft several times from 1639 to 1669, and Eunice Cole, a resident of Hampton, New Hampshire, who was first charged with witchcraft in 1656 and last charged in 1689.[44]

One of the most complex cases, however, was that of Mary Parsons. It began in 1649 when the Widow Marshfield of Windsor, Connecticut, brought suit for defamation against Parsons. The court found Parsons guilty and sentenced her to be whipped and to pay five pounds reparation to the Widow Marshfield. Two years later, in nearby Springfield, Massachusetts, following the death of two of her children and holding him responsible, Mary accused her husband, Hugh Parsons, of witchcraft. At about the same time, Hugh Parsons was suspected of seeking revenge on the town minister, George Moxon, by causing the death of two of his children after Parsons and Moxon had quarreled over brick work Parsons had done for him. Town residents offered some thirty-five depositions against Parsons in the matter, and he was indicted.[45]

Hugh Parsons was taken into custody on March 1, 1651, and examined. Mary was summoned as a witness, and she continued to insist that her husband was a witch, but she also spoke as though she were one. She admitted having spoken to the Devil, for example, and of having been persuaded by him to participate in a witches' meeting at which her husband was present. Not surprisingly, Mary was soon indicted as well. She was tried—the Widow Marshfield appearing as a witness against her—and found not guilty of witchcraft, but she was then indicted for the murder of one of her children. This time she confessed, and on May 13, 1651, she was sentenced to be hanged. There is no record of her having been executed, so she may have died in jail. Meanwhile, in 1652, a jury found Hugh Parsons guilty of witchcraft, but the General Court overturned the verdict and he was set free.[46]

One of the best-known cases of witchcraft in seventeenth-century New England was that of Anne Hibbins. Anne was the wife of the merchant William Hibbins, who also served in the Massachusetts General Court. Anne and her husband were highly regarded, and as both were members of the Boston church, neither seemed likely candidates for witchcraft charges. But then things started going wrong for Anne. In 1640, she was censured by her church for continuing to accuse a carpenter of overcharging for work he had done on her house, when the matter had been settled. Several months later, when she was still unrepentant, the church excommunicated her. Hibbins was widowed in 1654 and charged with witchcraft the next year. The jury returned a guilty verdict, but the judges refused to accept it, and a second trial took place in 1656. Once again, Hibbins was condemned, and this time she was executed.[47]

All of the preceding cases were limited in scope; they did not extend beyond the immediate family, and they seldom involved more than one person. The only witch-hunt prior to 1692 of any greater size occurred in Hartford, Connecticut, in the 1660s. It resulted in accusations against at least eight people, four of whom were executed. The Hartford witch-hunt began in 1662 when Ann Cole began to suffer what was deemed affliction. She accused Elizabeth Seager of tormenting her, and she was supported in her charge by her neighbors. She also named Rebecca Greensmith. Soon, an eight-year-old girl, Elizabeth Kelly, fell ill—an illness that eventually proved to be fatal—and she blamed Goodwife Ayres. Accusations were lodged against Mrs. Ayres's husband, who, when questioned, seconded Ann Cole's condemnation of Rebecca Greensmith, which soon led to the arrest of Rebecca's husband Nathaniel.[48]

In December 1662, the Greensmiths were indicted for having "familiarity with the Devil." Rebecca, described only as "aged," confessed and, in the process, implicated her husband. She also reported having attended meetings in the woods with Elizabeth Seager, Goodwife Ayres, Judith Varlet, and several others from the area. The reasons for Rebecca Greensmith's confession are unclear. Perhaps in her aging mind she had come to believe that she was familiar with the Devil. If she did it to escape execution, she was mistaken, because she and her husband were executed in early 1663.[49]

Mary Barnes, of nearby Farmington, whose connection to the case is likely but unclear, was executed at about the same time. The Ayres and Judith Varlet escaped to New York, but Elizabeth Seager was brought to court three times. In 1663, in two separate cases, she was found guilty of adultery but innocent of witchcraft. Two years later, she was charged with witchcraft again and this time convicted and sentenced to be hanged, but Connecticut Governor John Winthrop Jr. commuted her sentence. And all of this, historians surmise, may have begun over a disputed inheritance![50]

We shall conclude this brief sampling of seventeenth-century New England witch trials with two of perhaps the most influential cases of all on the Salem witch trials. They were the cases of Elizabeth Knapp and the Goodwin children. The details of the first were recorded by the Reverend Samuel Willard of Groton, Massachusetts, and published in Increase Mather's *Illustrious Providences* (1684); the second was covered and publicized by the Reverend Cotton Mather in *Memorable Providences* (1689).

The Knapp case began in 1671 in Samuel Willard's home with his servant, the sixteen-year-old Elizabeth Knapp. Knapp came from a respectable family. Her father was a prosperous farmer who had served several times as Groton town selectman, but even the daughters of respectable families were expected by their mid-teens to work as servants in neighboring homes. In late 1671, Knapp began to have fits, barking like a dog and speaking rudely in a gruff voice to the minister. The local physician diagnosed the illness as the effect of "foulness of the stomach and corruptions of her blood, occasioning fumes in her brain and strange fantasies," but when he could not effectively treat it, he declared it "diabolical" and left further remedies to Willard and other local ministers.[51]

Samuel Willard hoped to draw lessons from Knapp's affliction, and in those lessons, we can see firsthand how the ministry interpreted the appearance of witches in their midst and how they explained their presence to the people. Willard's first effort was a fast-day sermon, in which he sought to instruct the people of Groton on the spiritual significance of what had happened to Knapp. In that sermon, which was published for wider circulation in 1673, under the title *Useful Instructions for a Professing People in Times of Great Security and Degeneracy,* he urged the townspeople to respond to the event as "an awakening word of counsel." They were to take heed from it and engage in self-examination, whereby they should consider "what sins . . . have given Satan so much footing in this poor place." Willard admonished his flock not to focus on witchcraft, or the maleficia involved, which must certainly have been their first concern, but rather to consider of what sins they and their neighbors might have been guilty, thereby incurring God's wrath in the form of witchcraft. "Remember," he continued, "that God sits and rules over men and devils."[52]

Willard's description of Knapp and her affliction is instructive. Knapp, he observed, carried herself "in a strange and unwonted manner." Sometimes she would give sudden shrieks, and if he inquired as to the reason, "she would always put it off with some excuse and then would burst forth into immoderate and extravagant laughter, in such wise, as sometimes she fell onto the ground with it."[53]

Not surprisingly, Knapp claimed she was being afflicted by an older woman. What is surprising is that Willard and others, after questioning the accused, took no action, perhaps believing she was possessed. One evening when Willard was away, Knapp, who was sitting by the fire, suddenly cried out, "Oh my legs! and wrapped her arms around them. She cried, "Oh my breast!" and, according to Willard, "removed her hands thither; and forthwith [exclaimed], oh I am strangled, and put her hands on her throat," complaining that she could not breathe. The next day, Knapp sometimes wept, sometimes laughed, and at still other times made "foolish and apish gestures." At one point, she shrieked that she had seen two persons in the cellar, though they could not be seen by others, and she threw herself to the floor and threatened to fling herself into the fire, only to be restrained by those in attendance. And so it continued, for days.[54]

Knapp resisted ministerial counsel, Willard reported, but finally confessed that the Devil had often appeared to her, presented her with a covenant, and offered to her as an inducement to enter into the covenant with him such things as money, silks, fine clothes, and ease from her labor. The Devil's first visit had been three years before, she continued, following her expression of discontent, and for awhile his visits had been infrequent, but as of late they were more constant. He had presented her with "a book written with the blood of covenants made by others" and tempted her to murder her parents, neighbors,

Willard's children, and even Willard himself, but Knapp insisted that she had not succumbed to the Devil's entreaties.[55]

Willard would not pass final judgment on the source of Knapp's fits, but his account strongly suggests that he believed her possessed, not afflicted, thereby involving no others. He concluded with the following thoughts: First, the extreme nature of Knapp's fits evidenced that they were real. Second, her fits did not mimic, and therefore she did not seem to be acting out, possession. Third, despite the severity of her fits, she gained rather than lost weight, and when not afflicted retained her natural strength. Fourth, the functions of her mouth as well as what she had to say appeared to be beyond any of her control; her throat often swelled to the size of a fist, whereupon she occasionally produced at best guttural sounds, at worst reviling terms that he had never heard her utter at any other time, and therefore seemed attributable only to the Devil. And, fifth, she was therefore to be pitied. "I desire that all that hear of her would compassionate her forlorn state," he wrote. "She is (I question not) a subject of hope, and therefore all means ought to be used for her recovery. She is a monument of divine severity; and the Lord grant that all that see or hear, may fear and tremble."[56]

Elizabeth Knapp's possession ended almost as abruptly as it began. In the fall of 1674, she married and moved to Groton, where she lived a very ordinary and uneventful life.[57]

Cotton Mather's description of the Goodwin children's affliction appeared in 1689, only three years before events in Salem. It presented a case more clearly of affliction than of possession, and therefore it was even more influential than that of Elizabeth Knapp on what followed in 1692. As the Reverend John Hale, who was among the first to observe the young girls of Salem, wrote: They were "in all things as bad as John Goodwin's children in Boston in the year 1689. So that he that would read Mr. Mather's book . . . may read part of what these children and afterward sundry grown persons suffered by the hand of Satan, at Salem village and parts adjacent."[58] Several decades later, historian Thomas Hutchinson would observe that the conformity between the two was "so exact, as to leave no room to doubt the stories had been read by the New England [Salem] persons themselves, or had been told to them by others who had read them."[59] Instead of raising suspicion, however, the conformity only confirmed the reality of both episodes.

The Goodwin case began in 1688 in Boston, when four of John Goodwin's children—ages thirteen, eleven, seven, and five—began to display symptoms of diabolical affliction. Mather and other ministers were called in to pray for the children; he stayed to record his observations, much as had Samuel Willard, for whatever lessons it might provide the people of New England.[60]

The case followed the classic pattern of witchcraft charges in seventeenth-century New England. Martha, a thirteen-year-old child, accused the woman who did the family's laundry of stealing linens from them. Mary Glover, the mother of the laundress, responded to Martha with "harsh language," whereupon Martha's affliction began. When no physical cause or medical remedy could be found, Mary Glover and her daughter were arrested, but only Mary was put on trial.[61]

Mary Glover, who was Catholic and knew English, spoke Gaelic at her trial, leading Mather to comment that it was the result of a charm upon her. The evidence used against her included testimony that six years before the Goodwin children became ill she had bewitched a woman to death. Before she died, that woman told another by the name of Hughes that Glover was to blame. When Hughes prepared to offer this in testimony at Glover's trial, her son was stricken, and he claimed to have seen Glover's specter. In the end, Glover confessed to practicing image magic—the use of poppets—and she was executed on November 16, 1688.[62]

A number of points in Cotton Mather's report are helpful for our better understanding not only of the Goodwin case but of all cases in seventeenth-century New England, including Salem. To begin with, reflecting the widespread belief in witchcraft, Mather reported that when it became known that his children were stricken, Goodwin's neighbors urged him to use counter-magic, a suggestion Mather rejected. Second, Mather pointed out that the fits of the children continued even after Glover was executed. This might have led Mather and others to either continue the search for additional witches or revise their diagnosis from affliction to possession. Neither, however, occurred, although Mather at least considered the latter.[63]

Upon Glover's execution, Mather, observing that Martha Goodwin was "growing very far towards possession," took Goodwin into his home to heal her spiritually. When Martha reported that there were three other women witches in Boston besides Glover, he did not act, but rather kept the names to himself. Mather never abandoned the diagnosis of witchcraft, or affliction, and his belief in Glover's guilt, but his caution is notable, perhaps forestalling what might have become the Boston witch-hunt. Nevertheless, the case only served to confirm what he already believed concerning the reality of witches. Upon completing his observation of Martha Goodwin, he resolved "after this, never to use but just one grain of patience with any man that shall go to impose upon me a denial of devils or witches."[64]

Mather described John Goodwin as "sober and pious," and he concluded that the children were suffering from the effects of "stupendous witchcraft." He admitted that the children, as other children, had been tempted by the "temptations of idleness," but that there was no reason to believe that in this matter, they "dissembled" rather than being genuinely afflicted. Mary Glover, in contrast, according to Mather, was "an ignorant and a scandalous woman . . . whose husband before he died, had sometimes complained . . . that she was undoubtedly a witch," and who had long been a feared presence in the neighborhood. She had reacted to Martha Goodwin with the vilest of retorts and the result was "very grievous":

> Sometimes they [the children] would be deaf, sometimes dumb, and sometimes blind, and often all this at once. One while their tongues would be drawn down their throats; another while they would be pulled out upon their chins, to a prodigious length. They would have their mouths opened unto such a wideness, that their jaws went out of joint. . . . They would make most piteous outcries, that they were cut with knives, and struck with blows that they could not bear. Their necks would be broken, so that their neck bone would seem dissolved unto them that felt after it . . . their heads would be twisted almost round; and . . . they would roar exceedingly.[65]

Elsewhere, Mather wrote that when he prayed before them the children shrieked "they say we must not listen," and that upon occasion they had tried to throw themselves into the fireplace. He noted that it had been reported that upon occasion the children had flown "like geese," with "incredible swiftness . . . having but just their toes now and then upon the ground, and their arms waved like the wings of a bird," in one instance, about twenty feet without touching the floor. He reported that at mealtime they occasionally could not eat, but that usually they did, and, like Elizabeth Knapp, by evening their labors ceased and they slept all night "for the most part indifferently well."[66]

Mather reported that although John Goodwin accused Mary Glover, he "had no proof that could have done her any hurt." When summoned for questioning by the magistrates, however, Glover "gave such a wretched account of herself" that they saw cause to commit her. She did not deny she had "enchanted" the children, and when asked if she believed there was a God, Mather wrote, "her answer was too blasphemous and horrible for my pen to mention." On one occasion, when asked to recite the Lord's Prayer in English, she made "nonsense" of it, even with prompting. At another time, she did recite it in Latin "very readily," but "there was one clause or two always too hard for her, whereon she said she could not repeat it, if she might have all the world."[67]

And, finally, Mary Glover confessed. When presented with the poppets found in her home, Mather reported, she admitted using them and demonstrated how she could afflict the children with them. She admitted that the Devil was her prince, but that "because he had served her so basely and falsely, she had confessed all." When six doctors examined her and declared her *compos mentis,* she was sentenced to death.[68]

Mather visited Glover in jail as she awaited execution. She never denied her guilt, but she confessed little about the circumstances of her meetings with the Devil, except that she had four confederates. When she went to her execution, Glover said that, as there were others, the children would not be relieved by her death, "and it came to pass accordingly," Mather wrote, "that the three children continued in their furnace as before, and it grew seven times hotter than it was." Suspicion shifted to another woman in the neighborhood, but the new suspect died before she could be brought to trial. Almost immediately, the children showed signs of improvement and, by spring, the fires of which Mather spoke cooled.[69]

The Pattern of Witch-hunt Activity in Seventeenth-Century New England

As we have seen, historians of the Great European Witch-hunt have found a strong correlation between periods of substantial economic, political, social, and religious turmoil and significant increases in witch-hunt activity. They have found it to be true in New England as well, with two important qualifications. First, periods of increased witch-hunt activity followed but did not occur simultaneously with times of calamity. It is as if epidemics, hurricanes, crop failures, infestations, fires, and various other reversals channeled New Englanders' energies toward overcoming those obstacles at the same time that they built up resentment toward those they suspected of being responsible for their problems, but that their resentment could only be released when those obstacles had been overcome.[70]

The pattern began with the first significant period of witch-hunt activity in the late 1640s and early 1650s, and it continued through the end of the century. The second important qualification, however, is that in the nearly three decades after 1663, while the pattern continued, there was nevertheless an overall decline in the number of witchcraft prosecutions. In fact, between the Hartford witch-hunt and the outbreak of hostilities in Salem, the number of prosecutions fell from nineteen during the 1660s to six during the 1670s and eight during the 1680s. Only four of those prosecuted were convicted and only one was executed.[71] It was as if New England was experiencing the lull before the storm. And it was in that lull that New England, especially Massachusetts, faced its greatest reversals of fortune, building up unprecedented levels of frustration, anxiety, and resentment.

Focusing on Massachusetts, the final period of growing anxiety might be said to have begun in 1662 with the Massachusetts synod's adoption of the Half-way Covenant. In the face of declining church membership, the Massachusetts ministers authorized churches to baptize and thereby admit to partial membership the children of "half-way" members. "Half-way" members were the children of those who had had the conversion experience necessary for full membership, but who themselves had not yet qualified. For some, this was merely the recognition of reality, as many churches were already bending the law on this point, and this was one way through which to bolster their sagging rosters; for others, it was a sign of failing faith and loss of mission.[72]

Two years later, Massachusetts' long-standing concerns toward its loss of charter and political, as well as religious, authority were renewed. The Stuart Kings of England had not hidden their concern with what they saw as Massachusetts' abuse of their supposed independence from English law, and periodically they discussed revoking, or at least rewriting, the colonial charter upon which Massachusetts stood in its defense of such measures. With their restoration in 1660, that threat seemed, once again, all too real, and much as they feared, in 1664 Charles II appointed a special commission to investigate Massachusetts and its supposed violations of English law and rules governing the colonies. No action was taken, but few believed the threat had passed.[73]

Epidemics of measles, dysentery, influenza, and smallpox struck between mid-century and 1690. During the period 1677–1678 a smallpox epidemic took hundreds of lives; in 1690, it claimed over 150 lives. The colony was struck by a particularly destructive hurricane in 1675, and Boston suffered a devastating fire in 1676, in which over fifty homes and other structures, including the North Meeting House and Increase Mather's parsonage, were destroyed. Three years later, another fire consumed seventy warehouses and several ships in Boston's commercial sector, plus another eighty homes.[74]

And then there was King Philip's War. In one year, 1675–1676, in one of the most vicious wars of the century for New Englanders, Native Americans killed over 600 New Englanders (some estimates list 1,000 deaths), destroyed twelve towns, and looted and burned several others, at one point striking within ten miles of Boston. New Englanders killed as many as 3,000 Native Americans, wiped out entire villages, and sold hundreds of captives into slavery in the West Indies. For many Puritan New Englanders, King Philip's War was a just, if not holy, struggle against the Devil's legions, but for some it raised as well the question of why God, who controlled all things, even the actions of the Devil, had allowed such a thing to happen to his chosen people.[75]

In the decade prior to 1692, virulent epidemics of measles and smallpox reoccurred and hostilities resumed between New Englanders and their French and Native American neighbors. In response to the latter event, which began in 1690, Cotton Mather wrote, "The devils are stark mad that the house of the Lord our God is come unto these remote corners of the world; and they fume, they fret prodigiously." But perhaps the most devastating single blow came in 1684, when the Crown finally revoked Massachusetts' charter and two years later included Massachusetts in its newly conceived political unit of the eight northern colonies known as the Dominion of New England. For the first time, the colony of Massachusetts had thrust upon it a royally appointed governor, who ruled with a royally appointed council, rather than a popularly elected legislature. Revocation of the old charter called property rights into question, while the Dominion government assumed the authority to levy taxes without popular consent and to limit town meetings to only one a year, and then only for the election of local officials.[76]

When news of King James II's downfall reached their ears, New Englanders overthrew the Dominion. They arrested Governor Edmund Andros and created an interim government to administer the colony, largely under terms of the old charter. Nothing permanent could be established, however, until some more permanent settlement was reached with the new royal government of William and Mary. By the winter and spring of 1692, when the first signs of the Salem witch-hunt appeared, no such agreement had yet been reached.[77]

Finally, if only briefly, as it was addressed as a concept in the previous chapter on European context, New England on the eve of the Salem witch trials was experiencing the anxieties of modernization. Seventeenth-century New England, too, was struggling to deal with the problems that accompanied economic change from an agricultural or a traditional to a modern, or commercial, society. And as Paul Boyer and Stephen Nissenbaum have found, "if there was one place in late-seventeenth-century America that was witnessing in an extremely intense form the clash between the vanishing older order and the emerging modern order, it was the two Salems, village and town."[78]

Throughout this period of ill-fortune, Puritan ministers continually commented on and sought to find meaning in what was occurring. They did so in their sermons, treatises, and other forms of literature, thereby creating one of the earliest genres of American literature called the *jeremiad*. This second generation of New England Puritans found a golden age in the era of their forefathers—those who had settled New England. And with that golden age, they associated the ideas of faith and community, from which they believed the people of New England had strayed, if not fallen, thereby failing both their forefathers and God, who had chosen them for his errand.[79]

By the 1660s, there was a growing realization that the highest goals of the founding generation would not be achieved because of the shortcomings of the second generation. Fast-day and election-day sermons increasingly focused on New Englanders' lack of commitment, as compared to their predecessors, and on the divine punishment that would almost certainly result if they did not mend their ways. In 1662, the same year the Half-way Covenant was adopted, Malden minister and poet Michael Wigglesworth described God's reaction to the situation in "God's Controversy with New England":

> For think not, O Backsliders, in your heart,
> That I shall still your evil manners bear:
> Your sins me press as sheaves do load a cart,
> And therefore I will plague you for this gear
> Except you seriously, and soon, repent,
> I'll not delay your pain and heavy punishment.[80]

Wigglesworth's was only one of many public warnings with telling titles such as "New England Pleaded With," "The Day of Trouble is Near," and "The Only Sure Way to Prevent Threatened Calamity." Lay leaders often joined the clergy in their admonishments and underscored the need for reform. The Massachusetts General Court repeatedly called for fast days and publicly listed the sins of the people, along with a litany of external problems.[81]

In 1679, the General Court called for a synod to consider: "What are the provoking evils of New England?" The synod met in Boston and lamented "a great and visible decay of the power of godliness amongst professors in these churches." It listed the several misfortunes that had befallen them—King Philip's War, a smallpox epidemic, two major fires in Boston, and deteriorating relations with London—and attributed them to "holy displeasure." God's displeasure, the synod continued, was due to the moral failings of the second generation, generally described as a decline in godliness and in family discipline, and in the unwillingness of the people to embrace reform. More specifically, the synod cited an increased insubordination of the lower sorts to their betters, violations of the Sabbath, and various immoral and unethical acts, as well as a spread of heretics, contention in congregations, covetousness, and an "inordinate affection" for the world that included merchants who sold their goods at excessive rates and laborers who were "unreasonable in their demands."[82]

The frequent gatherings of New England clergymen thereafter routinely took up similar questions. The Reverend Samuel Parris of Salem village attended one such gathering in 1690 in Cambridge, at which ministers considered a question that illustrates the fundamental reason for the periodic self-flagellation of the Puritans: "What shall be done towards the reformation of the miscarriages for which New England now suffers by the heavy judgements of God."[83] If some were disposed to look within their own souls for the cause of their having lost their way, however, some, like Parris, would search for that evil in others.

Not coincidentally, it was in the 1680s that the New England clergy mounted a sustained campaign against magic. Beginning soon after the reforming synod of 1679, ministers attacked magic from the pulpit and in print. They berated members of their congregations for using magic and explained to them in detail why such practices were offensive to God. They had two fundamental objections to its use. First, they believed that magic relied on diabolical agency, and those who used magical techniques might believe that they themselves had somehow harnessed occult forces to bring about the desired effect, when in fact they had been duped by the Devil. Second, they insisted that those who used magic disregarded providential theology, which entrusted all knowledge and power to God. They were guilty of hubris, or pride, in that they refused to accept their allotted place in the world and sought to usurp God's rightful authority.[84]

People who used magic might not see those dangers, but, wrote the Reverend John Hale, the Devil was assuredly using such devices to seduce New Englanders, "that by sorceries, enchantments, divinations and such like, he may lead them captive at his pleasure." Moreover, he and others reminded their congregations that the Devil was not entirely responsible for their succumbing to his will in those matters. The Devil tempted people because they were already inclined toward sin and therefore fit candidates for his services. Those who succumbed to his temptations were impelled to do so by their own corruption, not by the Devil himself.[85]

In January 1692, only weeks before the discovery of witchcraft in Salem village, Parris addressed the subject of declension in a sermon in which he explained that Christ exercises "his church in spiritual obedience by manifold and various troubles, afflictions, and persecutions in this world." Christ had placed his church in the world as in a sea, Parris explained, "and [it] suffereth many storms and tempests to threaten its shipwreck, whilst in the meantime he himself seems to be fast asleep." Why would Christ, their mediator with a God angered by their sins, seemingly abandon his congregations of the elect? He did so, Parris answered, so as to "humble his church for their sins," to "make his church more watchful against sin," and to "make us more watchful to duty."[86]

In February, Parris returned to the subject again and told his congregation that God had abandoned them because of their "slightings" of Christ: "God is angry and sending forth destroyers." That was on February 14, and by that time the girls of Salem village, even within his own household, had begun to exhibit the afflictions that would plunge the village into a maelstrom of accusations. God had indeed begun "sending forth destroyers."[87]

If by the closing decades of the seventeenth century, some in New England were convinced that the unleashing of God's wrath was at hand, they nonetheless continued to believe that something could still be done to still His hand. New England Puritans believed that God would not abandon His chosen people. Therefore, *jeremiads* commonly ended with a ray of hope. If only they could realize their errant ways and recommit themselves to God's original design, all would be forgiven and they would once again enter God's good graces. That process of recommitment, however, would necessarily involve ferreting out the evil, not only within their hearts but also within their ranks.[88]

It is therefore puzzling why the number of prosecutions for witchcraft declined after 1663. Perhaps colonists lost faith in courts that failed to convict. The effect of the decline, however, is clear. In the midst of this lull before the storm, as their problems multiplied, the people of New England found themselves unable to protect themselves against the harm they believed was being done to them by witches, and they increasingly resorted to an alternative strategy that the clergy condemned as diabolical. As Richard Godbeer has found, "People turned from the law to informal channels such as counter-magic because they were not willing to leave a malefactor's punishment to God [or the courts]. If another human being was responsible for their condition, they wanted to know who it was, and they wanted revenge."[89] And although it may have been delayed during the 1670s and 1680s, in 1692 they had their revenge.

3

"The Evil Hand" Is Upon Them

Exactly why the witch-hunt of 1692 began in Salem village and not elsewhere in New England will perhaps never be fully explained. Historians of the Great European Witch-hunt, who have raised the question relative to other communities, have tended to focus on extraordinary strains with which those communities, for whatever reasons, were not able to cope. And to be sure, many New England communities had their fair share of strains. Several suffered from the economic, social, political, and religious dislocations of the modernization process of the Early Modern Period, but to a greater extent than others Salem village fell victim to warring factions, misguided leadership, and geographical limitations that precluded its dealing effectively with those problems.

A Glimpse At Salem's Past

In 1692, Salem village, now Danvers, had a population of about 600. It remained part of Salem town, but it had already earned the reputation of being one of New England's most contentious communities.

Not surprisingly, when accusations of witchcraft were made, they followed the lines formed by that contentiousness.[1]

Salem, located on the north shore of Massachusetts Bay, had always looked to the sea. Settled in 1626 as a fishing station and trading post, it became a principal destination for the great Puritan migration of the 1630s, among whom many became involved in trading networks that exported fur, fish, grain, and timber to ports in England, Spain, Africa, and the West Indies. Grants of land were made in the interior, including what was to become Salem village, and some measure of agrarian prosperity was achieved, but in general owners of interior lands increasingly became either dependent on, or isolated from, the town's commercial interests.[2]

By 1680, the probated estates of the town's merchants were almost ten times as valuable as those of its farmers. In the period from 1661 to 1681, the richest 10 percent of Salem's population, almost exclusively merchants, controlled 62 percent of the town's wealth, about three times as much as it had a generation earlier. And by about the same time, merchants gained control of town politics and church affairs, consistently winning a majority of the town's selectmen posts and seats in the General Court (the colonial legislature), as well as a majority on the town's church committee. Prior to 1665, for example, twice as many farmers as merchants were elected town selectmen; from 1665 to 1700, merchant selectmen outnumbered farmers six to one.[3]

Since its founding, four other areas, originally part of Salem—Wenham, Manchester, Marblehead, and Beverly—had been granted separate incorporation. Salem village had not, and likely, fearing the further loss of tax revenue, the town seemed committed to its separation. In 1672, the village had acquired permission to call its own minister, thus sparing villagers the as much as ten-mile trek to the town meetinghouse on the Sabbath, but that was granted only after repeated petitioning, and then with limitations.

Salem town allowed villagers to use their church tax to construct a meetinghouse of their own and to hire a minister. It did not authorize them, however, to establish an entirely separate congregation; thus, the minister of the village church could not distribute communion, baptize believers, or discipline its members, and those who attended retained their official membership elsewhere, mostly in the town church. Otherwise, villagers continued to pay all other town taxes; to have their constables and representatives to the General Court chosen by all town residents; and to have the town selectmen continue to set the prices at which their farm products could be sold, as well as to determine the location of new roads and the distribution of yet undistributed lands.[4]

Acting on what limited autonomy they had been granted, Salem village residents met on November 11, 1672, to elect a committee to plan the construction of their new church and to hire their first minister. Accomplishing both, however, did little to ease strained relations between the village and Salem town. Moreover, it exacerbated a growing rift within the village itself, between those who sought further independence from the town and those who opposed it. The establishment of a fully covenanted church and appointment of a like-minded minister became central to that quarrel.

Kinship was a primary determinant of social action in the seventeenth-century Puritan New England community, so it is not surprising that the contending Salem village factions were led by two dominant families, the Porters and the Putnams. The patriarchs of both families had arrived in Salem in the 1640s, and through marriage, business, and politics gathered around them an extensive network of family, partners, and allies. The second generation had grown wealthy, but the Porters, who owned land primarily on the east side of the village and maintained close commercial ties to the town, grew more prosperous. By 1681, the three Putnam brothers—Thomas Sr., Nathaniel, and John Sr.—whose lands lay primarily in the northwestern part of the village, paid the largest taxes in the village. When lands outside of the village were included, however, the Porters paid even more.[5]

Further, the Putnams, who relied almost exclusively on farming, faced a less-certain future. Not only did their land lack convenient access to markets by either land or water, but it was less arable, consisting in large part of hills and swampy meadows. Moreover, while the overall total of Putnam lands increased only slightly, it was being divided among a larger number of households. What was once distributed among three male Putnams, by the 1690s was being divided eleven ways.[6]

The families' political fortunes diverged as well. The Porters excelled in town politics, the Putnams in village affairs. As early as 1646, John Porter was elected to the first of many terms as a Salem town selectman. In 1668, he served as deputy to the General Court. In 1661, he became a deacon in the Salem town church and upon his death in 1676 left it a bequest. The second generation followed their father's example, the most prominent being Israel Porter, who from 1679 through the end of the century served almost uninterruptedly as a town selectman.[7]

Before 1672, the year the village church was established, the Putnams had been active in town affairs, even serving in town office. But thereafter, perhaps at first by choice but then almost certainly because of the rise to power of the town's commercial class, they focused almost exclusively on village affairs. From 1665 to 1673, for example, Nathaniel and John Putnam served a total of seven terms as town selectmen; for the next nineteen years, they served only five terms, and none of their sons took their places.[8]

The one notable exception to this family pattern was Joseph, the second son and only child of Thomas Putnam Sr., by his second wife Mary. Upon Thomas's death in 1686, he left to Mary and, upon his maturity, to Joseph, the larger part of his estate, including the family homestead. Joseph's step-siblings were by no means excluded from their father's will. Thomas Jr. and Edward were given farms of their own, but they were convinced that their father had favored the son of his old age and second love. In 1690, Joseph Putnam, by then the wealthiest of all of the third-generation Putnams, married Elizabeth Porter, entering into an alliance with his family's enemies to which he remained faithful to the end.[9]

Between 1672 and 1689, Salem village hired and then hounded out of office three ministers: James Bayley, George Burroughs, and Deodat Lawson. Bayley, a young Harvard graduate, came to the pulpit in October 1672. At first, all went well, but by 1679 a significant minority was in open rebellion. An appeal was made to the Salem town church to help resolve the conflict, whereupon the Reverend John Higginson concluded that because Bayley had the support of a majority of his parishioners all members should submit to him. The opposition did not submit, however, and at a village church committee meeting on September 11, 1679, the anti-Bayley faction managed to gather a sufficient number of votes to dismiss him by the end of the year. Several petitions to the General Court followed, in response to which the Assistants (members of the upper house) directed the village to continue to employ Bayley, only to have the Deputies (members of the lower house) limit the edict to one year, after which the church would be free to do what it wished.[10]

In an attempt to alleviate the problem, Bayley wrote a letter to village residents voicing his concern over the "uncomfortable divisions and contentions" that had existed among them. Although no doubt true, his letter only served to make matters worse. Soon he was charged with encouraging factions, theological unorthodoxy, and even neglect of family prayers. Although exonerated by the General Court,

Bayley stepped down in 1680, despairing of any comfortable future among such a divided lot.[11]

George Burroughs, Salem village's second minister and another Harvard graduate, had preached in Falmouth (Portland), Maine, on Casco Bay, until the settlement was destroyed by Indians in 1676, and thereafter in Salisbury, Massachusetts. Like his predecessor, it did not take long for the new minister to get into trouble with his divided congregation. And once again, it began over salary. From the start, Burroughs had not been fully paid, and when upon the death of his wife in 1681 he pressed the matter, some rebuked him for it. By early 1683, Burroughs stopped meeting his congregation, accepted an offer to return to the rebuilt community on Casco Bay, and departed.[12]

The Salem village committee, elected by village residents to manage the church tax, appealed to the Essex County Court to order Burroughs to return to settle his outstanding debts. On May 2, 1683, he returned to face his creditors, and apparently, without the knowledge of others, John Putnam Sr. had Burroughs arrested. When he could pay neither the debt nor his bail, he was jailed. In 1681, at the time of his wife's death, and again in 1682, Putnam had extended Burroughs credit, in the first instance to pay funeral expenses. Both sides agreed that the loan was to be an advance on Burroughs's salary, but as his salary was never paid, neither was Putnam. The various suits brought against Burroughs were settled out of court, and he returned to Maine, but the Putnams were not done with him, as we shall see.[13]

The third minister to answer Salem's call was Deodat Lawson. Lawson, English-born and Cambridge-educated, had served as minister to Martha's Vineyard before being called to Salem village. Upon his arrival in 1684, a period of calm descended on Salem village, but in 1686, controversy arose once again. It began with a renewed effort on the part of some residents to establish a fully covenanted church in their midst and to ordain Lawson as their first fully empowered minister. Leading the change were John Putnam and his nephew Thomas Putnam Jr., both of whom were members of the village committee. Leading the opposition were Joseph Hutchinson, Jeb Swinnerton, Joseph Porter, and Porter's brother-in-law Daniel Andrew. When the sides could not be reconciled, they agreed to submit the matter to five Salem town arbitrators: John Hathorne, Bartholomew Gedney, and William Brown Jr., three prominent merchants, and the Reverends John Higginson and Nicholas Noyes of the town church.[14]

Villager Jeremiah Watts described the affair as pitting "brother . . . against brother and neighbors against neighbors, all quarreling and smiting one another," and accordingly the arbitrators chastised both sides for their "uncharitable expressions and uncomely reflections tossed to and fro," and for their "settled prejudice" and "animosity." They also advised against a full covenanting, at least until residents' spirits had been "better quieted and composed." That not being accomplished, in 1688 Deodat Lawson departed.[15]

Finally there was Samuel Parris. Born in London in 1653, Parris moved with his family to Barbados, where his father became a sugar planter and merchant. He attended Harvard College, but in 1678, upon his father's death, he returned to the island, without his degree, as executor of his father's estate. He too became a merchant, but after about eight years, when his business was irreparably harmed by a devastating hurricane and a sustained drop in world sugar prices, Parris sold out and moved to Boston. He tried to compete with the city's already established men of commerce, but failing at that he opted for the ministry, and in November 1688, he preached for the first time in Salem village.[16]

Upon his first visit Parris so sufficiently impressed the congregation that they voted to accept him as their minister, but it took months of protracted discussion over salary to complete the hiring process, as well as to sow the seeds of future discontent. On June 18, 1689, Parris's contract was recorded in the Village Book of Record, but negotiations over compensation continued. In October, the village committee—consisting of Nathaniel and John Putnam, Jonathan Walcott and Thomas Flint (both connected to the Putnams by marriage), and Nathaniel Ingersoll—voted to grant Parris the deed to the village parsonage and two acres of land. In 1681, the property had been set aside for the support of the village's minister, with the provision that it not be given to him, but the committee voted to rescind the earlier action. It may have been legal, but the decision was not universally popular.[17]

At the same time Salem village was hiring Samuel Parris, Salem town finally granted the village permission to gather an independent congregation. Thus, on November 19, 1689, Samuel Parris, age thirty-six, became the village's first independent minister. On the occasion of its first gathering, twenty-five villagers joined Parris and his wife in signing the church's covenant. Three members of the village committee that had led the move for full establishment signed the covenant; none of the four who were opposed signed. Eleven of the Putnam clan signed the covenant; none of the Porters signed. The Porters would attend the village church, but they would remain members of the town meetinghouse.[18]

In his ordination sermon, the delivery of which he abbreviated because of the "sharpness" of the weather, the Reverend Parris proclaimed

Photograph of a portrait of Samuel Parris, a central figure in the Salem Witch trials. From the Massachusetts Historical Society.

the dawn of a new era. He acknowledged the disquiet that had plagued the congregation, but he urged his flock to put behind them all past controversies and indiscretions. The burden of leading members toward reconciliation would be his, he allowed, but if they were to seize the opportunity they must accept his leadership. They must treat him as an "ambassador of Christ Jesus" and abandon the "unchristian like behavior" they had exhibited toward their ministers in the past. In particular, Parris excused the extremes to which proponents of independence—and his supporters—had gone in the past, by suggesting that their cause was, after all, a just cause.[19]

Finally, in 1689, perhaps buoyed by their other successes, Salem villagers made another attempt for independence. The results, however, were disastrous. In July 1689, just two weeks after Parris's hiring, John and Nathaniel Putnam were elected town selectmen. In August, they led the village in their petition, but the town selectmen rejected it. One week after the election of 1689, Israel Porter, Daniel Andrew, and Timothy Lindall (related to the Porters by marriage) had resigned. Following rejection of the Putnams' petition, however, each was returned to office, where they were joined in March 1692 by another Porter kinsman by marriage, Thomas Gardner, and Philip English, a Porter ally, for a total of five out of seven town selectmen seats![20]

As a result of the village's continued quarreling, as well as his unseemly contractual haggling, Parris's ministry was in trouble from the start. His approach to his calling no doubt made matters worse. First of all, Parris resisted recent trends to open church doors to all comers of attestably sound character, a policy that followed upon adoption of the still much maligned Half-way Covenant of 1662. Parris continued to demand that candidates for church membership demonstrate, and have witnesses to, a work of "faith and repentance wrought in their souls," and that only those children of at least one such parent having entered into full communion with the church be eligible for baptism. For the first year, this did not seem to have been a problem. Church membership grew rapidly, and despite Parris's strictures on baptism, fifty-one children received the sacrament.[21] But then, just as dramatically, it stalled.

Second, Parris espoused the traditional Calvinist doctrine that all men were evil by nature, but that through Christ's sacrifice and atonement God had chosen some for salvation. Through self-scrutiny and with the confirming judgment of others, the elect could be assured that they had been chosen by God and could enter into the church of Christ as Parris intended it to be, namely a body gathered by separating the elect from the rest of mankind as Christ's "peculiar flock." Their task,

Parris reminded the elect, was not only to follow the teachings of Christ, but also to guard the church against its enemies, those followers of the Devil who existed everywhere and at all times.[22]

Parris's exclusion from the elect of those who could not, or would not, demonstrate their having been chosen by God, and his increasing tendency to include his enemies among the excluded, raised the ire of many village residents. The stall in new signers of the church covenant has been noted. But there was also an increase in the number of residents who began to absent themselves from worship, while some of those who attended, Parris complained, sat "as senseless as the seats they sat on," or as the "dead bodies they sometimes tread on." Finally, in September 1690, the village committee reported that 20 percent of the 1689/1690 church tax remained unpaid fourteen months after it had been assessed. In April 1691, the figure had increased to 29 percent.[23]

On October 16, 1691, members of the Porter faction—Joseph Porter, Joseph Hutchinson, Joseph Putnam, Daniel Andrew, and Francis Nurse—were elected to a majority of the village committee. Once in office, they promptly challenged the legality of Parris's ownership of the parsonage, and two months later they refused to assess taxes for the payment of Parris's 1692 salary. The Reverend Parris was in trouble, and he knew it. He announced from the pulpit that although through him Christ had "begun a new work" in Salem village, it was "the main drift of the Devil to pull it all down."[24]

It was not a new message for the Reverend Parris; it had evolved over the past two years in response to the growing challenge to his ministry. As early as January 1690, he had warned his congregation that although they may have pretended to be friends, the "rotten-hearted" were neither to be trusted nor expected to keep their distance. They could infiltrate even innocent communities, a point he returned to in February when he warned that there was "great guiltiness upon this account in this poor little village," and again in January 1692, when he charged that a "great hatred ariseth even from nearest relations."[25] In such sermons, Parris exacerbated the growing fear of one segment of his congregation of "outsiders," those of Salem town, but he also emphasized, to an even greater extent by 1692, the threat of internal subversion posed by those in their midst who were linked to those outsiders.

Although in retreat, the pro-Parris faction was by no means ready to accept defeat, and they marshalled their forces for what would prove to be one last devastating counterattack. In November 1691, the elders of the church, led by the Putnams, asked the village committee to levy a tax for the payment of Parris's salary. When the committee took no action, the elders sued the committee in county court. The committee countered by calling a village meeting on December 1 to investigate once again the legality of the action of 1689, whereby the parsonage and land was deeded over to Parris. No record of the meeting survives. It may never have happened, or if it did, nothing was resolved and there is no mention of any other village committee meetings until early March 1692, at which point the witchcraft hysteria had begun.[26]

By 1692, Salem village had reached the point of institutional, demographic, and economic polarization. The church served as the locus of one faction, the village committee served the other. Seventy percent of village church members supported the Reverend Parris, while only 13 percent opposed him. Of those who retained their membership in the town or other churches while worshipping in Salem village, only 56 percent supported Parris, almost all of the rest being listed among the opposition. Of the twelve wealthiest men of Salem village who made their opinions known, only four, all Putnams, supported Parris; eight, all Porters, opposed him. In contrast, of forty-six largely middle-class male residents whose positions were known, thirty-one backed Parris, while fifteen stood opposed. As Boyer and Nissenbaum have concluded, Parris's opposition constituted a minority in the village, but they owned as much property as his more numerous supporters.[27]

In geographic terms, Parris's opposition tended to come from those living on village lands nearest Salem town, especially along Ipswich Road, which connected the town to Boston. In that area, opponents outnumbered supporters by a ratio of six-to-one. Among residents of the northwestern half of the village, Parris's supporters led opponents four-to-one. In between lay an area in which proponents and opponents were more evenly divided, with an edge to Parris.[28]

Under such circumstances, that the witch-hunt of 1692 began at Salem makes more sense than it does at first glance. Historic frustrations had been translated into a life-and-death struggle over a way of life. Of the first four afflicted girls in Salem village, two lived in the Samuel Parris household and a third was Ann Putnam, daughter of Thomas Putnam Jr.; three of the afflicted girls who lived in the household of Thomas Putnam Jr. formally testified against at least twenty-five accused witches; and those same three girls were backed by adult members of the Putnam clan, seven of whom testified or signed complaints against thirty-nine of the accused witches, which could be no coincidence.[29]

We should recall, however, a point made at the outset: the people of seventeenth-century Salem believed in witches. Further, there is no direct evidence by which we can attribute those charges brought in the Salem witch trials entirely to factional politics or to a conscious effort

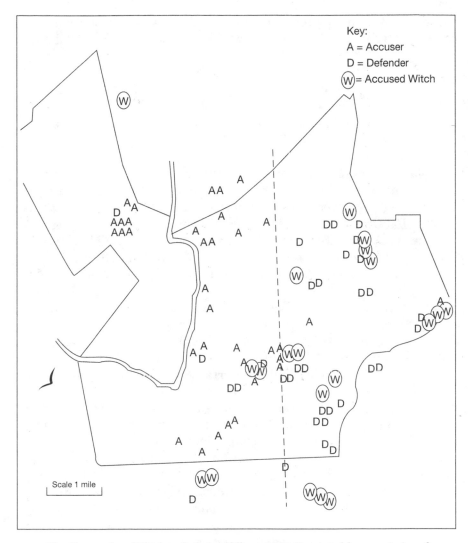

The Geography of Witchcraft: Salem Village, 1692. Reprinted by permission of the publisher from SALEM POSSESSED by Paul Boyer and Stephen Nissenbaum, Cambridge, Mass.: Harvard University Press, Copyright © 1974 by the President and Fellows of Harvard College.

on the part of one group to punish the other for economic and political wrongs. But in the end, even the young girls could not have been oblivious to the bitterness and resentment that had pervaded their own household.[30] When leaders of the pro-Parris faction, including Parris himself, resorted to denouncing their opponents as morally defective individuals—demonizing them, if you will—it was only one small step further to attribute their behavior to the influence of the Devil.

THE FIRST SIGNS OF THE DEVIL

Salem winters were long, and typically the children of the Reverend Samuel Parris's household were confined to their house for what must have seemed an eternity. They had little else to occupy their time but their chores and listening to the slave Tituba reminisce about her homeland, Barbados, and perhaps demonstrate the arts of fortune-telling and conjuring that she had brought with her from her Caribbean home. We may never know exactly what went on in the parsonage, but the Reverend John Hale of nearby Beverly later reported, "I know one of the afflicted persons, who (as I was credibly informed), did try with an egg and glass to find her future husband's calling, till there came up a coffin, that is, a specter or likeness of a coffin. And she afterward followed with diabolical molestation to her death."[31] Suspending an egg white in water to divine the future seems harmless enough, but at the time it was fraught with danger for the young and impressionable girls of Salem village. They had been warned that such dabbling could open their souls to the Devil!

At first, the circle Tituba entertained may have included only Betty, Parris's nine-year-old daughter, and Abigail, his eleven-year-old niece and probably an orphan. It soon widened, however, to encompass several other equally curious and bored young single women ranging in age from eleven to twenty. Perhaps the most dangerous of the group was Ann, the twelve-year-old daughter of Thomas and Ann Putnam.

We have already spoken of Thomas Putnam. Ann Putnam Sr. had come to Salem in 1672 with her sister Mary, wife of the Reverend James Bayley. Bayley's tumultuous years in the pulpit have already been noted; that the tumult took its toll on Mary Bayley has not. One pregnancy after another ended in death, and finally, severely weakened by her misfortunes, Mary herself died. Ann attributed her sister's physical adversities and death to the harassment the Bayleys had received at the hands of their enemies. Moreover, she too had lost babies and suffered in mind and body, and she believed she was about to discover the cause of all of her, and her sister's, misery.

Ann Putnam dreamed that her sister, her sister's children, and her own deceased offspring stood before her "in their winding-sheets, piteously stretching out their hands." They spoke to her, but she could not make out their words. When she learned of Tituba's activities, she resolved that with Tituba's help, through the medium of her daughter, she would learn what her spectral visitors had to say, or who was responsible for all that had befallen her. As one author has put it in describing Ann's approach to the parsonage door to join in its forbidden activities: "Ann had come on a serious, even a tragic errand."[32]

Twelve-year-old Ann was among the first stricken, but soon thereafter the Putnam household produced three more of the afflicted: Mercy Lewis, a servant of some seventeen years; seventeen-year-old Mary Walcott, a relative; and Ann Putnam Sr. In time, the girls formally testified against at least twenty-five alleged witches, and they were supported in their testimony by Ann Sr. and the Putnam men. A total of eight members of the Putnam family, drawn from all three branches, were involved in the prosecution of no fewer than forty-six witches![33]

As noted in the previous chapter, such "little sorceries," as Cotton Mather would call them, were commonly practiced in seventeenth-century New England, but they were nevertheless forbidden and increasingly denounced from the pulpit. Only those in league with the Devil, ministers explained, could successfully employ such powers. Not surprisingly, then, some time in January the pressure grew too great for the youngest of the group, Betty Parris, and she began to respond in a manner that deeply disturbed even those well acquainted with the most devastating maladies of the day. At first, Betty became uncharacteristically absentminded and at other times, often while supposed to be engaged in prayer, preoccupied, silently staring into space. She began to lapse into periods of weeping, and finally she succumbed to uncontrollable bouts of incomprehensible babbling, choking, barking like a dog, and writhing in pain as if being physically tormented by some mysterious invisible being. Abigail soon matched Betty's signs of affliction.[34]

Samuel Parris and other adults resorted, alternatively, to words of comfort and reprimand, but neither served the purpose, and when prayers were offered the two responded even more violently. Betty sobbed and at one point hurled a Bible across the room; Abigail covered her ears, stamped her feet, and roared at the top of her lungs. Understandably embarrassed as well as concerned, Parris tried to keep the matter quiet, but to no avail. Soon, people in increasingly large numbers were coming to the parsonage to see the girls in action, and once word of the affliction spread, still other girls, whose connection to Tituba was tenuous at best, also fell victim. Mary Walcott and Susannah Sheldon, age eighteen and the Walcott's servant, fell into convulsions, as did Mercy Lewis, Mary Warren, age twenty and servant to John and Elizabeth Proctor, and Sarah Churchill, also twenty, George Jacob's servant.[35]

Some in the girls' audience were no doubt merely curious as to the goings-on, but most were alarmed by what they saw as an evil portent. They no doubt remembered what had happened only four years earlier in Boston, when the Goodwin children succumbed to the wiles of Witch Glover. Parris called in those who might discover the cause of the girls' afflictions. He summoned Salem's own Dr. William Griggs, whose seventeen-year-old niece Elizabeth Hubbard was among the afflicted, and he confirmed Parris's worst fears. When he could neither find a natural cause nor prescribe effective medical treatment, Griggs concluded that "the evil hand" was upon them.[36] Parris appealed to area ministers for help, and although it was still mid-winter and roads and paths were barely passable, they responded. From Salem town came the Reverend Nicholas Noyes, who was hardly noted for his kindness to unrepentant sinners, but from Beverly came the more kindly Reverend John Hale.

In 1648, at age twelve, Hale was present at the execution of convicted witch Margaret Jones of Charlestown, and he later recalled that he was impressed by Jones's protestations of innocence unto death.[37] Since then, Hale had been called out on similarly troublesome missions, and in each case he had resisted considerable pressure and evidence to conclude that the Devil was responsible. Two such cases involved women to be charged during the Salem witch trials.

In 1670, Dorcas Hoar of Beverly confessed to practicing palmistry, only to have Hale send her on her way with a reprimand. Eight years later, he suspected Hoar and her children were helping his servant, Margaret Lord, steal from his house. His daughter admitted that she knew of the theft but chose not to tell him for fear of Hoar's power to "raise the Devil to kill her, or bewitch her."[38] And shortly thereafter, Rebecca Hale died.

Hale dismissed Lord, and there is no record of her prosecution. Hoar, however, was charged with stealing, and area residents testified to having witnessed various suspicious occurrences implying witchcraft. Hale recalled his daughter's testimony, adding that Hoar had shown Rebecca a book by which she could foresee what Rebecca might tell her father of Hoar's stealing. Still, Hale refused to accuse Hoar of witchcraft, and the court found her, her husband, and her daughters guilty of "entertaining" Margaret Lord, not the Devil, and of receiving stolen goods for which they were ordered to pay costs.[39]

In the second case, in 1687, Hale adjudicated a quarrel between Sarah Bishop and Christian Trask, both of Beverly. Trask accused Sarah and her third husband, Edward Bishop, both of whom were tavern keepers, of encouraging late night revels that included minors and disturbed the peace. On one occasion, Hale reported, Trask entered the tavern, and finding some at shuffle board, took the pieces, threw them into the fire, and reproved Sarah Bishop.[40]

Soon after, Trask showed remorse for her actions and asked Hale to inform the Bishops that she wished to become friends with them again. Before Hale could bring about any reconciliation, however, Trask became distraught and a month later she was found with her windpipe and jugular vein severed. A pair of scissors lay nearby. It was officially ruled a suicide, but some, including Hale, had their doubts. Seven years earlier, Bishop had been suspected of being a witch, and Hale recalled that Trask had believed himself bewitched by Bishop. But once again, neither he nor the court was willing to find Bishop culpable.[41]

Upon his arrival in Salem village, Hale's first task was to observe the children. He recorded what he saw:

> [The children] were bitten and pinched by invisible agents. Their arms, necks, and backs turned this way and that way, and returned back again, so as it was impossible for them to do so themselves, and beyond the power of any epileptic fits, or natural disease to effect. Sometime they were taken dumb, their mouths stopped, their throats choked, their limbs racked and tormented so as might move a heart of stone to sympathize with them, with the bowels of compassion for them.[42]

He and the other ministers presided over a day of fast and prayer and took spiritual measures to deal with the malady. Failing to elicit any positive response, the Massachusetts ministers also feared "the hand of Satan" was upon the children.

At that point, a diagnosis of possession was still possible. The girls, after all, had been dabbling with forbidden magic, and they could not name their afflicters. Possibly because of Hale's influence, the ministers initially urged Parris to proceed cautiously, to pray to God, and to await God's guidance, but the ranks of the afflicted were growing. Perhaps also wishing to protect the girls' reputation by ruling out possession, Parris would not be calmed. He began to demand of the afflicted the names of their tormentors.[43]

"Who torments you?" Parris asked of each girl, but at first none responded. He provided the names of old suspects, but still there was no response. Some of the village women took matters into their own hands, fighting sorcery with sorcery. On February 25, Mary Sibley, the aunt of one of the afflicted, Mary Walcott, directed Tituba and John Indian, Tituba's husband, in the baking of a "witch cake." Rye meal was mixed with the afflicted children's urine, and the mixture was baked and fed to a dog. If the girls were bewitched, it was believed, the creature would exhibit similar physical manifestations. When Parris found out about it, however, he flew into a rage, in response to which Betty uttered the name of Tituba and fell into a swoon. Abigail Williams, Elizabeth Hubbard, and Ann Putnam soon joined in the chorus, adding the names of Sarah Good and Sarah Osborne.[44]

With her exotic Caribbean background and well-known knowledge of the suspect arts, as well as her proximity to the afflicted, it was perhaps inevitable that Tituba would be charged. And as previously noted, she well may have entertained the girls with her "little sorceries." Sarah Good and Sarah Osborne, however, were also vulnerable. Kai Erikson once described Sarah Good as "a proper hag of a witch if Salem village had ever seen one," and if only by reputation that would seem to have been the case.[45]

The daughter of a prosperous Wenham inn keeper who drowned himself in 1672, Sarah was wrongfully denied her inheritance because of complications following the remarriage and death of her mother. Upon the death of Sarah's first husband, a penniless former indentured servant who left her in considerable debt, she married William Good. When they could not pay Sarah's creditors, William went to jail and they lost their property. Now among the landless poor, seen as eccentric and outspoken, melancholic and distracted, Sarah and her children followed William throughout the village seeking day labor and begging handouts. Only a few years before she had been suspected of spreading smallpox throughout the village.[46]

Much feared was the prospect that during her regular naps in neighborhood barns, Sarah Good's pipe would set the hay ablaze. Much resented was what people saw as her ungrateful response to their charity toward her or the unintelligible grumbling with which she departed those who turned her away empty-handed. Unintelligible muttering, however, was one thing; disorderly female speech, as it was known, was quite another. Disorderly female speech, or displays of insolence through verbal threats, scolding, cursing, or slandering, called attention to and helped condemn Good, as it had other women before and after. Such use of language by women both clashed with the Puritan construct of womanhood and was seen as a serious threat by a people who believed that words, especially those of someone trafficking with the Devil, could cause real physical harm.[47]

Sarah Osborne was not as poor as Sarah Good, but she shared in some of her other liabilities. She was considerably older, at age sixty, and her fortunes had declined in several ways. A native of Watertown, Massachusetts, in 1662 she had married Robert Prince, a Salem villager who owned a 150-acre farm next to Captain John Putnam Sr. Sarah Osborne's sister had married Putnam, and Sarah's husband allied himself with Putnam and the village independence movement as well.[48]

Soon after Prince died in 1674, Sarah's reputation suffered when she invited Alexander Osborne, a much younger Irish immigrant whose remaining indenture she had purchased for fifteen pounds, into her home to care for her and her property and, it was said, into her bed. Although in time Sarah married William and they both joined the church, the indiscretion was not forgotten. Moreover, her sons James and Joseph, from her first marriage, accused her of remarrying in an attempt to deprive them of their inheritance. In his will, Prince stipulated that his sons were to receive his lands when they came of age. He named John and Thomas Putnam executors of his will, and soon they were engaged in a protracted legal dispute with Alexander and Sarah Osborne over their attempts to give Alexander permanent legal control over Prince's land.[49]

Finally, perhaps all of these problems led her to commit another serious error, which was failing to attend church. At the time of her arrest, according to her husband and others, she had not been to church for over three years. She explained that she was ill, and indeed she had often been bedridden. Her marriage to Alexander Osborne seemed not to have been a happy one, and her mind was often depressed, if not deranged. But some no doubt wondered whether she was otherwise occupied, perhaps worshiping the Devil.[50]

On February 29 (it was a leap year), Thomas and Edward Putnam, Joseph Hutchinson, and Thomas Preston swore formal complaints against Tituba, Good, and Osborne, and arrest warrants were issued charging them with suspicion of witchcraft committed against Elizabeth Parris, Abigail Williams, Ann Putnam, and Elizabeth Hubbard.[51] The women were taken into custody and held in the nearby Ipswich jail until a preliminary hearing could determine if the evidence was sufficient to hold them for an appearance before a grand jury. John Hathorne and Jonathan Corwin, the town's assistants or delegates to the colonial legislature's upper house, were called to preside at that hearing.

As members of the General Court, Hathorne and Corwin were at least generally familiar with the law, if not formally trained as judges. As we have already seen, the Bible and British and colonial law were clear on one point: "Thou shalt not suffer a witch to live." Whereas British law was more detailed, however, colonial statutes were decidedly vague, especially in terms of evidentiary standards.[52]

The magistrates no doubt believed that they could recognize acts of witchcraft when they saw them, but just how would they define witchcraft as a punishable offense in a court of law? What testimony would be allowed? What evidence would be required for their ordering the accused held?

For their guidance the magistrates likely turned to the standard legal texts available to them, as well as to learned theological treatises by English divines who were conversant with the law. During the sixteenth and seventeenth centuries, English writers produced a considerable body of such literature. The literature represented a broad spectrum of opinion, from thinly veiled skepticism, especially as to the Devil's ability to physically intervene in human affairs, to those who doubted not the Devil's power. Puritans sided with the latter, among whom Joseph Glanvill and Richard Baxter produced a sufficient number of "relations" of supernatural incidents to establish the reality of witchcraft. Baxter's *The Certainty of the World of Spirits* (1691) was particularly useful on that count, but Glanvill provided the definition of a witch that was employed by authorities in both England and New England. In *Sadducismus Triumphatus* (*Sadducism Triumphant,* London, 1681), he wrote: "A witch is one who can do or seems to do strange things, beyond the known power of art and ordinary nature, by virtue of a confederacy with evil spirits."[53]

Two other influential studies of witchcraft as a legal problem were William Perkins's *Discourse on the Damned Art of Witchcraft* (1608) and Richard Bernard's *Guide to Grand-Jury Men* (1627). Their goal was to cleanse witch prosecutions of both pagan and "popish" errors (e.g., dunking) and to establish a straightforward procedure for trying witches that would rely on a few unexceptionable criteria. Perkins and Bernard argued that a confession was the most reliable proof of guilt. If the witch did not confess, however, conviction was justifiable only if two or more witnesses testified to having seen the witch either invoking the Devil or performing deeds that unquestionably relied upon diabolical agency. Further, there had to be at least two witnesses for each incriminating incident. Circumstantial evidence concerning illness or misfortune in the aftermath of an argument with the accused, considered maleficia, was welcome, but according to Perkins and Bernard it did not alone justify conviction.[54]

The New England magistrates adopted much of what Perkins, Bernard, and others recommended, but they interpreted and implemented it in their own way. They welcomed witnesses that could testify to suspect incidents that implied diabolical agency, not only recently but over time. Especially plentiful was testimony of willful malevolence on the part of the accused. Large numbers of people were willing to testify to instances of overt hostility on the part of the accused, followed by some unexpected misfortune, including in extreme cases the death of a family member. Whenever possible, authorities tried to buttress such testimony with multiple witnesses and physical evidence, such as the possession of poppets (puppets) or testimony as to the accused's having exhibited supernatural attributes such as superhuman strength or the ability to move from one place to another faster than seemed humanly possible. And they ordered the accused to recite a prayer or passage from scripture, anticipating that if the accused was guilty, he or she would stumble over the wording.[55]

The magistrates would bring the afflicted and the accused face-to-face, believing that if their eyes met and the latter was a witch, the afflicted would fall into a fit of agony, whereupon they would resort to the touch test. In the touch test, the afflicted, while suffering an attack, would be allowed to touch the accused, and, it was believed, if the accused was a witch the malignant fluid would flow back into the body of the witch. Magistrates ordered defendants to be stripped and searched for "witches' teats," any bodily excrescence, especially if found around the genitals, whereby witches could suckle their familiars. And they allowed spectral evidence.[56]

Spectral evidence involved testimony that physical harm to a person or property had been committed by the specter of a particular individual. Spectral evidence had long been admissible in prosecutions for witchcraft in England, but many authorities remained skeptical. Some believed that the Devil was not restricted to using only those with whom he had reached an accord, and that he could assume the shape of an innocent person. For that reason, most British courts had taken the position that such evidence might be treated as supportive but not conclusive, and that it was not to be used exclusively to convict.

By and large, the Salem magistrates and the jury that was dependent on the magistrates' interpretation of the law for their deliberations acted in a manner compatible with accepted legal procedures. Even their encouraging the accused to confess and name others as accomplices was not uncommon. That does not seem to have been the case, however, with spectral evidence, upon which they were too reliant. From the records of the hearings, it appears that the evidence, excluding that based on spectral sightings, was considerable, but it was largely circumstantial and not sufficient to merit in most cases the negative findings of the jury.[57]

Perhaps because they were not conducting formal trials where guilt or innocence was to be established, but only hearings to determine whether the accused were to be held for a grand jury, the magistrates did not consider themselves bound by the limitations jurists had placed on such evidence. They never admitted to that, of course, but it is difficult to avoid the conclusion that when the girls told the Salem magistrates that the specters of the three women "did grievously torment them," the magistrates believed them, and there was little the women could do to defend themselves.[58]

THE HEARINGS BEGIN

The preliminary hearings began on Tuesday, March 1. The magistrates arrived via the road from Salem town, gathering into formation around them the local constabulary and other prominent personages in a solemn yet impressive entourage. With "pennants flying and drums athrob," as one writer has described it, they arrived at Ingersoll's ordinary, where the court was to meet. Finding the space too small to accommodate the crowd that had gathered, the magistrates moved the hearing to the nearby meetinghouse. The Reverend Parris's chair was turned around, thereby providing a bar of justice for the prisoners, and the pulpit was moved back, making room for a large table for the magistrates and their secretary Ezekiel Cheever, later replaced by Parris. In contrast to today's judicial proceedings, the magistrates, in this case mostly Hathorne, conducted the hearings, and the defendants were left to defend themselves without benefit of counsel. In theory, in their search for the truth, the magistrates were to aid the accused in their defense against the charges.[59]

The magistrates called Goody Good (Puritan women of less than gentry rank were addressed as Goody), and two constables brought her, pregnant once again, before the court. Consistent with her reputation, Good would not be a model prisoner. She was often at odds with her jailers. Three times while en route between Salem and her Ipswich jail, she had leaped from her horse attempting to flee, and on one occasion she had tried to kill herself. When in court, Ezekiel Cheever described her responses to the magistrates as having been delivered "in a very wicked, spiteful manner, reflecting and retorting against the authority with base and abusive words." Neither was she convincing, it seems, as Cheever also reported that "many lies she was taken in."[60]

Good ardently, even belligerently, denied having made a "contract with the Devil," or even having "familiarity" with him. She rejected accusations that she had hurt the children or employed someone else to do it. "I scorn it," she replied, but the magistrates persisted. Why had

A painting by T. H. Matteson, titled *Examination of a Witch, 1855.* Photographer: Mark Sexton. From the Peabody Essex Museum.

she stopped going to church? "For want of clothes," she answered. Hathorne recalled that several villagers had complained that in the past, following her visits to their homes seeking handouts and her muttering retreat from them, evil and inexplicable things had occurred, and he called witnesses to testify that prior to such incidents she had spoken to them "in a very wicked, spiteful manner . . . with base and abusive language." "Why did you go away muttering from Mr. Parris's house?" Hathorne asked, citing one particular instance, but Sarah Good responded that she had only thanked Parris for what he had given her child. When Hathorne persisted with the similar testimony of others as to her muttering, she allowed, "If I must tell . . . it is the commandments." Later, she said it was a psalm, but when ordered to repeat one she could only mumble through a few lines.[61]

Seeking further proof of her effect on the children, Hathorne ordered Elizabeth Parris, Abigail Williams, Ann Putnam, and Elizabeth Hubbard to face Sarah Good, whereupon they were "dreadfully tortured and tormented." Hathorne pressed for a confession. Good retained her composure, insisted that she was innocent, and attempted to shift the blame to the other two accused women, naming Sarah Osborne in particular. Her efforts were doomed, however, as her six-year-old daughter Dorcas testified that she had seen her mother with black and yellow birds that had hurt the girls, and her husband William admitted that Sarah's behavior had led even him to believe that she was, or was likely to become, a witch. On one occasion, he testified, he had seen a witch's teat on his wife, "a little below her right shoulder," but otherwise he could offer no evidence of Sarah's having practiced witchcraft. He simply explained, "She acts badly toward me," and "I may say with tears that she is an enemy to all good."[62]

The court next called Sarah Osborne, only to have the departing Good cry out, "It is Gammer Osborne that doth pinch and afflict the children" ("gammer" being a term commonly applied to elderly women). Osborne, who probably ought to have been in bed, also arrived on the arms of two constables, but in her case it was for her physical support. Osborne took a different approach. She too denied having familiarity with the Devil and hurting the girls, but instead of presenting an aggressive defense, Osborne entered a plea of innocence that initially elicited some sympathy.[63]

Three witnesses testified that earlier that morning Osborne had said that she was "more like[ly] to be bewitched than that she should be a witch," and when Hathorne asked her what she had meant, she told him, in a rambling and often incoherent manner, of a vision or dream she had had in her sleep in which a "thing like an Indian, all black which did pinch her on her neck and pulled her by the back part of her head to the door of the house." The "thing" had told her to "go no more to meeting," but she had gone the following Sabbath, nonetheless. When Hathorne asked why she had not gone since to meeting, however, thereby apparently yielding to the Devil, she responded that she had been ill. Without admitting any guilt for what had happened, or any collusion with the Devil, Osborne portrayed herself not as the victimizer but as the victim.[64]

When the girls responded to her presence in the room, as they had to Good's, by falling into fits, Osborne continued to deny that she was the cause. When Hathorne asked how it had happened that in their moment of torment she had appeared to the girls, she offered that the Devil must have employed her likeness without her knowing it. It was perhaps a more sophisticated challenge to the girls' spectral evidence than Hathorne expected, at least at the moment, because he did not seek an explanation.[65]

Tituba's defense was different, yet again. When first charged, Tituba had stood firm. She had explained that her former mistress in

Barbados had taught her "some means to be used for the discovery of a witch and for the prevention of being bewitched," but that she was not a witch and had not hurt the girls. Although only about twenty-five years old, Tituba quickly learned, however, no doubt from Parris's badgering, to tell her accusers what they wanted to hear and to use the court's prejudices to her advantage. According to Robert Calef, a contemporary critic of the trials, Tituba later recanted her confession, explaining that Parris had beaten her until she confessed and named others. Given her slave status, that is entirely possible. It is certainly the case that the specifics of witchcraft she included in her confession were English, not Caribbean.[66]

In confessing, Tituba earned a least a temporary reprieve from her tormentors, but, unwittingly or not, she also took revenge on them by feeding their fears of a diabolical conspiracy. Indeed, she set an example for about fifty of the accused who would follow her in that she confessed and named names, whereupon the no doubt startled afflicted girls fell silent. She testified for three days and at times became "very much afflicted" herself. She spoke of familiars like red cats, one of which had two legs, wings, and a woman's head, whereupon Abigail Williams testified that she too saw the same creature and that it turned into the shape of Goody Osborne.[67]

Sarah Good had a cat, and Tituba reported that she had sent it to harm Elizabeth Hubbard, one of the afflicted. Tituba spoke of a yellow bird that she saw nursing between fingers of Sarah Good's right hand; of a creature that accompanied Osborne, that walked on two legs but was only two-to-three-feet high, and that sported a long nose and hair all over; and even of a black dog. All of the familiars entreated her with "serve me," as did a tall man from Boston with white hair who wore black clothes, proclaimed he was God, tempted her with pretty things, and announced he would kill the children and, if she did not serve him, kill her as well.[68]

Having established the existence of those who led her into her fallen state, Tituba explained that she was to serve the tall man by tormenting the children. "I would not hurt Betty. I love Betty," she testified as having protested, but Good and Osborne had forced her to do it anyway, as they also appropriated her spectral shape to pinch Elizabeth Hubbard and to attack Ann Putnam with a knife. Witnesses confirmed Tituba's recollections concerning Ann Putnam, testifying that at about the same time Tituba reported the incident to have happened, the twelve-year-old had been visited spectrally, that her visitors had tormented her, and that Ann "did complain of a knife—that they would have cut her head off with a knife."[69]

Tituba explained how she had come to know the Devil. She testified that in mid-January a man had come to her contending that he was God and promised that if she would serve him for six years, he would give her "many fine things," including "a little bird something like green and white." Unconvinced that he was actually God, Tituba resolved to consult the Reverend Parris, but the man angrily stopped her. To appease him, Tituba called him God and he disappeared only to return to the parsonage five nights later with four other witches. While the unsuspecting Parris sat in one room, her visitors made Tituba pinch Betty Parris. They told her to go into the other room and if Parris were to read to her from the Bible and to ask her what she recalled, she was to reply that she recalled nothing.[70]

Tituba had finally succumbed, she told the court, because of the Devil's threats and because he promised her "pretty things" and a familiar. Under duress, she rode with other witches "upon a stick or pole" and performed evil deeds. In what would prove to be the most damaging testimony of all, however, Tituba announced that other witches were at work in the community. In the just-noted instance, she said there were four other witches active in Salem village, two besides Good and Osborne that were from Boston and unknown to her. Moreover, she continued, the tall man had with him a book in which she was induced to make her mark, and in which she saw the names of nine people. Tituba could not read, but when pressed for the names of those signed in the book, she announced that Good had told her she had signed. Osborne had not. "She was cross with me," Tituba explained. The Devil had told Tituba, however, that the other signers were from Boston and Salem.[71]

Tituba reported that although she had attended witches' Sabbaths, she did not recognize the locations. She did recall, once again, the occasion upon which the four witches and the previously mentioned diminutive upright hairy familiar had appeared to her in the parsonage, prevented her from hearing the Reverend Parris's prayers, and convened a meeting. And, she added that the tall man, presumed to be the Devil, had warned her that if she told anyone about him, he would cut off her head.[72]

At one point in her testimony, the children worked themselves into another fit, whereupon Hathorne ordered Tituba to reveal to the court who was hurting the children. Tituba first responded that she saw the shape of Sarah Good, a sighting with which the girls agreed, but when pressed further she exclaimed, "I am blind now. I cannot see," perhaps knowing that continued or second sight was denied those who renounced their calling by the Devil. Her testimony, nevertheless, continued through March 5, and in the end the court found sufficient evidence to hold all three women.[73] On March 7, they were sent to prison in Boston, where before she could be brought to trial, on May 10, Sarah Osborne died, as would the newborn of Sarah Good.

Several depositions taken in Good's case after the hearing, in preparation for her trial, added damaging evidence. Sarah and Thomas Gadge, for example, recalled that subsequent to denying Good entrance to their home and Good's muttered response, one of their cows died in a "sudden, terrible, and strange manner." William Griggs reported that at his house during the evening after the first day of examinations, the doctor's niece, Elizabeth Hubbard, had cried out that Sarah Good was pinching and pricking her. Samuel Sibley deposed that upon a later occasion when Hubbard visited him, she had screamed that Good "with all her naked breast and barefooted and barelegged" was standing on a table near him. He swung his staff in the direction to which Hubbard pointed, and, according to Hubbard, he struck the specter. Sibley saw no signs of blood at the time, but the next morning Constable Joseph Herrick examined Good and found that one of her arms was bloody. Herrick further reported to the court that the night before he had placed Good under three guards at his home, barelegged and barefooted, but that in the morning they reported that she had been gone much of the night![74]

And finally, during the evening of March 1, William Allen and John Hughes reported that when they were walking through the village, they heard an unusual noise ahead of them. As they got closer, they spotted a strange beast but it quickly vanished. So too did three women, flying, who they took to be Sarah Good, Sarah Osborne, and Tituba. The following night, the women visited the men in their bed chambers. Allen had retired for the night when Good appeared and sat on his foot. She was accompanied by an unusual light, and when he tried to kick her, both vanished. Hughes had also gone to bed, only to awake to a "great light" and "a large gray cat" at the foot of his bed.[75]

Such testimony, presented to a grand jury on May 2, 1692, led to Good's and Tituba's indictment. Both were returned to jail and placed in irons (witches needed extraordinary manacles), but that did not end the afflicteds' suffering. Tituba's testimony confirmed for many, probably most, that diabolical doings had indeed gone on in their midst, but the incarceration of the accused, and even a series of fasts conducted by the Reverend Parris and other area ministers, failed to reestablish calm. The circle of the afflicted only widened and the net to catch their tormentors was cast further afield. If the matter had concluded with the condemnation of the three Salem village women, it would not have been a markedly different affair from the dozens of other cases in seventeenth-century New England. To that point, the Reverend John Hale observed ten years later, it "was small, and looked on . . . as an ordinary case which had fallen out before at several times in other places and would be quickly over."[76] That, however, was not to be the case.

4

"Is Not This a Brand Plucked From the Burning?"

March 11, 1692, was a day of fasting and prayer, not an inappropriate response to the turmoil in which Salem village found itself. Once again, area ministers returned both to assist Parris in this day of divine petition and to consult with him. It was in their presence that the fourth witch was named. The charge came from Ann Putnam Jr. and the accused was Martha Corey, who was the first member in good standing of the village congregation to be singled out. It was an important point psychologically, because in striking out against Corey the signal was sent that witchcraft accusations were no longer to be limited to the powerless, the outcast, and the already victimized.

The Cases of Martha and Giles Corey and Dorcas Good

Martha Corey made the ideal transitional figure for the accusers. Her claim to respectability has already been noted, but she had also earned the reputation of being opinionated and outspoken, and several years earlier she had given birth to an illegitimate mulatto who still lived with Martha and her second husband Giles. Martha and Giles had become prosperous, and she was recognized in the community as "a stout professor of the faith." In 1690, she had been received into the village church, and she had already become a woman of some consequence therein.[1] When the accusations began, however, she chose the wrong side and made no attempt to hide it. For many, not to be on the side of the witch-hunters was paramount to being among the witches, so at least to them it came as no surprise when Ann named her.

Being the first of a new breed of suspects—those who had professed their faith in God and been admitted to the church—Martha Corey received a greater measure of care than those previously charged. On March 12, the magistrates sent Edward Putnam, Ann's uncle, and Ezekiel Cheever, clerk in the initial hearing, to discuss the charges brought against her. Before they left, perhaps as a test of Ann Putnam's reliability, they asked Ann to describe what Martha's specter was wearing. Ann, likely sensing a trap and taking a page from Tituba's testimony, refused: "I am blind now; I cannot see."[2]

When Putnam and Cheever reached Corey's house, they found her alone in the kitchen, spinning. She greeted them with a smile, they reported, and said, "I know what you are come for. You are come to talk with me about being a witch, but I am none. I cannot help people's talking of me." As noted, Martha was well-known for being outspoken and even of taking the words out of one's mouth, but this was even more than her visitors expected. "Did she tell you what clothes I have on?" she continued, and when the men provided the details of what had transpired, Martha, they noted, "seemed to smile at it as if she had showed us a pretty trick."[3]

Martha, however, was not in a joking mood. She reminded her visitors that "she had made a profession of Christ and rejoiced to go and hear the word of God and the like." She then let her visitors know that she had had enough of the loose talk circulating in the village and of the malicious gossip and scandal mongering. She did not think that there were any witches, Martha announced, which, although she may not have intended to rule witches out entirely, was tantamount to blasphemy and heresy. When Putnam and Cheever reminded her that the magistrates had found sufficient cause to believe that Tituba, Good, and Osborne might be witches, she replied, "Well, if they are, I could not blame the Devil for making witches of them, for they were idle slothful persons and minded nothing that was good." She was not of their ilk, she assured them.[4]

On March 14, Martha Corey was summoned to confront her accuser, Ann Putnam, in her home. As soon as she stepped into the house, Edward Putnam reported, Ann fell to the floor in a fit. She complained of being choked and blinded, her "feet and hands twisted in a more grievous manner," and she charged Martha Corey, to her face, with having afflicted her. Ann reported that she had seen Corey nourishing her familiar, a yellow bird, between her middle and fore-finger. Corey invited Ann to more closely examine her hand, and even placed a finger in the space where Ann reported seeing the bird, but her rubbing the spot only caused the child to go blind and collapse. When she regained her sight, Ann cried out that she saw Corey turning a spit with a man on it in the fireplace. The Putnam's maid, Mercy Lewis, seized a stick and tried to strike the apparition, only to scream "with a grievous pain in her arm" as if herself struck. The Putnams ordered Corey to leave, but later that night, Edward Putnam reported, Lewis was:

> drawn toward the fire by unseen hands as she sat in a chair and two men had hold of it. Yet she and the chair moved toward the fire though they labored to the contrary. Her feet going foremost and I seeing it, [I] stepped to her feet and lifted with my strength together with the other two and all little enough to prevent her from going to the fire with her feet foremost, and this distress held until about eleven of the clock in the night.

Martha Corey, of course, was blamed for the inexplicable phenomenon. Elsewhere the same day, Abigail Williams cried out against Martha Corey as well, and when Ann Putnam's mother fell victim, Edward Putnam and Henry Kenney filed a complaint. On March 19, 1692, a warrant was issued for Corey's arrest.[5]

Martha Corey's arrest warrant was issued on a Saturday, and because it could not be served on the Sabbath, she would not be taken into custody until Monday morning. On Sunday, she attended church service as usual. Deodat Lawson, the former minister of Salem village, was to preach. He had arrived in Salem the day before and had taken up lodging at Ingersoll's ordinary. There he met Mary Walcott, who complained of pain in her arm and bore teeth marks on her wrist. He proceeded to Samuel Parris's home, where he observed Abigail Williams at her best, or worst. She ran about the house, he later noted, flapping her arms in an attempt to fly, and then she quite dramatically entered into shadow play. A specter entered the room, which only Abigail could see, and she gave it a name—Goodwife N[urse].[6]

"Do you see her?" Williams asked of Lawson. "Why there she stands." Williams acted as if she were pushing some invisible and dreadful object from her, which was certainly the case, he learned, when she shrieked, "I won't, I won't, I won't take it. I do not know what book it is. I am sure it is none of God's book! It is the Devil's Book, for all I know!" Finally, Williams grew hysterical, Lawson concluded, and ran into the fireplace. She returned with firebrands, hurled them about the house, and dashed back to the hearth in an attempt to fly up the chimney before being restrained.[7]

It can hardly be doubted that Williams's performance was ingrained in Lawson's memory when he climbed into the pulpit the next morning, March 20, but his trials had not ended. Williams arrived and sat quietly, but so too did Martha Corey, setting the congregation abuzz both at what seemed to them to be her temerity and in anticipation of what the confrontation between the accused and her accuser would bring. Almost immediately, Ann Putnam and the other girls responded. Corey's specter went about its business pinching and choking the girls, and they shrieked and wailed.[8]

At the point at which Lawson was scheduled to deliver his sermon, Abigail Williams shouted, "Now stand up and name your text," and when he did, she responded, "It is a long text!" Lawson proceeded, but the pandemonium caused by the afflicted only grew worse. A young married woman, Bethshaa Pope, a recent addition to the ranks of the afflicted, became overcome and yelled, "Now there is enough of that." "Look where Goody C[orey] sits on the beam suckling her yellow bird betwixt her fingers," Williams shouted, and the entire congregation sat transfixed, straining unsuccessfully to confirm the sighting. Ann Putnam reported that the bird had flown to the minister's hat, which was hanging on a peg in the pulpit, but in time the adults restored order and Lawson was able to complete the morning service.[9]

When the afternoon service began, Martha Corey was once again in attendance. She had remained above the fray all morning, choosing to ignore the girls' actions, though they were aimed at her, and she continued to do so into the afternoon. She made her purpose in being there clear. "I will open the eyes of the magistrates and the ministers," she is said to have explained. Abigail Williams greeted Lawson's opening of his afternoon sermon with, "I know no doctrine you had. If you did name one, I have forgot it," but relative calm prevailed and the service proceeded to its conclusion.[10]

Corey's hearing began at about noon on Monday, March 21, to a packed house; once again, the magistrates were forced to move the hearing from Ingersoll's ordinary to the meetinghouse. As were her predecessors, Martha was escorted into the meetinghouse by two constables. She entered defiantly, by all reports, and faced her accusers, the ranks of whom had now grown to include the above-mentioned

Pope, Sarah Bibber, and "an ancient woman" named Goodell, likely Eliza Goodell, the oldest women in Salem village. The Reverend Nicholas Noyes opened the hearing with a prayer, whereupon Martha asked permission to pray as well. The magistrates refused, responding that they were not there to hear her pray but to examine her.[11]

In response to Hathorne's usual opening questions, Corey denied being a witch and hurting the girls, insisting that she was a gospel woman. But rather than belabor the point, as he had wont to do, Hathorne promptly raised questions from Putnam's and Cheever's deposition about their visit to Corey's home. In a series of questions, he asked how she knew the two men were coming to see her and that they had asked Ann Putnam to describe her clothes. She answered that she had heard the children had offered such testimony. When pressed, she said her husband had told her about the procedure, but Giles denied he had said any such thing, whereupon Martha finally offered that she understood such testimony was used in the cases of others and that it would likely be employed in hers.[12]

Hathorne referred to depositions wherein Corey was quoted as saying that the Devil could not "stand" before her, but she denied having said it, whereupon three or four witnesses insisted that she had. Hathorne asked what she meant when she said that "the magistrates' and ministers' eyes were blinded," and that she would open them, whereupon Corey laughed and denied having said that as well. And finally, referring to Ann Putnam's testimony, Hathorne asked her what she was turning on the spit in the fireplace. But Corey denied turning anything on the spit, much less a man.[13]

Hathorne turned to the moment at hand and asked Corey why she afflicted the girls. Martha replied that she did not afflict them. He asked Corey if she believed the girls were bewitched, to which Corey responded that they may well have been, but that she had had no part in it. When she said she did not know that there were any witches in the area, Hathorne asked, if that were true then who was it that had tormented the girls, to which Martha answered, "How can I know?" And when Hathorne asked what book she had presented to Mary Walcott, Corey again denied having done any such thing, adding that perhaps the Devil had appeared in her shape. Corey continued to insist that it was impossible for her to afflict the children because she was a gospel woman, but the girls responded with a chorus of "She's a gospel witch" and fell into fits. When Hathorne ordered her to explain their torment, she being the apparent cause, Corey answered, "If you will all go hang me, how can I help it."[14]

Martha Corey called upon the magistrates not to believe the "distracted children," but the girls were not done with her by any means. They mimicked her every move. When she shifted her feet, so did they. When she bit her lips, they summoned the magistrates to show how their lips bled. And when Corey, clearly weary of the affair, leaned against the minister's seat—the prisoner's bar—Pope reacted as if she had excruciating pain in her bowels and threw her muff and shoe at Corey, the latter hitting Corey in the head. It was at that point that the Black Man, first described by Tituba as the witches' ringleader, reappeared. The girls spotted him whispering in Martha's ear. They heard the pounding of a drum in the distance, and when they looked out the window they reported seeing several witches assembling for worship outside the meetinghouse. "Don't you hear the drum beat?" one of the girls cried. "Why don't you go, gospel witch? Why don't you go too?"[15]

The magistrates called Martha Corey's husband to the stand, but he would neither confirm Martha's testimony on Putnam's and Cheever's visit, nor offer effective testimony in her support. Like Martha, Giles Corey, seventy-two years of age in 1692, was a religious man, having been received into the Salem town church one year earlier. Unlike Martha, he seemed to have been caught up in the excitement of the moment and even became a believer in the witch-hunt. If, at that point, Giles Corey believed his wife was a witch, it was not clear, but in his attempt to be scrupulously honest in his testimony he only added to her condemnation. He admitted, for example, that ever since Martha had removed the saddle from his horse as he was preparing to attend a session of the hearings, he had been suspicious about her intent. He reported that during the past week he had found it hard to pray unless Martha was nearby. Once, in the middle of the night, he had found her kneeling silently on the hearth, but he could hear nothing nor determine for sure what it was she was doing. On one occasion, upon fetching an ox, the animal had lain down and resisted rising, dragging "his hinder parts as if he had been hip shot." And, at another time, their cat had suddenly grown ill, whereupon Martha had encouraged him to put it out of its misery, only to have it recover.[16]

The testimony against Martha Corey was impressive by seventeenth-century standards. It was made worse by her repeated outbursts of laughter at Hathorne's questions and the actions of the afflicted, for which Hathorne reprimanded her. "You can't prove me a witch," Martha cried as she was led from the meetinghouse, but that was not the issue. They had found good reason to try, and as she herself had observed, "If you will all go hang me, how can I help it?" As the

Reverend Noyes later wrote of the affair: "It was the judgment of all that were present, they [the girls] were bewitched, and only she, the accused person, said they were distracted."[17]

Martha Corey's hearing lasted only one day, and in the end she was packed off to prison to await trial, but before that would occur she was joined by her husband. The magistrates issued a warrant for Giles Corey's arrest on April 8.[18] Having accepted the idea of his wife's guilt, perhaps out of his own piety and limited intelligence more than as a result of any intended harm, and maybe because he had denounced those of his sons-in-law that defended Martha, Giles now found himself standing among the accused.

Giles Corey had a substantial criminal record, including theft, though largely of minor items such as food and tobacco, for which he was charged and found guilty on at least two occasions. Of a more serious nature, John Proctor held Corey responsible for setting fire to his house, but he could never prove it, and Corey provided evidence that he was at home the night of the fire.[19]

Corey was well-known for his quick temper. Court records make reference to his arguing with or threatening neighbors over fences, sawmills, horses' fetters, and even his reputation. One frequent antagonist referred to him as "a very quarrelsome and contentious bad neighbor." And, not surprisingly, there are reports of Corey's having been the victim, and agent, of violence. In 1651, records show that John Kitchin, seeking revenge for some perceived or real slight, pinched, choked, and kicked Corey, tossed "stinking water" on him, and threw him out the door. Corey tried to escape, but Kitchin chased him down, threw him off a rail fence he had climbed, and beat him "until he was all bloody." Twenty-four years later, Corey so badly beat with a stick his servant Jacob Goodale that Goodale apparently died from the wounds. During the several days the servant lay dying, however, he refused to contradict Corey's explanation that he had fallen—neither did a neighbor, who had broken up the beating, but when Goodale died, an inquest was held. Although no evidence was found to directly link Corey to the beating, he was nevertheless fined for abuse.[20]

Some of Corey's neighbors came to believe that he possessed occult powers. In one quarrel, Robert Moulton testified, Corey had told him that his "sawmill should saw no more," and sure enough, shortly thereafter, it did not. Still, as noted, Corey had recently become a member of the Salem town church, and the church records attest to a remarkable change in his behavior. They report that although he had been "a scandalous person," God had "awakened him upon repentance" and he had made a confession of those evils that had been held against him. Therefore, "he was received into the church with the consent of the brethren."[21]

When he appeared before the Salem magistrates, the circle of accusers responded to Giles Corey as they had to his wife and others of the accused, condemning him, one by one. Parris reported, "All the afflicted were seized . . . with fits, and troubled with pinches." The magistrates ordered Corey's hands tied, and Hathorne exclaimed, "What! Is it not enough to act witchcraft at other times, but you must do it now, in the face of authority?" Still bewildered, all Giles could say was, "I am a poor creature and cannot help it." He moved his head, and the girls' heads and necks were sorely afflicted. One of his hands was let go, and several reacted in pain. "He drew in his cheeks, and the cheeks of some of the afflicted were sucked in."[22]

Perhaps better sensing his predicament, Corey began to come out of his bewildered state. The turning point occurred when some of the afflicted testified that Corey had said that he had seen the Devil in the shape of a black hog and was afraid. Jolted back to his senses, Corey snapped that he had never seen such an image and, he added, "I do not know that I ever spoke that word [afraid] in my life." Corey was accused of having said that "he would make away with himself, and charge his death upon his son," a statement that must have seemed plausible to those who knew of the controversy he had created within his family over the role he had played in his wife's condemnation.[23] The magistrates, however, had heard enough. They ordered him off to prison, setting the stage for perhaps the most bizarre episode of the Salem witch trials, to which we will return in chapter eight.

Soon after the magistrates ordered Martha Corey held for trial, they packed off to prison the youngest of the accused witches of the Salem witch trials, Dorcas Good. According to Mary Walcott and Ann Putnam Jr., Dorcas, the daughter of Sarah Good, or at least her specter, had been running about the countryside "like a mad dog, biting the girls" in retaliation for what they had done to her mother. A warrant was issued for her arrest. At her hearing, whenever Dorcas looked at the girls, they screamed, accused her of biting them, and displayed teeth marks on their arms. Otherwise, the hearing was brief, and she was jailed. Two days later, Hathorne, Corwin, and Salem town minister John Higginson visited Dorcas Good in prison, where she told them that she "had a little snake that used to suck on the lowest joint" of her forefinger. She pointed to the spot and explained that the snake had been given to her by her mother. Five-year-old witches were not hanged in seventeenth-century New England, but following her release several months later, Dorcas was never quite the same again.[24]

THE CASE OF REBECCA NURSE

↣ If Martha Corey was the first church member in good standing to be accused of witchcraft, Rebecca Nurse was even more saintly and better-placed. She certainly represented a higher rung on the social ladder, and the greatest challenge to date to the as-yet-perfect onslaught of the accusers. At seventy-one years of age, Rebecca was the oldest of the Towne sisters and the matriarch of the Nurse family. Although she worshipped in the Salem village church, she remained a member of the town church, and in the eyes of many she was the very essence of the Puritan mother—pious and beloved. That is not to say, however, that she did not have her weaknesses or her enemies.[25]

Rebecca was one of eight children of William Towne of Topsfield, who died in 1672 leaving a small estate. She had married Francis Nurse, who had risen from an obscure artisan to landed yeoman with the acquisition of a 300-acre farm near Ipswich Road. Not everyone looked with favor upon such rising above one's station in the Puritan community, least of all the Nurses's neighbor Zerubel Endicott, whose family once owned the 300 acres on which the Nurses and their four sons and four daughters all married, resided, and prospered. Few questioned the decent God-fearing character of the Nurses, but to some their growing prosperity was suspect. Perhaps a few recalled that years earlier Rebecca Nurse's mother had been accused of witchcraft, although she was never arrested or brought to trial.[26]

The Nurses did not yet own their property. They were in the process of buying it, in twenty yearly installments, from the Reverend James Allen. Allen had gained possession of the 300 acres through his marriage to an Endicott woman, but when his wife died, rather than return the land to the Endicotts as Jerubel Endicott would have liked, he sold it to the Nurses. A boundary dispute between the Nurses and Endicott ensued, as did a brawl over the cutting of wood on overlapping property. Both conflicts had long been settled but probably not forgotten by 1692, at which point the Nurses had only six years of payments left.[27]

Beginning half a century earlier and lasting for many years, a boundary quarrel had ensued between the residents of Salem village and Topsfield, among whom the Townes were prominent. In response to one of the most vehement resolutions passed at a meeting of the inhabitants of Salem village in that affair, Samuel Nurse, Rebecca's eldest son, and Thomas Preston, her son-in-law, lodged a formal objection. And on another occasion, Rebecca's husband, Francis Nurse, Samuel Nurse, Preston, and another son-in-law issued a protest. Living in Salem but siding with the Topsfield group no doubt created lasting ill will against the Nurses.[28]

And, finally, Rebecca Nurse had some personal flaws, most of which were largely attributable to her age, such as her poor hearing. She often failed to hear and therefore did not respond to what was said to her by her neighbors. She was known to lose her temper. Witnesses recalled that on one occasion, when a neighbor's hogs got free and trampled her flax garden, Rebecca had lashed out at the neighbors in no uncertain and un-Christian terms. They also recalled that the neighbor had died shortly thereafter and that his wife had never stopped talking about the coincidence.[29]

Ann Putnam Sr. was one of the first to name Rebecca Nurse, and there may have been reasons, if subconscious, why she did so. To begin with, the Nurses belonged to the party that had opposed the Reverend Bayley and, as previously noted, Bayley was Ann Putnam's brother-in-law. Second, Nurse was connected to the protracted boundary dispute between the residents of Topsfield and Salem village, which included claims made against lands belonging to the Putnam family. Third, during the 1670s, while residing in Salem village, Francis Nurse, Rebecca's husband, had been involved in a dispute with Nathaniel Putnam over some mutually bounded acreage. And, fourth, over the years, Francis Nurse had grown closer, politically, to the Porter faction. The reader will recall that he was one of the four Porterites to be elected to the village committee in October 1691, at the expense of the Putnamites, and that the committee had challenged the Putnamites' decision in 1689 to transfer ownership of the village parsonage to the Reverend Parris.[30]

On March 23, two days after Martha Corey's examination, the Reverend Lawson visited Ann Putnam. She had been severely tormented by apparitions, including that of Martha Corey's, for several days. On two occasions, she reported, Corey was accompanied by Rebecca Nurse. The first visit was brief; during the second, however, Nurse appeared to Putnam early in the morning, clad only in her shift and nightcap. She brought with her a "little red book," which she urged Putnam to sign, threatening to tear her soul out of her body if she did not. Nurse, Putnam told Lawson, had blasphemed by denying God and the power of Jesus Christ to save her soul, as well as by denying several passages from scripture of which Putnam informed her in order "to repel her hellish temptations."[31]

Putnam asked Lawson to pray for her, and he did, but as he began his prayers Ann suffered a fit. Her husband tried to help her from her bed to kneel and pray, but "she could not be bended," and soon she began to move frantically about the room, arguing with Rebecca Nurse's specter. "Goodwife Nurse be gone!" she cried out. "Are you not ashamed, a woman of your profession, to afflict a poor creature so? What hurt have I ever done you in my life?" Putnam told Nurse that she was to live only two more years, Lawson reported, whereupon her soul would become the Devil's, for "your name is blotted out of God's Book, and it shall never be put in God's Book, again." Again Putnam ordered Nurse away, adding, "I know what you would have [Lawson assumed she meant her soul] but it is out of your reach; it is clothed with the white robes of Christ's righteousness." And finally, engaging Nurse's shape in a discussion of scripture, Putnam exclaimed that Nurse could not remain if Lawson were to recite the third chapter of the Book of Revelation. Lawson started to read it, and before long, Nurse disappeared, leaving Ann Putnam in peace.[32]

On the same date, March 23, Edward and Jonathan Putnam (son of John) filed complaints with the presiding magistrates, and they ordered Nurse's arrest for practicing "certain detestable acts called witchcraft" on Ann Putnam, Mary Walcott, Elizabeth Hubbard, and Abigail Williams. Before taking Nurse into custody, however, the magistrates sent Israel and Elizabeth Porter to speak to her. Israel Porter we have already met; Elizabeth was John Hathorne's sister.[33]

Nurse had been ill for about a week, the Porters found upon their arrival, but, in the company of her sister Sarah, Sarah's husband, Peter Cloyce, and a friend, Daniel Andrew, all of whom served as witnesses, they were able to visit Nurse in her bedroom. Unlike Martha Corey, Rebecca Nurse had no idea why the Porters had come. She smiled, they later reported, and sat up as best she could. They asked how she was feeling, to which Nurse replied that "she blessed God" for her illness because "she had more of his presence" in her sickness than she sometimes had when she was well, "but not so much as she desired." She had resolved, Nurse continued, thereafter "with the apostle [to] press forward to the mark."[34]

As one might expect, Nurse inquired about the status of the afflicted village children. She expressed her grief for the Parris family, and when told that the children did not fare any better as of late, Nurse offered that she "went to God for them." She also said, however, that she had heard that some of the accused "were as innocent as she." The Porters must have been more than a little startled by Nurse's comment, but they pushed on. They told her that, in fact, she had been named, whereupon Nurse replied, "Well, if it be so, the will of the Lord be done." She sat silently for a moment, as if in a trance, and then added, "As to this thing I am as innocent as the child unborn; but surely, what sin hath God found out in me unrepented of, that he should lay such an affliction upon me in my old age?"[35]

Unlike all who had gone before her, when Rebecca Nurse entered the meetinghouse to meet her judges on March 24, 1692, the response was one of marked compassion, even among the magistrates who had otherwise become quite hardened to their deadly serious task. One by one, however, the girls accused Nurse of having tormented them, and Ann Putnam, the younger, fell in pain to the floor, crying that Nurse was afflicting her. Hathorne turned to Nurse and asked what she had to say in response to the girls' charges, and she replied, "I can say before my eternal father, I am innocent, and God will clear my innocency." Hathorne, perhaps genuinely impressed, responded, "Here is never a one in the assembly but desires it; but, if you be guilty, I pray God discover you."[36]

Henry Kenney testified that, following a visit by Nurse to his home, he had been seized "with an amazed condition," but Nurse refused to take responsibility. "Would you have me belie myself?" she answered. Hathorne did not respond. Instead, he read her the most serious charge, that which had been sworn to by Ann Putnam Sr. Little children in their winding sheets had been appearing to Ann, calling her aunt and telling her dreadful things, namely that Rebecca Nurse had caused their death. When asked to respond to the charge, all Rebecca could say was, "I cannot tell what to think."[37]

When other witnesses confirmed that Rebecca had indeed tormented the accusing girls, Rebecca once again maintained her innocence and explained that she had not been able to leave her house for the past eight or nine days. The girls, however, would have none of it. One by one, they had convulsions. Above it all the voice of the elder Ann Putnam could be heard. "Did you not bring the Black Man with you? Did you not bid me tempt God and die? How often have you eaten and drunk your own damnation?" Bedlam ensued at the unexpected outburst, and Putnam's agony was so great that the magistrates gave her husband permission to take her from the meetinghouse. Only the near-deaf, and likely confused, Rebecca Nurse failed to respond, at which point the girls explained that she was being distracted by the "Black Man," who was whispering in her ear. When Hathorne pressed her for an explanation, all Nurse could say was, "Oh, Lord help me!"[38]

The girls mimicked Rebecca Nurse's every movement and gesture, and they cried out in pain as if she were practicing her art on them in punishment for their actions against her. Hathorne watched closely and noticed that throughout all of it, Rebecca Nurse, despite her protests and unlike many of the other women in the meetinghouse, had not cried. Tears, he recalled, were not possible for a witch. "It is awful for all to see these agonies, and [to see] you an old professor thus charged with the Devil by the effects of it," he commented, "and yet to see you stand with dry eyes where there are so many wet." "You do not know my heart," Rebecca responded, but Hathorne ignored the response and told her that she would do well to confess if she were guilty and to give glory to God.[39]

Perhaps because she had expressed earlier such concern for the girls, Hathorne asked Nurse why she had never visited the afflicted. "Because I was afraid I should have fits too," she answered. Did she believe, then, that they were bewitched? "I do think they are," she responded. Unlike Martha Corey, whose response to a similar question suggested that she did not believe the girls were bewitched or that witches were present in Salem village, and even implied that she did not believe in witches, Nurse remained among the considerable majority of the populace who believed in witches and the possibility of all three assertions. Nevertheless, she maintained her innocence, and when Hathorne reminded her that it was her specter that continued to torment the girls, Nurse could only answer, "I cannot help it. The Devil may appear in my shape."[40]

The magistrates returned Nurse to jail and broke for the day around noon so Deodat Lawson would be able to use the meetinghouse that afternoon to deliver the Lecture Day sermon. Lecture Day sermons on most occasions were well-attended; under the peculiar circumstances of March 1692, the sermon attracted a capacity crowd, including area ministers and, of course, the afflicted girls. The arrest of Martha Corey and Rebecca Nurse had raised new and serious questions concerning the trials, which if not resolved could threaten their continuation. Both Corey and Nurse had asked whether spectral evidence was trustworthy. Both suggested that the Devil had assumed their shape without their knowledge or permission, and some observers wondered whether it was indeed possible for the Devil to employ the specters of innocent people. Corey and Nurse had been professed and respected members of the church, and some found it difficult to believe that they, who had made a covenant with God, would, or could, break that covenant and enter into one with the Devil. It was up to Deodat Lawson to provide answers to their questions.[41]

DEODAT LAWSON'S LECTURE DAY SERMON

Deodat Lawson's activities from his arrival in Salem village on March 19 through his tumultuous Sunday sermon to his tempestuous visit with Ann Putnam Sr. on Wednesday, March 23, have already been noted. On March 24, Lawson attended the examination of Rebecca Nurse but left one hour early to complete his Lecture Day sermon. He had seen enough, and he chose as the title of his sermon, "Christ's Fidelity the Only Shield Against Satan's Malignity." For his text, he selected Zechariah 3:2: "And the Lord said unto Satan, the Lord rebuke thee, O Satan. Even the Lord that hath chosen Jerusalem rebuke thee. Is not this a brand plucked from the burning?"

Lawson began his sermon by reviewing the well-known story of Satan's rebellion and descent from heaven with his "accursed legions." He reminded his listeners that, as a result, the Devil was committed to a continued struggle with "the infinite and eternal God" and was "filled with envy and malice against all mankind," God's creation. The "Grand Enemy of all mankind," he explained, is always seeking "to catch, devour, and destroy souls." To that end, he employs various tactics, including confusion, in which he surrounds people in "mists of darkness"; "frightful representations" in people's imaginations; "violent tortures of the body"; and, in certain cases where he receives people's assistance, possession of human souls.[42]

Lawson pointed to recent adverse developments as God's righteous punishment for a people who had forgotten the commitment of their fathers—the founding fathers of New England—to Christ. "We all, even the best of us," Lawson announced, "have by sin a hand and share, in provoking God, thus to let Satan loose." In particular, he suggested that God might have been exercising his "righteous judgment" in sending "this fire of His holy displeasure" upon them, "to put out some fires of contention" that had been among them.[43]

On the one hand, Lawson offered that what had occurred was only the opening salvo of a prolonged conflict with the Devil for the spiritual allegiance of New Englanders. He said:

> You are therefore to be deeply humbled, and sit in the dust, considering the signal hand of God in singling out this place, this poor village, for the first seat of Satan's tyranny, and to make it (as it were) the rendezvous of devils where they muster their infernal forces appearing to the afflicted as coming armed to carry on their malicious designs against the bodies, and if God in mercy prevent not, against the souls of many in this place.[44]

On the other hand, Lawson offered comfort and some reassurance to the congregation. Even in its darkest hour, he explained, God would not abandon Salem, one of the Puritan cities in the wilderness, a Jerusalem chosen by God. Surely, in the end, God would rebuke and destroy their adversaries, even if they were the legions of the Devil.[45]

Lawson answered those who questioned the apparent guilt of the visibly godly, like Corey and Nurse, and in doing so lent support to the use of spectral evidence. He reminded those present about the nature and superhuman powers of the Devil, who did not have to, but often did, employ human mediums in his attacks on mankind. He "contracts and indents" with such persons, Lawson explained, so that they might be "the instruments by whom he may secretly affect and afflict the bodies and minds of others." To prevail upon those that make a visible profession to God, he continued—like Corey and Nurse, although he did not name them—may be the best, covert way to pursue his diabolical enterprise, and thereby to more effectively "pervert others to consenting unto his subjection." In that manner, as he had in Salem village, the Devil "insinuates into the society of the adopted children of God," winning over "the visible subjects of Christ's Kingdom," because "it is certain that he never works more like the Prince of Darkness than when he looks most like an angel of light."[46]

But, he added, in reference to spectral evidence, "so far as we can look into those hellish mysteries, and guess at the administration of that kingdom of darkness," people become subject to the Devil's use, or become witches, only upon their swearing allegiance to him, or by "subscribing to a book or articles, etc." Then having them "in his subjection, by their consent"—and their no longer being innocent—the Devil can "use their bodies and minds, shapes and representations" to his purposes. In sum, the Devil could not assume the shape of an innocent person.[47]

At that crucial moment in the Salem witch trials, when serious doubts existed as to its validity, the highly regarded Deodat Lawson stepped forward to allay fears that the magistrates' emphasis on spectral evidence had been misplaced. Further, he made it clear that the people of Salem village were engaged in no ordinary battle, but in one of cosmic importance. What had occurred was to serve as a "solemn warning and awakening" to all of the "direful operations of Satan," which God had permitted to occur in their midst. "Awake, awake then," he beseeched them, "remain no longer under the dominion of that prince of cruelty and malice, whose fanatical fury we see thus exerted against the bodies and minds of the afflicted persons":

> I am this day commanded to call and cry an alarm to you. Arm! Arm! Arm! Handle your arms . . . as faithful soldiers under the Captain of our salvation . . . [and] be faithful unto death in our spiritual warfare. . . . Let us admit no parley, give no quarter."[48]

Lawson urged those in attendance not to be divided, not to "rashly censure" even those they believed had accused innocent people, because that would "give . . . place to the Devil." The "grand accuser" would take advantage of such divisions, as he "loves to fish in troubled waters." If innocent people were suspected, Lawson offered, "it is to be ascribed to God's pleasure, supremely permitting, and Satan's malice, subordinately troubling." In other words, it was better to accuse the innocent, if in the process it was assured that the guilty would not go undetected![49]

Lawson's sermon was rushed into print with the signed endorsement of the Reverends Increase and Cotton Mather, Samuel Willard, James Allen, John Bayley, and Charles Morton. Lawson dedicated it to the "worshipful and worthily honored" magistrates who had presided over the hearings thus far, including not only Hathorne and Corwin but also Bartholomew Gedney, who had been irregularly present, as well as the Reverends John Higginson and Nicholas Noyes of the Salem town church, who had lent their considerable support. He addressed the preface to his "Christian friends and acquaintances, the inhabitants of Salem village."[50]

Sarah Cloyce Is Charged

The magistrates were ready to proceed, and as was often the case in such matters, the charges brought against Rebecca Nurse raised suspicion against others in her family, in this case, her two sisters. The next to fall would be Sarah, age forty-eight and the wife of Peter Cloyce. Perhaps paving the way for suspicion regarding Sarah was her decided and open antipathy toward the pastors of Salem village and Salem town for their not having protected Rebecca, one of their most devout parishioners. The triggering event, however, occurred on March 27, three days after Lawson's sermon.

It was Sacrament Sunday, and Sarah Cloyce, despite her ill will toward Parris, sought communion in the village church, which she had joined in 1690. The service opened peacefully, even though the afflicted girls were present. But perhaps because Lawson had prepared the way, Parris sought to advance the call to arms against the Devil's minions. He chose as the title of his sermon: "Christ knows how many devils there are in his church and who they are," and he named as his text Christ's response to Judas's pending betrayal in John 6:70: "Have I not chosen you twelve and one of you is a devil." Upon his naming his text, Sarah Cloyce stormed from the meetinghouse, slamming the door behind her (some said the wind blew it shut), and as if on cue, the girls promptly fell into fits, claiming that Cloyce's specter afflicted them.[51] Calm was restored, and Parris continued his sermon, but the moment was not forgotten.

In his sermon, Parris built upon the theme that Lawson had employed and had been developing for more than two years. The Devil, Parris explained, had breached the security of their covenanted congregation of God's elect. He had done so by employing those "vile and wicked" sinners within their ranks, of whom there may be one, ten, or twenty, and none of those "vile and wicked" sinners were worse "than those that have been good, and are naught." Weeks earlier, he had expressed confidence that the church had been guaranteed safe passage by God over troubled seas, secure at least within its doors from the corrupting influence of the Devil. Now, he concluded that the church consisted of good and bad, like a garden of both flowers and weeds, or like the apostles, of saints and an apostate. Much as Christ knew who the apostate was among the apostles, however, so too Christ knew the sinners in their midst, so he warned, "Let none . . . build their hopes of salvation merely upon this, that they are church members. This you and I may be, and yet devils for all that." And as far as people like Rebecca Nurse were concerned, or Sarah Cloyce—he did not identify anyone in particular—"the Devil would represent the best saints as devils if he could," and he could if they were to abandon their faith, if only secretly.[52]

Given the sources of conflict between Salem town and Salem village and of the factionalism that divided Salem village, it is important to note that Parris went beyond attributing the outbreak of witchcraft to the growing power of the Devil to include "the pervasiveness of lust," or greed. Much as Judas had betrayed Jesus for thirty pieces of silver, so too were some of the people of Salem sacrificing their loyalties for worldly possessions. Covetousness, he explained, or that which prevented people from giving themselves wholly up to Christ, "sorely prevails in these perilous times." And oftentimes, he insisted, covetousness and witchcraft were manifestations of the same diabolical menace. Christ knows, he declared, "who they are that have not chosen him, but prefer farms and merchandise above him and above his ordinance."[53]

Parris nevertheless followed up his remarks with a most interesting decision. He recalled Mary Sibley's action, upon hearing of the initial affliction of Parris's household, whereby she had sought to counter that affliction with magic or sorcery of her own—a witch's cake. Parris condemned such "diabolical actions" as contrary to the gospel. He pointed out that similar actions on the part of others had raised the Devil amongst them and that God only knew when he would be silenced again. But, he allowed, Sibley had meant well. She had acted out of ignorance, confessed, expressed sorrow for her actions, and promised "future better advisedness and caution." He therefore recommended that members of the congregation allow her to continue in their holy fellowship, and they did so unanimously.[54] It is true that no one had accused Sibley of doing any harm, and that she had employed witchcraft in an attempt to help the afflicted, but in view of his conduct toward other practitioners of similar sorceries and the temper of the times, it was an extraordinary gesture on Parris's and the congregation's part. Unfortunately, it was their last such gesture.

On April 4, Jonathan Walcott and Nathaniel Ingersoll filed complaints against Sarah Cloyce "for high suspicion of sundry acts of witchcraft," and on Friday, April 8, the magistrates issued a warrant for her arrest. Much like her sister Rebecca, there was nothing in Sarah's background to make her particularly suspect as a witch, save her being Rebecca Nurse's sister, her criticism of the charges brought against Rebecca, and her action in the Salem village meetinghouse. She and her husband Peter were of average means. They and their five children lived on a small farm about two miles from the meetinghouse, which they rented from Daniel Andrew. Peter had been among the original signers of the new church covenant of 1689, but there is no record of his having ever taken sides in any of the church's disputes over its various ministers.[55]

On Monday, April 11, Sarah Cloyce appeared before the magistrates, this time at the meetinghouse in Salem town. The hearing had been moved to accommodate representatives of the colonial government who had decided to investigate the developments in Salem. Among the guests were Deputy Governor Thomas Danforth and four prominent members of the General Court: James Russell, Isaac Addington, Samuel Appleton, and Samuel Sewall. Massachusetts continued to operate without a charter, but it had reinstalled their former governor, Simon Bradstreet, who was then living in Salem. The evidence suggests that even at this early stage Bradstreet looked with concern, if not disfavor, on the Salem witch trials, but he was eighty-seven years old and had left most of the executive functions of his job to Deputy Governor Danforth. Danforth did not share in Bradstreet's misgivings.[56]

Danforth took control of the examination, and he called forward Sarah Cloyce's accusers: John Indian, Mary Walcott, Abigail Williams, Mercy Lewis, and Ann Putnam Jr. Indian was the first to speak. He claimed that Cloyce had come to him "a great many times" and had choked, bit, and pinched him. Cloyce called him "a grievous liar," whereupon Indian fell to the floor and tumbled about in pain. Danforth

turned to the afflicted girls, and they too condemned Cloyce. Mary Walcott claimed that Cloyce had brought her "the book" and bid her "touch
it, and be well." She then fell into a fit, but after touching Cloyce and
regaining her composure, Walcott added that Cloyce had not come to
her alone, that she was at various times in the company of Rebecca
Nurse, Martha Corey, and "a great many" she did not know.[57]

Abigail Williams testified that she had seen Cloyce at a gathering of about forty witches at the Reverend Parris's house. Cloyce and
Good had served as deacons and assisted in the sacrament wherein
they told Williams that the group partook of "our blood . . . twice a day."
She confirmed Walcott's report that Cloyce's specter had accompanied
"a white man," or "a fine grace man," to Ingersoll's tavern, and that all
the witches did tremble in his presence.[58]

The testimony weakened Sarah Cloyce's resolve. Cloyce asked for
water and sat down, only to have the girls cry out that they saw the
Black Man standing beside her whispering in her ear, and a yellow
bird, obviously her familiar, flying about her head. When Cloyce nearly
fainted, they announced that her spirit had gone to prison to visit her
sister, Rebecca Nurse.[59]

The magistrates ordered Sarah Cloyce held for trial. "It is no wonder that they are witches," John Putnam is reported to have said upon
Cloyce's being sent off to prison, "their mother was a witch before
them." But perhaps Putnam was too outspoken on that occasion. Soon
thereafter the shapes of Rebecca Nurse and Sarah Cloyce fell upon
Putnam's eight-week-old child, he reported, torturing it "enough to
pierce a stony heart" until it died.[60]

Mary Easty Is Summoned

To complete our story of the Towne sisters, we must take some lib-
erty with the chronology to which we have been faithful, thus far by a
few weeks. The third and last of the sisters to fall was Mary Easty of
Topsfield, and the warrant for her arrest was issued on April 21. Mary
was fifty-eight years old, the mother of seven children and the wife of
Isaac Easty. The Eastys owned a large and valuable farm and, it should
be noted, they had been active with the Nurses in the Topsfield-Salem
village boundary dispute.[61]

Mary Easty's hearing began on April 22 in Salem village, the
original Salem magistrates presiding once again. She approached the
court in a different manner from both of her sisters. Much younger

than Rebecca, she did not enter so failingly, but perhaps because she was several years older than Sarah, neither did she appear defiant. Instead, as one source has put it, she "carried herself with such grace, courage and good sense," that even Magistrate Hathorne was given pause.[62]

"Does this woman hurt you?" Hathorne asked the girls, who had initially either fallen silent or had fallen into fits in Easty's presence. Abigail Williams was the first to respond that she did, but Mary Walcott, Ann Putnam, and John Indian followed her lead. Easty protested her innocence, but when she tilted her head to one side as if trying to understand what was happening, the girls' heads tilted as well into positions so unnatural, it was reported, that it seemed their necks would break. "Oh, Goody Easty, Goody Easty!" Ann Putnam screamed in pain, "You are the woman! You are the woman!" When the magistrates asked Easty if she was responsible for the girls' torments, she maintained her innocence. Hathorne inquired about how far she had complied with the Devil, to wit she responded, "I never complied, but prayed against him all my days." When pushed to confess, she answered, "What would you have me do?" She was innocent and she would insist to the end that she was "clear of this sin."[63]

Once again, Hathorne asked the girls if they were certain Easty was the woman that had afflicted them, and once again they fell into fits. Overcome by it all, Easty clasped her hands together, only to have Mercy Lewis's hands become clenched and the ritual of physical mimicking begin again. When calm was restored, Hathorne again asked Easty what she thought of the girls' torment and whether she believed it was the result of witchcraft. She replied, clearly understanding the intent of his question, "It is an evil spirit, but whether it be witchcraft I do not know."[64]

Mary Easty was imprisoned along with her sisters, but there the story took a curious twist. Unlike many of the others, including her sister Sarah, Mary resisted railing against her accusers and appears to have been so gentle in her manner that her jailers took up her cause. The magistrates responded by interviewing the girls again, and this time they demurred; they were no longer certain. On May 18, the magistrates ordered Easty's release, and she returned to her home in Topsfield. On May 20, however, Mercy Lewis, the only person among Easty's accusers who had not cleared her, was taken violently ill. While at the home of John Putnam Jr., Lewis first experienced considerable pain, then lapsed into a coma from which she awoke only long enough to utter her prayers and then suffer a relapse. "Dear Lord, receive my soul," she pleaded aloud, and "Lord, let them not kill me quite."[65]

Word spread that Lewis was dying, and it was clear to her observers that Lewis's agony had been brought about by Mary Easty. Still, the magistrates were reluctant to act without further evidence. Samuel Abbey, John Putnam's neighbor, who was present at the Putnam's home on the morning of the twentieth, provided a detailed account. Abbey reported that he had found Mercy Lewis in "a terrible condition, crying with piteous tones of anguish." She had urged that those nearby pray for the salvation of her soul "for they [the specters] will kill me outright." Abbey reported that he was asked to summon Ann Putnam, the younger, to see if she could determine who it was that hurt Lewis. Finding Abigail Williams with Ann Putnam, Abbey brought both back to John Putnam's home, but even before they arrived they cried out that they saw the apparition of Mary Easty afflicting Lewis. When they arrived at Lewis's bedside, they added the names of John Willard and Mary Whittredge.[66]

Mary Walcott was summoned, and she saw Easty "pressing upon her [Lewis's] breasts with both hands," putting chains about Lewis's neck and choking her. When Elizabeth Hubbard was brought in, she offered much the same testimony. Walcott explained that they had had second thoughts concerning Easty, because she had blinded them. Not being able to blind her, Walcott added, Easty chose to kill her![67]

When Lewis's state grew critical—when, as some reported, it seemed she would not live to see the next day—Marshall George Herrick was summoned. He found Lewis, in his own words, "in a very dreadful and solemn condition, so that to our apprehension she could not continue long in this world without a mitigation of those torments we saw her in." John Putnam Jr. and Benjamin Hutchinson made a formal complaint, and Magistrate Hathorne ordered Easty's arrest. That evening, Easty was taken into custody again, but Lewis's torment did not subside. It was only the next afternoon, after Easty had been arraigned and "laid in irons," that Lewis's agony lessened and she fell into a deep, natural, and healing sleep.[68] The magistrates had learned their lesson; they would not again let their sympathies for the accused risk the lives of the afflicted.

THE PACE QUICKENS

The cases of Martha Corey and Rebecca Nurse, the sermons of Deodat Lawson and Samuel Parris, and the participation of the visiting colonial officials made it clear to many in Salem village that they were engaged in a major, perhaps cosmic, as Lawson had termed it,

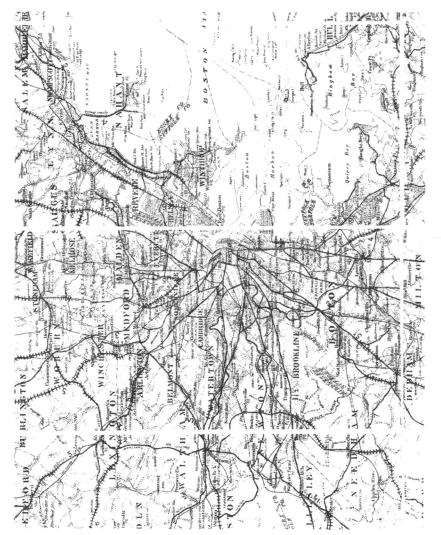

A map of the Salem/Boston area (eastern Massachusetts). (Part A) Detail showing North Andover to Salem. From Walker Lithograph & Publishing Co., ca 1910. Courtesy Peabody Essex Museum, Salem, MA.

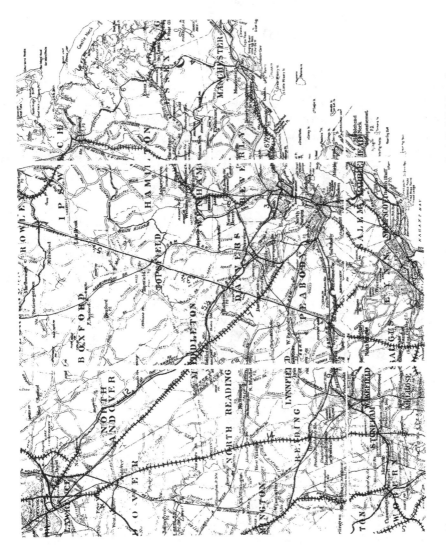

(Part B) Detail showing Salem to Boston. From Walker Lithograph & Publishing Co., ca 1910. Courtesy Peabody Essex Museum, Salem, MA.

battle with the forces of evil, and that those forces could be found in their midst, even in the House of the Lord. Not only was the battle raging all around them, but their last refuge from the Devil had been lost. Almost anyone could, and would, become suspect.

The pace thus far had been slow. By the first of March, only three witches had been named. By early April, six had been charged, but then the pace quickened, and the geographic area involved expanded. Four were arrested on April 18, nine on April 21, five on April 30, eight on May 14, and eleven on May 28. Seventy people stood accused by June 2, including not only twenty-five from Salem village, which retained the dubious distinction of being the hub of witch-hunting activity, but ten from nearby Salem town; seven from Topsfield; four from Reading; three each from Beverly, Billerica, and Lynn; two from Charlestown, Malden, and Woburn; and one each from nine other towns in eastern Massachusetts. By the time the trials ended, at least 160 people stood accused from an even larger area.[69]

Three general points concerning the numbers of the accused should be made, however, lest they get lost in the narrative. First, as the geographical distribution suggests, to a degree it is misleading to refer to what happened in 1692 as the Salem witch trials. The trials may have begun in Salem village, but charges soon spread throughout Essex County, eastern Massachusetts, and even into other parts of New England. The first twelve to be accused lived in or near Salem village, and the afflicted girls of Salem were instrumental in the charging of suspected witches near and far. By June 2, however, and increasingly thereafter, more of the accused lived outside of Salem village, and even Salem town, than within the community where it all began. Of the approximately 150 that were formerly charged, fewer than 20 percent came from Salem village. Fewer than 30 percent of the accused resided in either Salem village or Salem town, while roughly only half of those executed came from one or the other.[70]

Second, in the types of people involved and the nature of the charges made, what happened until March 1, 1692, fit the pattern for other individual and small-scale witch-hunts in England and New England prior to 1692. Thereafter, especially beginning in April, in their intensity—measured by the number of people accused, tried, condemned, and hanged in such a brief period of time—the witch trials tended to reach beyond the usual group of suspects. They began to follow the rules, if not the pattern, of much larger hunts, like that of mid-seventeenth-century England and of various locations on the Continent.

Tituba, Sarah Good, and Sarah Osborne fit our definition of those who were most likely to be suspected of witchcraft in limited witch-hunts. Those who followed increasingly did not. More men than usual would be charged, as would greater numbers of those from a distinctly higher social class. Two of the three who were accused in March (the third being Dorcas, the daughter of Sarah Good) were highly regarded church members and the wives of relatively prosperous freeholders. Included among those accused in April were Philip English, one of the wealthiest men in New England, and a minister, George Burroughs.

By the end of the summer, as we shall see, some of the most prominent people in the colony would be named, if not officially charged, including the wife of Governor Phips! As Thomas Newton, prosecuting attorney for the Court of Oyer and Terminer, was forced to conclude: "The afflicted spare no person of what quality so ever."[71] It is true that three-quarters of those charged with witchcraft in 1692 continued to be women, and that most of them were of the lower-middling sort, and that few of those suspected people of quality were ever brought to trial, much less executed. The overall direction of the accusations was clear, however, and the reader may be tempted to speculate where, if the trials had not been so abruptly terminated, it all might have led. But then perhaps that is why the trials came to such an abrupt halt. As Cotton Mather wrote a decade later:

> The more there were apprehended, the more were still afflicted by Satan; and the number of confessors increasing, did but increase the number of the accused. . . . [T]hose that were concerned, grew amazed at the number and quality of the persons accused, and feared that Satan by his wiles had enwrapped innocent persons under the imputation of [witchcraft].[72]

And, third, no matter how far afield the witch trials spread, the girls remained at center stage. In 1711, nearly twenty years after the fact, the Massachusetts General Court described some of the girls as having "proved themselves profligate persons, abandoned to all vice," and others as having since "passed their days in obscurity and contempt."[73] But that was not the perception of most in 1692; indeed, it was quite the opposite. It was decided early on that the girls were not possessed, but afflicted, and from that point on the trials relied almost exclusively on the evidence only they, as the afflicted, could provide.

Historians have been of different minds in assessing the behavior of the young accusers. Charles Upham was among the first to suspect fraud, but he allowed that "credulity, hallucination, and the delirium of excitement" contributed to the girls behavior as well.[74] Most other historians have been more single-minded, some insisting that the girls should have been charged with fraud, others offering psychological, sociological, and even physical interpretations. Attempts at establishing physical causation have largely failed.[75] Few are no longer willing to pronounce the girls possessed or afflicted in seventeenth-century terms.

Nevertheless, some historians have defended the girls—or at least some of them, like Elizabeth Parris—as being seriously troubled or victims. Ernest Caulfield, for example, has pronounced them the victims of "the worst sort of mental distress—living in fear for their very lives and the welfare of their immortal souls."[76] And Chadwick Hansen has agreed, calling the girls hysterics, in that they were not merely overexcited, but mentally ill.[77]

John Demos has cited intergenerational conflict and child-rearing practices as lying at the core of the girls' problems. To read Paul Boyer and Stephen Nissenbaum, we might conclude that they were merely pawns in the deadly game of community crisis politics in which their parents were engaged. And from Carol Karlsen, we might see the girls as being used by the enforcers of traditional gender roles against those who would violate them. But as with so many questions raised by the study of the Salem witch trials, we are not likely to ever know for sure what led the girls to act the way they did.

As the story unfolds, readers will be left to draw their own conclusions regarding the accusing girls' motives, but some further observations might be in order on this point as well. Elizabeth Parris was the first to crack, but soon there were four among the original accusers. Elizabeth and Abigail dropped out of the proceedings relatively early, but they were replaced by several others, most of whom had nothing to do with whatever happened in the Parris house during the winter of 1691–1692.[78]

Further, if members of Parris's household—Betty Parris and Abigail Williams—were indeed young, ages nine and eleven respectively, those who followed were drawn increasingly from their older female and even male neighbors. Ann Putnam Jr. may have been only twelve and Elizabeth Hubbard only seventeen, but soon most were in their late teens, some in their twenties and thirties, and a few even older. If, as most allow, Betty and Abigail were traumatized by something that happened that winter and Ann Putnam was caught up in the nearly insane obsessions of her mother, what motivated the rest?

Of this we may never be certain, but it is clear that once involved, except for Parris and Williams, the accusers were swept along by the tide they helped create, but which they could not control and from which they could not extricate themselves. And they did not act alone. They had to have some help, if only to accuse the many with whom they had no previous acquaintance. Perhaps the accusers simply availed themselves of local gossip or the unintentional, but nonetheless deadly, asides of those attending to them. It is also possible, however, although the evidence remains circumstantial, that they were prompted by individuals with more nefarious intentions.

5

"If They Are Let Alone We Should All Be Devils and Witches"

Although in April 1692 most of the inhabitants of Salem village were convinced that the Devil was in their midst, not all were so persuaded and at least a few were willing to make their sentiments known. When Joseph Putnam learned that his brother's wife, Ann Putnam, was adding to the list of the accused, he is reported to have warned her that if she dared touch with her "foul lies" anyone belonging to his household, she would "answer for it."[1] George Jacobs, whose servant Sarah Churchill was among the possessed, called them "bitch witches."[2] But the best known of the early critics was John Proctor, whose case has been popularized (and fictionalized) by Arthur Miller in *The Crucible* (1952).

THE CASES OF ELIZABETH AND JOHN PROCTOR

In 1692, John Proctor was sixty years old and a prosperous landowner and tavern keeper on Ipswich Road. A native of Ipswich, he came to the area in 1666, while in his mid-thirties, leasing one of the area's largest farms, at some 700 acres, lying just beyond the village's southeast corner. Upon the death of his father, Proctor inherited a one-third share in an estate of more than 1,200 pounds, about 60 percent of the value of which consisted of houses and lands that he rented.[3]

Proctor was moderately active in Ipswich, Salem, and Boston area affairs, through which he made a number of close friends. In a legal document of 1689, which arranged for the disposition of his estate upon his death, the four "trusty and well-beloved friends" he named as trustees included one man from Concord, two from Salem town, and Israel Porter of Salem village. After his imprisonment in 1692, thirty-two Ipswich residents, including minister John Wise, signed a petition on his behalf.[4] Proctor had avoided most of Salem village's squabbles. When the witch trials began, however, Proctor's servant, Mary Warren, was among the afflicted, and he was opposed to her participation. In one early instance he reported to a neighbor that he had cured Mary Warren of her fits by sitting her down at her spinning wheel and threatening her with a thrashing if she stirred from it, afflicted or not. He protested her continued use by the court, but to no avail. "She must have her fits again," Proctor concluded in frustration.[5]

Arriving in the village to pick up his servant on the day after Deodat Lawson's call to arms, Proctor once again made his objections clear. "They should rather be had to the whipping post," he said of the girls. "If they are let alone we should all be devils and witches." As for him, he would "fetch his jade [Mary Warren] home and thrash the Devil out of her," and, if given the chance, he would do the same with the others. Witches were not to be found among decent women, he insisted, but they may well be discovered among the afflicted girls![6] At a time when the people of Salem were being forced to take the side of God or risk being seen as having sided with the Devil, Proctor's was an unwise, or at least an unsafe, position to take. When the afflicted girls struck back, however, they began with his wife.

Elizabeth Proctor, John's third wife, was as well respected as her husband. Married to John for eighteen years, she was pregnant with his seventeenth child in April 1692. Elizabeth ran the family tavern, while her husband tended to their other business, and therein lies the only shadow cast upon her reputation. On two occasions, she had quarreled with Robert Stone over "a reckoning" and with Hugh Jones over a pint of cider for which he had not paid. Many years earlier, Elizabeth's grandmother, Ann Burt of Lynn, had been suspected of witchcraft, but no mention of the case appears in the records of Elizabeth's hearing.[7]

Only a few days after John's outburst against the girls, on Monday, March 28, 1692, one of the girls then at Ingersoll's ordinary (perhaps Mercy Lewis, but the record is unclear) cried out against Elizabeth Proctor. "Goody Proctor . . . Old Witch! I'll have her hang." In this instance, Sarah Ingersoll, Daniel Elliot, and William Raymond immediately charged her with lying, whereupon she "came out of her trance" and explained, "It was for sport. I must have some sport."[8] Similar developments, however, occurred the next day at the home of Thomas Putnam. Ann Putnam Sr. and Jr., as well as their nineteen-year-old servant Mercy Lewis, suffered fits. Lewis called out Elizabeth Proctor's name, but when questioned by those present, Lewis replied that if she had done so, she had done it "when she was out of her head." Complaints were made nevertheless, and a warrant was issued for Proctor's arrest on April 8, the same day the magistrates ordered Sarah Cloyce arrested. The two would stand trial together.[9]

Elizabeth Proctor appeared before the magistrates on April 11, her husband John standing by her side. Perhaps John's show of support had some effect initially on those who would bear witness against Elizabeth, because the questioning did not follow its usual course. Deputy Governor Danforth inquired as to whether she understood the charges that had been brought against her ("sundry acts of witchcraft"), to which she did not immediately respond, or at least her response was not included in the record. Danforth asked Mary Walcott whether Elizabeth Proctor was the woman who had hurt her, but Walcott replied, "I never saw her so as to be hurt by her." He asked the same question of Mercy Lewis, Ann Putnam, and Abigail Williams, but none responded. According to the records, Lewis's "mouth was stopped," Putnam "could not speak," and Williams's "hand was thrust in her own mouth."[10]

John Indian was the first to make a positive identification. "There is the woman who came in her shift and choked me," he said, and brought him a book to sign. The girls continued to remain silent, "by reason of dumbness or other fits," but Elizabeth Proctor broke her silence. "I take God in heaven to be my witness, that I know nothing of it, no more than the child unborn," she pleaded, but that only seemed to release the pent-up energies of the young girls. Ann Putnam was the first to find her tongue, but then all of the girls began to cry out against Proctor. Each testified that Proctor had been after them to sign the book, Williams adding that she had "made her maid [Mary Warren, not present] set her hand to it." "Dear child, it is not so," answered Elizabeth, and she warned, "There is another judgment, dear child." Neither Abigail nor the court, however, was concerned with any later call to the bar of justice. The girls merely fell into fits and pointed to Proctor's specter, perched on a beam above the gathering of amazed people.[11]

Danforth employed the Lord's Prayer test on Elizabeth Proctor, and as expected, she stumbled twice in ways that were meaningful to the court. In the first instance, instead of saying "deliver us from evil," she said "deliver us from all evil." And when asked to try again, where she should have said "hallowed be thy name," she prayed, "hollowed be thy name." Upon her first error, the court reasoned that Proctor had "prayed against what she was now justly under"; and, in the second, they concluded that her words were "a depraving" of the real words, making them void and even "a curse rather than a prayer."[12]

Although it does not appear in the records, it is possible that John Proctor expressed his indignation over the attack on his wife, because at one point in the hearing the girls turned on him. Ann Putnam and Abigail Williams called him a wizard and fell into fits. Some of the girls (their names were not listed in the record) cried, "There is Proctor going to take up Goody Pope's feet," and Pope's feet were immediately taken up, whereupon she immediately fell into a fit. When asked to explain the girls' fits while in his presence, John Proctor could only say, "I know not. I am innocent."[13]

Danforth was not impressed. "You see, the Devil will deceive you," he responded. "The children could see what you were going to do before the woman was hurt. I would advise you to repentance, for the Devil is bringing you out." Repent he did not, however, and if the Devil did not bring him out, others did. Benjamin Gould testified that he had seen the Proctors, Giles and Martha Corey, Cloyce, Nurse, and Goody Griggs in his chamber that past Thursday evening. Abigail Williams once again cried out that Proctor was going to hurt Goody Bibber; and indeed, Bibber fell into a fit. Williams and Putnam both tried to strike Elizabeth Proctor, but they were held back by an invisible force. As Williams's fist came near Proctor, it was forced open and it alighted only lightly on him, whereupon she cried out that her fingers burned.[14]

By the end of the day, John Proctor joined his wife, Rebecca Nurse, Sarah Cloyce, Martha Corey, and Dorcas Good in a cart bound for Boston and for prison. The accusers, however, were not yet done with the Proctors. In one of the most extensive cases of family culpability in the records of the Salem witch trials, four of the Proctor children were accused of witchcraft. Three were the subject of arrest warrants: Sarah Proctor on May 21, Benjamin on May 23, and William on May 28. Joseph Proctor was named but there is no record of his arrest. All of the warrants made essentially the same charge. The Proctors' children were accused of afflicting, causing "great hurt" to, or committing "sundry acts of witchcraft . . . upon the bodies" of Mary Warren, Abigail Williams, Elizabeth Hubbard, Mary Walcott, Ann Putnam, the younger, Sarah Churchill, and others. If they were ever tried, the records of their trials have not survived, so we have no information regarding what followed. We do know, however, that unlike their father, they at least escaped with their lives.[15]

One of the more interesting elements of the Proctor children's story involves a letter written by John Proctor and other prisoners on July 23, 1692, to the Reverends Increase Mather, James Allen, Joshua Moody, Samuel Willard, and John Bayley. The trials had begun, and Proctor's principal goal was to gain the support of those notable ministers for either a change of venue to Boston, where they believed they would be more fairly treated, or failing that, for the replacement of the judges that were sitting on the Court of Oyer and Terminer. The current judges had condemned them even before their trials had begun, Proctor insisted. The judges "being so much incensed and enraged against [them] by the Devil," they would settle for nothing less than their "innocent blood."[16]

John Proctor also made one of the few surviving references to the use of torture in the Salem witch trials. Torture, it will be recalled, was not permitted under British law. Proctor, however, charged that two (Richard and Thomas Carrier) of the five people who had recently confessed and accused others had done so only after they had their necks and heels tied "till the blood was ready to come out of their noses." Proctor's son William received the same treatment, "until the blood gushed out at his nose," and he would have been left tied in that painful position for twenty-four hours, Proctor added, if "one, more merciful than the rest, had not taken pity on him, and caused him to be unbound." Nevertheless, William did not confess.[17]

Given the presence of the colonial luminaries, the Cloyce and Proctor cases of April 11 constituted another important step in the development of the Salem witch trials. In their presence and with their approval, both of the defendants were deemed sufficiently suspect to be held for trial. Samuel Sewall recorded his thoughts in his diary: "Went to Salem, where in the meetinghouse the persons accused of witchcraft were examined; was a very great assembly; 'twas awful to see how the afflicted persons were agitated." In the margin, sometime afterward, he added in Latin, *Vae* or "Alas," three times![18] What had begun as a village or at best a town affair was no longer so parochial.

But even more interesting developments followed upon the Proctor hearings. It seems that perhaps because of John Proctor's stern reproaches, or maybe because of some affection she may have had for him if not his wife, Mary Warren, Proctor's twenty-year-old servant, began to recant her earlier testimony and to suggest that others among the afflicted may have lied.[19]

MARY WARREN TRIES TO RECANT

The reader will recall that Mary Warren had not taken part in the cases brought against her master and mistress, and that at their hearing on April 11, from which Warren was absent, Ann Putnam and Abigail Williams had accused Elizabeth Proctor of having forced Mary Warren to sign the Devil's book. Quite likely, the girls anticipated Warren's defection and to protect themselves they were prepared to turn against their former compatriot. And sure enough, on April 18, Mary Warren was among those listed on a new warrant for arrest.[20]

On April 19, Warren appeared before the magistrates in Salem village, this time on the other side of the bar of justice. Hathorne led the questioning and as usual began by informing her of the charges brought against her. Warren pleaded innocent, whereupon Hathorne asked the girls if Warren had hurt them. "Some were dumb," Parris's official notes read, but Elizabeth Hubbard cried out against Warren and fell into a fit. Hathorne turned to Warren and asked, "You were a little while ago an afflicted person; now you are an afflicter. How comes this to pass?" Mary Warren, in the presence of her judges, neighbors, and former accusing sisters, was rattled. "I look up to God, and I take it to be a mercy of God," she responded. "What!" Hathorne exploded, no doubt surprised by what he had heard. "Do you take it as a great mercy to afflict others?"[21]

Warren seemed even more confused, and much to everyone's surprise she fell into fits, writhing in pain and seemingly unable to control herself any longer. Some of the afflicted cried out that Warren was going to confess, the records continue, "but Goody Corey and Proctor and his wife came in, in their apparitions, and struck her down, and said she should tell nothing." For the moment Warren could not speak, but soon she cried out again, "I will speak! Oh, I am sorry for it! I am sorry for it!" She wrung her hands and again fell into a fit, only to recover and add, "Oh Lord help me! Oh, good Lord, save me!" and, later, "I will tell! I will tell!" A great struggle had broken out within Mary Warren, and just as suddenly as it had begun she became speechless, swooned, and had to be carried from the meetinghouse.[22]

Some time later, Warren was recalled, but once again she lapsed in and out of fits, speaking when she could. In an extraordinary move on the part of the court, the magistrates granted Mary Warren a private hearing. The records of that interview suggest a woman who was in and out of reality, or of a woman who was alternately trying to confess to having lied and then falling back in fear of the repercussions that confession would bring about for her. "I will, I will speak, Satan!" she exclaimed. "She saith she will kill me! Oh, she saith she owes me a spite and will claw me off. Avoid, Satan, for the name of God, avoid!" Who was "she"? Elizabeth Proctor? Perhaps, but Mary Warren did not actually name her.[23]

As one author has said, Mary Warren was no Joan of Arc, and even Joan of Arc could not stand the pressures upon her to tell the truth come what may. Like Joan, Warren was sent to prison, but the possibility that she might have lied to the magistrates was potentially damaging enough to persuade the magistrates to continue her questioning for the next several weeks. Reports about her behavior in prison were just as disturbing. It seems that when she was alone, she behaved as rationally as anyone. In her discussion with her fellow prisoners, against whom her former afflicted colleagues had borne witness, she even reasserted her skepticism—her disbelief in the truthfulness of those who had cried out against them. Four of those prisoners— Edward and Sarah Bishop, Mary Easty, and Mary English—prepared a deposition in which they offered the following report:

> We have heard Mary Warren several times say that the magistrates might as well examine Keyser's daughter that has been distracted many years, and take notice of what she said, as well as any of the afflicted persons. 'For,' said Mary Warren, 'when I was afflicted, I thought I saw the apparitions of a hundred persons,' [but] she said her head was distempered that she could not tell what she said. And the said Mary told us, that, when she was well again, she could not say that she saw any of the apparitions at the time aforesaid.[24]

Mary Warren's meetings with the magistrates, which took place between April 21 and May 12, were marked by periodic fits and moments of lucidity, but they always ended with her confessing. Perhaps she was just confessing to whatever they wanted to hear; maybe she was telling the truth, at least as she saw it. In either event, her confession took place in stages. On April 21, she said John Proctor had brought her a book, but she denied having signed it "unless putting her finger to it was signing." When asked whether she had seen a spot in the book where she had put her finger, she answered that there was indeed a black spot. And when asked if John Proctor had threatened to run hot tongs down her throat if she did not sign, she answered that he had threatened to "burn her out of her fits."[25]

At one point, Warren testified that her master had "put her hand to the book," whereupon she "was undone body and soul and cried out grievously." Her interrogators told Warren that she must have touched the book voluntarily, because the Devil could not have forced her to do so against her will. She had succumbed, they insisted, "for the ease of her body, not for any good of her soul," to which she did report that John and Elizabeth Proctor had threatened to drown her and "to make her run through the hedges" if she did not.[26]

On May 12, Warren reported that upon one occasion when she was afflicted, John Proctor had said to her, "If you are afflicted, I wish you were more afflicted and you and all." When she asked why he had said such a thing, she said, he had responded, "Because you go to bring out innocent persons." Warren protested that "that could not be"; whether the Devil had taken advantage of her to afflict them, however, she did not know.[27]

Mary Warren was more specific and damning in her testimony against Elizabeth Proctor than she was against John. Warren reported having seen suspicious objects in Elizabeth's house and in her possession, including ointments, a poppet stuck with pins, and strange books. One poppet, she responded, was for either Ann Putnam or Abigail Williams, she could not be certain, but Warren had upon that occasion, while Elizabeth Proctor had the poppet, stuck a pin into it. Those revelations seem to have been enough to provoke Elizabeth Proctor, because on at least one occasion in the presence of the magistrates, on April 21, Warren had to fight off her specter. Once again, she cried out, "I will tell! I will tell! Thou wicked creature, it is you that stopped my mouth, but I will confess." This time, however, she added, "Oh Betty Proctor, it is she. It is she I lived with last." Elizabeth Proctor had undone her, "body and soul."[28]

Warren salvaged her credibility by adding to the evidence gathered against several of those already charged, including Rebecca Nurse, Sarah Cloyce, Sarah and Dorcas Good, Giles and Martha Corey, and others. She also explained the supernatural causes of the death of a man on a vessel in Salem harbor, the falling of a man from a cherry tree, and even the mysterious casting away of a ketch or small ship.[29]

Having heard what they wanted from her, the magistrates considered Mary Warren free of the Devil's grip. They released her from jail and allowed her to rejoin the girls in court. Mary never again led the demonstrations, but neither did she question what was being said or done. Although readmitted to her circle of friends, she was no doubt viewed with suspicion thereafter. Although she had recanted her earlier confession of having dissembled, there were some who continued to believe that Warren had in fact told the truth, and although she had in the end told the magistrates what they wanted to hear, it could hardly have been the case that they or others, animated by the spirit of finding the witches in their midst, were any longer totally comfortable with her as an informer.[30]

Bridget Bishop and Abigail Hobbs Are Charged

On April 19 three others joined Mary Warren in the Salem meetinghouse: Giles Corey, of whom we have already spoken; Bridget Bishop of Salem village; and Abigail Hobbs of Topsfield. Bridget Bishop's was a classic case in that she had been suspected for some time and actually charged ten years earlier.[31] It was also unique, however, in that on some key points the evidence used against her constituted a case of mistaken identity, an error not brought to light until 1981 by David L. Greene.

Greene discovered that the testimony offered by Sarah Churchill and Susannah Sheldon was taken from details provided by the Reverend John Hale in the case of Sarah Bishop of nearby Beverly. The references by Churchill and Sheldon to Bridget Bishop, the tavern keeper who had permitted young people to gather all hours to play shuffleboard and to make so much noise that they disturbed the neighbors, as well as to her having worn "a red paragon bodice" and other flashy apparel, had nothing to do with Bridget; they originated with Hale's testimony concerning Sarah Bishop.[32]

What we do know about Bridget Bishop is that she was somewhere between fifty-five and sixty years old and that she had been married three times. She was the widow Wasselbe on July 26, 1666, when she married Thomas Oliver, a widower with three children. They brought another daughter into the world, but their marriage was a troubled one. In January 1670, Bridget and Thomas were found guilty of fighting with one another and sentenced, barring payment of a fine, to be publicly whipped. At their trial, a neighbor testified that Bridget's face had been bloodied on one occasion and made black-and-blue on another. Thomas Oliver protested that Bridget had given him "several blows."[33]

In January 1678, Bridget was back in court for calling her husband names on the Lord's Day, but authorities obviously found fault with Thomas as well, because they sentenced both to stand gagged in the marketplace, a sign on their heads indicating their offenses. Thomas's daughter paid her father's fine, which released him from punishment, but there is no record of Bridget's having been released.[34]

In 1680, Bridget Oliver was charged with witchcraft. Little is known of the case except that there is no record of conviction. The charge came from a man described as "Wonn, John Ingerson's Negro," who told a story of frightened horses, the vanishing shape of Bridget Oliver, the appearance of an unknown cat, and mysterious pinchings and pain. John Lambert, Jonathan Pickering, and "some youths" corroborated Wonn's testimony regarding the horses, offering that they believed them to have been bewitched. The charge came soon after the death of Bridget's husband in 1679. Because Thomas had died without a will, Bridget was appointed executor of his estate. Thomas's sons by his first wife, and their daughter, Christian, received twenty shillings each, but Bridget was ordered to pay her deceased husband's debts. She was granted permission to sell a ten-acre lot to pay those debts and to provide for herself.[35]

Sometime before 1687, Bridget married Edward Bishop. In 1687, Thomas Stacey charged her with stealing his brass. She was arrested on December 14, but her hearing did not take place until the following March. The only person to testify against Bishop was William Stacey, presumably Thomas's son, but John Hathorne, presiding, ordered Bridget Bishop to jail until "her trial at the next Sessions of the Peace." Edward Bishop and William Reeves posted bond for her release, but there is no record of the case ever having been heard.[36] She did not return to court until April 19, 1692.

On April 19, Bridget Bishop stated her case directly: "I take all this people to witness that I am clear." In a second account of the examination, Bishop is reported to have said: "I never did hurt them in my life. I never saw these persons before. I am as innocent as the child unborn." She further swore that she had never even ventured into Salem village center. But the girls fell into their fits, and when Hathorne asked Bishop if it troubled her to see the girls so tormented, she simply said, "No."[37]

The girls testified that upon one occasion, when Bridget Bishop's shape appeared to them, they had pointed to the spot where she stood and Mary Walcott's brother Jonathan had struck her with his sword. Walcott cried out that Jonathan had hit Bishop and torn her coat. Hathorne had Bishop's coat examined, and although some disagreement followed on what they saw, Cheever's records read that they did find a tear that "seems to answer what was alleged was found."[38]

Marshall Herrick stepped forward to ask how Bishop had come to be in his bedchamber one morning, asking whether he had any curtains to sell her. She denied having been there, only to have the afflicted retake the floor and recall the earlier charges of murder that had been brought against her. "They say you bewitched your first husband to death," Hathorne continued, but Bishop replied that she knew nothing of it. She said she was not guilty, but as she did she shook her head and said "the afflicted were tortured." She turned up her eyes, and the eyes of the afflicted rolled in their sockets. Indeed, the girls fell into such torment that Hathorne could no longer take it. He asked that if it were true that she was not a witch, then why did her "appearance" hurt the girls: "Why, you seem to act witchcraft before us!" "I know nothing of it," she replied. "I am innocent to a witch. I know not what a witch is."[39] The magistrates ordered Bridget Bishop held, and she too was carted off to prison.

And then there was Abigail Hobbs, described by one historian as "a wild creature" and by another as "deranged." Her mother, Deliverance Hobbs, had once said that "she little thought to be mother of such a dafter." Hobbs had long shocked the people of Topsfield by her rambling about the woods at night. One of her accusers, in commenting on her behavior, had explained that whereas others might be afraid to wander in the forest at night, she was not, because she believed "she had sold herself body and soul to the old boy."[40]

Abigail, however, perhaps because she was "a dafter," was a match for her accusers. Not only did the girls fail to alarm her in the least, but she added to the mayhem by confessing to "crimes enough to have hanged her a dozen times." She admitted to having met the Devil and signed his book three or four years earlier at Casco Bay (Maine), where the Hobbs had lived in the late 1680s. He was "like a black man with a hat," she recalled, and he had told her that if she consented he would hurt people in her shape. She described in detail the witches' Sabbaths in Parris's pasture. She named nine witches who had been present, as well as the Boston woman Tituba had seen who was dressed in a silk mantle. And she confessed to having hurt Mercy Lewis and Ann Putnam.[41] The tables having been turned, the girls could only watch in awed silence.

One witness reported that during a conversation with Abigail about "her wicked carriages and disobedience to her father and mother," Hobbs had said that "she did not care what anybody said to her, for she had seen the Devil and had made a covenant or bargain with him." Another testified that upon one occasion in her mother's presence, Abigail had asked the woman if she was baptized. When she said yes, Abigail offered, "My mother is not baptized, but I will baptize her," whereupon she sprinkled water in her mother's face "in the name of the Father, Son, and Holy Ghost."[42]

On April 20, Abigail Hobbs continued her self-condemnation. She declared that Judah White, who recently arrived from the Isle of Jersey and who had lived with Joseph Ingersoll at Casco Bay but had since moved to Boston, had appeared to her in apparition. White had advised her to flee and to not go to the examination, but if she did go, not to confess to anything. Hobbs confessed that the Devil, in the shape of a man, had come to her and pressed her to afflict the girls. He had brought with him wooden images in their likenesses with thorns she could stick into them, and she had, whereupon the girls cried out in pain. The magistrates returned Hobbs to jail, but Hobbs was still not done. When the magistrates visited her, she confessed to murder. "Were they men or women you killed?" the magistrates asked. "They were both boys and girls," she responded. And when they asked if she was angry with them at the time, she answered, "Yes, though I do not know why now."[43]

On April 21, 1692, the Salem magistrates issued warrants for the arrest of Mary Easty (whose hearing we have already discussed), Edward and Sarah Bishop, Deliverance and William Hobbs, Sarah Wildes, Mary Black, Nehemiah Abbott Jr., and Mary English, all of whom Abigail Hobbs had named in her testimony. The Bishops were from Salem village and English was from Salem town, but Easty, the Hobbs, Abbott, and the Wilds were from Topsfield.[44]

Seven of the Nine Are Formally Charged

The Bishops had several strikes against them. Edward Bishop, age forty-four, was the stepson of the above-mentioned Bridget. His wife, Sarah, age forty-one, was also the sister of the accused Sarah Wildes. Edward owned land in Topsfield as well as in Salem village, and he had been one of the Topsfield men who had come into conflict with Salem villagers. In 1690, Sarah had left the Salem village church to join the church at Topsfield, and finally, in the wake of Bridget's hearing, Edward Bishop had the temerity, courage, or lack of good sense to whip John Indian and to call for the same treatment of the other afflicted persons in order to bring them back to their senses.[45]

Sarah Bishop was the tavern keeper to which the Reverend John Hale referred in his testimony concerning Christian Trask. The specifics of that story have already been reported. What most concerned Hale in its retelling in Salem, however, were his renewed doubts about Bishop's innocence. He recalled how Trask had become distracted soon after she had formally complained about Sarah Bishop, and had then taken her life, or so it appeared at the time. Moreover, he now realized, Trask's distraction was much like that of the afflicted girls of Salem who had charged Sarah Bishop with witchcraft.[46]

While continuing to be the subject of considerable mental anguish, Hale reported, Trask had taken steps to reconcile with Sarah Bishop, so he had dismissed Bishop as having had any role in Trask's death. He concurred with others that it must have been suicide, but the circumstances of Trask's death continued to trouble him. Hale explained that Trask had died of three wounds, described as "a piece of her windpipe cut out, another wound above that through the windpipe and gullet, and the vein they call jugular [cut]." At the time, he questioned whether such wounds could have been self-inflicted—that Christian Trask, "with so short a pair of scissors" as they found near the body, could "mangle herself so without some extraordinary work of the Devil of witchcraft."[47] In April 1692, he was even more doubtful. We know little else about the Bishops' hearing, but whatever additional testimony—if any—was offered was enough to persuade the jury to return Edward and Sarah Bishop to jail, from which, it was later reported, they escaped!

Deliverance and William Hobbs were the parents of "the dafter," Abigail. Both were characters in their daughter's fantasies. Deliverance was brought to court first, on April 22, and although she struggled to keep her composure, she gradually succumbed. At first, she denied the girls' charges, but when they rolled on the floor at her feet, she could only say, "I am amazed! I am amazed!" whereupon, she too confessed, offering the court all they could want of her. She began by asserting that she was among the afflicted. "Last Lord's Day in the meetinghouse," she reported, "I saw a great many birds and cats and dogs, and heard a voice say 'Come away.'" Thereafter, she continued, she had seen the shapes of several people. Hobbs admitted to having signed the Devil's book only "the night before last" when it was brought to her by Goody Wildes, who threatened to tear her to pieces if she did not sign, and admitted also to having participated in several acts of maleficia.[48]

Like Abigail, Deliverance Hobbs named others, but only those who had already been accused. One notable example of this will suffice. On April 22, Hobbs identified several suspected witches, but not George Burroughs. Burroughs was already under suspicion in some quarters, but he had not been formally or publicly charged. On May 3, after news of his arrest warrant was made public, but before he arrived in Salem, Hobbs was examined again and this time she included Burroughs. In particular, she reported that although in prison she had visited, spectrally, a meeting of witches and wizards in Parris's pasture, which included the Proctors, Rebecca Nurse, the Coreys, Sarah Bishop, and George Burroughs, as their preacher. Burroughs had exhorted those present to bewitch all in the village, "telling them they should do it gradually, and not all at once, but also "assuring them that they should prevail." Burroughs had administered the sacrament, Hobbs continued, "using red bread and red wine like blood;" and Sarah Osborne, Sarah Good, and Rebecca Nurse had assisted in their distribution.[49]

Finally, Deliverance Hobbs reported that "a man in a long-crowned white hat" had sat next to George Burroughs during the sacramental celebration and that "they filled out the wine in tankards." At one point, she continued, Abigail Williams ran out of the nearby parsonage to speak to them, but by the time she came anywhere near the group, Hobbs was struck blind. Thus, Hobbs never saw with whom Williams spoke. The record of Deliverance Hobbs's prison examination ends with a reference to Deliverance's daughter being brought before her mother. Abigail was "immediately taken with a dreadful fit," whereupon the examiner asked Deliverance who afflicted her. She answered, Goodman Corey: "She saw him and the gentlewoman of Boston striving to break her daughter's neck."[50]

William Hobbs responded quite differently from his wife and daughter. When confronted by the girls' uncontrollable reaction to his presence, he insisted that he was innocent. "I can speak in the presence of God safely, as I must look to give account another day, that I am as clear as a newborn babe." When Hathorne asked if he could "act witchcraft" at that moment and by "casting" his eyes "turn folks into fits," he answered, "You may judge your pleasure. My soul is clear." He denied being able to see who was afflicting the girls, and when Hathorne asked how he could deny responsibility for their torment, Hobbs replied, "I can deny it to my dying day!" And he did.[51]

Although he admitted to not having attended church for "a pretty while," because he was ill, Hobbs insisted that he worshiped God only and that he knew nothing about witchcraft. He denied, as had been charged by his daughter, that he left the room whenever the family read from the scriptures and that he prayed to the Devil. Hobbs testified that he had not known his daughter was a witch and knew nothing about that to which his wife had confessed. But the magistrates did not believe him, and they ordered William Hobbs held as well.[52]

Quickly dispatched among those charged on April 21 were Sarah Wildes, who insisted she was innocent but was condemned by several of the afflicted, and Mary Black, a slave owned by Nathaniel Putnam but who lived with his son Benjamin. There is little reason to dwell on Wildes's hearing,[53] but Black's testimony, given her status in the community, is worth exploring briefly.

Unlike the slave Tituba, who quickly adapted to the situation before her, Mary Black seemed to have been confused by what had happened to her and unable to defend herself. She stood silently when first asked if she was a witch, but more often than not she replied to the magistrates questions with, "I do not know" or "I cannot tell":

Magistrates:	How long have you been a witch?
Black:	I cannot tell.
Magistrates:	But, you have been a witch?
Black:	I cannot tell you.
Magistrates:	Why do you hurt these folks?
Black:	I hurt nobody.
Magistrates:	Who does?
Black:	I do not know.[54]

To be sure, the girls acted against her, but so too did her master. Nathaniel Putnam reported that "a man sat down upon the form [bench]" with Black about one year earlier. The record does not explain what was intended by the statement, but clearly the magistrates saw it as being suspicious. They asked Black what the man had said to her, but she replied only that he had said nothing. Mary Black denied hurting the girls. At one point, Hathorne asked her if she "pricked" the girls with sticks, as they had charged, only to have Black reply, innocently and also comically, if the stakes had not been so high, "No, I pin my neckcloth." Hathorne directed her to take out her neckcloth pin and put it back in. She did so, and the girls cried out in pain as if pricked, even showing blood running from their wounds. Black was ordered held.[55]

Nehemiah Abbott, an elderly weaver and church deacon, was brought to the bar. John Hathorne estimated Abbott's age to be nearly 100, but he may have been younger. Larry Gragg has found evidence that he lived until 1701, which would have been remarkable if Abbott was 100 in 1692. Whatever his exact age, Mary Walcott testified that she had seen his shape, and Ann Putnam spotted him on a beam of the meetinghouse. The magistrates urged Abbott to confess, as his guilt "was certainly proved," and to "find mercy of God." "I speak before

God," he replied, however, "that I am clear from this accusation . . . in all respects."[56]

At that point, another curious turn of events occurred. Ann Putnam remained resolute in her charges, but Walcott began to waiver. "He is like him, [but] I cannot say it is he," she allowed. Mercy Lewis testified that Abbott was not the person who had afflicted her, and the rest of the girls remained silent. The magistrates ordered the girls to examine him more closely, even moving them outside to take advantage of the daylight. But they still could not identify him, admitting only that "he was like that man, but [that] he had not the wen [cyst or blemish] they saw in his apparition." Putnam, perhaps sensing her isolation and wishing to explain her mistaken identification, quickly shouted at Abbott, "Did you put a mist before my eyes?"[57]

Nehemiah Abbott was discharged, but what happened thereafter is unclear. Unlike Mary Easty, he may never have been charged again, but that is not certain. In her testimony of August 25, 1692, the accused witch Sarah Briggs remarked that she had heard "of but one innocent man imprisoned yet for witchcraft and that was Abbott of Ipswich." No first name is recorded, but it may well have been Nehemiah. Abbott's son, however, also named Nehemiah, was charged with witchcraft, although the records concerning the case have been lost. No Abbott, however, was ever hanged during the Salem witch trials.[58]

The Ordeal Begins For Mary and Philip English

Also indicted on April 21 was Mary English of Salem town, the wife of the wealthiest man in Essex County and one of the wealthiest men in New England, clearly setting a new mark for the circle of accusers. Mary English, born Mary Hollingsworth, could trace her ancestry to the founding of the Massachusetts Bay Colony and to the founder of a considerable shipping business. The Hollingsworth fortune failed after 1674, but the reversal had little effect on Mary, who in 1675 married Philip English. In marriage, she added to her husband's already well-supplied estate a Hollingsworth wharf, warehouse, and tavern.[59]

On the one hand, Mary English was a professor of the faith. She regularly attended the Salem town church, was admitted to full communion in 1681, and had her children baptized there. On the other hand, she developed a reputation for exhibiting an aristocratic bearing toward those she considered beneath her.[60] Moreover, Mary had a very disagreeable mother, Eleanor. Eleanor Hollingsworth is said to have come from a prominent English family with ties to the Crown— a point, according to her fellow townspeople, she continually flaunted. By one account, she never left home in the evening without a servant walking before her and another behind her. But then, the failure of the Hollingsworth fortunes in the 1670s changed all of that. Eleanor was forced to run the family's tavern, but she was obviously not temperamentally suited for the job. One disgruntled customer called her "a black-mouthed witch and a thief." The assailant was fined for his verbal assault, but Eleanor's reputation survived. In 1692, she was cried out against again as being a witch, but she had been dead for two years! Mary, however, was still very much alive.[61]

The warrant of April 21 ordered Mary English arrested "for high suspicion of sundry acts of witchcraft done or committed . . . upon the bodies" of Ann Putnam, Mercy Lewis, and Mary Walcott. According to a granddaughter, the Salem town sheriff and his deputies arrived with their arrest warrant at Mary English's house at about 11:00 P.M., by which time Mary and Philip had retired for the evening. When the arresting officers entered the chamber and ordered Mary to accompany them to the local jail, she refused, insisting that they return in the morning. The sheriff, according to the account, reluctantly agreed but left his men to guard the house. When he returned, Mary went with him, but only after having joined her family at breakfast, bid farewell to her servants, and instructed Philip on the education of their children.[62]

How much of this account is true we may never know, but Mary English did appear before the magistrates on April 22. The records of her examination have been lost, but she was ordered held, and eight days later a warrant was issued for Philip English's arrest for afflicting the same three girls and Abigail Williams and Susannah Sheldon.[63] Philip was clearly an outsider, or, as defined in chapter one, an intruder, as well as a prominent and representative figure of the economic and social transformation that was overtaking Salem in the late seventeenth century.

Philip English—his name an anglicization of the French L'Anglais—was born on the Isle of Jersey in the English Channel. The date and circumstances of his arrival in Salem are unclear, but by the time he married he had become a successful independent shipmaster with business connections throughout the British colonies in the Western Hemisphere and in Europe. His marriage to Mary Hollingsworth added to his fortune, so by 1692 he was believed to be the richest man "on the coast." He and Mary lived in what was commonly called English's "great house." It was the largest and most opulent in Salem, and it was staffed by fifteen to twenty servants.[64]

If Mary was universally called "haughty," Philip English received mixed reviews as a person. He was variously described as "high-spirited" and "impulsive" but "not ungenerous," and "at times choleric" and "not overly conciliatory to his peers" but "kind to the poor."[65] Perhaps his best-known but irritating quality, however, was his litigiousness. Already soundly condemned by those who mourned the loss of community it signaled, litigiousness was on the rise in Salem, especially among those in the business community. In 1683, out of 556 men listed as taxpayers in the town of Salem, 62 were involved in court cases. Of a sample of 506 men who appeared in court in the twenty-year period from 1672 to 1692, 357 appeared an average of four times and 216 of that number were always plaintiffs. Philip English was in court seventeen times, usually as a plaintiff![66]

By 1692, there were over two dozen families with husbands of Jersey extraction in Salem. Philip English was not only the most prominent among them, but he was also responsible for many of their passages to Salem, having arranged their indenture. They tended to live apart from the local populace, several residing on Philip English's land, and they were seen as "rapacious swindlers" or as acting in collusion against the rest of the community. Animosity between the Jerseyans and the English Salemites peaked in the years immediately preceding the witch trials, when there was a sudden influx of French Huguenots and renewed war with France. The Huguenots, French Protestants, began to arrive in 1686 with France's revocation of the Edict of Nantes, which had guaranteed their religious freedom, and the much-despised Governor Edmund Andros welcomed them and accorded them the rights of British citizenship.[67]

In 1689, when King William's War began, however, tensions in the British colonies of New England led to a growing fear of those of French extraction in their midst. In 1690, in one particularly incendiary incident, Jerseyan Isaac Morrill was accused of plotting the overthrow of British rule in New England with the help of other Jerseyans, 500 Indians, 300 French troops, and a French fleet. In October 1692, in the midst of the Salem witch trials, the Massachusetts General Court proposed that armed parties be used to search all French communities within their borders for powder and arms and that an oath of allegiance be required of those people. As part of the measure the legislature resolved that "sundry" of the French who lived in the region were "enemies to their majesties and the weal of the province."[68]

Not surprisingly, then, several Jerseyans became the victims of the hysteria of 1692, but indirectly. Most Jersey men were not charged, but their English wives were. The native Salem women who married them may have been lifelong members of the community and therefore insiders, but their actions had caused their loyalties to be suspect and them to be even more distrusted, feared, or hated than their husbands. Among those women to be charged with witchcraft were Mary De Rich, Mary De Riels, Mrs. Zachariah White (Le Blanc), and Mary English (L'Anglais).[69]

Philip English was Anglican. He regularly attended services in Salem's First Church with Mary, and he agreed to have his children baptized there. He joined other leading citizens in supporting the construction of a larger structure, and he seemed to have stayed out of any open conflict that may have resulted from his religious preferences, at least until after 1692. But Philip English was definitely not a Puritan, and he never made any attempt to become one.[70]

Finally, Philip English, the successful man of commerce, the man of many lawsuits, the outsider, and the Anglican, became even more vulnerable when he entered politics. Despite his shortcomings, he was highly regarded in Salem's commercial circle, which was beginning to dominate town politics, and not surprisingly English allied himself politically with the Porter faction. He held various town offices and, perhaps not coincidentally, on March 8, 1692, less than two months before his wife's arrest, he and four other Porter kinsmen were elected town selectmen. The election, the reader will recall, was of considerable importance in the struggle between the Porters and the Putnams.[71]

In a document attached to the April 30 arrest warrant, Susannah Sheldon testified that while attending a service in the town church on Sunday, April 24, "being afflicted in a very sad manner," she saw Philip English's specter step over his pew and pinch her. Later, when Sheldon was returning home, Philip English and "a black man with a high crowned hat on his head" approached her, the latter with book in hand. Philip English told Sheldon that his companion was her God and that if she would touch the book English would not pinch her anymore, nor would anyone else. The next day, she continued, English appeared to her again, this time threatening to kill her if she did not sign the book. In both instances, Sheldon refused.[72]

Philip English had been visiting Mary in jail, but when a warrant was issued for his arrest, he disappeared. On May 2, Essex County Marshall George Herrick reported that English had fled. Guessing that he might have gone to Boston where his wife was being held and where he had influential friends, the magistrates on May 6 procured a second warrant for his arrest in that city, where he was apprehended. Philip English was returned to Salem on May 30, and he appeared before the magistrates the next day, but the records of Philip English's examination have disappeared.[73]

In the meantime, the case against the Englishes grew worse. On May 12, a further complaint was made against Mary English for afflicting the same girls noted above and others from Salem village. On May 23, Susannah Sheldon testified that a dead man, Joseph Rabson, had appeared to her, told her that Philip English had murdered him by drowning him at sea, and ordered her to convey that information to Magistrate Hathorne. English's specter, however, warned Sheldon that if she did so he would cut off her legs, and that if he were to be arrested he would "kill ten folks in Boston before the next six days," as well as the governor, whom he called his "greatest enemy."[74]

On June 1, it will be recalled, Mary English was among those who testified that Mary Warren had confessed to lying in court. On June 2, the girls struck back. In one complaint, Susannah Sheldon reported that Mary English had appeared to her with Bridget Bishop and Giles Corey, and that English had "a yellow bird in her bosom." When Sheldon refused to touch the book Bishop offered her, English joined the others in biting her. The next day Corey and Mary English returned, and following a similar confrontation, Philip English appeared as well. He too urged Sheldon to touch the book, and when she refused he bit her. And, finally, that night, Mary English, Giles and Martha Corey, and Bridget Bishop visited Sheldon yet again, for the same purpose, but on this occasion English told Sheldon that she had been a witch for twenty years, a point confirmed by the "black man" in attendance.[75]

Just as damaging was the testimony of William Beale. On August 2, 1692, Beale testified before an Essex County grand jury that in March 1691, while he lay sick in bed, Philip English had appeared to him. The next day, his son James, who had been recovering from smallpox, complained of a pain in his side and died. At that same hour, the previous January 23, another of Beale's sons had died of "a stopping in his throat"; he too had been recovering from smallpox.[76] What Beale intended by this testimony requires some explanation.

On January 12, 1693, Beale appeared before a grand jury to explain the circumstances of his first meeting with Philip English. He explained that in 1690 English had asked Beale to show him the boundaries of English's land in Marblehead. Beale told English he knew nothing about his land, but English insisted he did and offered to pay him "a piece of eight" and part of nearby land owned by Richard Reede for his services. Beale refused and, suspecting that English's proposal was part of a plan to defraud Reede of his land, said he would testify against English if called. English called Beale a liar and an argument ensued. That fall, Philip English had Richard Reede arrested in a dispute over the same piece of land. Beale set out to tell Reede's son of his earlier encounter with English, but while passing through Lynn he had a massive nosebleed that continued until he arrived in Marblehead.[77]

Further testimony against Philip and Mary English was offered, but by early August the Englishes took matters into their own hands. Due to their station in life, it is said, while in the Boston jail they were given certain privileges, including permission to leave the jail upon occasion, as long as they returned at an appointed hour. One Sunday, on the eve of their return to Salem for trial, the Englishes attended a service at Boston's First Church, led by the Reverend Joshua Moody. Moody, a critic of the Salem witch trials, chose as his text Matthew 10:23: "If they persecute you in one city, flee to another." Following the service, Moody and his associate Samuel Willard visited the Englishes in prison to impress upon them the meaning of Moody's sermon. According to the English's granddaughter, Philip English resisted their entreaties, but his wife did not. She is said to have told him, "Do you not think the sufferers innocent? Why may not we suffer also?" Mary had contracted consumption (tuberculosis) during her ordeal, and when Moody and Willard urged him to escape for her sake, Philip finally agreed.[78]

Legend has it that Philip and Mary English were assisted in their escape by Moody and Willard, as well as by Governor Phips of Massachusetts and Governor Fletcher of New York. There is no proof of such collusion, but the Englishes did flee to New York City, where they were joined by other escapees. Once again, an unconfirmed account offers that at one point the Englishes sent a ship with 100 barrels of flour or corn to Salem to feed those who were starving because of the disruption the witch trials had caused in planting and harvesting.[79] It is not legend, however, that Massachusetts officials made no attempt to extradite the Englishes, a point to which we will return momentarily.

THE "BLACK MINISTER" IS APPREHENDED

Perhaps the most important person to be formally charged during the Salem witch trials was George Burroughs, who became known as the "black minister." References to the "black minister" appear in the earliest records of the Salem witch trials, usually in the context of the witches' Sabbath. According to testimony of the afflicted girls and confessions of several of the accused, the "black minister" led meetings of witches and wizards in the Reverend Parris's pasture.

Witnesses reported that at midnight a horn was sounded from Parris's pasture, which although inaudible to most, summoned witches from near and far. They arrived on foot or through the air on brooms, whereupon the ceremony began. The diabolical rites performed in seventeenth-century New England were far less dramatic than those reported to have occurred in Europe, but they nonetheless horrified local residents. Dedicated to the Devil, participants sat in an orderly fashion, reminiscent of seating arrangements in the meetinghouse. They partook of communion, the bread being red and the wine being real blood. They listened to a sermon in which the "black minister" exhorted them to bring others to the Devil. He promised them wealth, power, and other worldly pleasures, as well as release from the rigid confines and perceived intolerance that marked the Puritan community.[80] But who was the "black minister" that did the Devil's bidding and around whom the witches and wizards rallied? And was it possible to put an end to the entire affair without his apprehension? No, he had to be found.

Clues about the "black minister's" identity were gathered from the record, but the major break in the case came on April 20, when Ann Putnam Jr. reported seeing him gathering his flock in the Reverend Parris's pasture. In her father's presence, and that of others, she cried, "Oh dreadful, dreadful! Here is a minister come! What, are ministers witches too? Whence dreadful here is a minister come. What is your name for I will complain of you, though you be a minister."[81]

Ann did not recognize the minister, so she questioned him: "Oh dreadful, tell me your name that I may know who you are." At first he avoided the question, tortured her, and pressed her to write in his book, but when Ann persisted he gave her not only his name but a list of his crimes! It was George Burroughs, and he told her that he had had three wives, that he had bewitched the first two to death, and that he had killed Deodat Lawson's wife because she was unwilling to leave Salem village. He also admitted to having killed Lawson's child because Lawson had gone "eastward" to preach to the soldiers. Burroughs confessed to having "bewitched a great many soldiers to death at the eastward," meaning the frontier where the British colonists were gathered to fight the French and Indians. And, finally, Putnam reported that Burroughs had told her that he had made Abigail Hobbs and several others witches, and that "he was above a witch. He was a conjurer."[82]

The identification, though surprising to most and clearly of major import, was perhaps not entirely unexpected. In the quarrel over the ministers of Salem village, the Putnams and George Burroughs had not been on the best of terms. Burroughs and his family had lived for some time with John Putnam and his family while the parsonage was being repaired. They carefully watched Burroughs's every move and made their failings well-known to the village. They gossiped about his supposed mistreatment of his wife, his condemnation of her harmless gossiping, and his refusal to allow her to write to her family. When, within a year of his arrival in Salem village, Mrs. Burroughs died, the Putnams blamed her death on George's severe treatment of her. And, as it has already been noted, upon Burroughs's leaving Salem but being forcibly returned, John Putnam had had him jailed for a debt Burroughs had incurred as part of his wife's funeral![83]

On April 21, Thomas Putnam, Ann's father, wrote a note to the magistrates in response to something he had heard. He began with "humble and hearty thanks" for "the great care and pains" that the magistrates had taken in the hearings thus far, for which the people of Salem would never be able to repay them but for which they would receive recompense from "the Lord God of Israel," whose cause and interest they had espoused. "Beholding continually the tremendous works of Divine Providence," Putnam continued, he deemed it his duty to inform the magistrates of something he believed they had not heard, of something "high and dreadful," of "a wheel within a wheel at which our ears do tingle." He did not elaborate, perhaps preferring to reveal the details in person.[84]

What Thomas Putnam did not know was that on the same day he composed his brief message to the magistrates, Abigail Williams had already named George Burroughs. Standing just outside Ingersoll's ordinary, Williams had told Benjamin Hutchinson that she saw Burroughs or, as she put it, the "little black minister that lived at Casco Bay." She told Hutchinson of Burroughs's amazing feats of strength, called him a wizard, and also reported that he "had killed three wives, two for himself and one for Mr. Lawson." Hutchinson asked where she saw Burroughs, and Williams pointed to a rut in the road nearby. Hutchinson threw a pitchfork at the spot, whereupon Williams fell into a fit, but when she came out of it she reported that she had heard the pitchfork tear Burroughs's coat.[85]

When Williams entered the ordinary where people were gathering for a Lecture Day Sermon, she spotted Burroughs again, and this time Hutchinson struck at the spot with his rapier. Williams reported that the specter disappeared, but that a gray cat had taken its place. Hutchinson struck once again and Williams fell into a fit, but when she recovered she reported that he had killed the cat, whereupon the specter of Sarah Good had carried it away. The Lecture Day service continued without interruption, but upon its completion the room filled with specters flying in through the windows "as thick as horse-flies." Abigail Williams and Mary Walcott saw the Hobbs among the spectral visitors, as well as an unidentified Indian. Eleazur Putnam joined Hutchinson in the fight to ward off the specters, and between them they killed three, including "a great black woman of Stonington and an Indian who came with her." The floor ran red with blood, the girls reported, although only they could see it, and the witches quickly removed the bodies of the dead, assembling outside of the ordinary to mourn their losses.[86]

The magistrates had two separate and independent sources of testimony, yet still they held back. It was no mean thing to arrest a minister, a man of God, as the leader of witches and the servant of the Devil. But then the revelations of Ann Putnam and Abigail Williams were quickly followed by the confessions of some of the most recently accused witches, including Deliverance and Abigail Hobbs. As we have already noted, although she had not identified him earlier, magistrates went to Deliverance to see if she could see what the girls had witnessed, and she concurred. She too saw the small "black minister" presiding over the witches' Sabbath. George Burroughs was indeed the man they sought.[87]

Because Burroughs lived in Maine, some distance from Salem but then still part of Massachusetts, steps toward his arrest had to be taken in Boston. Upon the request of the Salem magistrates, Boston magistrate Elisha Hutchinson issued a warrant for Burroughs's arrest. He addressed it to John Partridge of Portsmouth, New Hampshire, Field Marshall of the provinces of New Hampshire and Maine. It was dated April 30, and it included the order to arrest George Burroughs for having been "suspected of a confederacy with the Devil." Partridge was directed to deliver him to the custody of the marshall of Essex County, or directly to the Salem magistrates.[88]

Soon thereafter, while Burroughs and his wife were at home dining, it was reported, men bearing the summons burst into the house and took him into custody. He had time neither to finish his meal nor to pack his belongings. The charges may not have been totally clear either, but the Burroughs no doubt knew enough about what was happening in Salem to fear the worst. In fact, when the third Mrs. Burroughs learned specifically what had happened, she took everything of value in the house, found a buyer for George's books, and lent the money for interest. Then she took her own daughter and left, leaving George's children by his earlier marriages, the eldest of whom was seventeen, to fend for themselves.[89]

Partridge returned Burroughs to Salem on May 4, but he was not examined until May 8. Burroughs was held in a room in the house of Thomas Beadle, where he received visitors. In Salem town, at least, he had some defenders. One was Captain Daniel King, who urged his friend Elizur Keyser to visit Burroughs. "If you are a Christian," King said, "go see him. . . . I believe he is a child of God, a choice child of God, and that God will clear his innocency." Keyser did not share in King's confidence in Burroughs, but he agreed to visit him anyway. Once in Burroughs's company, he later testified, Keyser was bothered by the minister's fixed stare and by the spell of his evil eye, and not surprisingly, he later began to have visions. He saw "something like jelly" in his chimney that did "quaver with a strange motion" and a light "about the bigness of my hand." Keyser summoned his maid, who saw it as well, but his wife could see nothing. Keyser was convinced it was Burroughs's doing.[90]

On the evening of May 5, Ann Putnam, the younger, in the presence of her father and her Uncle Edward, had yet another vision of George Burroughs. Once again, he tortured her and urged her to write in his book. In this instance, however, Burroughs told Putnam that his first two wives would appear to her and tell her "a great many lies," but that she was not to believe them. The wives did appear "in winding sheets, and napkins about their heads." They faced Burroughs, "looked very red and angry," and told him that "he had been a cruel man to them, and that their blood did cry for vengeance against him." When they announced that they should be "clothed with white robes in heaven, when he should be cast into hell," he vanished.[91]

The two women turned toward Putnam and provided further details on what Burroughs had told Putnam on April 20. They confirmed that Burroughs had murdered them. The first wife announced that while she lived in the Salem village parsonage he had stabbed her under the left arm and put a piece of sealing wax on the wound. The second wife offered that Burroughs had killed her aboard a vessel as she was coming from Maine to see her friends. Both told Putnam to tell the magistrates in Burroughs's presence what she had learned from them, and if he denied the charges they would reappear. Later, Putnam added, Deodat Lawson's wife and her daughter Ann appeared, telling her that Burroughs had murdered them, as did a woman who identified herself as Goodman Fuller's first wife. She reported that Burroughs had killed her "because there was some difference between her husband and him."[92]

Given his elevated position, on May 9 Burroughs was granted a preliminary hearing with Hathorne and Corwin, as well as magistrates William Stoughton of Dorchester and Samuel Sewall of Boston, who had come to Salem especially for Burroughs's hearing. They so-licited from Burroughs some damaging admissions. They found him not entirely sound in doctrine on some points not connected with witchcraft, but certainly part of his calling to the ministry. He admit-ted that he had attended communion service on only one or two occa-sions recently, even though he remained a member of the Roxbury Church, and that only his eldest of eight children had been baptized.[93]

When Burroughs appeared before the afflicted girls, they shrieked in terror and fell to the floor where they were so tortured the magistrates ordered their removal. "It is an amazing and humbling providence," Burroughs responded, when Stoughton asked for his as-sessment of the affair, "but I understand nothing of it." He neverthe-less denied the specific allegations that had been made against him. His house on Casco Bay had not been haunted, for example, although it was surrounded by toads. (Toads were widely held to be capable of diabolical affliction. They were mentioned in the Book of Revelation as coming from the mouth of the Apocalyptic Beast, and they were known to inhabit the Reverend Parris's pasture where witches' Sabbaths, it was reported, had been held.) His family had not been "affrighted" in their house by a white calf, as had been alleged, and he had not for-bidden any of his wives to write to their parents. He denied having killed his first two wives, or even having abused them in any way. And when the ministers had him bodily searched for the Devil's mark, they could find none.[94]

Adding to the negative side of the ledger of evidence in the Bur-roughs case, however, Mary Webber, of Casco Bay, testified that as Bur-roughs's neighbor in the mid-1680s his second wife had informed her about "much of her husband's unkindness to her." She had pleaded with Webber to write to her father to apprise him of the situation, be-cause Burroughs had forbidden her to write to him. Hannah Harris, who lived with the Burroughs in Maine, reported that Burroughs had often scolded his third wife, and once when she was ill he held her in an open doorway exposing her to the elements until she nearly died.[95]

On May 5, Ann Putnam dutifully reported what she had been told by her spectral visitors, and much as they had promised, when Bur-roughs denied the story the specters of Burroughs's first two wives flew into the room to corroborate her testimony. Susannah Sheldon at least saw them, and perhaps Ann Putnam, but she fell into convulsions and had to be taken from the room. Abigail Williams's reference to George Burroughs's great strength was recalled on April 21. Burroughs's strength was legendary, and in friendlier times he had taken some pride in the various physical feats attributed to him. At this point, however, the stories he heard were greatly exaggerated. One eyewitness, Thomas Greenslit, attested to Burroughs having lifted a "gun of six-foot barrel" with one finger stuck in the muzzle and a barrel of molasses above his head with only two! It was implied that Burroughs's great strength was made possible by his collusion with the Devil.[96]

There were witnesses to strange, perhaps occult, happenings associated with Burroughs. As part of her testimony, Casco Bay neighbor Mary Webber recalled Burroughs's wife telling her about a strange noise that had awakened her and her husband one night. George and a slave had pursued the specter, Mrs. Burroughs told Webber, and when they reached the bottom of the stairs it had taken on the appearance of a white calf. (Burroughs denied the appearance of a white calf during his private hearing with the magistrates.) On another occasion, Burroughs's wife reported to Webber that an invisible spirit had come into her bedroom and breathed on her. Struck with fear, she had tried to awaken her husband but could not rouse him until the visitor had left. Webber was suggesting, of course, that George Burroughs was responsible for those strange occurrences, an implication made worse by testimony to his having led the witches of Salem.[97]

Mercy Lewis was a particularly damaging witness. At age fourteen, upon the murder of her parents by Indians, Burroughs and his first wife had taken her into their home in Maine. They brought her to Salem but left her with Thomas Putnam when they moved away. Lewis had taken close mental notes of what went on in the Burroughs's household, and she was prepared to report on it, or at least on her version of what had happened. Burroughs had admitted to Lewis, she had testified, that he could raise the Devil and that he had bewitched people. When she asked him how he could bewitch people at such great distances (Maine to Salem), he told her the Devil was his servant, and that he had sent the Devil in his shape to do it. Burroughs had taken Lewis to his study and asked her to sign a "new fashion" book, and when she refused, Burroughs, much like Satan to Christ, had taken Lewis to a mountaintop and tempted her by showing her the kingdoms of the earth, threatening to throw her from the mountaintop if she should continue to refuse. Burroughs denied having done any such thing, but it meant little.[98]

The other girls reported that although he had failed with them, he had boasted of converting several in the area to the Devil's cause. Abigail Hobbs and Mary Warren were brought forth to testify. They identified Burroughs as being the man who was leading the witches' Sabbath in Parris's pasture. It was this "black minister," Warren explained, who gave the blast on the spectral trumpet at midnight that summoned the witches. It was Burroughs who preached at the meeting and "pressed them to bewitch all the village," and it was he who assured those gathered that they would prevail.[99]

What else need be said? The leader of the Devil's disciples had been found, and he was sent off to prison with those he had led. A minister in whom the people of New England had placed their faith as their primary defender against the Devil turned out to be the Devil's follower. What hope remained for those faithful to God's word?

DORCAS HOAR IS JAILED

Before concluding this chapter, we might pause briefly to consider the case of still another person subjected to an arrest warrant on April 30. The reader will recall our earlier discussion of Dorcas Hoar and her brush with the law in Beverly, where largely through the good graces of the Reverend John Hale she had been able to avoid being charged with witchcraft. Much as Hale had been drawn into the crisis at Salem, so too had Hoar, but Hoar was brought to the village under arrest. Upon her appearance before the Salem magistrates on May 2, the girls immediately fell into fits. Elizabeth Hubbard cried out that Hoar was pinching her and displayed the wounds, whereupon Mary Walcott, Abigail Williams, Ann Putnam, and Susannah Sheldon made similar complaints. Hathorne demanded to know why Hoar hurt the girls, whereupon she answered that she had never hurt any child in her life. When Hathorne responded that if it was not her it was her "appearance," she pleaded, "How can I help it?"[100]

Abigail Williams and Ann Putnam charged Hoar with having choked a woman in Boston, and according to the records, a chorus of voices accused her of having killed her husband. But when Williams, Susannah Sheldon, and Mary Walcott exclaimed that they saw a "black man" whispering in her ear, Hoar shot back, "Oh, you are liars, and God will stop the mouths of liars!" The magistrates were outraged at Hoar's outburst. They ordered her to not speak in such a manner in court, but she persisted, "I will speak the truth as long as I live." How long Dorcas Hoar was to live, however, was about to be decided. She too was sent to jail.[101]

6

"God Will Deliver Us Out Of the Hands Of Unmerciful Men"

The actual Salem witch trials began in May 1692, and we will turn to those trials in the next chapter. Before doing so, however, we will spend one last chapter on the preliminary hearings, about which we know much more. (The trial records have disappeared.) We will select from those that remain the hearings which either more fully develop themes introduced in previous chapters or provide an additional dimension to what we have learned so far. The cases discussed in this chapter will include three other individuals who at first supported and then turned against the witch-hunt and paid a dear price; three cases of prominent figures who were charged, two of whom escaped; and the single largest group of witchcraft charges outside of Salem, namely those of Andover, Massachusetts.

The Case of George Jacobs Sr.

In the previous chapter, we discussed the case of Mary Warren, whose second thoughts concerning her role in the Salem witch trials exposed her to the wrath of her young compatriots. We shall now turn to the cases of Sarah Churchill, another member of the accusing circle who tried to pull back, and Margaret Jacobs, who confessed to being a witch and in the process condemned her own grandfather, only to seek forgiveness in the end. Both cases involve the bringing of charges against George Jacobs Sr.

By 1692, George Jacobs had lived in Salem for over thirty years, most recently on a moderate-sized farm about two miles south of the Salem village meetinghouse. He was eighty years old, and he walked on two staffs, but he nevertheless continued to cut an imposing figure. Jacobs was uncommonly tall and wore his white hair long, perhaps reminding some, one historian has quipped, of the "man in a long-crowned white hat" to whom Deliverance Hobbs had referred in her testimony.[1]

Age had not diminished George Jacobs's formidable reputation. He lived modestly, but he was widely known in Salem village as a tough, quick-tempered man who had been involved in a number of public quarrels and even physical confrontations. In 1677, for example, he landed in court for physically attacking John Thompkins. Witnesses testified that he simply lost control of himself and struck Thompkins and would have done so repeatedly if he had not been restrained.[2]

A warrant was issued for George Jacobs's arrest on May 10, 1692. He was immediately taken to Thomas Beadle's ordinary in Salem town for examination. Things did not go well for Jacobs from the start. Prior to his hearing, Sheriff George Herrick and Constable Joseph Neale examined Jacobs and found a witch's teat under his right shoulder, "about a quarter of an inch long or better with a sharp point drooping downwards." Herrick thrust a pin into the growth and noted that Jacobs was "not in the least sensible" to it. Further, "there was neither water, blood, nor corruption, nor any other matter" in the growth.[3]

When Jacobs entered the hearing room, he did not do so meekly. When told of his accusers, he said, "Well, let us hear who are they and what are they." When Abigail Williams was presented, identified him, and fell into a fit, Jacobs laughed and exclaimed that he had been falsely accused. "Do you think this is true?" he asked the magistrates, and when they asked him who he thought was responsible for the girl's affliction, he replied, "I never did it. . . . Don't ask me."[4]

Prominent among George Jacobs's accusers was Sarah Churchill, his servant. Standing before the court, Churchill testified that the night before Jacobs had afflicted her while she was at Ingersoll's ordinary. Perhaps sensing the damage the testimony of someone so close to him might cause, Jacobs appealed to the magistrates, "Pray, do not accuse me. I am clear as your worships; you must do right judgments." But the magistrates persisted, even leading Churchill in her testimony.[5]

"What book did he bring you, Sarah?" the magistrates asked, drawing on an earlier deposition. "Did he not appear on the other side of the river and hurt you?" "Yes, he did," Churchill responded, whereupon the magistrates turned to Jacobs and again pressed him to respond. "What would you have me say? I never wronged no man in word nor deed," to which he added, "You tax me for a wizard, you may as well tax me for a buzzard. I have done no harm." When the magistrates asked Jacobs how he would explain the appearance of Churchill's afflicter in his shape, he, as others before him, suggested that the Devil could take any likeness. The magistrates countered that the Devil could not do so without a person's consent, but Jacobs did not pursue the matter. All he said was that with which he had been charged was untrue: "I am as silly about these things as the child born last night."[6]

Churchill charged Jacobs with having lived "a wicked life," to wit she offered testimony that only one who had lived with him, if only as a servant, could offer. She testified that Jacobs only prayed when he was alone and never with his family, and that he had pressured his son, George Jacobs Jr., and his granddaughter, Margaret (George Jr.'s daughter), into signing the book. The elder Jacobs explained that he did not pray with his family because he could not read, but that he did pray. When the magistrates ordered him to repeat the Lord's Prayer, however, he repeatedly stumbled his way through it.[7]

Jacobs's hearing was extended into the next day, May 11, at which time Ann Putnam and Abigail Williams charged him with hurting them and showed the magistrates their hands with pins stuck in them. Mary Walcott testified that he had beaten her with one of his staves, and Putnam reported that Jacobs had told her that he had been a witch for forty years.[8] His fate was sealed. George Jacobs Sr. was sent to prison, but problems soon arose for the prosecution due to the second thoughts of Sarah Churchill and to his granddaughter's recantation.

In a deposition sent to the magistrates after Jacobs's hearing, Sarah Ingersoll reported that Churchill had come to her "crying and wringing her hands, seemingly to be much troubled in spirit." When Ingersoll asked what troubled her, she answered that she had "undone herself . . . in belying herself and others in saying that she had set her hand to the Devil's book, whereas . . . she never did." When Ingersoll asked why she had lied, Churchill answered that she had done so "because they threatened her, and told her they would put her into the dungeon . . . along with Mr. Burroughs."[9]

Ingersoll reported that Churchill had repeated the confession several times and that when she asked Churchill why she still would not admit her error, she explained that she simply had "stood out so long in it" that she dared not stop. She also added, tellingly, that she had not attempted to clear the record because "if she told Mr. Noyes [Salem town minister] but once she had set her hand to the book he would believe her; but if she told the truth, and said she had not set her hand to the book a hundred times, he would not believe her." The deposition was endorsed by Ann Andrews, Jacobs's daughter.[10]

On the one hand, the deposition did not explicitly state that Sarah Churchill had admitted to having lied in her testimony against Jacobs. It did report, however, that more than once she had spoken of "belying herself and others," and such an admission in ordinary circumstances would certainly cast a shadow on the entirety of her testimony. The magistrates, however, did nothing about it, and Jacobs remained in jail. Further, although it was clear Churchill had felt remorse for her role in condemning her master and others, much as had happened to Mary Warren, the girls had threatened her and the authorities were unsympathetic. She would go no further in her recantation, and she would live to testify another day.

Margaret, George Jacobs's granddaughter, had been named in the May 10 arrest warrant and examined as well. Her records have not survived, however, so we know little about her hearing except that she confessed and in the process condemned her grandfather and George Burroughs. In August, after both had been tried and condemned to execution, however, she recanted both about her own guilt and about those against whom she had testified. She explained that a combination of fear and bewilderment at the accusations made against her, intimidation by the magistrates, and a desperate hope to save her life and gain her freedom had led her to falsely incriminate them.[11]

"The Lord above knows I knew nothing, in the least measure, how or who afflicted them," she admitted, but the magistrates had told her that if she did not confess she would be jailed and hanged. If she did, she would save her life. So she confessed. It was "altogether false and untrue," however, she continued, that very night she had been "in such horror of conscience" that she could not sleep, "for fear the Devil should carry me away, for telling such horrid lies." Thus her recantation. "What I said was altogether false against my grandfather and Mr. Burroughs," she wrote. Further, she was not guilty "in the least measure of the crime of witchcraft, nor any other sin that deserves death from man." Margaret sought and received the forgiveness of her grandfather and George Burroughs. Jacobs soon added Margaret to his will, leaving her ten pounds in silver. Burroughs went so far as to pray with her and for her, but even Margaret's recantation did not alter their fate.[12]

On April 20, the day after her grandfather was executed, Margaret wrote a letter to her father once again asserting that her confession had been "contrary to [her] conscience and knowledge" and "wounding of [her] soul." She wrote of "the terrors of a wounded conscience" she bore, relief from which she prayed to God. She noted that the magistrates had not believed her recantation, and that she expected soon to be put to death as well. She begged her father's prayers and prayed to God that they would one day have "a joyful and happy meeting in heaven." Fortunately for Margaret, she became so ill while in prison that she could not stand trial in September. By the time she did appear in court, a new tribunal with a different charge, which we have yet to discuss, set her free.[13]

Finally, as yet another example of family guilt by association, on May 14 warrants were issued for the arrest of George Jacobs Jr., the elder George's son, and the younger George's wife, Rebecca. George Jr. escaped and did not return until the trials ended. The story is that he took up residence "in a foreign country," perhaps Canada. Rebecca, George's wife and the mother of four children, was slightly—perhaps more than slightly—insane. With her daughter and father-in-law already in jail and her husband charged but having escaped without her, she was much overwrought. She did not flee, however, but was apprehended and jailed.[14]

Rebecca Jacobs's mother (Rebecca Fox) petitioned the governor and his council for her release, apprising him of Rebecca's debilitating mental condition. She described her daughter as "well known to be a person crazed, distracted, and broken in mind." She had been that way for twelve years or more, her mother reported, but she had grown even worse while in prison. "Christianity and nature do each of them oblige your petitioner to be very solicitous in this matter," she wrote, "and although many weighty cases do exercise your thoughts, yet your petitioner can have no rest in her mind till such time as she has offered this her address on behalf of her daughter." Rebecca's mother insisted that she was not capable of doing that with which she had been charged, and she begged the government to grant her release. The governor did not respond, but on January 3, 1693, when the mood had changed, a grand jury acquitted her.[15]

JOHN WILLARD CHANGES SIDES

On the day the magistrates examined George and Margaret Jacobs, they issued a warrant for the arrest of John Willard. Willard's origins are unclear, but he lived for a time during his youth in Lancaster, Massachusetts. In the 1680s, he and his wife resided in Groton. His wife, however, was a third-generation member of Salem village's large Wilkins family, which occupied much of the western part of the village. It was his wife who brought Willard to Salem village.[16]

For a time the Wilkins family operated a logging and lumber processing operation. The business failed, however, and at one point Bray Wilkins, the family patriarch, was arrested for stealing hay to feed the oxen that he used to transport the lumber to town. They were forced to return two-thirds of their land to its original owner, who later seized other Wilkins's assets as well. By the 1680s, though not impoverished, their fortunes had declined rather precipitously.[17]

The Wilkins family openly and actively supported the Putnams and the village autonomy movement. They joined the village church soon after its establishment in 1689. Only one Wilkins appeared to have been opposed—one of Bray's younger sons, Thomas, who had married a niece of Rebecca Nurse. Thomas Wilkins became one of the four "dissenting brethren" who led the anti-Parris movement within the village church, and subsequently his father disinherited him. Thomas Wilkins did not join his family in its attack on John Willard.[18]

Margaret Knight Willard was the first Wilkins to not marry a Salem village resident. Moreover, rather than being a farmer, her husband was a land speculator. In March 1690, John Willard purchased a village lot totaling between 400 and 500 acres, which he subdivided and sold for a considerable profit. It might have been his land speculation that caused the Wilkins family to distrust Willard, but that is difficult to prove. What is known is that when John Willard was accused of witchcraft at least ten members of the Wilkins family testified against him![19]

The principal reason for including Willard's story here is that he had the distinction of being both a participant in and opponent to the Salem witch trials. He was a Salem deputy constable during the early days of the trials. As such, in March, he had brought in for trial several of the accused. Then, however, he had a change of heart, and he made his sentiments known. In one instance, at the house of a relative, he is quoted as having said in reference to the girls, "Hang them, they're all witches!"[20]

In April, rumors of Willard's criticism of the hearings and of his involvement in the diabolical conspiracy began to circulate. Reportedly, he went to Bray Wilkins and asked Wilkins to pray with him, but Wilkins put him off, explaining that he had other business to which he must attend. Bray did say that he would consider praying with Willard if he returned home early enough, but he did not and Willard, quite likely taking offense, never again asked him for his help.[21]

Soon after, Willard planned a trip to Boston with Henry Wilkins Jr. for election week. Wilkins's son, seventeen-year-old Daniel, who had heard the rumors concerning Willard, urged his father to not go. The two went anyway, as did Bray Wilkins and his wife, though separately. Daniel Wilkins's fears notwithstanding, his father's and John Willard's trip to Boston passed uneventfully, as did passage for the eighty-two-year-old Bray Wilkins and his only slightly younger wife. On Election Day, all were invited to dine with Richard Way in Dorchester, the Reverend Deodat Lawson and others in attendance. Willard arrived later than the rest, however, and upon his entrance Bray Wilkins thought he saw unpleasantness if not anger in Willard's countenance, which may well have been the case. Shortly, Bray experienced considerable suffering. He was, to use his own words, "like a man on a rack."[22]

Bray Wilkins believed Willard was responsible for his torment. He told his wife, "Mr. Lawson and others there were all amazed," and knew not what to do for him. It took him three or four days to recover sufficiently to return home, and he still needed to be in bed. Moreover, Bray found his grandson Daniel gravely ill. His family and neighbors suspected foul play, and they summoned the Reverend Samuel Parris. Parris brought with him Mercy Lewis and Mary Walcott. When they entered Daniel Wilkins's room, the girls saw Willard's specter and that of "Old Mrs. Buckley" crushing the boy's throat and chest, and they could not stop them. The boy soon died. Lewis and Walcott were taken to Bray Wilkins's room, where Lewis reported seeing John Willard sitting on Bray's belly. Bray later reported that at that very moment he had experienced "grievous pain in the small of [his] belly."[23]

A coroner's jury was called to rule on Daniel Wilkins's death. The records of its ruling have been lost, but the comments of those involved in the case suggest that the jury ruled that Wilkins had died of strangulation, which they, if not the jury, attributed to Willard and Buckley. Bray Wilkins, for example, answered those who later held him responsible for Willard's conviction that it was not his testimony "but the testimony of the afflicted persons and the jury" concerning the murder of his grandson that had made the difference. In the church records, the Reverend Parris's comment on the jury's verdict was brief but to the point: "Dan Wilkins. Bewitched to death."[24]

On May 10, the magistrates issued a warrant for John Willard's arrest for "sundry acts of witchcraft . . . committed on the bodies" of

Bray Wilkins, Samuel Wilkins, and others. Constable John Putnam Jr. went to Willard's house but could not find him. Willard's relations and friends told him that he had fled. On May 15, a second warrant covering the entirety of the colony was issued, and Willard was found near Lancaster, forty miles away, and delivered to the Salem magistrates.[25]

Upon Willard's entering the examination room, on May 18, the girls fell into fits. The magistrates informed him that his fleeing from the law constituted an acknowledgement of guilt, but they nonetheless urged him "to confess the truth." Willard explained that he had fled out of fear, but that he also feared not, but that "in his due time" the Lord would make him "as white as snow." The magistrates told Willard that in addition to afflicting the girls he had been charged with "dreadful murder," and that if he desired mercy from God, he should confess. But he would not. He was accused of "murdering and bewitching" his relations and of bewitching his grandfather because he had prayed that the Kingdom of Satan be "thrown down." Willard began to explain, only to be cut off by the magistrates with "we do not send for you to preach."[26]

Susannah Sheldon's deposition was entered, wherein she testified that the apparitions of "William Shaw's first wife, the widow Cooke, Goodman Jones, and his child" had appeared to her and claimed that Willard had murdered them. Similarly, Ann Putnam Sr. deposed that the shapes of Samuel Fuller and Lydia Wilkins had told her that Willard had murdered them, and that Willard himself appeared to her admitting to have murdered Fuller, Wilkins, and eleven others![27]

Ann Putnam Jr. testified that Willard had appeared to her, threatening to kill her, as he had her little sister Sarah, if she did not sign his book. She also reported having seen the apparition of John Wilkins's first wife, who said Willard had had a hand in her death. Then being transported to Willshill, Putnam had witnessed John Willard's apparition afflict both his grandfather Daniel Wilkins and Rebecca Wilkins. Willard told Putnam, upon that occasion, that he would kill Daniel Wilkins if he could, but that he did not have enough power to do so. He would go to George Burroughs to get it![28]

Finally, a deposition from Lydia Nichols was read. Nichols reported that Mrs. Willard had told her "how cruelly her husband had beaten her," whereupon Benjamin Wilkins testified of Willard's "unnatural usage" of his wife, and Peter Prescot told the magistrates that Willard had admitted to him that he had beaten her. At that point, Susannah Sheldon leaped forward to point out that the "Black Man" was whispering in Willard's ear, telling him not to confess, and soon the rest of the afflicted girls screamed that those Willard was accused of murdering had gathered about him.[29]

The magistrates asked if Willard thought the girls were bewitched. "Yes, I really believe it," he responded. They asked why if in other instances their identification of their afflicters had been found to be true that would not be the case with him, but Willard only continued to insist that he was "as innocent as the child that is now to be born." The examination ended with Willard's repeatedly trying to recite the Lord's Prayer, stumbling each time. "It is a strange thing," he said. He could say it without error at other times. "I think I am bewitched as well as they," he said and laughed, but the magistrates saw no humor in it: "No, it is no strange thing that God will not suffer a wizard to pray to him."[30] They ordered Willard jailed.

DANIEL ANDREW IS CHARGED

Daniel Andrew, whom we met earlier, was one of Salem village's wealthiest men in 1692. Andrew had been born in obscurity in Watertown. At age twenty-five, in 1669, he moved to Salem town where he purchased two small but valuable house lots near the center of town, one of which contained an apothecary shop. In 1671, he was paid to teach school in his home, but soon afterward he took up housebuilding. Officially he was known as a bricklayer, but in practice he made considerable money building some of the town's finest homes and a new meetinghouse. Andrew married Sarah Porter, the youngest child of John Porter, and the sizable inheritance from her father upon his death included a large tract of land in Salem village. The Andrews moved to the village, close to Joseph and Benjamin Porter, where Daniel undertook some shrewd land purchases and continued his success as a contractor.[31]

In February 1692, Andrew purchased a town landing wharf at the point where the Frost Fish Brook, flowing southward through the eastern part of Salem village, traversed Ipswich Road and widened into the navigable Frost Fish River. From his dock, Andrew could transport supplies both into the village from town markets and out, in the latter case floating to town farm products from farms on the east side of Salem village near Ipswich Road. In time, Daniel Andrew became politically active as part of the same Porterite faction that sought the Reverend Parris's removal, and beginning in 1685 he was elected to town selectman five times, including the election of March 1692 to which we have already referred.[32]

On May 14, while he was both a member of the village committee and a town selectman, a warrant was issued for Daniel Andrew's arrest. The constable searched his home, but Andrew was not found. On the same day George Jacobs Jr. disappeared, Andrew too "found refuge in a foreign country."[33]

THE CARYS ESCAPE

That George Jacobs Jr. had escaped to parts unknown no doubt concerned many of the proponents of the Salem witch trials. More worrisome was the prominent Daniel Andrew's escape, but he too left no trace of where he had gone. Most troubling were the prominent individuals, like Philip and Mary English, who had fled but whose whereabouts were known and yet nothing was done. Such was the case with Elizabeth Cary, the wife of Captain Nathaniel Cary, a wealthy shipmaster and shipbuilder from Charlestown.[34]

In mid-May, rumors began to circulate that Elizabeth Cary was about to be cried out against. On May 24, she and her husband Nathaniel attended a session of the magistrates at the Salem village meetinghouse. In his account of the visit, Nathaniel made his intentions for going to Salem clear—"Being much disturbed" by rumors that his wife had been accused of witchcraft and "by advice," he had gone "to see if the afflicted did know her." The Carys were only spectators, and no one had taken any notice of them except for once or twice when the girls came to Elizabeth and asked her name. Perhaps emboldened by this, Cary asked the Reverend John Hale, whom he already knew, if he might be allowed to speak to those who had accused his wife. After the examination Hale reported he could, but that it would not be at the Reverend Parris's home, as Hale had promised earlier, but at Ingersoll's ordinary.[35]

The Carys went to the nearby ordinary, Cary wrote, where John Indian waited on them and with minimal coaxing and a drink of cider showed them several scars that he said had been caused by witchcraft. He told them of his wife Tituba, who had been imprisoned for witchcraft, but soon Indian was upstaged by the dramatic entry of the young girls. They "began to tumble down like swine," Cary continued, and to cry out the name Cary, and almost immediately a warrant was delivered summoning his wife to appear before the magistrates, who were sitting in chambers nearby."[36]

Two girls stepped forward as Elizabeth Cary's chief accusers. Elizabeth declared that she had never seen them before, but the magistrates ordered her to stand with her arms outstretched. Cary requested permission to hold one of her hands, but the magistrate denied his request. "She desired me to wipe the tears from her eyes, and the sweat from her face," Cary reported, but when she grew faint and wished to lean against him for support, Magistrate Hathorne replied that if she had strength enough to torment the afflicted, she should be strong enough to stand unassisted.[37]

Nathaniel Cary spoke out against what he described as "their cruel proceedings," but the magistrates commanded him to be silent or be removed from the room. John Indian was brought in and "he fell down and tumbled like a hog," Cary noted. The magistrates asked the girls who had afflicted Indian, and they answered Elizabeth Cary. The justices ordered Elizabeth to touch Indian, with her face turned away lest she make matters worse by looking at him. The guards guided her hand toward Indian, but he held her hand and pulled Elizabeth to the floor. Indian's hand was removed and hers put on his, whereupon "the cure was quickly wrought."[38]

Once again, Nathaniel Cary spoke out. "Being extremely troubled at their inhumane dealings," Cary "uttered a hasty speech," he reported, wherein he prayed "that God would take vengeance on them" and "desir[ed] that God would deliver [his wife] out of the hands of unmerciful men." God did not, at least at the moment, and Elizabeth Cary was ordered jailed. She was sent to a Boston prison, but her husband managed to get her moved to Cambridge in his own County of Middlesex. After one night in a Cambridge jail, she was put in leg irons weighing about eight pounds, Cary continued, and the combination of those weights and "her other afflictions soon brought her into convulsion fits," such that he thought she might die that night. He sought in vain to have the irons removed, but Elizabeth survived.[39]

Realizing that it was now certain his wife would stand trial for witchcraft, Nathaniel Cary visited a session of the Court of Oyer and Terminer (to be introduced in the next chapter) "to see how things were managed." Finding that "the specter evidence was there received, together with idle, if not malicious stories, against people's lives," he knew what the fate of all of the accused, including his wife, would be. "I acquainted her with her danger," Cary explained, "and that if she were carried to Salem to be tried, she would never return." And when he could not persuade authorities to move Elizabeth's case to his home county of Middlesex, Nathaniel arranged for her escape.[40]

At the end of July, Elizabeth Cary fled to Rhode Island, but fearing that she would not be safe there, she continued on to New York "along with others that had escaped the cruel hands" of Massachusetts' officials. (The Englishes escaped to New York at about the same time.) New York's Governor Benjamin Fletcher, Nathaniel reported, was "very courteous" to her. Nathaniel remained behind, and upon Elizabeth's escape, some of his goods were seized. Nathaniel was imprisoned for half a day, but when he was released, he joined Elizabeth in New York, where they remained until the trials ended.[41]

JOHN ALDEN IS ARRESTED

A warrant was issued for John Alden's arrest on May 28. He had been a resident of Boston for over thirty years and a member of the Puritan Church. During that time, he had distinguished himself for his service during the French and Indian Wars, and as commander of Massachusetts' armed vessels, and as late as 1690 he had been chosen to represent the British in their negotiations with the Indians. Alden, now age seventy, was wealthy and powerful, but the reader may better remember him as the firstborn of the same John and Priscilla Alden mentioned in the more romantic histories of Plymouth Colony. Longfellow had not yet spoken of the Aldens, but John Alden of Boston was already making a name for himself. How his name came to the attention of the Salem girls, however, is unknown.[42]

Alden's physical stature reminded some of testimony offered by Tituba weeks ago. Was he the tall man from Boston that Tituba had seen but had not been able to identify? Officials had been puzzled and worried about this unknown person, second only to the "black minister" in importance, but to date they had had little to go on. Perhaps Alden was their man! That very possibility alone may have led the Salem magistrates to issue the order for Alden's arrest, but officially they issued the warrant upon the complaints of Mary Walcott, Mercy Lewis, Abigail Williams, Elizabeth Booth, Ann Putnam Jr., and Mary Warren.[43]

On the same day Philip English faced the magistrates, May 31, Alden strode into the courtroom. According to his own account of the affair, Alden did not move directly to the front of the room. Instead, he stood near the rear where he could observe his accusers without making his presence obvious. The girls, who had never met him, were already afflicted—screaming, crying, and rolling about the floor—but when the magistrates asked them to identify their assailant, they first pointed to another person! Only after a man, who held up the unidentified girl to see over the crowd, whispered something into her ear did she get it right. "How did you she know it was

Alden?" a magistrate asked. "The man told me so," she responded, according to Alden.[44]

The magistrates were skeptical of such an identification, so they ordered the girls and Alden outside where they were to pick him out from among several others in the sunlight. "There stands Alden!" one cried. "A bold fellow with his hat on before the judges." He sells powder and shot to the Indians and French, and "lies with the Indian squaws and has Indian papooses." Alden was immediately taken into custody and his sword was taken from him, as he afflicted the girls with it. When returned to the meetinghouse, he asked the magistrates how they could believe he would come to the village to afflict those he had never known or even seen. Further, he asked why his looking at the magistrates did not affect them as it had the girls, but the magistrates did not respond.[45]

Joining Magistrates Hathorne and Corwin for the hearing was Alden's friend, Bartholomew Gedney, in whom he trusted for a reasoned response to events. He must have been more than a little surprised, therefore, when Gedney urged Alden to "confess and give glory to God." "I hope to give glory to God, but not to gratify the Devil," Alden responded, and he challenged anyone who ever knew him to step forward and testify that they had ever suspected him of being a witch. Gedney admitted he had known Alden for many years and had always looked upon him as "an honest man," but said he had seen enough that day to change his mind. Gedney joined Hathorne and Corwin in ordering Alden to be taken to jail.[46]

Imprisoned in Boston, John Alden was visited by his friends Cotton Mather, Samuel Willard, and Samuel Sewall. It was a daring gesture on their part, but then they must have found the charges against John Alden difficult to accept. On July 20, those three and others prayed for Alden. Some may have also proposed a course of action, because Alden would not remain much longer in jail.[47] In his firsthand account of his ordeal, Alden put his escape matter-of-factly:

> To Boston Alden was carried by a constable. No bail would be taken for him, but was delivered to the prison-keeper, where he remained fifteen weeks; and then, observing the manner of trials, and evidence then taken, was at length prevailed with to make his escape.[48]

In September, Alden escaped to Duxbury, Massachusetts, where his relatives resided. He is reported to have made his appearance there late at night and begged shelter and protection from the Devil who was pursuing him. Whether he remained there or went on to other climes, which is more likely, we do not know. Unlike the others, who remained away until the trials had ended, however, Alden returned while they were in their final stages. As previously noted, the climate of the hunt had changed by that time, so even though he was bound over to the Superior Court at Boston for trial, on the last Tuesday of April 1693 he was discharged.[49]

THE ANDOVER WITCH-HUNT

Also in May the first resident of Andover was taken into custody. Already the number of charges being made outside of Salem was surpassing those made in the town, but Andover would soon top them all. By the end of July, more than fifty of its residents would be jailed and several hanged, making Andover the single largest venue outside of Salem. Andover, therefore, is worth pursuing in some detail at this point. It provides a good comparative case study of another community caught in the grip of the witchcraft hysteria.

Martha Carrier was ordered arrested on May 28 upon the complaints of Joseph Holton and John Walcott, both of Salem village. When she was taken into custody, four of her children were taken with her. The records of what happened to them have been lost, but we do know that they were all eventually released. The confessions of three of the Carrier children have survived. Sarah Carrier, age eight, admitted to having been a witch since the age of six, when her mother made her "set [her] hand to a [red] book." After touching the book, her mother baptized her in Andrew Foster's pasture in the presence of Elizabeth Johnson Jr., her Aunt Toothaker, and her cousin. Those present promised her a black dog, Sarah continued, but she had never received one. She had been given a cat instead, but they told her the cat would tear her to pieces if she did not set her hand to the book.[50]

Sarah could not recall ever having seen the Devil or the "Black Man," but she did provide some details on the witches' Sabbath, during which she had been baptized. Her mother had baptized her saying, "Thou are mine forever and ever. Amen." Further, she had taught Sarah how to afflict people, and thereafter she had pinched people—spectrally, not in person—and traveled through the air, often carried by her mother, who at times took the form of a black cat.[51]

Richard Carrier was the second of Martha Carrier's children to confess. He too offered evidence that helped condemn his mother, as well as his brother Andrew. Richard had succumbed only five weeks before, he reported, in the presence of Mrs. Bradbury, and since then he had joined in the affliction of others. At another time, the child added, he had seen a dozen gathered witches, including Elizabeth How, Rebecca Nurse, Sarah Wildes, the Proctors, Martha Corey, Bridget Oliver (Bishop), and John Willard. Once again, however, he had not seen the "Black Man."[52]

Thomas Carrier offered much the same report. He, too, confessed that his mother had baptized him into the craft. He had been a witch for only one week, but during that brief time he had afflicted others. The process had begun, he explained, when a yellow bird appeared to him, followed by his mother who brought him a book. She said that "it would do him good" if he set his hand to the book, but if he refused, she would tear him to pieces. He did so and was baptized in the Shaw Shin River, his mother proclaiming that "he was hers forever." He too named Elizabeth Johnson.[53]

The testimony of the children was devastating to Martha Carrier's case. As Cotton Mather concluded, "This rampant hag was the person of whom the confessions of the witches, and of her own children among the rest, agreed that the Devil had promised . . . would be queen of hell." The record of Carrier's examination, dated May 31, provides some insights into Mather's choice of the phrase "rampant hag"—she spoke her mind quite openly and at times offensively to the magistrates. Nevertheless, she denied the girls' charges that she had tormented them or threatened to cut their throats if they refused to sign the Devil's book, and when one of the accusers cried out that Carrier was sticking pins into her, and another that the "Black Man" had appeared near her, Carrier replied that she saw no black man but the magistrates![54]

Whenever Carrier looked at the girls they fell to the floor, so Hathorne asked if she could look at them without such a result. "They will dissemble, if I look upon them," she explained coolly, but "it is false; the Devil is a liar. I look upon none since I came into the room but you." When Susannah Sheldon testified that Carrier had murdered thirteen people, Carrier appeared to have lost her composure. She rebuked the magistrates, charging, "It is a shameful thing that you should mind those folks that are out of their wits." And to her accusers, Carrier added, "You lie. I am wronged."[55]

The record of Carrier's hearing closes with the following comment:

> The tortures of the afflicted were so great that there was no enduring of it, so that she was ordered away and to be bound hand and foot with all expedition, the afflicted in the meanwhile almost killed to the great trouble of all spectators, magistrates, and others.

The Reverend Samuel Parris simply added that Mary Walcott had told the magistrates that Carrier had been a witch for forty years.[56]

If the arrest of Martha Carrier planted seeds of suspicion about other witches in Andover, nothing resulted until July. At that point, Andover started down the path already blazed by Salem village. The wife of John Ballard became seriously ill, and her local doctor was unable to alleviate her suffering. The untoward events of Salem having provided an explanation for several similar afflictions, and having found the alleged witch Martha Carrier in their midst, John Ballard decided to seek another type of diagnosis for his wife's illness. He feared the "Devil's hand" might be upon her.[57]

Ballard let his plan be known to his fellow townspeople, and soon he had considerable support. Goody Ballard was not the only person ill in Andover, and the others were willing to share the expense Ballard would incur in bringing one of the young women to town to investigate the matter. Local minister Thomas Bernard, several church deacons, and Justice of the Peace Dudley Bradstreet, son of the retired governor, all lent their support and representatives were sent to Salem. They returned with Ann Putnam Jr. and Mary Walcott.[58]

Putnam and Walcott were welcomed with near reverence, their success as instruments in uncovering the presence of the Devil having preceded them. When taken to the bedside of Goody Ballard, the girls fell into fits of pain and accused Andover residents Mary Lacey Sr., Mary Lacey Jr., and the three sons of Martha Carrier. They were taken into other homes, where they visited the long-term ill, the blind, and the lame, all of whom awaited the girls' arrival, as one historian has put it, much as others in other times would welcome faith healers. And the girls did not disappoint them.[59]

When Putnam and Warren entered the sickrooms of the afflicted, their response was invariably the same. They saw one witch at the head of the bed, another at the foot. It was as Ballard and others had suspected; the "Devil's hand" was upon the afflicted, and it was being exercised by people within their midst. Because the girls were not familiar with the people of Andover, however, they could not place names with the faces they saw in their visions. It was necessary to provide what we might today call a police lineup.[60]

Several local residents were blindfolded and brought before Ann Putnam and Mary Warren, in the throes of full possession, to undergo the touch test. It is not known how they were chosen, but if previous crises provide any guidance, they were probably suspect because of previous behavior. It may be that some were not, and that they were included as a testing measure, but that is mere speculation, perhaps tainted by our knowledge of modern judicial proceedings.[61]

Regardless of how those led before the young girls were chosen, as each was led to touch the girls they ceased their struggling, indicating that the spirit of the Devil had been drawn off. There were very few exceptions. Six of those condemned in the process later described the incident:

> After Mr. Bernard had been at prayer, we were blindfolded, and our hands were laid upon the afflicted persons, they being in their fits, and falling into their fits at our coming unto their presence, as they said: and some led us, and laid our hands upon them; and then they said they were well, and that we were guilty of afflicting them. Whereupon we were all seized as prisoners. . . . [62]

The naming of names through confessions of the accused followed, and soon dozens were charged. Between July 15 and the end of September, Magistrate Bradstreet issued at least forty warrants, and the list would have been longer had he not let it be known at that point that he would not issue any more based on such evidence. The effect of such revelations on the town of Andover was much as it had been on Salem village. The accused were bewildered. "We were all exceedingly astonished and amazed and consternated and affrighted, even out of reason," the same six women who were noted above later recalled. Some were even persuaded by the course of events to consider the possibility that they might, in fact, be guilty, and they searched their memories for the moment at which they may have unwittingly or not made their pact with the Devil.[63]

Mary Osgood, whose husband was a church deacon, recalled that eleven or twelve years earlier, when she was "in a melancholy state and condition" following the birth of a child, she had been led into the arms of the Devil. She recalled how when she was walking in her orchard a cat had diverted her from praying, "about which time" she made a covenant with the Devil. The Devil appeared as a Black Man, and Osgood laid her finger on his book, leaving a red spot. Upon her "signing," the Devil told her "that he was her god, and that she should serve and worship him," and, the record of her examination reads: "she believes she consented to it."[64]

Two years later, Osgood continued, she "was carried through the air" to Five Mile Pond, where she was baptized by the Devil. He "dipped her face in the water and made her renounce her former baptism and told her she must be his, soul and body, forever, and that she must serve him." She promised to do so and confessed that thereafter she had afflicted several people "by pinching her bed clothes, and giving consent the Devil should do it in her shape." Upon further questioning, Osgood admitted that she did not believe the Devil could take the shape of an innocent person. She further admitted that although the Devil had promised her "abundant satisfaction and quietness in her future state," she had only grown more miserable and discontented.[65]

Samuel Wardwell remembered that about twenty years earlier, he too was so "much discontented" that he could not get any work done. The source of his discontent, he admitted, was his unrequited love for one "Maid Barker." He "had been foolishly led along with telling of fortunes," he allowed, and he had often used the phrase "the Devil take it" when his fields were invaded by various creatures. The Devil, he suggested, may have used his discontent and indiscretions to take advantage of him. During one moment of his being in a "discontented frame," he had witnessed an assemblage of cats and a man among them who called himself "a prince of the air" and promised Wardwell a comfortable life if he would "honor him." Wardwell promised to do so, signed the man's book by making "a mark like a square" with a black pen, and pledged that he thereby covenanted with the Devil until he turned sixty. He was forty-six.[66]

The most notable confession of the Andover accused, however, came from William Barker, likely the husband of the above-mentioned maid. His confession revealed what was no doubt behind many of those who resisted the seventeenth-century Puritan world in which they lived. He confessed that the Devil, who appeared in the shape of a black man with a cloven foot, had seduced him some three years earlier. Barker explained that "he had a great family, [that] the world went hard with him," and that, although he had gone into debt, he was "willing to pay every man his own." The Devil had offered to pay all of his debts and to guarantee that he would live comfortably if Barker would "give up himself soul and body unto him," which he did. Barker signed the Devil's book by dipping his finger into blood that was brought to him and making his mark. At the same time, however, the Devil told Barker that he intended to abolish all of the churches in the land, to put an end to resurrection and judgment and to punishment and shame for sin, and to provide for a future wherein all under the Devil's rule would be equal and "live bravely."[67]

Barker provided the most detailed account among the accused of Andover of the witches' Sabbaths. A trumpet summoned about 100 participants from as far away as Connecticut to the meeting, Barker recalled. George Burroughs presided, and he administered communion with bread and wine. "It was proposed at the meeting to make as many witches as they could," Barker reported, "and the Black Man exhorted them to pull down the kingdom of Christ and set up the kingdom of the Devil."[68]

Barker explained why Salem village had been chosen for attack. It was, he revealed, "by reason of the people being divided and their differing with their minister." The Devil's design, however, was not to stop there. It was to destroy Salem village, beginning with the minister's house, and thereafter "to destroy the Church of God, and to set up Satan's kingdom" throughout the land, whereupon all would be well. Barker reported that he had been told "by some of the grandees" among the witches that there were "about 307 witches in the country," and that they were "much disturbed" with the afflicted because they had been "discovered by them." Further, the witches "cursed the judges" because by their actions "their society" had been "brought under." And, finally, Barker offered that he thought the afflicted individuals were innocent victims, that authorities were doing "God's good service," and that he did not know, nor had he heard of, even one innocent person that had been put in prison.[69]

If any of the Andover accused were reluctant to confess, there were many to urge them on. Instructive were the cases of Ann Foster, her daughter Mary Lacey, and her granddaughter, also named Mary Lacey—hereafter referred to as Lacey Sr. and Jr. All were charged with tormenting Goody Ballard. Ann Foster was the first to succumb. On July 15, after four separate examinations, she offered a detailed confession. She reported that the Devil had appeared to her several times in the shape of a bird, and that ever since she had the "gift" of being able to afflict people. When asked how she could tell the bird was the Devil, she answered, "because he came white and vanished black, and that the Devil told her that she should have this gift, and that she must believe him."[70]

On July 16, Foster revealed that it was Martha Carrier (already condemned) who made her a witch. Carrier had come to her some six years earlier and threatened that "the Devil would tear her to pieces, and carry her away," if she refused to serve him. She reported that she had attended a meeting of some twenty-five witches at Salem village and that Carrier had informed her of the meeting, urged her to go, and ridden with her to the meeting "upon sticks." George Burroughs had officiated, Foster added.[71]

Foster admitted to having injured those who had lodged complaints against her. She afflicted Timothy Swan by tying a rag in a knot and throwing it into a fire, and she choked others "by squeezing poppets like them." Moreover, she reported that she had heard tell from other witches that there were 305 witches "in the whole country, and that they would ruin that place, the village." Their purpose in ruining Salem village, she explained, as had William Barker, was to "set up the Devil's kingdom."[72]

Mary Lacey Sr. was brought up on charges, and on July 21, upon finding herself in the same room with her confessing mother, she cried, "We have forsaken Jesus Christ, and the Devil hath got hold of us. How shall we get clear of this Evil One?" She too proceeded to confess. She readily confirmed that her mother was a witch and that she was as well.[73]

Mary Lacey Sr. reported that she, her mother, and Martha Carrier had ridden together to Salem village on a pole, and that three or four years earlier she had seen "Mistress Bradbury, Goody How, and Goody Nurse baptized by the Old Serpent at Newbury Falls." He dipped their heads into the water and then said they were his, and he had power over them." Six were baptized on that occasion, Lacey continued, including "some of the chief or higher powers," with nearly 100 in attendance. When asked how she got to Newbury Falls, she answered that "the Devil carried her in his arms."[74]

On July 21, Lacey's daughter, Mary Jr., confessed. After her confession, the record reads, Mary Warren, whom Lacey Jr. had afflicted, "came and took her by the hand and was no way hurt." Lacey Jr. asked Warren's forgiveness, and according to the records, "both fell a weeping together." Apparently, Mary Lacey Jr. was alone during her confession, however, because, the records continue, at that point Mary Lacey Sr. and Ann Foster were summoned once again. The moment was dramatic, to say the least. Upon the arrival of the two other women, the magistrates announced, "Here is a poor miserable child, a wretched mother, and grandmother," whereupon Mary Lacey Jr. "broke forth" with "O mother, why did you give me to the Devil twice or thrice over." Her mother said she was sorry for having hurt her, but that she had done so because of "that wicked one."[75]

Lacey Jr. offered the same lament to her grandmother, whereupon the magistrates interjected that because Mary Lacey Jr. had so thoroughly repented of her actions, there was "an argument of hope" that she would be "snatched out of the snare of the Devil." Turning to the two older women, they continued, "We desire you therefore to be free in the presence of God and tell us the truth in this matter. Will you play with devouring fire and will you share everlasting flames and the society of this devouring lion that has so ensnared you." They would not. Both deeply lamented their having covenanted with the Devil, but all three were nevertheless taken to jail.[76]

Less dramatic but instructive as well was the case of another Andover resident who was persuaded to confess in quite another manner. Upon her arrest, Martha Tyler later reported to Increase Mather, "she had no fears upon her, and did think that nothing could have made her confess against herself." When she was taken to Salem by her brother, Jonathan Bridges, and Andover schoolmaster, John Emerson, however, she was pressured into doing so. Mather recorded her recollection of the affair:

[W]hen she came to Salem, she was carried to a room, where her brother on one side, and Mr. John Emerson on the other side, did tell her that she was certainly a witch, and that she saw the Devil before her eyes at that time (and, accordingly, the said Emerson would attempt with his hand to beat him away from her eyes); and they so urged her to confess. . . .

When she refused, Emerson threatened to withdraw, declaring her "undone, body and soul, forever," but her brother persisted. Mather continued:

Her brother urged her to confess, and told her that, in doing so, she could not lie, to which she answered: 'Good brother, do not say so, for I shall lie if I confess, and then who shall answer unto God for my lie?' He still asserted it, and said that God would not suffer so many good men to be in such an error about it, and that she would be hanged if she did not confess; and continued so long and so violently to urge her to confess, that she thought, verily, that her life would have gone from her, and became so terrified in her mind that she owned, at length, almost anything that they propounded to her.[77]

"These several weeks later," Mather concluded, Tyler had come to believe that in confessing "she had wronged her conscience," and that "she was guilty of a great sin in belying herself and desired to mourn for it so long as she lived." She reported all of this, Mather noted, "with such affection, sorrow, relenting grief, and mourning, as that it exceeds any pen to describe and express the same."[78]

There were other recantations among those who confessed in Andover, as elsewhere. Samuel Wardwell's recantation provides a second example. After being charged with practicing witchcraft, he confessed that he had met the Devil and been baptized by him, whereupon he was imprisoned. While in prison, however, he met John Proctor, whose resistance to the trials caused Wardwell to have second thoughts. Wardwell then renounced his confession, but as was the case with others who recanted, Wardwell remained in jail, and on September 22 he was executed.[79]

The witch-hunt in Andover was shorter than that in Salem, but its intensity was greater. It came on suddenly, and because Salem had paved the way, it built to a climax more rapidly. Even dogs in the street were suspected of having been bewitched, one by John Bradstreet, another son of the ex-governor. Bradstreet fled to New Hampshire, but the dog was executed. And when, at about the same time, his brother Dudley refused to sign any more warrants, he was cried out against. His accusers charged him with nine murders, whereupon he fled.[80]

The Andover witch-hunt ended as abruptly as it had begun, largely because of the courage and intelligence of an individual who became one of the most visible and effective critics of the witch trials. The Andover accusers charged Robert Calef, a Boston merchant who was already known for his skepticism. In his defense, Calef resorted to a tactic often used in the past by those accused of witchcraft but that had not yet been employed in the Salem cases. He brought suit against his accusers; he filed a 1,000 pound defamation suit against them. As it had been in the past, the threat of such legal action was effective, especially when others among the accused were prepared to take the same steps. The accusers fell silent, not only against Calef, but altogether, at least in Andover. Unfortunately, however, much damage had already been done, and at least fifty people were in prison awaiting trial.[81]

We are about to turn to the actual trials, but before leaving Andover one last point needs to be made. It has been noted that the various episodes in the Great European Witch-hunt occurred in communities in conflict. Stephen Boyer and Paul Nissenbaum have persuasively made the case for Salem village. Chadwick Hansen's research, however, suggests that Andover was an exception. Accusations flourished in Andover in the absence of such conflict. Andover, a largely homogeneous farming community without the agrarian-commercial strains noted in the case of Salem village, or any other noticeable difficulties, was known for its harmony. The witchcraft hysteria nevertheless struck Andover, as it had Salem, with as great, if not greater, ferocity, and by the time it ended in that model community nearly 10 percent of its residents stood accused.[82]

7

"God Will Give You Blood To Drink"

Soon after George Burroughs's hearing ended, the frigate *Nonesuch* entered the port of Boston from England, thereby ending a period of anticipation and anxiety as great as that which ended with the finding of the "black minister." On board were Increase Mather, who was returning to Massachusetts with the new colonial charter he had been sent to secure, and Sir William Phips, his handpicked first Royal Governor.

Increase Mather, best known today perhaps for being the father of Cotton, but then president of Harvard and pastor of Boston's Second Church, had been away for four years. He had been sent to England to resecure the old charter, but when that was denied by the new King and Queen, William and Mary, he made the best that he could of creating a new one. It contained some compromises, with which many Massachusetts Puritans would not be pleased, but it had much to commend it as well. "Take it with all its faults," Mather explained, "and it is not so bad but when I left New England the inhabitants . . . would gladly have parted with many a thousand pounds to have obtained one so good." Andros would not return, Mather pointed out, and the new charter did not meddle with local government, as some had feared it would if precedents set by the Andros Administration were honored. Taxes would still be levied by the General Court, wherein, again in contrast to what had happened during the Dominion Period, the people would be duly represented. And all of the general privileges of English citizenship that Andros had called into question were confirmed.[1]

As the arrival of Sir William Phips indicated, the people of Massachusetts would no longer elect their governor; he would be appointed by the Crown. Moreover, the electorate would no longer be limited to those in covenant with the Church. Nearly all adult male Christians (save Roman Catholics) who owned property would be enfranchised. It is true that it had long been the case that those living outside of the covenant in Massachusetts greatly outnumbered those living within, but the Puritan leadership did not feel obligated by that to make any changes. After all, to be in the majority was not necessarily to be among the godly, and it was the godly who were to rule their "City on a Hill," their "Bible Commonwealth."[2]

Certainly a major point of saving grace in Mather's return with a new colonial charter was his companion Sir William Phips. If the people of Massachusetts were to have to live with no longer being able to select their own governor, they would take solace in having picked for them a man in whom they had as much faith as any. Phips was no stranger to Massachusetts. In fact, he was one of them. He had been born and raised in New England. He was a man of common ancestry, rather than of aristocracy, but he had worked his way to the top without alienating those he passed along the way.[3]

Phips had been born in 1651 in what was to become Maine. His father was a gunsmith, and William grew up in the wilderness without any formal education. Reaching adolescence, he apprenticed himself to a ship's carpenter, and having mastered the trade he moved to Boston. Phips provided himself with at least a rudimentary education, became a ship's captain and shipbuilder, and at age twenty-one married a "lady of good fashion." His bride was the widow of Captain Roger Spencer and the daughter of John Hull (whereby she was related to Samuel Sewall), and it would seem she rested content in the match, which in time resulted in considerable wealth and prestige.[4]

In 1687, Phips raised from its watery grave off the coast of Haiti a Spanish galleon loaded with thirty tons of silver and gold. For his toil, James II knighted him and awarded him a 11,000-pound share of the booty. Phips was knighted when Massachusetts was incorporated into the Dominion of New England and straining under the rule of the royally appointed Governor Edmund Andros. The story is told that when, upon his being knighted, James asked Phips what favor he would ask of the King, Phips requested the restoration of New England's charters and privileges. The King would not concur. He did make Phips high sheriff of New England, but it was a post without much authority, as neither Andros nor Phips had any use for the other.[5]

Upon his return to Massachusetts from England, Phips was baptized by Cotton Mather and became a member of Mather's Second Church. When asked why he had not taken advantage of his well-earned fame to live in England, he explained, in words that must have been music to New Englanders' ears, and which they no doubt recalled as he later returned to them as governor, "I knew that if God had a people . . . it was here, and I resolved to rise and fall with them."[6]

Phips further proved himself to his fellow New Englanders in his courage in battle against the French and Indians on the Maine frontier. In 1690, he obtained command of an expedition that captured Port Royal in Nova Scotia. That success led to his selection as commander of an amphibious assault on the French stronghold of Quebec, but that ended in defeat and in the loss of over 200 of his 2,000 men. Phips nevertheless sailed to London, where he hoped to obtain another royal military commission. While there, he lent his support to the efforts of Increase Mather on behalf of the Massachusetts charter.[7]

Mather seized the opportunity of Phips's presence to suggest that if Massachusetts were to have a royally appointed governor, it should be Phips—one whom both parties, England and New England, trusted. It had been done, and now both men were returning to a colony racked by events about which they knew nothing. Perhaps Phips, neither to the manor nor governing born, believed himself less than fully qualified to deal with what he expected as governor; he was even less prepared to deal with what he did not expect, but found nevertheless. He expected to have to implement a less than universally welcome charter and to govern a colony of strong-willed Puritans; he did not expect to have to deal with witches.[8]

The *Nonesuch* sailed into Boston Harbor on Saturday evening May 14, 1692, and Phips and Mather disembarked with as much pageantry as the Sabbath's eve would allow. On Monday, the governor was sworn in, and he assumed his duties. Simon Bradstreet, the aged interim governor who had ruled since Andros's overthrow, was relieved of duty. Bradstreet had been inactive, if not paralyzed, by events and old age, leaving matters to his second-in-command, Thomas Danforth. It was under Bradstreet that matters at Salem reached a fevered pitch, but, as his defenders have pointed out, no trials took place under Bradstreet's watch, perhaps reflecting his resistance to the entire affair.[9] In either event, on May 16 Bradstreet stepped aside.

The Court of Oyer and Terminer Is Established

In one of the great "what if" moments of history, Sir William Phips arrived at the moment when he might have been able to make a significant difference in the course of the Salem witch trials. Twenty-seven were being held for trial, but none had as yet gone to court. Whether or not they would be tried, and if they were, how their trials would be conducted, was dependent in large measure on Phips's actions. It may be the case that had Phips acted forcefully at that point, history would have been different. But he did not.[10]

Phips later reported that he was bewildered by what he found upon his arrival in Massachusetts. The province was "miserably harassed with a most horrible witchcraft or possession of devils," he wrote. "Scores of poor people were taken with preternatural torments, some scalded with brimstone, some had stuck pins in their flesh, others hurried into the fire and water, and some [were] dragged out of their houses and carried over the tops of trees and hills for many miles together." Phips was no skeptic when it came to witches. He made it clear that he was a believer and took the threat that had been described to him seriously. With the "loud cries and clamors of the friends of the afflicted" in his ears and the advice of Deputy Governor William Stoughton and his closest advisers, he felt compelled to act.[11]

As long as the colony had no charter and the legal basis of their laws and court was suspect, the people of Massachusetts had been reluctant to proceed to trial. With a new charter in effect providing a legal basis for both, they insisted that Phips act, and act quickly, and that he constitute a court by which the accused would be tried. Phips turned to his councilors for advice, and they recommended establishing a Court of Oyer and Terminer, commonly used in England. On May 27, the governor, through his Council, issued a commission for the creation of such a court, "for discovering what witchcraft might be at the bottom" of what had transpired, as Phips later put it. Because it was commonly believed that witches could ply their wares even from prison if they were left unshackled, Phips also ordered those already jailed to be placed in chains. That accomplished, he set out for the frontier to fight the French and Indians—enemies with whom he was better acquainted. Deputy Governor Stoughton was left in charge.[12]

Phips made his motives clear in the text of the commission. He referred to the "many criminal offenders" in custody; to their having long suffered the "many inconveniences attending the throngings of the jails," especially "at this hot season of the year"; and to there being "no judicatories or courts of justice yet established." Unwittingly, however, Phips exceeded his authority in establishing the Court of Oyer and Terminer. The new Massachusetts charter gave the provincial legislature the power to create such a special court, but Phips would not convene that body until June. Further, until the new legislature could meet, none of the laws adopted under the old charter could be confirmed. Thus, the Court, which had been improperly constituted, proceeded without a statute against the crime it was impaneled to inveigh. Only one extenuating, and much debated, explanation has been offered, which is that as British colonies the proceedings were covered by the English statute of 1603, and by that act those convicted of witchcraft could be sentenced to death.[13]

Phips named as judges of the Court of Oyer and Terminer seven men "of the best prudence and figures" that he could find, as he put it. All were members of the Governor's Council. We have already met Deputy Governor William Stoughton, who was named to preside. A graduate of Harvard and Oxford, he had served some fifteen years in the General Court and as a member of Governor Edmund Andros's Council. Also introduced earlier was Bartholomew Gedney, a Salem physician, who had been a member of the General Court and who had joined Hathorne and Corwin in presiding over some of the preliminary hearings in Salem.[14]

Other appointees to the Court included John Richards, a wealthy Boston merchant, who had served as captain of the militia, town selectman, and treasurer of Harvard College; Nathaniel Saltonstall of Haverhill, an experienced Essex County judge and a member of the provincial Court of Assistants; Wait Winthrop of Boston, grandson of the colony's first governor, a major general in the militia, and a member of the Governor's Council; Captain Samuel Sewall of Boston, destined to become Chief Justice of the (Massachusetts) Superior Court; and Peter Sergeant, a prominent Boston merchant who had been active in the opposition to depose Governor Edmund Andros.[15]

According to Thomas Hutchinson, Phips listed John Hathorne and Jonathan Corwin among prospective judges.[16] Later historians, however, Charles Upham being the first, did not include them among those who took seats on the bench (Corwin would later be appointed to replace Nathaniel Saltonstall).[17] The records of the Court of Oyer and Terminer having disappeared, there is no way to document their absence, but Upham is probably correct. Hathorne and Corwin were already well occupied in the preliminary hearings that would continue even after the trials began, and perhaps Governor Phips wanted to ensure a measure of objectivity by appointing people not directly involved in those hearings.

Other people directly associated with the Court of Oyer and Terminer, but not as judges, were Stephen Sewall and Thomas Newton. Sewall, of Salem town, served as Clerk of the Court. He was closely tied to events in Salem if only through the presence of Betty Parris, who had been entrusted to him for safekeeping by her father. Newton, of Boston, the King's Attorney General, had no such connection. His job was to prepare the cases for the state.

Their considerable legal experience notwithstanding, the judges of the Court of Oyer and Terminer no doubt considered those various standard sources on witchcraft law, mentioned earlier in reference to the Salem magistrates. One of the judges, John Richards, asked Cotton Mather for his advice. In a lengthy letter, Mather attributed the troubles at Salem to a "horrible witchcraft," but he also pleaded for caution and discretion in the Court's actions. He urged the judges to use spectral evidence with care. "It is very certain," Mather wrote, echoing objections raised by a number of the defendants already, "that the devils have sometimes represented the shapes of persons not only innocent, but also very virtuous." He believed that spectral evidence could offer an important "presumption" of guilt, but that it should not be the basis for conviction. For that a credible confession, as opposed to one issued by "a delirious brain, or a discontented heart," was best, but confessions, he admitted, could be difficult to obtain. Mather rejected the use of torture and instead recommended "cross and swift questions." If that should fail, the judges could always order the accused to recite the Lord's Prayer or to be examined for evidence of the Devil's mark, or to have their personal property searched for evidence, such as poppets. In sum, his reputation for prosecutorial zeal notwithstanding, Mather's advice was well within the law and standard legal procedures of the day.[18]

Although it might have chosen to act otherwise, the Court of Oyer and Terminer opted to follow those procedures established by the Salem magistrates. On May 31, Thomas Newton went to Salem to observe seven examinations, and he returned convinced that the hearings had been conducted fairly. What reservations he retained, more as to who had been charged than how, he made clear in a letter to Isaac Addington, Secretary of the province, that same day. He noted that he had sent to Addington the names of the prisoners he wished to try first.

All had been formally indicted following their preliminary hearings by a grand jury. However, Newton continued:

> I fear we shall not this week try all that we have sent for; by reason the trials will be tedious, and the afflicted persons cannot readily give their testimonies, being struck dumb and senseless, for a season, at the name of the accused. I have been all this day at the village, with gentlemen of the council, at the examination of the persons, where I have beheld strange things, scarce credible but to the spectators and too tedious here to relate; and, amongst the rest, Captain Alden and Mr. English have their mittimus [had been ordered held by the magistrates]. I must say, according to the present appearance of things, they [the members of the council] are as deeply concerned as the rest; for the afflicted spare no person of what quality soever, neither conceal their crimes, though never so heinous.[19]

The Court of Oyer and Terminer treated the records of the preliminary hearings as its primary source of information. The records were to be entered as evidence, and the Court would proceed from there. It would add to the record depositions gathered since the preliminary hearings and call forth witnesses who had still other information to convey, after which the case would be submitted to the jury. Newton recommended that at least some of those who had confessed be used to testify against other defendants. In the above-mentioned letter to Isaac Addington, Newton asked that Tituba, for example, and "Mrs. Thatcher's maid" be "transferred as evidence," and that they not appear in court with the prisoners present but by herself.[20]

Physical evidence, such as poppets and the Devil's marks, would be allowed, as would the testimony of those acquainted with the accused and of the afflicted girls, who claimed they had seen the specters of individuals doing them harm. Moreover, although never specifically stated, or even admitted—and contrary to Cotton Mather's advice—the Court of Oyer and Terminer would treat as spectral evidence more than presumptive evidence. Cotton Mather may have described the process best when he wrote, in the case of Bridget Bishop, "there was little occasion to prove the witchcraft, this being evident and notorious to all beholders."[21]

BRIDGET BISHOP IS TRIED

Bridget Bishop was the first to be tried by the Court of Oyer and Terminer. The journal of the Court having disappeared, however, what transpired in Bishop's and all other cases can only be reconstructed from the surviving related documents and from the comments of contemporary observers. Bishop's trial began on June 2, 1692, bringing to the Court as its precedent-setting case one of the most notorious defendants of the lot. As one historian has said, failing to allow for the case of mistaken identity noted in Chapter five, given her "smooth and flattering manner" with men and the notorious goings-on in her tavern, even if the question of witchcraft had not provoked it, Bridget Bishop was a woman the Puritan community would almost certainly have been bound to investigate, sooner or later.[22]

As was customary, Bridget Bishop had no counsel when she stood before the Court. Thomas Newton entered as evidence records from Bishop's appearance before the Court of Assistants on witchcraft charges in 1680, as well as the testimony solicited for her April 19 examination before the Salem magistrates, including the charge that she had bewitched her first husband to death. Newton then brought forth new evidence. One day, while walking by the town meetinghouse it was reported, although under guard, Bishop had glanced at the town's meetinghouse. At that very moment, her guards reported, a clatter arose within, whereupon investigators found "a board which was strongly fastened with several nails transported into another quarter of the house."[23] Bishop, it was assumed, had offered one last dramatic act of defiance.

Interestingly, given the relative lack of emphasis on sexual matters in the Salem witch trials (as compared to those in Europe), perhaps because of her reported dress and occupation, much of the testimony that had been gathered since Bishop's hearing and which was now to be presented to the Court of Oyer and Terminer suggested a certain concern with Bishop as a provocateur. William Stacey, for example, presumably the same person who charged her with stealing from Thomas Stacey in 1688, deposed on May 30 that when he was twenty-two years old, some fourteen years earlier, he had come to admire Bishop, largely because of the extraordinary love she had professed for him when she cared for him while he had smallpox.[24]

Later, however, Stacey overheard considerable malicious gossip concerning Bishop, including the accusation that she was a witch. Bishop had tried to discourage him from paying any attention to that gossip, but he began to experience some inexplicable mishaps. Money given to him by Bishop disappeared from his pockets, and his wagon wheel sank in a hole, only to have the hole disappear when he climbed down to free it. In another instance, as he approached his barn, Stacey "was suddenly taken and hoisted from the ground and thrown against a stone wall [and] after that taken up again and thrown down a bank at the end of his house."[25]

Stacey told the court that he believed Bishop was responsible in 1690 for killing his daughter, who had thrived but suddenly been taken ill and died. And he revealed that Bishop's specter had visited him in his bed-chamber and kissed him while he slept. Her lips pressed so hard against his and were so cold, he reported, that he awoke and sat upright on the bed. Bishop, wearing a black hat and red coat, sat at the foot of the bed, and it suddenly became as light as day. She then hopped from the bed, about the room, and out, whereupon darkness returned. When Stacey reported this incident to others, Bishop confronted him and asked him if what she had heard concerning his story was true. Stacey insisted it was. He dared her to deny it, and, although she grew even angrier, she did not.[26]

Similar reports of nocturnal visits were made by John Cook, Richard Coman, and John (Jack) Louder. Cook, age eighteen, testified that one morning five or six years earlier, Bishop had appeared in his chamber by the window. She looked at him and grinned, but then struck him on the side of the head, "which did very much hurt," and disappeared through "a little crevice [under the window] about so big as I could thrust my hand into." Later that day, the Sabbath, Cook continued, Bishop reappeared and as she walked across the room an apple that he was holding flew out of his hand into his mother's lap. His mother, who sat some six or eight feet away, and several others present, however, did not see Bishop.[27]

Coman, age thirty-two, deposed that eight years earlier, while he was in bed with his wife, he was awakened by Bishop's entering the room with two strange women. Bishop, dressed in the "red paragon bodice" that had been attributed to her, sat on his chest and so oppressed him that he could neither speak nor stir, not even to awaken his wife. The next night, the three women reappeared, and Bishop "took hold of him by the throat and almost hauled him out of the bed." They reappeared on the third night, but this time Coman had asked his kinsman William Coman to keep a vigil with him. One of the three spectral visitors grabbed Richard's sword, with which he hoped to defend himself, but he would not let it go. He called to William, his wife, and another visiter, Sarah Phillips, and they all heard him but could neither see the specters nor even stir until they had disappeared.[28]

That Bishop appeared so wantonly to these men was one thing; that she responded to their rejection of her as she did was quite another. When they repelled her advances, the men reported, their children paid the price. Coman reported that during one such visit by Bishop, she had approached the cradle of a sleeping child nearby with something in her hands, whereupon the child "gave a great screech." Soon thereafter, the child died, as did Tracey's daughter.[29]

John Louder, also age thirty-two and John Gedney's servant, told the Court that about seven or eight years earlier he had had a quarrel with Bishop over some of her fowl that had strayed into the Gedney orchard or garden. Soon thereafter, in the "dead of the night," Louder felt "a great weight" upon his breast. It was Bridget Bishop, or her likeness, and when he tried to push her off she grabbed Louder by the throat and almost choked him to death. He explained, "I had no strength or power in my hands to resist or help myself."[30]

Susannah Gedney, Louder's mistress, and Louder confronted Bishop. Bishop denied the accusation, however, and threatened Louder. Sometime after, Louder, not feeling well and staying home on the Sabbath with the doors shut, saw a black pig in the room, coming toward him. He kicked at it, and it disappeared. Still later, "a black thing" with a body that looked like a monkey but "with the feet of a cock and a face of a man" jumped in Louder's window. The visitor told Louder that he had been sent to tell him that if he would "be ruled by him, he should want for nothing in this world." Louder indignantly responded that he would kill the intruder. He struck it, but "could feel no substance," and it jumped out of the window. It reentered by the porch, though the doors remained shut, and said, "You had better take my counsel," whereupon Louder struck at it again and met no corporeal resistance. The figure vanished, not to return, but when he opened the door he saw Bridget Bishop in her orchard walking toward her house. Seeing her, he "had no power to set one foot forward" in pursuit.[31]

Samuel and Sarah Shattuck added a charge of murder to Bishop's list of crimes. They told the Court that beginning in 1680—the year she first faced witchcraft charges—Bishop had often visited them for "very slight reasons" and always "in a smooth flattering manner." With the increasing frequency of Bishop's visits, their eldest son grew progressively ill. He often fell onto the floor or ground, "as if he had been thrust out by an invisible hand," doing even further harm to himself, and in time he declined to the point where he was "stupefied and void of reason." The Shattucks began to believe that their son suffered from "some enchantment," a diagnosis confirmed by a stranger who also found him "bewitched" and declared "a neighbor that lives not far off" responsible. When he said the witch was one with whom the Shattucks had quarreled, they recalled having once had such a disagreement with Bridget Bishop.[32]

The Shattucks and the stranger devised a test whereby Bishop's culpability would be determined. The Shattuck's son would take the stranger to Bridget Bishop's tavern, ostensibly to buy a pint of cider.

While there, the stranger would "fetch blood of her" for an occult test, about which the records offer little information. When the two knocked on her door, however, Bishop immediately sensed a trap, chased the stranger away with a spade, and scratched the boy's face, calling him a rogue and accusing him of bringing strangers to plague her. Thereafter, the boy's condition grew worse yet, and local physicians were forced to conclude that he was "under an evil hand of witchcraft."[33]

Deliverance Hobbs, who had since Bishop's hearing turned informer, and the girls added to the new evidence as well. Hobbs reported that while she was a witch, she had seen Bridget Bishop help administer the sacrament on the witches' Sabbath, and that after she herself had confessed, Bishop's specter had beaten her with iron rods in an attempt to get her to recant. Mary Warren, Susannah Sheldon, and Elizabeth Hubbard, who had already done much to condemn Bishop, simply demonstrated their support for all they heard, including charges that Bishop had murdered several children. Sheldon added that she had seen Bishop suckle her familiar, a snake.[34]

As was common procedure, Bridget Bishop's house had been thoroughly searched, and poppets stuck with pins had been found in the cellar. John and William Bly testified that Edward and Bridget Bishop had hired them to remove a cellar wall in a house in which she had once lived, and that they had found therein several poppets "made up of rags and hogs bristles with headless pins in them with the points outward." When confronted with this evidence, the records show, Bishop had no explanation that was "reasonable and tolerable." A surgeon and eight women examined her for witch marks, twice—just before and right after the trial—in the first instance finding a "preternatural excrescence of flesh between the pudendum and anus much like a witch's teat," in the latter discovering that it had disappeared.[35]

We do not know for certain what Bridget Bishop had to say in her defense. Her stepson Edward Bishop and Edward's wife Sarah attacked the credibility of the girls, especially Mary Warren, who, they told the Court, while in Salem Prison had frequently contradicted statements she had made to the magistrates at Bridget's hearing.[36] The judges of the Court of Oyer and Terminer, however, were aware of Mary Warren's travails, and they were not tempted to place much emphasis on any equivocation on her part.

Thus, the case was sent to the jury. As part of his jury instruction, Stoughton explained that Bishop had been charged with five counts of witchcraft, against Abigail Williams, Ann Putnam Jr., Mercy Lewis, Mary Walcott, and Elizabeth Hubbard. But, he continued, according to Robert Calef, a guilty verdict did not require that the prosecution

prove that the five actually suffered the torments of which they complained—that they had actually been consumed, wasted, and tormented—but rather, that they had not suffered from their afflictions
"naturally"! That is to say, if Calef's account is correct, the jury could
assume that the afflictions were genuine and could merely decide
whether they were natural or not. If not, given the testimony, the accused were to be found guilty.[37]

The jury quickly returned a guilty verdict, and the judges sentenced Bridget Bishop to be hanged, but a legal problem arose to delay
her execution. The General Court, which had only just convened, following implementation of the new charter, still had not adopted those
laws passed by the Legislature under the previous, now nullified, charter, including that wherein witchcraft was made a capital crime, punishable by death. It did so on June 8, and the sentence was reinstated.[38]

Two days later, Bridget Bishop earned the dubious distinction of
being the first of the accused of the Salem witch trials to be hanged.
Sheriff George Corwin took Bishop to the top of what has variously
been called Gallows Hill or Witches' Hill, described as a barren and
rocky elevation on the western side of town. A hood was probably
placed over her head, and she was hanged "from the branches of a great
oak tree." Although the records do not indicate it, a brief sermon was
most likely offered, drawing lessons from the tragic affair for those assembled. The minister in attendance probably exhorted Bishop one
last time to confess and repent, but he likely did not offer any prayers
specifically for Bishop. The records show that following her execution
her body was thrown into a pit or hastily dug grave, which was refilled
and left unmarked.[39]

Although meriting our attention because it was the first, the case
of Bridget Bishop may not have been representative. As one historian
has said, "Bridget Bishop was too special a case, too marked a character, for her fate to govern the fate of all the rest."[40] Quite different, although she suffered the same fate, was Rebecca Nurse. Nurse's case,
however, was delayed until June 28. In the meantime, the number of
the accused awaiting trial continued to grow. This the general public
could see and no doubt wonder about. What they did not know was
that the Court had divided over the use of spectral evidence in the
Bishop case, and that it could not proceed against Nurse until the matter was resolved.

At least one member of the Court of Oyer and Terminer, Nathaniel
Saltonstall, was troubled by the fact that Bridget Bishop had been condemned almost exclusively on the basis of spectral evidence. Had the
use of such evidence been limited, he and others believed Bishop's

behavior would not have merited conviction for witchcraft and execution. An authoritative unequivocal statement on the matter was needed. Governor Phips was seldom in town, continuing to deal with matters on the frontier, and even if he had been present it is unlikely that he had the educational preparation either in law or theology to provide such a statement. As it would take too long to write to England for a ruling, the matter was entrusted to the New England ministry.[41]

On June 15, twelve Boston area ministers, including Samuel Willard and Increase Mather, met to prepare a response to the Court of Oyer and Terminer. Serving as their amanuensis was Cotton Mather. In the way of a preamble, the ministerial committee expressed sympathy for those who had suffered "by molestations from the invisible world." It issued "a very critical and exquisite caution, lest by too much credulity of things received only upon the Devil's authority there be a door opened for a long train of miserable consequences." The ministers voiced their concern with the boisterous and disruptive outburst of the afflicted and urged that future proceedings be "managed with an exceeding tenderness" toward those who might be charged, especially if they were persons formerly of unblemished reputation."[42]

Addressing the specific issue of evidence, the ministers, much as Cotton Mather had done earlier, warned that spectral evidence should be handled with care, especially, in a most crucial allowance, because the "demon may assume the shape of the innocent." Conviction, they continued, should be based upon evidence "certainly more considerable than barely the accused person being represented by a specter unto the afflicted." Even the touch test, the ministers added, was not infallible. It too was liable to be abused by "the Devil's legerdemain." Nevertheless, the ministers thanked colonial authorities for their "sedulous and assiduous endeavors" in ferreting out the culprits and recommended that the proceedings be vigorously pursued.[43]

The ministers provided the Court of Oyer and Terminer with their statement in the form of a confidential memorandum. It differed from the advice offered by Cotton Mather to John Richards, only in a few particulars and in tone. Whereas previously Mather had approved of tests, such as that of the Lord's Prayer, for example, he and the other ministers now warned that they could be cunning devices used by the Devil to deceive the Court. And although in his earlier letter Mather had struck a note of caution in his instructions to the Court, the tone of the second document was even more cautionary. It nevertheless concluded with words in response to which the Court would take refuge and not change its ways. All previous criticism notwithstanding, the ministers recommended "unto the government the speedy and vigorous prosecution of such as have rendered themselves obnoxious, according to the direction given in the laws of God, and the wholesome statutes of the English nation, for the detection of witchcrafts."[44]

In sum, despite its many sound points, the document was less than decisive. Indeed, it was equivocal to the extent that the judges were free to interpret it as they wished. Perhaps the ministers were themselves uncertain about the guilt or innocence of the accused or about the height or depth to which the trials had reached. Maybe, as the opening words of caution suggest, they saw those of a previously unblemished reputation as being innocent, but others as being guilty, thereby reflecting a prejudicial double standard with which the Court came to be charged. But it was not the document for which some had hoped.

"The Return of Several Ministers Consulted," as it was titled, was to be used at the judges' and jury's own discretion. And despite its note of caution, the judges read into this memorandum confirmation of what they had already done, or of the procedures they had adopted in trying Bridget Bishop. Stoughton clearly took this position, and it would seem that he carried the rest of the Court with him. Nathaniel Saltonstall remained the sole dissenter, and he resigned from the Court.[45]

Saltonstall's resignation is not surprising, as he had agreed to participate with reluctance in the first place. The previous March he had excused himself from the Essex County Court, when it heard the case of Rachel Clinton, and he had refused to sign the witchcraft charges brought against three Haverhill women. It is probably not a coincidence that after his resignation from the Court of Oyer and Terminer, Saltonstall took to heavy drinking. Moreover, the girls, perhaps sensing the reason for his resignation, which was not made public, began to cry out against him and to report that they had seen him, or his specter, under incriminating circumstances. He was never charged, however.[46]

THE COURT COMPLETES ITS FIRST SESSION

When the Court of Oyer and Terminer reconvened on June 29, it heard the cases of Sarah Good, Sarah Wildes, Elizabeth How, Susannah Martin, and Rebecca Nurse. It was expected that Sarah Good would be quickly condemned, and she was, although someone did step forward to defend her, albeit unintentionally. During her trial, one of the girls accused Good of attacking her with a knife; she even produced a part of the blade that was used against her, the knife having been broken in the attack. The evidence seemed quite conclusive until a young man stepped forward out of the audience. He recognized the blade as that which had broken off his own knife the previous day and which he had thrown away in the presence of the afflicted, whereupon he produced the matching other part. Tellingly, although the girl seems to have made no attempt to contradict the young man's story, the judge merely reprimanded her for lying, told her to stick to the facts, and then let her continue to testify.[47]

Elizabeth How was less suspect than was Sarah Good, but the Court did not labor much longer in her case. How's two daughters and her blind husband remained faithful to her, as did a few friends, some of whom were prominent in the community. Deacon Ingersoll of Salem village, for example, was willing to testify about her good character, as were the ministers of Rowley, who had even gone so far as to trace and expose the source of much of the gossip about How. Most of that gossip, although malicious, was not relevant to the case made against her. As with others of the accused, however, there were types of evidence that were germane and unassailable, namely that of the girls, and How was duly convicted.[48]

The testimony in Sarah Wildes's case was mixed. Some reported that she was capable of outbursts of temper when she felt she had been wronged and that mayhem often followed. Others testified that they had seen no such behavior on her part, but as with the others, the negative testimony fit that brought by the afflicted, so Wildes too was condemned, as was Susannah Martin.[49]

Marion Starkey has described Susannah Martin as "every inch a witch, bright of eye, salty of tongue, and the central figure of every marvelous event that had happened in Amesbury for going on three decades." She had been formally charged with being a witch as far back as 1669. It seems she had bewitched a neighbor, but for some unknown reason she was never put on trial. At her preliminary hearing, Martin displayed contempt for the Court and ridicule for the afflicted, and when the girls who accused her burst forth in pain, she startled the Court by laughing! "Well may I laugh at such folly," she said when the magistrates reproved her. "What do you think ails them?" they asked when Martin denied hurting them, to which she only shrugged and said, "I don't desire to spend my judgment on it." "Don't you think they are bewitched?" the magistrates persisted, to wit she answered, "No, I do not think they are! If they be dealing with the black arts, you may know as well as I."[50]

The magistrates directed Martin to touch the afflicted so the Devil might be drawn from them, and he was, but Martin was not impressed. Instead, when confronted with her various alleged diabolical deeds, she commented, "He that appeared in the shape of Samuel, a glorified saint, may appear in anyone's shape." She was referring, of course, as the magistrates, ministers, and better-educated individuals knew, to the Witch of Endor, who had caused the shape of Samuel to appear before Saul. Her meaning, they also knew, was that the Bible itself (1 Sam. 28) seemed by this scene to make it clear that the Devil could assume the specter of an innocent person, much as he had her.[51]

The charges against Martin seem minor when compared to those brought against others, like Rebecca Nurse. She had done no real harm except to scare some people half to death. Mostly she was charged with committing several pranks, but certainly no murders, save John Allen's oxen. But neither did she exhibit any remorse or concern for what others thought of her. Cotton Mather merely verbalized what no doubt many others were thinking when he wrote: "This woman was one of the most impudent, scurrilous, wicked creatures in the world," and what made it even worse was that when asked what she had to say for herself, she had had the audacity to reply "that she had led a virtuous and holy life."[52] That was pretty much the case for the three decades she had been under suspicion, but in the end that did not matter. She had been an unpleasant person, perhaps even a dangerous person to cross, and she had afflicted the girls of Salem village. Therefore, the judges condemned her along with the rest.

As we have already seen, Rebecca Nurse's was among the most troubling of the preliminary hearings, and it would prove to be among the most difficult cases for the Court of Oyer and Terminer. It may have been the result of Nurse's good reputation; it may also have been the jury's response to the ministers' document on spectral evidence, or both. The charges brought against Nurse were formidable. Since her preliminary hearing, Ann Putnam Sr. had testified that Nurse had visited her on several occasions, afflicted her, and pressed her to sign the book. Nurse had told her during one visit that she had killed Benjamin Houlton, John Fuller, and Rebecca Shepard, and that she and her sister Sarah Cloyce had killed John Putnam's child as well. Putnam continued:

> Immediately there did appear to me six children in winding-sheets, which called me aunt, which did most grievously affright me; and they told me that they were my sister Baker's children of Boston; and that Goody Nurse and Mistress Cary of Charlestown, and an old deaf women at Boston, had murdered them, and charged me to go and tell these things to the magistrates, or else they would tear me to pieces, for their blood did cry for vengeance. Also there appeared to me my own sister Bayley and three of her children in winding-sheets, and told me that Goody Nurse had murdered them.[53]

Mary Walcott and Abigail Williams charged Nurse with having committed several murders, assisted in three instances by Sarah Cloyce. Sarah Houlton offered that three years earlier Nurse had killed her husband in retaliation for his not preventing his hogs from trampling her garden. Upon that occasion, despite all Houlton's attempts to pacify her, Nurse "continued railing and scolding a great while together," calling to her son Benjamin to get a gun and kill his pigs, and let none out of the field. Shortly thereafter, Sarah Houlton continued, upon his return from an early morning venture out of doors, Benjamin Holton "was taken with a strange fit . . . struck blind and stricken down two or three times, so that when he came to himself, he told me he thought he should never have come into the house anymore." He languished for the rest of the summer, "being much pained in his stomach, and often struck blind," and then he died. About two weeks before he died, Houlton added, her husband "was taken with strange and violent fits, acting much like our poor bewitched persons when we thought they would have died," and of course the doctor could not find any physical cause for the malady. In the end, she concluded, "he departed this life by a cruel death."[54]

Only a few days before her trial, Nurse was found to have a witch's teat. On June 28, however, Nurse wrote to the judges of the Court of Oyer and Terminer calling to their attention the dissenting vote cast on that occasion by one of the women who was "known to be the most ancient, skillful, prudent person of them all." She had found nothing, Nurse reported, "but what might arise from a natural cause." Although hers was the sole dissenting voice, Nurse petitioned the Court to order a second examination, employing women that were "most grave, wise, and skillful," but the Court did not honor Nurse's request.[55]

Much of the evidence used against Rebecca Nurse was spectral, and as we have seen, that was exactly the kind of evidence the Massachusetts ministers had suggested be treated with "exquisite caution." Further, the minsters had urged the Court to exercise "exceeding tenderness" toward those "persons formerly of an unblemished reputation." Not only did Rebecca Nurse have an unblemished reputation, but her husband Francis brought to court petitions signed by thirty-nine village residents attesting to her upstanding character, including the Porters and Putnams, although not Thomas and Ann Putnam. The petition attested to Nurse's having led "her life and conversation . . . according to her profession [of faith]," and to the fact that they had never had "any cause or grounds to suspect her of anything as she is now accused."[56]

In a separate document, even Nathaniel Putnam Sr. testified that in the forty years he had known Nurse, "her human frailties excepted," her life and conversation had been "according to her profession," and that she had raised "a great family of children" and had educated them well, so that "there is in some of them apparent savor of godliness." He had known her to "differ with her neighbors," Putnam continued, but he "never knew or heard of any that did accuse her" of being a witch.[57]

For a brief time, the behavior of the children in court was suspect. At one point, in response to the children's demonstrating affliction in Nurse's presence, Sarah Nurse, Rebecca's daughter, came forward to explain that she had seen Goody Bibber inflict her own pain. When Bibber cried out, she explained, Sarah had seen Bibber pull pins from her clothes and hold them between her fingers and then clasp both hands around her knees, crying as she did that Nurse had pinched her.[58]

The jury took all of this into consideration and returned a not guilty verdict. At that moment, any courtroom decorum that may have existed collapsed into bedlam. The girls roared in pain and their bodies jerked and spasmed in what one historian has described as an "unearthly choreography." The judges and jury members were no doubt stunned, while the packed house was divided between those, probably a minority, who were thrilled by the verdict and the many more who were outraged.[59]

Chief Justice Stoughton, characteristically, took control. "I will not impose on the jury," he began in addressing Thomas Fisk, jury foreman, "but I must ask you if you considered one statement made by the prisoner." Stoughton referred to the response Nurse had offered when Deliverance Hobbs and her daughter, both of whom had confessed to their guilt, were brought into court to testify, namely, "What do these persons give in evidence against me now? They used to come among us." Fisk could not answer the question. He explained that several jurymen were willing to deliberate further, but that upon their leave they "could not tell how to take her words . . . till she had a further opportunity to put her sense upon them."[60]

Stoughton asked Nurse to explain herself. Nurse, by all reports, oblivious not only to what was going on around her but even to he who stood before her and asked her about the statement, made no reply. She later explained that being "hard of hearing and full of grief" she had not realized that she had been addressed. She simply stared ahead as if in a trance, her mouth silently working as if in prayer. This time the jury, no doubt both suspicious of Nurse's failure to respond and leery of the effect their initial verdict had had on the girls, reversed itself. It assumed that by saying that Hobbs "used to come among us," Nurse had admitted that she had seen Hobbs at a witches' Sabbath, and it pronounced Nurse guilty as charged.[61]

Since she was a member of the Salem town church, there was still another step to be taken. Nurse must be cast out, or excommunicated. Nicholas Noyes, assistant pastor of the town church, but to whom, because of John Higginson's advanced age, most of the work had accrued, moved swiftly. The ceremony took place on July 3, the first Sabbath after Nurse's condemnation. Nurse, who had collapsed after her trial, was carried into the meetinghouse in a chair. Both Noyes and Higginson entered the pulpit, and the two deacons and the ruling elders sat before them. Noyes read the sentence of the congregation to her. Acting on God's behalf, the members of God's church, by denying her access to his church, condemned Nurse to eternal damnation.[62]

If the rest of the community accepted Rebecca Nurse's condemnation, however, her family did not. They went to Boston to visit Governor Phips. Phips agreed to meet with them, and they provided him with a summary of the Court's proceedings and a number of other documents, including: the petition of those who had spoken in her favor; their view of the jury's highly unusual reconsideration and reversal of their initial verdict; their explanation of Rebecca's silence when asked to explain herself; a challenge to Deliverance Hobbs's right to testify, being a fellow prisoner; and Rebecca's appeal for a second physical examination to clarify the disputed evidence of the witch's teat discovered in the first.[63]

Clearly moved by what he read and heard, Phips signed a reprieve for Rebecca Nurse, but it was met with an uproar of opposition. Immediately upon his having issued the reprieve and Nurse's release, the girls were once again afflicted. Some of them were dying, it was reported, and if they died the governor would be held responsible. Phips recalled his reprieve and left once again to fight the enemies he understood on the northern frontier.[64]

THE FIRST MASS EXECUTION AND ITS EFFECTS

The stage was set for the most dramatic day thus far in the history of the Salem witch trials. On Tuesday, July 19, 1692, the first mass execution of witches occurred. Sarah Good, Elizabeth How, Sarah Wildes, Susannah Martin, and Rebecca Nurse were hanged on Gallows Hill. Many of the residents of Salem town were in attendance, as it was common for such public acts of discipline, and it was an appropriately solemn occasion—with one exception. Sarah Good would not go quietly.[65]

When the Reverend Noyes made one last appeal to her to save her immortal soul by confessing, again a common procedure, insisting that she was indeed a witch, Good responded, "You're a liar! I am no more a witch than you are a wizard! If you take my life away, God will give you blood to drink." Good was hanged, nonetheless, but some believe her prophecy came true. Years later, Noyes died of a hemorrhage. Perhaps Good's words came back to haunt him in his final moments.[66]

The bodies of the witches were buried in a shallow grave on Gallows Hill; they could not be interred in a sacred graveyard. The body of Rebecca Nurse, however, did not remain there. Her children, so the story goes, returned that night, dug up the body, and took it home. No one knows where they buried Rebecca; no one outside of the family would be told. Years later, however, a granite marker was erected for her under a tree on the Nurse's property. Another marker was erected nearby honoring all who had defended her in a day when to do so was to jeopardize their own lives.[67]

It should be noted that the executions of July 19 had a profound effect on the other witches awaiting trial. If people such as Rebecca Nurse, with all of the support she seemed to have in the community, could be executed, what chance did they have to escape the hangman's noose? And perhaps symbolically, but in a development the impact of which could not have been missed by all of those concerned with the course of events in Salem, in July, with the witchcraft fervor at its height, a special election was held in Salem town. Daniel Andrew and Philip English, not surprisingly, as well as Timothy Lindall and two other selectmen associated with the Porters were voted out of office. Five new men (four of whom had never served in that office before) took their place. The moderator of the election was John Putnam. The counterattack had reached its greatest point.[68]

Most, if not all, of those facing trial no doubt despaired of their fate. Those who could, took fate into their own hands, and flights from the law began. Nathaniel Cary smuggled his wife from prison and escaped to New York. Edward and Sarah Bishop fled, but it is not known where. Philip and Mary English resisted almost until the day of their trial, but then they too left for New York. And John Alden disappeared. In all, Larry Gragg found that thirteen individuals had escaped, seven men and six women, five from Salem and eight from seven other communities.[69]

Four points should be added in reference to those who escaped prosecution. First, it was quite likely the conduct of the Court of Oyer and Terminer in its first session that precipitated their flight. Second, although Alden, Andrew, Cary, and the Englishes were prominent among the fugitives, and although another escapee, Dudley Bradstreet, was a man of wealth, as many others maintained a decidedly lower public profile and were of modest means. Third, given the less than physically secure nature of most prisons, as well as the absence of systematic supervision, it is surprising that even more did not escape. Obviously some prisoners were more closely guarded or physically unable to flee, but other factors kept the number down. Some believed that running would be an admission of guilt, which they found unacceptable, and at least until January 1693, confession afforded a safer way of avoiding execution.[70]

Fourth, it is interesting, but perhaps not especially surprising, that although there was much talk about the escapees, the judges made little effort to pursue those fugitives who fled beyond their immediate jurisdiction. Extradition from one British colony to another was legally possible, but unless it was attempted secretly there is no record that it was even tried. This led Thomas Brattle to charge that the Carys, Alden, and the Englishes had not been pursued because of their status. Rather than prompt the Court to action, Brattle intended his comments to ridicule the proceedings as a whole. And, although only true in part (the Court did not seek to extradite those of lesser means, either), his charges did lend substance to a message that was gaining support in many quarters. People were beginning to believe that being rich, wellborn, and powerful not only protected some from the charges the young girls made against them, but also that if formally charged it would be sufficient to ensure that they would never be tried, much less executed. Execution, it was believed, would be the fate of those of lesser wealth, birth, and power.[71]

8

"What A Sad Thing It Is To See Eight Firebrands of Hell Hanging There"

Having successfully withstood the challenge posed by the pious and highly regarded Rebecca Nurse, the Court of Oyer and Terminer reconvened on August 5 to face six more defendants: George Burroughs, John and Elizabeth Proctor, George Jacobs Sr., John Willard, and Martha Carrier. Burroughs and Proctor challenged the court in different yet powerful ways, but both failed. All six were condemned and, with the exception of Elizabeth Proctor, all were executed two weeks later.

The Case of George Burroughs

As was the case in many of the trials, most of the evidence used against Burroughs was gathered from his preliminary hearing. Yet, again, witnesses testified to the amazing feats of strength the little man had performed. He had held out a gun with a seven-foot barrel with one finger stuck in the muzzle, it was recalled, and he had carried a barrel full of cider with only one finger stuck in the opening (the details varied with each telling). Burroughs responded that such incidents had been much exaggerated. He added that an Indian had done much the same thing, but perhaps that was not a wise comparison for him to make, because his accusers soon pointed out that Burroughs was not only "the Black Man" but that he also looked like an Indian![1]

Witnesses again testified that Burroughs had been known to travel from place to place in a shorter time than was humanly possible, without the assistance of the Devil. Burroughs pointed out that upon the occasion cited another man had accompanied him, only to have his accusers suggest that the other person must have been the Devil. Additional depositions were offered attesting to Burroughs's "unkindness," or abusive treatment, of his wife. Once again the Court heard of his wife's laments to neighbors that Burroughs would not let her write to her father, and that she suspected him of dealing with, or at least having direct knowledge of, evil spirits.[2]

As the mid-eighteenth-century historian Thomas Hutchinson said: "Upon the whole, he [Burroughs] was confounded, and used many twistings and turnings, which, I think, we cannot wonder at."[3] Cotton Mather recorded one such "twisting and turning" at the hands of Chief Justice Stoughton and upon the failure of several of the afflicted to bear witness in George Burroughs's presence:

> The chief justice asked the prisoner who he thought hindered these witnesses from giving their testimonies; and he answered, he supposed it was the Devil. The honorable person then replied, 'How comes the Devil so loath to have any testimony borne against you?' Which cast him into very great confusion.[4]

George Burroughs was not an entirely passive victim. He came to court prepared to defend himself. He called into question a concept central to the definition of witchcraft itself. In a written statement he presented to the jury, he wrote that "there neither are nor ever were witches that having a compact with the Devil can send a devil to torment other people at a distance." We do not know the judges' response to Burroughs's statement, but we can well imagine what it was. We do know that the jury was not impressed. Neither was Cotton Mather, who determined that the statement had been taken from *A Candle in the Dark* (1656), written during the days of the English (Stuart) Restoration following the witch-hunt of the 1640s by Thomas Ady, a notorious English skeptic.[5]

The jury was more impressed by the tooth marks the afflicted girls showed them, testifying that Burroughs's specter had bitten them only the night before. To prove the case, the judges had Burroughs's mouth pried open, and upon close inspection of his teeth as well as those of others in the courtroom, they declared that indeed his teeth were responsible for the marks.[6] The jury no doubt recalled that Burroughs had tried to seduce the girls into witchcraft by offering them fine clothes, and that he had told them of his plan to pervert the whole of Salem village. Having revealed so much to them, only to have them resist his entreaties, the court reasoned, Burroughs had no choice but to act to silence them. Burroughs was condemned.

THE PROCTORS ARE CONDEMNED

On July 23, two weeks before he arrived in court, John Proctor took the offensive by having delivered to five Boston area ministers a petition on his behalf and on behalf of others of the accused. In that petition, Proctor urged the ministers to use their authority to have the cases moved from Salem to the Boston area, or failing that, to have the judges replaced by others. The sitting members, he explained, had already condemned them, their being "so much enraged and incensed against us by the Devil." The petition, it will be recalled, also alleged the use of torture in eliciting confessions from some of the accused.[7]

The direct results of the Proctors' petition, at least in the short run, were no doubt disappointing. The petition was sent to the Reverends Joshua Moody and Samuel Willard, both of whom had displayed some sympathy for the accused, as well as to the Reverends James Allen, John Bayley, and Increase Mather. None took any immediate action. Perhaps Moody and Willard remained cautious despite their already well-known opposition to the trials. Further, although there are indications that he was beginning to grow uneasy with the course of events, Increase Mather was still recouping his lost fortune among the general population for his role in the writing of the new colonial charter. In time, Moody and Willard did act decisively in opposition to the trials, and Mather did investigate Proctor's allegations of torture, but if they did anything at the time, it did not alter John Proctor's fate.[8]

Indirectly, two developments might well have resulted at least in part from John Proctor's petition. First, apparently in retaliation, Proctor's relatives in Lynn were immediately cried out against and arrested.[9] Second, Increase Mather decided to visit Salem to see for himself how the trials were conducted. He witnessed the trial of George Burroughs, but his observations after the trial ended, as we shall see, were less than supportive to the defendant's cause.

A few days before their trial, two additional petitions were offered to the Court of Oyer and Terminer on behalf of John and Elizabeth Proctor. In one petition, thirty-one residents of Ipswich, and in the second, twenty others who lived nearby, attested to the Proctors' good conduct. In the first, apparently written by the Reverend John Wise of Ipswich, the signatories explained that out of charity, whereby they should "do as [they] would be done by," they had decided to do what they could to clear their neighbors' names. They noted that they had come to suppose that "it may be a method within the severer but just transactions of the infinite majesty of God, that He sometimes may permit Satan to personate, dissemble, and thereby abuse innocents." Therefore, they testified to the innocence of their neighbors. They reported that they:

> never had the least knowledge of such a nefarious wickedness in our said neighbors, since they have been within our acquaintance. Neither do we remember any such thoughts in us concerning them, or any action by them or either of them, directly tending that way, no more than might be in the lives of any other persons of the clearest reputations as to any such evils. What God may have left them to, we cannot go into God's pavilion clothed with clouds of darkness round about, but, as to what we have ever seen or heard of them, upon our consciences we judge them innocent of the crime objected.[10]

In the second statement, the signatories offered a briefer confirming paragraph, noting that they had no reason to suspect the Proctors either, as they had "lived Christian-like in their family, and were ever ready to help such as stood in need of their help."[11]

Once again, the petition did no good. Neither did the previously mentioned testimony of the Proctors' servant Mary Warren, which was offered in evidence at the Proctors' trial. Warren had recanted her testimony against John and Elizabeth Proctor, only to recant her recantation. So in the end, John and Elizabeth Proctor were condemned. Elizabeth, however, was pregnant and the judges chose not to condemn her unborn child as well, even though it was begotten by two convicted witches! They granted Elizabeth a stay of execution until the baby was born.[12] As it turned out, although she gave birth only about two weeks after her scheduled date of execution, the delay was sufficient to save her life.

THE CASES OF GEORGE JACOBS SR., JOHN WILLARD, AND MARTHA CARRIER

Once again, nearly all we know of the trials of George Jacobs Sr., John Willard, and Martha Carrier comes from the records of their preliminary hearings and pre-trial depositions. Most of that has already been reported, except for their ultimate fate, at which the reader can likely guess. The reader will recall the sad tale of Jacobs's son and daughter-in-law, as well as the fascinating stories of Jacobs's servant Sarah Churchill and his granddaughter Margaret Jacobs. Sarah too had recanted her recantation, and although Margaret persisted in telling the Court that she had lied, it made little difference. George Jacobs Sr. was condemned.

At John Willard's trial, Susannah Sheldon testified that on one occasion, while at Ingersoll's ordinary, she had been visited by four apparitions: "William Shaw's first wife, the Widow Cook, Goodman Jones and his child." Among them came the specter of John Willard, to whom the four said, "You have murdered us," whereupon they all "turned as red as blood." Turning to Sheldon, the visitors became "as pale as death," and they ordered Sheldon to tell Hathorne what she had heard. Willard, however, pulled a knife, saying that if she did he would cut her throat.[13]

The apparitions visited Sheldon twice more in the same day, telling much the same story. Upon their third visit, Sheldon inquired about the locations of the specters' wounds. They answered that an angel from heaven would soon appear and show her, and soon one did. Sheldon asked the angel who the "shining man" was, and the angel told her his name was Southwick. Then "the angel lifted up his winding-sheet, and out of his left side he pulled a pitchfork tine, and put it in again." Likewise, "he opened all the winding-sheets [of the others], and showed all their wounds." And once again, the angel ordered Sheldon to tell Hathorne what he had told her, and then vanished. In a second deposition, Sheldon testified that she had seen Willard "suckle the apparitions of two black pigs on his breasts," that Willard had told her that he had been a wizard for twenty years, and that she had witnessed Willard and other wizards and witches kneeling in prayer "to the black man with a long-crowned hat." John Willard was sentenced to be hanged.[14]

Finally, the Court called Martha Carrier. The Reverend Francis Dane of Andover appeared in her defense. He told the Court that Carrier had been the victim of malicious gossip, but his testimony was suspect. Although he was a minister of God, three of his female relations had been arrested for witchcraft! Moreover, there were new depositions to add to the list of those who had already spoken out against her. Benjamin Abbott testified that in March 1691 he had had some land granted to him by the town of Andover. The lot, however, bordered on that of the Carriers, and when Martha concluded that Abbott's lot encroached on hers, she was very angry. She said she "would stick as close to [him] as the bark stuck to the tree," and that he would "repent of it afore seven years came to an end."[15]

What exactly befell Abbott is unclear, but he did report suffering from a swollen foot and a pain in his side that "bred to a sore which was lanced by Dr. Prescott and [from which] several gallons of corruption did run" for some six weeks. He experienced soreness in his groin, which was treated in a similar manner but which almost caused his death. He concluded by noting that Dr. Prescott was never able to cure him, but that once Martha Carrier was imprisoned he began to heal. As he continued to be in good health since, he had "great cause to think that the said Carrier had a great hand" in it all.[16]

John Rogers deposed that about seven years earlier he had quarreled with Martha Carrier, his neighbor, at which time "she gave forth several threatening words as she often used to do." A short time later, two of Rogers's "lusty sows" disappeared. Rogers found one dead and with both ears cut off, near the Carrier's home, but he never found the other. One of Rogers's cows stopped giving milk in the morning, as she formerly had, and produced only at night.[17]

And Phoebe Chandler, about twelve years of age, reported that on one occasion while carrying food to workers in the field, she had heard a voice she thought was Martha Carrier's coming from the bushes, asking her what she was doing there and where she was going. Chandler saw nobody but was frightened, nonetheless, and ran. Later in the day she made the same trip and upon returning she heard the same voice, this time saying that she would be poisoned within two or three days. Soon Phoebe suffered from a swollen right hand, excruciating pain in her face, and the feeling of "a great weight" upon her breast and legs.[18]

The jury returned a guilty verdict in Carrier's case, and their work on those first summoned by Thomas Newton was done.

THE HANGINGS OF AUGUST 19

On August 19, 1692, five more witches, four men and one woman, were taken to Gallows Hill and hanged. To a person, Thomas Brattle reported, they forgave their accusers. They also spoke "without reflection on jury and judges, for bringing them in guilty, and condemning them," and their words were "very affecting and melting to the hearts of some considerable spectators." At the same time, however, they continued to insist that they were innocent. "The condemned," Brattle wrote, "went out of the world not only with as great protestations, but also with as good shows of innocency, as men could do." They "declared their wish, that their blood might be the last innocent blood shed."[19]

According to Robert Calef, Cotton Mather was present upon the occasion of the mass hanging of August 19, and he made record of an incident that has remained indelibly ingrained in the history of the Salem witch trials, forever exemplifying in most minds Mather's zealous role therein. First, Calef reported, the condemned asked Mather to pray with them. Then George Burroughs, the "black minister," climbed the ladder and all eyes were upon him. He was allowed to speak, and he once again proclaimed his innocence "with such solemn and serious expressions as were to the admiration of all present." He even repeated the Lord's Prayer—flawlessly! Indeed, to quote Calef directly, Burroughs's recitation "was so well worded, and uttered with such composedness and such (at least seeming) fervency of spirit, as was very affecting and drew tears from many."[20]

Those in attendance were dumbstruck. Was it possible they had condemned an innocent man? The moment cried out for an explanation, lest some, who had even been moved to tears, lose their resolve and hinder the execution. The accusers, Calef reported, insisted that another "black man" stood nearby and dictated the prayer to Burroughs, and then Cotton Mather stepped forward to provide his explanation. Dressed all in black, Calef reported, Mather rose in the stirrups upon his horse and addressed the crowd. He began by declaring that Burroughs was not an ordained minister, a statement based, most historians agree, on a technicality but nevertheless intended to counter any last-minute second thoughts on the matter. Further, without making specific reference to it, he recalled a point made several weeks earlier by the Reverend Deodat Lawson, namely that the Devil is never more subtly himself than when he most appears like an angel of light. Burroughs, he explained, was like an angel of light, but he was not what he appeared to be. The noise of the crowd subsided, Calef continued, and Burroughs was hanged. Burroughs had been silenced, but his last words were not forgotten. Even Cotton Mather lived to regret the day, as he later wrote that he wished he had never heard "the first letters of his [Burroughs's] name."[21]

The reader should understand that Robert Calef's account of the August 19 hanging was the only contemporary description that mentioned Mather's role in Burroughs's hanging. Thomas Brattle's and Samuel Sewall's, for example, do not, although in his diary on August 19, 1692, Sewall did write that Burroughs "by his speech, prayer, and protestation of innocence, did much move unthinking persons."[22] Given Calef's hostility toward Mather and the dramatic nature of the event upon which the others were almost certain to have commented, Calef's account must be viewed with some skepticism. That is not to suggest, however, that Mather was not persuaded of Burroughs's guilt. Upon Burroughs's execution, Mather recorded the following passage in his diary:

> God had been pleased so as to leave this George Burroughs, that he had ensnared himself by several instances which he had formerly given of preternatural strength, and which were now produced against him.[23]

Even his father, Increase—commonly seen as considerably less zealous than his son, and who had attended Burroughs's trial—found the evidence against Burroughs compelling. He concluded that it showed that "the Devil had been Burroughs's familiar," and that if he had been on the jury he would not have quarreled with their verdict.[24]

Calef described the hanging of August 19 in the following manner:

> When he [Burroughs] was cut down, he was dragged by a halter to a hole, or grave, between the rocks, about two feet deep; his shirt and breeches were pulled off, and an old pair of trousers of one executed put on his lower parts. He was so put in [the grave], together with Willard and Carrier, that one of his hands and his chin, and a foot of one of them, were left uncovered.[25]

Tradition, however, describes a different end for the body of George Jacobs. According to historian Charles Upham, the body "having been obtained at the place of execution, was strapped by a young grandson on the back of a horse, brought home to [his] farm, and buried beneath the shade of his own trees." Two "sunken and weather worn stones" marked the spot, Upham continued, and there Jacobs rested until 1864, when his remains were exhumed, his identity confirmed, and he was reburied in the same place.[26]

In the 1950s, when the Jacobs home was abandoned after a series of fires, George Jacobs was exhumed a final time by the town of Danvers (formerly Salem village) and put into storage, to be reburied in 1992 in the Rebecca Nurse graveyard. The stone is decorated with angels' wings on both sides of a skull, which was common in the late seventeenth century, and is inscribed with "Here lies buried the body of George Jacobs Sr., Deceased August the 19th, 1692. Well! Burn me or hang me, I will stand in the truth of Christ."

THE TRIALS OF SEPTEMBER: THE CASES OF MARTHA COREY
AND MARY EASTY

The Court's perfect record of conviction thus far spurred it on. On September 9 it tried and condemned six more witches, and eight days later nine more. Of the fifteen, eight were hanged on September 22: Martha Corey, Mary Easty, Alice Parker, Ann Pudeator, Margaret Scott, Wilmot Reed, Samuel Wardwell, and Mary Parker. Of the seven who escaped hanging, five had confessed and were at least temporarily reprieved: Rebecca Eames, Abigail Hobbs, Mary Lacey Sr., Ann Foster, and Dorcas Hoar. The execution of Abigail Faulkner, daughter of Francis Dane, was postponed because of her pregnancy, while Mary Bradbury of Salisbury escaped. Ninety-three neighbors had signed a statement on Bradbury's behalf, indicating how beloved she was of her neighbors in Salisbury, and when she escaped it is quite likely, given her infirmity, that she had help. Once she disappeared, authorities made little attempt to find her.[27]

Of those cases included in the previous list, we might pause to bring two of those introduced earlier to completion—those of Martha Corey and Mary Easty. In the most significant deposition entered for her trial, Edward Putnam and Ezekiel Cheever reviewed the previous detailed charges brought against Corey by Ann Putnam Sr., as well as what had transpired upon their visit to Martha Corey's house on March 12.[28] But further testimony was added to the evidence.

Elizabeth Booth testified that the apparition of George Needham had appeared to her and had said that Martha Corey had killed him because he would not mend her spinning wheel. Elizabeth Hubbard reported that not only had Corey afflicted her, but that she had seen Corey torment Mercy Lewis, Abigail Williams, and Ann Putnam Jr. Lewis confirmed that Corey had tortured her and added, "I believe in my heart that Martha Corey is a most dreadful witch, and that she hath often afflicted me [and] several others by her acts of witchcraft."[29] The Court agreed. On September 11, the day after Martha Corey was condemned, the Reverend Samuel Parris wrote:

> Sister Martha Corey—taken into the church 27 April 1690—was, after examination upon suspicion of witchcraft, 27 March 1692, committed to prison for the fact, and was condemned to the gallows for the same yesterday; and was this day in public, by a general consent, voted to be excommunicated out of the church, and Lieutenant Nathaniel Putnam and the two deacons chosen to signify to her, with the pastor, the mind of the church herein.

Parris added that three days later, Putnam and the two deacons visited Corey in prison. They found her as unrepentant as before, "justifying herself, and condemning all that had done anything to her just discovery or condemnation." He concluded, "[A]fter prayer—which she was willing to decline—the dreadful sentence of excommunication was pronounced upon her."[30]

About Mary Easty we know only a little more than what has already been reported. The previously noted outpouring of emotional support concerning what many believe was Easty's innocence continued at her trial. Immediately preceding her appearance before the Court of Oyer and Terminer, a petition written by Easty and her sister Sarah Cloyce was read to the Court. In it, they made the following requests. First, "seeing that we are neither able to plead our own cause, nor is counsel allowed to those in our condition," they asked the judges to counsel them "wherever we may stand in need."[31]

Second, whereas they were still convinced of their innocence and whereas people "of good report" had deposed that they had never been guilty of "any other scandalous evil or miscarriage inconsistent with Christianity," they requested that some of those deponents offering evidence favorable to their case, including the pastor and others of the town and church of Topsfield, be allowed to testify before the Court of Oyer and Terminer. And finally, the two asked that the testimony of the confessed witches and of the afflicted not be used to condemn them "without other legal evidence concurring," a point consistent with accepted legal procedures but with which the Court seemed little concerned.[32]

All of the petitions in her favor notwithstanding, Easty was condemned, but she made one last appeal. It was not only for herself, but for those yet to stand trial. Her appeal is worth quoting at length, because it reflects a perceptive and sensitive assessment of the Court's actions thus far. To the Governor, members of the Court of Oyer and Terminer, and "the Reverend Ministers" she wrote that having seen "plainly the wiles and subtlety" of her accusers, she despaired of any more favorable outcome for the rest of the accused than had resulted in her case:

> I petition to your Honours, not for my own life, for I know I must die, and my appointed time is set; but . . . if it be possible, that no more innocent blood be shed, which undoubtedly cannot be avoided in the way and courses you go in. I question not but your Honors do to the utmost of your powers in the discovery and detecting of witchcraft and witches, and would not be guilty of innocent blood for the world; but by my own innocence, I know you are in the wrong way. The Lord in his infinite mercy

directs you in this great work; if it be his blessed will, that no more innocent blood be shed, I humbly beg of you that Your Honours would be
pleased to examine these persons strictly, and keep them apart some time,
and likewise to try some of these confessing witches, I being confident
there are several of them have belied themselves and others. . . . They say
myself and others have made a league with the Devil. . . . I know and the
Lord He knows . . . they belie me, and so I question not but they do others. The Lord above, who is the searcher of all hearts knows, as I shall answer it at the Tribunal Seat, that I know not the least thing of witchcraft;
therefore I cannot, I dare not, belie my own soul.[33]

On Thursday, September 22, Martha Corey, Mary Easty, Alice
Parker, Ann Pudeator, Margaret Scott, Wilmot Reed, Samuel Wardwell, and Mary Parker were taken by cart to Gallows Hill and executed. When all had been hanged, the Reverend Nicholas Noyes was
heard to say, "What a sad thing it is to see eight firebrands of hell hanging there." The number of executed had now reached nineteen, not including one of the most notorious cases of all—that of Giles Corey.[34]

THE ORDEAL OF GILES COREY

We started the story of Giles Corey in chapter four with some discussion about his arrest and appearance before the Salem magistrates.
He was jailed and subsequently indicted by a grand jury. He spent one
month in the Salem jail, but when his specter continued to appear
regularly to Mary Warren he was ordered removed to Boston.[35] On
September 19, following the condemnation of his wife but before her
execution, Giles Corey was crushed beneath a pile of rocks. Why he was
so treated merits some explanation.

On or about September 16, the Court of Oyer and Terminer ordered the sheriff to pile rocks on Giles Corey because he had chosen
not to stand trial. Because his records have not survived, it is not
known exactly what happened, but nearly all of the historians who
have investigated the matter believe that sometime soon after September 9, when he was called to face the Court, Corey either entered
a plea of not guilty and refused to place himself on trial, or he remained
silent altogether.[36]

David C. Brown has made a persuasive case for the former. First,
Brown has pointed out, Robert Calef, who has provided the most complete account of his trial, has specifically stated that Corey pleaded
not guilty and refused to "put himself upon trial by jury." The other

accounts, Brown has reasoned, likely merely shortened their reference to the two-step procedure by simply saying he refused to enter a plea. Second, Brown continued, if Corey had both refused to enter a plea and stood mute, under the law the Court would have had to impanel a jury to determine whether he had stood mute "of malice" or "by the visitation of God," having been struck dumb. If decided as being the former, Corey would have been treated as if he had "put himself on the country." If as the latter, the Court would have ordered the trial to proceed as if Corey had pleaded not guilty. In either event, there is no evidence that any additional hearings took place.[37]

Under English law, "standing mute" after entering a not guilty plea prevented a court from ordering a person to stand trial. He could be tried only if he "put himself on the country" or agreed to a jury trial "by God and my country." His not having done that, the Court was forced to proceed against Corey in another manner. The judges resorted to *peine forte et dure*, a seldom-used procedure whereby they hoped to force Corey to agree to stand trial.

What Corey intended by his unusual action is also unclear. Most believe that by refusing to stand trial, he hoped to protect his property from confiscation. After his arrest, Corey had deeded his land to his two sons-in-law, William Cleeves and John Moulton. Martha, after all, was to be executed, and, as he put it, he lay "under great trouble and affliction" and knew not how he would "depart this life." By "standing mute," many historians have argued, he would at least prevent the Court from finding him guilty and confiscating his property. David Brown, however, has found that in 1692 forfeiture of one's estate upon conviction for witchcraft was illegal.[38]

Witchcraft was a felony under seventeenth-century English law, and felonies were punishable by death, corruption of blood, confiscation of one's belongings, and forfeiture of one's lands. Corruption of a felon's blood meant that he could not own any property or convey property to his heirs. "Standing mute" and avoiding conviction was one way to avoid such repercussions, although in England personal goods could still be confiscated. Under English law, however, witchcraft was a special felony for which provisions for corruption of blood and forfeiture of real property did not apply. And as early as 1641 in its Body of Liberties, the Massachusetts General Court abolished laws of forfeiture for all felonies. Goods or "moveable property" could still be confiscated, if expressly permitted by law, in this case meaning laws passed in regard to witchcraft, but no such provision for confiscation has been found.[39]

On June 15, 1692, the Massachusetts General Court under its new charter passed an act continuing all laws adopted under its previous charter, which would have included the laws abolishing forfeiture. No attempt was made to establish a law of forfeiture or confiscation in cases of witchcraft until December 14, 1692, about three months after Corey's death, and it was disallowed by the Privy Council as "repugnant to the laws of England." David Brown has argued that the bill of December 1692 may well have been a failed attempt to sanction those confiscations that had already taken place.[40]

If Brown is correct, either Giles Corey was aware of the law and stood mute for another reason, or he was not and he wasted his life. Brown favors the first interpretation, suggesting that Corey refused to "put himself on the country" out of contempt for the Court of Oyer and Terminer. But as even Brown admits, legally or not, confiscations had occurred, as we shall see in the final chapter, and regardless of the letter of the law, it is entirely plausible that Corey believed his property would be in jeopardy if he were to be convicted.[41]

Whatever he might have intended, on September 17, Sheriff George Corwin ordered "great weights" to be piled on Giles Corey, one at a time, until he changed his mind. The sheriff placed rocks on his chest in the field beside the Ipswich jail, to which Corey had been returned to stand trial. Under English law, his only sustenance during the ordeal would have been alternating days of bread ("three morsels" was prescribed) and water ("three draughts"). However, Giles Corey never did change his mind, and as legend has it his only comment was, "More weight." On or about September 19 (the date is unclear), Corey's body yielded to the weight pressed upon him. As Robert Calef put it, his tongue protruded from his mouth until an official forced it back with his cane. Exaggerated or not, it was undoubtedly not a pretty scene. And upon his death, the sheriff threatened to confiscate Corey's property until he was paid eleven pounds, six shillings by his sons-in-law.[42]

David Brown, who has found so much irregularity already in the proceedings against Giles Corey, has argued that even *peine forte et dure* was illegal. In Massachusetts, he has pointed out, there were no laws expressly providing for it, and to his way of thinking, based on provisions in the laws of 1641, confirmed in 1692, it would have been precluded as cruel and unusual punishment. There was only one other case in Massachusetts history where a prisoner was threatened with *peine forte et dure,* and that occurred in the winter of 1638–1639, when Dorothy Talbye, a one-time member of the Salem town church, was indicted for murdering her three-year-old daughter. She stood mute, but when told what was in store for her, she not only changed her mind but confessed and was hanged! Thus, Giles Corey retains the dubious distinction of being the only person ever pressed to death by law in the history of the United States.[43]

The ordeal of Giles Corey is well-known. Less well-known is what happened while he was being pressed to death. At exactly the same hour, it was reported, Ann Putnam was nearly crushed by a group of witches. They laid on Ann's chest, much as did the rocks upon Corey's, and they pledged that she would die before Corey. Ann was saved, her father reported, only when an apparition in his winding-sheet appeared to her. He drove the witches from her, and when Ann expressed some compunction concerning Corey's fate, he explained to her why Corey had to be pressed to death.[44]

Corey, the mysterious savior told her, had once pressed a man to death with his feet—the very man who now stood before her (perhaps Jacob Goodale, as noted in chapter four)! At the time of his diabolical compact, the specter continued, Corey had reached agreement with the Devil wherein the Devil had promised that he would not hang. So it came to pass. In the end, although he would pay the price for his transgression, God had hardened his heart against the advice of the Court, which would have at the least arranged for an easier death. And, as the visitor concluded, that was as it should be: "It must be done to him as he has done to me."[45]

On September 18, the Reverend Nicholas Noyes made the following entry in the records of Salem's First Church:

> Giles Corey was excommunicated. The cause of it was that he being accused and indicted for the sin of witchcraft, he refused to plead, and so incurred the sentence and penalty of *peine forte et dure;* being undoubtedly either guilty of the sin of witchcraft, or of throwing himself upon sudden and certain death, if he were otherwise innocent.[46]

In the end, Corey was "damned if he did and damned if he didn't," but he would nonetheless be memorialized for posterity in the following ballad:

> *Giles Corey was a wizard strong,*
> *A stubborn wretch was he,*
> *And fit was he to hang on high*
> *Upon the locust tree.*
>
> *So when before the magistrates*
> *For trial he did come,*
> *He would no true confession make*
> *But was completely dumb.*

'Giles Corey,' said the magistrate,
'What have thou here to plead
To these who now accuse thy soul
Of crimes and horrid deed?'

Giles Corey—he said not a word,
No single word spoke he.
'Giles Corey,' said the magistrate,
'We'll press it out of thee.'

They got them then a heavy beam,
They laid it on his breast.
They loaded it with heavy stones,
And hard upon him pressed.

'More weight,' now said this wretched man,
'More weight,' again he cried.
And he did no confession make
But wickedly he died.

Dame Corey lived but three days more,
But three days more lived she,
For she was hanged at Gallows Hill
Upon the locust tree.[47]

THE MOOD IN SEPTEMBER 1692

The Court of Oyer and Terminer adjourned on September 22, fully expecting to reconvene soon to continue through the trials of the dozens of indicted who remained in jail. The fever had peaked. The months of accusations, examinations, indictments, trials, convictions, confessions, and executions had given some pause to reflect on what was happening. Many others, however, became more zealous in their support of the trials. They revised their earlier estimations of the extent of the problem that New England faced. They no longer saw what was happening as a conspiracy against a single congregation or community. It had become an all-out war between the forces of Christ and the Devil.

On August 4, in a sermon subsequently included in his *Wonders of the Invisible World*, Cotton Mather, who had urged caution in certain procedural matters before the Court, offered an apocalyptic vision of the crisis facing not only Salem but also New England. Building on the jeremiads that had been so popular before the Salem witch trials,

Mather interpreted the witchcraft episode of 1692 as another example of a just divine punishment for a wayward people. "A variety of calamity has long followed this plantation," he explained, "and we have all the reason imaginable to ascribe it unto the rebuke of heaven upon us for our manifold apostasies." Mather's interpretation of events led him to conclude that the Second Coming was near and that the Devil had seized the brief time he had remaining to launch an attack on New England. Mather's objective was to reveal the Devil's plot against New England and to muster the opposition in preparation for that fateful day.[48]

On September 11, the Reverend Samuel Parris placed recent events into the context of the 1,700-year-old war waged by "the Devil and his instruments" against Christianity. He chose as his text Revelation 17: 14: "These shall make war with the lamb, and the lamb shall overcome them; for he is Lord of lords, and King of kings; and they that are with him are called and chosen and faithful." He titled his sermon: "The Devil and his instruments will be warring against Christ and his followers."[49]

During Jesus' own life on earth, Parris explained, the Devil sought his destruction, from his "manifold temptations of Christ in the wilderness" to his putting "it into the heart of one of Christ's disciples to betray him." Thereafter, over the centuries, the Devil had employed many agents to subvert the church. "In our land," he continued, the Devil has instigated multitudes of witches and wizards "with utmost violence to attempt the overthrow of religion."[50]

Parris put the matter directly before the members of his congregation. "There are but two parties in the world," he pointed out, "the Lamb and his followers, and the dragon and his followers." There are no "neuters." "Everyone is on one side or the other." Parris professed his confidence in the outcome of their struggle, as the Lamb's victory was assured. "Devils and idolaters will make war with the Lamb and his followers," he warned, but to join the Devil's troop was "to take the weakest side," and to "fight for him" was to be paid "no other wages than [that] of being your eternal torturer."[51]

Parris's purpose was to not only speak out about the danger of the Devil's threat, but also "to reprove such as seem to be so amazed at the war the Devil ha[d] raised among [them] by wizards and witches, that they altogether den[ied] it." If ever there were witches, men and women in covenant with the Devil, he lectured skeptics, there were "multitudes" in New England. It was, Parris added, a problem faced by the chosen people of God on both sides of the Atlantic, to wit he quoted from Richard Baxter's *The Certainty of the World of Spirits* (London,

1691). Baxter sought to expose "the Devil's prevalency in this age," and after noting that authorities had discovered hundreds of witches in one English shire, he wrote:

> If fame deceives us not, in a village of fourteen houses in the North, are found so many of this damned brood. Heretofore only barbarous deserts had them, but now the civilest and religious parts are frequently pestered with them. Heretofore some silly ignorant old women, etc. but now we have known those of both sexes, who professed much knowledge, holiness, and devotion, drawn into this damnable practice.[52]

At the same time, and for the first time at least publicly, Parris implied that absolute victory over the Devil and his minions might not be possible in this world. Thus, he concluded his sermon by shifting his focus from the battle in the natural world to the final triumph in the Hereafter. "After this life the saints shall no more be troubled with war from devils and their instruments," he offered. "The city of heaven, provided for the saints, is well-walled and well-gated and well-guarded, so that no devils nor their instruments shall enter thereunto."[53] Perhaps the enormity of the forces arrayed against him was beginning to take its toll, and he was tiring or even despairing of its outcome. Or maybe Parris was aware of the skepticism of a growing number of people regarding the Salem witch trials and what that skepticism portended.

Mather and Parris, and no doubt others who did not articulate their fears, had come to believe that they were the victims of a cosmic plot involving an unprecedented, at least in New England, number of witches. The details of the plot—indeed the sheer enormity of it—were made clear by the equally unprecedented number of confessions. At least forty-three by one estimate,[54] fifty-five by another,[55] of the accused "voluntarily" or "freely" revealed the details of an incredible diabolical conspiracy to destroy New England. The impact of those confessions should not be underestimated. John Hale credited them with being the factor "which chiefly carried on this matter [the trials] to such a height."[56] Before concluding this chapter, then, some further discussion of the confessions is necessary regarding both their probable cause and meaning.

THE CONFESSIONS OF 1692

Earlier reference was made to John Proctor's complaint that authorities had tortured Richard and Andrew Carrier, as well as his own son William, in an attempt to get them to confess. Thomas Brattle and

Robert Calef offered similar accounts. Brattle claimed that the accused faced "violent, distracting, and dragooning methods" and repeated "unreasonable urgings."[57] Calef wrote that there were many tedious interrogations with questioners taking turns to persuade them until "the accused were wearied out by being forced to stand so long, or for want of sleep, etc. and so brought to give an assent to what they said."[58] In some such cases, the records indicate, not only did the confession result in relief for the afflicted, but also in their embracing the accused in tearful forgiveness of their tormenters.[59]

As we have seen, there were even more subtle, yet equally effective, methods employed. We have already referred to the six women from Andover who confessed that because "some gentlemen" so often and forcefully told them they were witches, they came to believe it. There was the case of Sarah Churchill, who was persuaded to confess, first by the threat that she would otherwise be thrown into the dungeon with George Burroughs, whom she had helped condemn, and second by realizing that she could deny having signed the book a hundred times and no one would believe her, but if she admitted it only once she would be left alone. And there were those who confessed because their families and friends urged them to, especially when it became clear that the confessed would not be hanged, at least not immediately. One group of six confessed witches made this motive clearer: "Our nearest and dearest relations . . . apprehending that there was no other way to save our lives . . . but by our confessing . . . they out of tender love and pity persuaded us to confess what we did confess."[60] Of the over fifty people who confessed, none was executed.

Such measures may not have constituted torture, as it was known on the continent of Europe, but they were sufficiently harsh to prevent historians from accepting the Court's position that the confessions were freely given. Moreover, they were very effective in soliciting a sufficient number of confessions to lend substance and credibility to the witch trials for several weeks. But what exactly did the confessions say? What common elements did they contain that might tell us something about the Salem witch trials and the culture that produced them?

Larry Gragg, for one, has found a revealing pattern in the confessions of 1692. The Devil, the confessions suggest, disguised as a cunning black man, approached people at vulnerable times in their lives. A number were experiencing financial difficulties. William Barker, for example, was finding it difficult to provide for his family. A few had frustrated love lives: Mercy Wardwell was convinced that no young man would ever love her. Some were experiencing guilt over their actions, like Rebecca Eames, who was despondent over an adulterous relationship and an attempted suicide. Others had lost their faith, like Hannah Bromage, who "had been under some deadness with respect to the ordinances for the matter of six weeks." And still others had developed uncontrollable fears of the various worldly threats to life and limb with which they were surrounded. Mary Toothaker, for example, was terrified by the repeated rumors of renewed Indian attacks.[61]

To such troubled individuals, the Devil offered resolution, but to even more he promised other rewards: fine clothes, a comfortable life, "happiness and joy," "a pair of French fall shoes," and even "crowns in Hell." Whatever the ploy, the confessors reported that the Devil had been persuasive, recruiting some of the accused as much as twenty years earlier. Moreover, he had even been able to attract the young, like twelve-year-old Mary Bridges, to cite just one example not mentioned earlier.[62]

Similar to what was reported in Europe in the seventeenth century, joining the Devil, the New England confessors of 1692 revealed, involved two important rituals: signing the Devil's book, or at least making one's mark, and being baptized by him. Some signed with pen and ink. Others made their mark with pricked and bleeding fingers and in a number of other ways. Once they had signed, however, the Devil took them to a pond or a river and baptized them, either by partial or total immersion, whereupon the baptized renounced Christ and yielded to Satan their "soul and body."[63]

Once baptized, the Devil's recruits were obligated to attend witches' meetings, that had occurred, confessors testified, in places such as Samuel Parris's field or in Andover at either Chandler's garrison or Joseph Ballard's home. The meetings could be observed only by those who had covenanted with the Devil, because, as Mary Lacey Jr. explained, the Devil "puts a mist before" the eyes of ordinary people and "will not let them see." Witches traveled to their meetings, or went about their diabolical business, on foot or by horseback or wagon, or they flew on sticks or poles.[64]

Confessors' estimates as to the numbers of those attending witches' Sabbaths in the area ranged from a handful to twenty-five, seventy-seven, "six score," or even 200—305, 307, or even 500 were seen at Sabbaths elsewhere. George Burroughs often presided, as did the Devil himself, and the ceremony included a sermon and a mock communion. During the sermon, the presider called upon those gathered to advance the Devil's triumph over Christianity by afflicting others, thereby weakening their allegiance to Christ's kingdom. He prophesied that the Devil would triumph over Christianity. The communion involved white or brown bread and blood-red sacramental wine, often drawn from pots or barrels in earthen cups.[65]

Notably missing from the confessions of 1692, Richard Godbeer has pointed out, are references to sex, certainly as compared to the sexual preoccupation of continental Europeans during the Great European Witch-hunt. It may be recalled from chapter one that according to the European model, once the formal business of the witches' Sabbath was concluded, participants "broke into lascivious dancing and soon fell upon each other in a frenzy of sexual abandon." Witches engaged in various sexual acts, and the Devil worked his way through the company copulating with all present, men and women alike.[66]

Whereas sex with the Devil was a central characteristic of witchcraft lore on the continent, it was not in England—save for some of the confessions that resulted from the prosecutions of Matthew Hopkins during the 1640s—or in New England. Prior to 1692 in New England, Godbeer has found, only two women who confessed to witchcraft claimed that they had engaged in sexual acts with the Devil. During the Salem witch trials, such confessions were entirely absent. Only two of the depositions given by hostile witnesses even hinted at sexual relations between witches and the Devil. Edward Bishop claimed that the Devil had "come unto" his wife Bridget, that she was "familiar with the Devil," and that "she sat up all the night long with the Devil." Similarly accused witch Rebecca Eames testified that although she did not know Sarah Parker (one of the accused) to be a witch, she had heard that Parker had been "crossed in love" and that "the Devil had come to her and kissed her."[67]

Carol Karlsen has found evidence to suggest that there existed a connection in some seventeenth-century New England cases between accusations of witchcraft and prior illicit sexual behavior. She has estimated that twenty-three women accused of witchcraft had also been "explicitly charged with sexual excesses, either during their witch trials or during the years preceding the accusations."[68] In two of the Salem cases, a connection was made between illicit sexual behavior and witchcraft. Evidence given against Bridget Bishop and Susannah Martin suggests that male neighbors and acquaintances found them sexually provocative and linked that perception to suspicions of witchcraft. Male deponents claimed that Bishop and Martin had visited them at night and subjected them to various physical actions that could be seen as being of a sexual nature. About Bishop's activities along this line, we have already spoken. Martin visited Bernard Peach's bedroom one night and "lay upon him about an hour and a half."[69] Such explicit references, however, were few, exceptional, and comparatively tame.

The emphasis on sex in European accounts, Godbeer has argued, was intended to reinforce an official campaign against sexual license. Its absence from descriptions in New England could have been the result of a lesser concern for such behavior, but Godbeer has suggested that it might also have been intended to emphasize the similarity between witches' and Christian Sabbath activities, thereby posing a very different sort of challenge to official values. Witch behavior in Europe was portrayed as the inversion of order, sanctity, and virtue. As such, it was used by authorities in a campaign to acculturate and subordinate the peasantry. By portraying an ideological polarity between Christian order and diabolical disorder, authorities could better teach peasants that all forms of behavior fell into one of those two categories, and that the first was possible only by rejecting the second.[70]

In New England, rather than inverting orthodox behavior, Godbeer has pointed out, accounts drawn from confessions portray witch behavior that actually mimicked that of the Puritan community. Instead of using its opposite to validate acceptable behavior, the stereotype that emerged "equated the godly and diabolical communities," or, as the Reverend Deodat Lawson put it, made the Devil's "Kingdom and Administrations to resemble those of our Lord Jesus Christ." This congruity, Godbeer has argued, "constituted a thinly veiled attack on Puritan orthodoxy itself." Satanism and Puritanism were interchangeable. The black figure was analogous to the Puritan minister; the Devil's book to the Bible; his rituals of worship, including the consumption of bread and wine, to those of good Christians; and the signing of the diabolical pact and related rituals to Christian baptism.[71]

Once again, in contrast to what occurred in Europe, Godbeer has concluded that the creation of this stereotype was attributable to the confessors only, not to the ministry. The ministers, after all, could only stand to lose by it. Confessors stood to gain in that while taking advantage of a way to escape execution, suspects could attack their prosecutors by suggesting that the society they were accused of having joined and the society that sought to reclaim or destroy them were essentially one and the same. "By equating the godly and the diabolical, confessors transformed an act of surrender into one of resistance and defiance," and in the process shocked and insulted authority.[72]

Finally, perhaps most terrifying to those who listened and believed, was the confessors' common insistence that the Devil had employed them in order "to pull down the Kingdom of Christ." According to William Barker, the reader will recall, the Devil had selected Salem village to begin his campaign because the people had been divided and differed with their ministers. After destroying the village church, Barker commented, the Devil would move to Salem town "and so go through the country." The Devil would "make as many witches" as he could and eventually establish his kingdom. In that kingdom, confessors explained, the Devil promised "happy days." In a direct challenge to all for which Puritan New England stood, and that no doubt appealed to many who had become disillusioned with the rigorous Puritan ideals of the Bible Commonwealth, "all persons should be equal; there should be no day of resurrection or of judgment, and neither punishment nor shame for sin."[73]

Cotton Mather, like many of his clerical contemporaries and predecessors in Old and New England, was willing to dismiss some of the confessions as being little more than the "delusions of Satan." But he argued that most should be believed. They had been made by "intelligent persons of all ages, in sundry towns, at several times," and often they were "harmonious."[74] As Thomas Brattle wrote to a friend on October 8, 1692:

> The great cry of our neighbors now is what, will you not believe the confessors? Will you not believe men and women who confess that they have signed to the Devil's book? That they were baptized by the Devil; and that they were at the mock-sacrament once and again? What, will you not believe that this is witchcraft, and that such and such men are witches?[75]

Many did believe the confessors, including the judges of the Court of Oyer and Terminer. But, by October, some had begun to have their doubts.

9

"It Were Better That Ten Suspected Witches Should Escape, Than That One Innocent Person Should Be Condemned"

Perhaps it is appropriate that we begin our discussion about the end of the Salem witch trials with the spectral appearance of Mary Easty. On September 22, 1692, the same day she was hanged and the Court of Oyer and Terminer adjourned, the ghost of Mary Easty appeared in Wenham, Massachusetts, to a seventeen-year-old girl, Mary Herrick. "I am going upon the ladder to be hanged for a witch," Easty said, "but I am innocent and before a twelfth-month be past you shall believe it." Then Easty vanished.[1]

Wenham, although close to Salem, had escaped the ravages of the witchcraft hysteria. Nevertheless, Mary Herrick no doubt was informed about what was happening, and she quite likely had heard of Mary Easty. Whether or not she sympathized with Easty we cannot tell, but Herrick said nothing at first regarding her visit. Soon after, however, she began to experience pains. No physical cause could be found, but when the specter of the wife of the Reverend John Hale appeared to her, Herrick assumed Mrs. Hale was her tormentor. Hale appeared regularly, and Herrick concluded that it was her hand that pinched and choked her.[2]

At length, Mrs. Hale spoke, "Do you think I am a witch?" "No! You be the Devil!" Herrick replied. Easty, who then reappeared, had successfully carried out her ploy. She explained to Herrick that "she had been put to death wrongfully," that she was innocent, and that she had come "to vindicate her cause." She cried, "Vengeance! Vengeance!" and ordered Herrick to tell the Reverend Hale and her own pastor, Joseph Gerrish, what she had witnessed, whereupon she, Easty, would rise no more and the specter of the innocent Mrs. Hale would no longer afflict her.[3]

Mary Herrick understood the lesson she had been taught, and she followed Easty's orders. She told Gerrish about the "delusion of the Devil" she had witnessed, and the two met with, and informed, the Reverend Hale. Hale was no doubt stunned by Herrick's report. He knew his wife was innocent, and if her specter could appear, if she could be cried out against and evidence offered against her that the Court could use to condemn her, might not others have been wrongfully condemned? Although he may have had doubts prior to this point, Hale resolved that the continued use of spectral evidence was wrong. Clearly, as some had warned all along, God could permit, and no doubt had permitted, the Devil to use the shape of the innocent to delude those obsessed with his presence among them.[4]

VOICES ARE RAISED IN OPPOSITION TO THE TRIALS

The ghost of Mary Easty, of course, was not the only, or even the most consequential, factor contributing to doubts concerning the witch trials. For various other reasons—including the integrity of the accused and their admirable behavior even though condemned to an almost certain death—a growing number of people began to have second thoughts. As summer ended, one of the leading causes of discontent was the sudden rush of recantations.

Several of the recantations have already been noted. Tituba admitted she had lied, blaming it on Parris's mistreatment of her, but in notable contrast to her confession little was made of it.[5] Thomas Brattle reported that in late summer several confessors "recanted their confessions, acknowledging, with sorrow and grief, that it was an hour of great temptation with them."[6] When Increase Mather visited the Salem jail on October 19, he found that most of the several confessors there (he noted eight by name) were eager to renounce their earlier testimonies. He reported that those who had confessed were filled with horror and anguish at what they had done, both to themselves and to others they had implicated, and that they were willing to renounce those confessions even though it might well lead to their execution.[7]

Public petitions to the Court and open criticism of its procedures became more frequent. By early October, almost 300 people had offered support, largely through petitions, for one or more of the accused, and critics such as Robert Calef, Thomas Maule, and Thomas Brattle began to make their sentiments known. Calef's criticism has already been noted. A Salem Quaker, Thomas Maule, stated that he believed the entire affair had been fabricated from the petty hates and envies of the community, and that it all could be brought to an end if people would simply obey the injunction, "love your enemies." Maule further asked his fellow Salem residents who could count themselves among the wholly guiltless in matters of witchcraft. It was, he offered, like the biblical story of Jesus' response to those who would stone the woman taken in adultery (John 8:7), to wit, he wrote, "He that is wholly clear of every degree of witchcraft may cast a stone at witches."[8]

Thomas Brattle offered his thoughts on the Salem witch trials. Brattle, a successful, wealthy, and well-regarded Boston merchant, who was also a mathematician, an astronomer, a member of the Royal Society, and an experienced traveler, stated his ideas in the form of a public letter, dated October 8, 1692, to an unnamed correspondent of the clerical profession. Brattle characterized Oyer and Terminer Chief Justice William Stoughton as "very zealous" in the proceedings and "very impatient" of criticism. He had great respect for Stoughton in most matters, Brattle allowed, but in this matter "wisdom and counsel are withheld from his honor." Brattle claimed that the judge's class bias prevented him from dispensing justice to all of the suspects and that the rich often escaped punishment. In particular, he cited Margaret Thatcher, Judge Jonathan Corwin's sixty-seven-year-old mother-in-law, who had been named by several of the afflicted but had never been formally charged, as well as escapees Elizabeth Cary, Philip and Mary English, and John Alden, who had never even been pursued.[9]

Brattle denounced the use of spectral evidence, but he went even further, abandoning the tact others had employed. He described the testimony that the afflicted and confessed offered of witches' Sabbaths, the Devil's baptisms, and mock sacraments as "nothing else but the effect of their fancy, depraved and deluded by the Devil." He accused the judges of having allowed testimony from the Devil himself, through witnesses who swore to what they said the Devil communicated to them. And he condemned the judges for excusing the accusing girls and confessing witches when they contradicted each other by saying that the Devil in such circumstances had momentarily taken away their memory, obscured their brains, and misled them.[10]

It was a disgrace, Brattle continued, that the magistrates had based their judgments on such evidence as common gossip, irresponsible confessions, and the pretensions of the afflicted girls. He charged the girls with lying, but he also denounced those "Salem gentlemen" who had encouraged them in the prosecutions, as well as those of Boston who had supported them. To make his point, Brattle made it clear that he believed the charges brought by the accusing girls had been fraudulent, but he also pointed out that in some cases they could not have been the ones generating the accusations. "[S]everal persons," he wrote, "have been apprehended purely upon the complaint of these afflicted, [and] to whom the afflicted were perfect strangers."[11]

Brattle, as well as any, saw the predicament in which the Court found itself, and he did not minimize it. "I am sensible that it is irksome and disagreeable to go back when a man's doing so is an implication that he has been walking in the wrong path." "However," he concluded, "nothing is more honorable than, upon due conviction, to retract and undo (so far as may be) what has been amiss and irregular."[12]

Unlike others who had thus far either written anonymously, or used only their initials, Brattle signed his full name to his letter. Open defiance without fear of reprisal was now possible. Moreover, he ended his open letter by reporting that he knew several people "about the Bay" of intelligence, judgment, and piety, who had also come to condemn the proceedings.[13]

Contrary to what is commonly believed, some of the most effective opposition to the Salem witch trials came from Massachusetts ministers. To be sure, the Reverend Samuel Parris played a key role in the outbreak of the witchcraft hysteria, as did the Reverends Nicholas Noyes and Deodat Lawson. They may have been true believers, or perhaps, as has been charged, they merely sought to reestablish their lost authority, but there were few others who openly supported the trials. Many stepped forward to defend the accused. There were, for example, the Reverend Dane, who managed to turn the tide of opinion in Andover; ministers Payson and Phillips of Rowley, who defended Elizabeth How; and the Reverend Wise of Ipswich, who spoke out on John Proctor's behalf. Unsung and largely forgotten ministers in Marblehead, Topsfield, Salisbury, and elsewhere did much the same, the case of the Salisbury minister being representative.[14]

On August 9, 1692, "R. P."—Salisbury minister Robert Pike—drafted a letter to Judge Jonathan Corwin. At first, Pike had only followed events in Salem from a distance. When Nathaniel Saltonstall resigned from the Court of Oyer and Terminer and Corwin took his place, however, Pike visited Salem to make some firsthand observations. Later he became involved in the cases of Mary Bradbury of Salisbury and Susannah Martin, the latter who was known there. Pike had taken the formal depositions of the residents of the town in those cases, but he was skeptical of what he had heard. Thus he joined dozens of Bradbury's neighbors in petitioning the Court of Oyer and Terminer on her behalf.[15]

The Burroughs trial had just ended, and Pike wrote that he had come to believe that the trials had left the lives of innocent people "to the pleasure and passion of those that are minded to take them away." The witnesses were not only informers, he continued, "but sole judges of the crime." Pike emphasized the "doubtfulness and unsafety" of admitting spectral evidence "against the life of any that are of blameless conversation, and plead innocent," and he asked just how witchcraft was to be proved under such circumstances. Were reports of witches' Sabbaths in Parris's pasture to be trusted? Was it appropriate that the testimony of what appeared to him to be erratic witnesses carry such weight in condemning others who had seemed quite innocent? Had not the Devil once carried Christ himself from place to place to tempt him and yet left him innocent? Might witch marks simply be a product of nature? And had not confessions often been "necessitated"?[16]

Implying that the girls might be possessed, not afflicted, Pike asked who it was that had pointed out to the Salem girls things that they could not see, but the Devil, especially when some things that they had reported were false and mistaken. "Is the Devil a competent witness in such a case?" he asked. And how reliable was the touch test on which the judges had placed such emphasis? Was it likely that the accused, appearing in a court of law where they had been charged with witchcraft, would in full view of all practice their arts openly? Such actions would only contribute to their condemnation, he reasoned, leading him to conclude that if that were the case the Devil had "become a reformer to purge . . . witches out of the world"![17]

Although written in the form of a personal letter, Pike's having addressed such leading questions to a member of the Court of Oyer and Terminer was a daring move. But even more prominent ministers stepped forward to oppose the trials, including some who had previously supported the witch-hunt. Samuel Willard was typical of this group. In March, Willard publicly endorsed Deodat Lawson's famous Salem sermon that drove the prosecutions forward, but by late summer he began to express his doubts to the three judges of the Court of Oyer and Terminer, who were also members of his congregation. In

October, he published, although anonymously and in Philadelphia, a work titled *Some Miscellany Observations on Our Present Debates Respecting Witchcraft in a Dialogue Between S and B* (Salem and Boston, or possibly Chief Justice William Stoughton and Thomas Brattle).

In his *Dialogue, B,* Willard's mouthpiece, called the accusers in the Salem witch trials "scandalous persons, liars, and loose in their conversation," as well as disqualified as reliable witnesses by the fact of their affliction. By Willard's observation, the girls, with their extraordinary sight, predictions, and discovery of secrets, rather than supporting the proposition that they were afflicted, had only shown themselves to be either witches or possessed. Such powers, he insisted, were necessarily the result of one or the other, and, he wrote, "I charitably believe the latter of them [that they were possessed]."[18]

That when the girls had been brought before the accused they were struck down by a mere glance and raised up by a touch of the hand Willard called an illusion, and use of it as evidence "utterly unlawful" and "exceedingly fallacious"—to say nothing, he reminded his readers, of being "borrowed from Popish exorcists"! And Willard too renounced the use of spectral evidence. "If the fact may be done and yet the persons doing it be innocent of the crime," he reasoned, "the verdict is merely conjectural, and the man dies by will and doom; whereas God hath not granted to man such a power over others' lives."[19]

The reaction to Willard's critique was predictable, even by Willard. "You are an admirable advocate of witches," S responded to B, as had been the response to others who had raised questions concerning the trials. And indeed Willard would be cried out against soon thereafter, but he was never formally charged and his opposition to the trials only grew, as did the criticism of others.[20]

On October 12, seven Andover residents petitioned the General Court to have their wives and children released on bond "to remain as prisoners in their own houses," where they might be "more tenderly cared for." The petitioners spoke of the "distressed condition in prison" of the condemned, their grief, and the prospect of the descending winter cold dispatching "such out of the way that have not been used to such hardships."[21] On October 18, twenty-four Andover residents led by ministers Francis Dane and Thomas Bernard, addressed a similar memorial to Governor Phips and the General Court. In that petition, the Andover residents acknowledged that they considered what had happened "the heavy judgment" of a "righteous God" upon them from which they wished to be purged. They explained that they did not want to be seen as defending those who "should be found guilty of so horrid a crime" as witchcraft, but that they believed it was possible that some among the accused had been misrepresented, and they wished to speak on their behalf, "having no other design therein, than that the truth may appear."[22]

The petitioners reported that most of the accused had never given them the least occasion to be suspected of witchcraft. Several of the women were members of the church in full communion and were well-regarded for "their walking as becometh women professing godliness." It was true, they allowed, that many of the accused had confessed, and if such confessions had been freely given, the petitioners continued, they had nothing to plead. But, they added, the petitioners had reason to believe otherwise—namely that "the extreme urgency" that had been used with some of them by their friends and others who had privately examined them, and the fear they were then under, may have induced them to confess, only to later repent their actions.[23]

Finally, the petitioners called the accusing girls "distempered persons" and protested the position of authority they had assumed in court. If that were not changed, they reasoned, the colony's troubles were likely not only to continue but even to grow worse. "We know not who can think himself safe," they warned, "if the accusations of children and others who are under a diabolical influence shall be received against persons of good fame."[24]

Phips Dismisses the Court of Oyer and Terminer

In October 1692, in the midst of this growing opposition to the Court of Oyer and Terminer, Governor William Phips returned once again to Boston. What he no doubt hoped would be settled in his absence had only grown worse. His own wife had been accused, but not yet formally charged! Thomas Brattle may have described Phips's predicament best. On October 8, he wrote, several men of "understanding, judgment, and piety, inferior to few" had publicly condemned the proceedings as likely to "utterly ruin and undo poor New England." Included on Brattle's list were former Governor Simon Bradstreet, former Deputy Governor Thomas Danforth, Increase Mather, Samuel Willard, and Nathaniel Saltonstall. Except for the Reverends Hale, Noyes, and Parris, Brattle continued, "almost [everyone] throughout the whole country . . . [was] very much dissatisfied."[25]

Brattle may have overstated the case, but it is clear that Phips had little choice but to act. On October 12, he reported on what had happened thus far to William Blathwayt, clerk of England's Privy Council, charged with advising the Crown on matters related to the colonies. Phips made it clear from the start that once having established the Court of Oyer and Terminer, and while the trials were proceeding, he had been occupied in the service of the Crown "in the eastern part of the country." He noted that upon his arrival in May, he had encountered "a province miserably harassed with a most horrible witchcraft or possession of devils," but that he had left Boston with confidence in the judgment of the Court to resolve matters. When he returned, however, he had found "many persons in a strange ferment of dissatisfaction which was increased by some hot springs that blew up the flame."[26]

Phips reported that the Court of Oyer and Terminer had convicted more than twenty people of practicing witchcraft, and that some of the convicted had confessed their guilt. He explained that he had been told (quite likely by Cotton Mather from whom he had commissioned a report on the affair), that the Court had begun its proceedings with the accusations of the afflicted girls but added to it "other humane evidences" to strengthen each case. As that was the source of some contention, however, Phips had inquired into the matter and found that "the Devil had taken upon him the name and shape of several persons who were doubtless innocent" and to his knowledge of good reputation.[27]

As a result, Phips had forbidden any further incarceration of those who might yet be accused "without unavoidable necessity" and any further action taken against those already committed "wherein there may be the least suspicion of any wrong to be done unto the innocent." Phips also banned any further printing of statements for or against the trials that might kindle "an inextinguishable flame." Phips ended his letter by lamenting that there were those who were seeking to place all of the blame on him for what had happened, but that he was not willing to go any further than he had until he heard from their majesties.[28]

Nevertheless, Phips and the colonial legislature did act prior to their having received instructions from England. On October 26, the Massachusetts General Court called for a fast and for a "convocation of ministers" that they might "be led in the right way as to the witchcraft."[29] Those ministers, including the most prominent clerics in Massachusetts, gathered in Cambridge. Cotton Mather was present, as was Samuel Willard, but all deferred to Increase Mather to prepare their response, which was subsequently published under the title *Cases of Conscience Concerning Evil Spirits Personating Men* (1693).

Increase Mather, who like Willard had endorsed Lawson's Salem sermon and who would express his approbation of his son's defense of the Salem witch trials in *The Wonders of the Invisible World*, did not qualify his belief in witchcraft. He acknowledged that there were bewitched, as well as possessed, individuals. In reference to the girls of Salem, he did not specifically rule out the latter, but he implied the former, explaining that there was a seemingly unending diversity of ways by which God permitted the Devil to afflict his people. Drawing upon a number of important texts, including his own *An Essay for the Recording of Illustrious Providences* (1684), he confirmed the power of the Devil and his minions to, among other things, "steal money out of men's pockets and purses, or wine and cider out of their cellars," to throw "fire on the tops of houses, and to cause a whole town to be burnt to ashes." God had allowed the Devil "to violently carry away persons through the air, several miles from their habitations," he wrote, as well as to cause the dead to appear before the living. In sum, Mather insisted, the Devil was an ever-present reality in their lives. But, he continued, the Devil was also a master of deception, and all might not be as it appeared, especially regarding those believed to be associated with him:

> The father of lies is never to be believed. He will utter twenty great truths to make way for one lie. He will accuse twenty witches, if he can but thereby bring one innocent person into trouble.[30]

As he and his ministerial colleagues, including his son Cotton, had done in the past, Increase Mather warned against relying on spectral evidence. Although "such things are rare and extraordinary, especially when such matters come before civil judicature," he wrote, the Devil can "represent an innocent person." He offered examples from scripture of the Devil taking an innocent's shape, and he argued that the Devil could employ the afflicted as instruments to destroy the innocent and even the saints of God. Since the Devil "has perfect skills in optics," he explained, he could cause the afflicted to see whatever he wished, making things "appear far otherwise than they are." The afflicted could see things "through diabolical mediums," and therefore the Devil could impose on their imaginations. He could cause them to believe that an innocent person was afflicting them when the Devil himself was responsible.[31]

Mather allowed that spectral evidence could be admitted in a limited way as evidence in a court of law—that it could be used, for example, to raise suspicion—but that it should not be used as the basis for conviction. "To take away the life of anyone, merely because a specter or devil in a bewitched or possessed person does accuse them," he wrote, "will bring the guilt of innocent blood on the land." Further,

Mather denounced the use of the sight and touch tests. He pointed out that there was substantial evidence to show that people fall into fits for a variety of reasons—"at the sight of brute-creatures, cats, spiders . . . [or even] at the sight of cheeses, milk, [or] apples." He insisted that no one person had the "natural power" to look upon others and bewitch them nor to touch them and cure their affliction. Such powers were supernatural, he insisted. Those who depended on them for evidence were relying on occult techniques, and, he concluded, "we ought not to practice witchcrafts to discover witches."[32]

Still, Mather did not directly criticize the judges of the Court of Oyer and Terminer. Neither did he state specifically that it had erred in condemning those they had already found guilty. By his estimation, the judges were "wise and good men," and they had "acted with all fidelity according to their light" and had "out of tenderness" declined doing some things with which the ministers would have been dissatisfied. He did not quarrel with the judges' assertion that they had not convicted anyone "merely on the account of what specters ha[d] said, or of what ha[d] been represented to the eyes or imaginations of sick bewitched persons." And in the only trial he actually witnessed, that of George Burroughs, Mather not only concurred but admitted that he would have found Burroughs guilty as well.[33]

Nevertheless, Increase Mather, on behalf of the fourteen prominent New England Puritan divines who signed their names to what he had written, including Cotton Mather, called into question much of the evidence upon which the Court of Oyer and Terminer had relied. Coming at a time when there had already been considerable doubt cast upon its proceedings, that alone may have been sufficient to cause authorities to move against the Court. But, then, there were Mather's closing words—those that signaled an important turning point in the thinking that had guided the Salem witch trials thus far. In response to those, like Deodat Lawson, who had argued that to ensure that none of the guilty go free, it might be necessary to condemn some of the innocent, Mather wrote, "It were better that ten suspected witches should escape, than that one innocent person should be condemned."[34]

If *Cases of Conscience* was not sufficient to cause authorities to act against the Court of Oyer and Terminer, it received help from a quite unexpected quarter. In late October, Governor Phips received opinions about issues related to the Salem witch trials from four Dutch and French Calvinist ministers living in New York: Henry Selijns, Peter Peiretus, Godfrey Dellius, and Rudolph Varich. Their views had been solicited and sent to Phips by Joseph Dudley, former Deputy Governor of Massachusetts, under Edmund Andros, who, since Andros's removal and his release from prison in that bloodless coup, had left Boston for an appointment as New York's Chief Justice. Dudley remained a Bostonian at heart, but for a time he was unpopular. Perhaps he saw this as one way of regaining favor.[35]

Dudley was clearly well-informed on events in Salem, from his correspondence as well as from the firsthand experiences of those who had fled to New York as fugitives, like the Englishes and the Carys. With that information, Dudley posed a series of questions relevant to the trials and sent them to the above-mentioned ministers, who although not English were highly regarded by Puritan divines. As noted in Chapter two, there had been few witch trials in seventeenth-century New Netherlands, because Dutch theologians and public officials had tempered their fear of witches, or thereafter in New York, under British rule. A skeptical response to what was happening in Salem was therefore to be expected, but more importantly what they had to say served to confirm what had been offered by Increase Mather and the other Massachusetts ministers, as well as the Court's several other critics.[36]

In brief, Dudley asked if spectral evidence could be trusted. "By no means," the ministers responded. God often permitted seemingly inexplicable things to happen to good people, and He has often demonstrated that He would use "any instrument to turn evil into good." Therefore, no one should be surprised if God allowed the Devil to abuse the specter of an innocent person, and to convict on the basis of such evidence would be "the greatest imprudence."[37]

Dudley asked about evidence of previous malice, but once again the ministers were skeptical. Honest men could have their fallings-out, they responded, but the Devil, subtle as he was, would take pains to avoid performing under such obvious circumstances. Although it was possible, it was not probable that a person whose whole life had been otherwise outwardly virtuous would be guilty of witchcraft. "An honest and charitable life and conduct of long continuance, such as meets with universal approbation," therefore, would "probably" remove any suspicion of criminal intent on the part of those who had been accused of witchcraft by the afflicted.[38]

Regarding the afflicted girls, the New York divines were kind but firm. Whereas Brattle, for example, had denounced them as liars, the New York divines allowed that their affliction could be real enough, and yet not physical at all. At the same time, if they were deluded by the Devil, they were in the worst possible position to identity the cause of their affliction. And on it went, until the New York ministers had called into question all of the principal procedural points and elements

the Court of Oyer and Terminer had relied in its trials and
ctions.[39]

)onse to the General Court's calling for a fast and for a con-
ministers to consider "the right way" to be taken by the
people of Massachusetts in the witch trials, Samuel Sewall wrote in his
diary, "The season and manner of doing it is such that the Court of
Oyer and Terminer count themselves dismissed."[40] And sure enough,
three days later, on October 29, in receipt of all of the foregoing critical commentary, Governor Phips dismissed the court.

THE JAILS ARE EMPTIED

In some respects, the repercussions of Phips's actions were immediate. Through the end of October, charges continued to be brought
against suspected witches, but the rate of accusations slowed to a
trickle. To cite just one example, in October, the residents of Gloucester, Massachusetts, having reason to believe that things diabolical
were afoot in their community, summoned the Salem girls to investigate. The girls found four witches in their midst. In November, the girls
returned to complete the job but were simply ignored. Try as they may,
the girls' fits failed to result in any arrests.[41]

In other ways, however, Phips's actions were less immediately effective. Dismissing the Court of Oyer and Terminer may have brought
about a temporary halt to the trials, and his other edicts may have
slowed the course of the arrests, but at least fifty—and quite likely
more—remained in jail awaiting trial or execution. Perhaps the single
largest group among those still in jail consisted of those whose fate remained particularly unclear—those who had confessed. The Old
Testament and European tradition made it clear: "Thou shalt not suffer a witch to live" (Exodus 22:18). In November 1692, however, in the
cases of the confessed, the directive had not yet been implemented.

The principal reason for the stays of execution was to provide for
the continued testimony of the confessed against their more recalci-
trant fellow travelers. At some point, however, their testimony would
no longer be needed, and then what? Paul Boyer, Stephen Nissenbaum,
and Carol Karlsen have concluded that the judges planned to execute
the confessors once their testimony was no longer needed. The English
divine, William Perkins, whom New England Puritans found instructive on several related matters, had written that those who confessed
to witchcraft should be given time to examine their souls, but then justice was to be done.[42] Larry Gragg, however, has suggested that the
Court may have been preparing to spare the lives of those who had con-

fessed and repented. As evidence, he has cited the case of Mary Lacey Jr., wherein the judges told her that if she would freely confess and repent, she would "obtain mercy . . . [and] be saved by Christ," as well as the judges' instructions to John Willard, "If you can therefore find in your heart to repent, it is possible you may obtain mercy." He has referred to the case of Dorcas Hoar, wherein upon her confession Hoar's execution, the date of which had already been set, was postponed "until further notice," but even Gragg has admitted that at the end of October the fate of the confessed remained unclear.[43]

Winter was in the air, and prisons in Salem, Ipswich, Boston, Cambridge, and Charlestown, already dark and dank, unheated and unhealthy, were overflowing to the point where private contractors were being hired to care for many of the prisoners in their homes, barns, or other buildings. No such crime wave had ever hit the colony and the system was simply not prepared for it. The conditions of their incarceration, which included their being heavily manacled, broke the spirit and health of many. Sarah Osborne and Roger Toothaker of Billerica, Ann Foster of Andover, and Sarah Good's newborn had already died in captivity, and others were seriously ill. Phips was not ready to see the death toll rise any further.[44]

Phips turned to the petitions he had received for the release of various prisoners. Some were quite young, like Dorothy and Abigail Faulkner, who were ten and eight years old, respectively; Stephen and Abigail Johnson, who were thirteen and eleven years old, respectively; and Sarah Carrier, who was eight years old. Others were the mothers of large families, and it was reported that their incarceration had placed a burden on their communities to care for their children. The list of such special petitions was long, and Phips found it persuasive. He reconsidered the evidence used in those and other cases, and when it was only primarily spectral he released those prisoners on bond into the custody of their families. Some remained in jail, but Phips made their care and well-being the responsibility of the judges. They were not to be allowed to suffer.[45]

In his second letter to the Privy Council, dated February 21, 1693, Phips continued to explain what he had done. He reported that in the weeks after his October communication, he had grown even more skeptical of the Court of Oyer and Terminer's procedures, especially of their use of spectral evidence, and he had begun to fear that, as many had charged, it had condemned innocent people. Indicating that he was not the only person to have reached that conclusion, Phips wrote that the Deputy Governor and Chief Justice Stoughton had nevertheless "persisted vigorously in the same method, to the great dissatisfaction and disturbance of the people," forcing Phips to put an end to the Court, fearing that if he did not "many innocent people might otherwise perish."[46]

There being at least fifty people who were still in prison (but quite likely many more) suffering from "the extreme cold" and too poor to take better care of themselves, Phips continued, he resolved to take two further steps.[47] First, as has been noted, he released on bail those against whom only spectral evidence had been used. Second, he decided to bring all of the outstanding cases to resolution. As certain judges of the Court of Oyer and Terminer had acknowledged that "their former proceedings were too violent and not grounded upon a right foundation," and intimated that if they were to sit again they would proceed differently, Phips was encouraged to establish a second court. First, however, they found it necessary to clarify the law concerning witchcraft.[48]

THE SUPERIOR COURT of JUDICATURE

On December 14, the General Court passed a new measure intended to provide a better "explanation of the law against witchcraft," "more particular direction" for its execution, better restraint of such offenses, and more severe punishment for those found guilty of such crimes. At the same time, however, following the example set by England in its legislation on witchcraft, Massachusetts recognized that the uses to which witchcraft could be made varied in terms of the degree of harm done, and that the punishment in each case should vary as well, befitting the crime.[49]

In summary, those who were found to invoke any evil or wicked spirit; covenant with such spirit; raise from the grave any dead person; use any part of the body of a deceased individual in any manner of witchcraft; or practice any witchcraft, whereby any person would be killed, wasted, or lamed, "shall suffer pains of death." Anyone who was convicted of employing witchcraft to discover treasures; provoke anyone to "unlawful love"; destroy or impair the property of others; or hurt another person would be imprisoned for one year and made to stand in the pillory wearing on his or her breast a sign announcing the nature of the crime.[50] If this law had been in effect earlier, it would likely have made a difference for some of the condemned. It would also have made a difference in the future, if the trials to come had resulted in guilty verdicts and the law applied in sentencing, but that was not to be the case.

On December 16, the General Court appointed special sessions of the Superior Court of Judicature to finish the trials. Appointed to the Court were Oyer and Terminer holdovers William Stoughton, who would once again preside, and Samuel Sewall, John Richards, and Wait Winthrop. Added was Thomas Danforth, who had from time to time sat with Hathorne and Corwin in the preliminary examinations, but who had subsequently become a critic of the Court.[51]

Three major procedural changes were made. First, the location of the trials of the Superior Court would no longer be limited to Salem, but rather circulated from Essex County to Middlesex and Suffolk counties, according to the origin of the defendant. Second, the jurors impanelled in each location would be new and different, and as per the terms of the new colonial charter, not drawn exclusively from the Puritan church membership rolls. And third, the judges would limit their use of spectral evidence and the tests of sight and touch. Such evidence could be admitted as presumptive evidence, but it was no longer to be used exclusively, or even primarily, to convict.[52]

The Superior Court met on January 3, 1693, to consider the indictments of some fifty-two of those charged with witchcraft. It met in Salem until January 13, in Charlestown on January 31, in Boston on April 25, and in Ipswich in May (the exact dates were not recorded). In a notable reversal of the pattern set by the Court of Oyer and Terminer, wherein all who appeared before the Court were convicted, forty-nine of the fifty-two cases heard by the Superior Court resulted either in acquittal or dismissal. In Salem, the Superior Court handled twenty cases between January 4 and 13! Only three cases resulted in conviction, and that was on the basis of statements made by the accused themselves. They were Sarah, the wife of Samuel Wardwell, who had confessed; Mary Post, called "senseless and ignorant," but about whom little else is known; and Elizabeth Johnson Jr., whom her grandfather Francis Dane called "simplish at best."[53]

Before leaving Salem for Charlestown, Chief Justice Stoughton turned to five of those who had been condemned by the Court of Oyer and Terminer but who had been temporarily reprieved. Elizabeth Proctor had delivered her baby and was ready to be hanged. The rest were confessing witches. Their testimony, being almost entirely spectral, was no longer needed, and Stoughton appears to have intended to end the Court's practice of sparing those who confessed. They had, after all, admitted their guilt. Governor Phips, however, was hesitant to allow even those convictions to proceed. He sought the advice of the King's Attorney General, Thomas Newton, who concluded that the evidence against them hardly differed from that used against those who had already been cleared, whereupon Phips signed reprieves for all eight.[54]

Stoughton took Phips's action as a direct rebuke of his conduct of the trials. When on January 31 Stoughton, who was sitting on the bench in Charlestown, heard what Phips had done, Phips wrote, he was so "enraged and filled with passionate anger" that he left the bench.[55] According to Robert Calef, Stoughton was overheard to explain that they (the judges) "were in a way to have cleared the land" of witches, but that they had been prevented from doing so. "Who it is that obstructs the course of justice I know not," he continued, but, he concluded, "The Lord be merciful to the country." At that point, Stoughton "went off the bench and came no more to that court," Calef reported. He did return, however, on April 25, when the Court convened in Boston to hear cases from Suffolk County.[56]

In Stoughton's absence and even after his return, the Superior Court continued without fail to clear all who were brought before it. Eighty-one-year-old Sarah Daston was freed, against whom, one of the judges later admitted, there was more evidence than any who had been hanged, as was another of the confessors, Mary Watkins. Watkins, an intermittently deranged indentured servant, upon being caught trying to strangle herself, had volunteered that she was a witch. Reminiscent of the Rebecca Nurse preliminary hearing, the jury of the Superior Court in the Watkins case initially returned an innocent verdict, and the judges returned the verdict to the jury for reconsideration. In this case, however, the jury stood its ground.[57]

Finally, in May, Governor Phips issued a proclamation of general pardon, providing for the release of those still in jail and for the return of refugees from the law. A mere pardon, however, was not enough in some cases to free everyone from prison. Prison fees remained to be paid. In seventeenth-century Massachusetts, prisoners paid for their expenses—food, fuel, clothes, and transportation to and from court, for example—while they availed themselves of the local prison accommodations. Even if they were found not guilty, they still could not leave until they had paid those fees and another fee to cover their discharge. Prices varied from prison to prison, but by one estimate, based on an average stay of four and one-half months, a prisoner faced fees totaling just over four pounds, six shillings. Some, however, were forced to pay much more. Tituba's fee, for example, was about seven pounds.[58]

Given the modest means of most families of the accused, such bills were considerable. Farms had to be mortgaged in some cases to pay for the release of loved ones, but a few had no farms to mortgage and still others had no families to act on their behalf. No one, for example, was interested in the previously mentioned Sarah Daston, who, although found not guilty, remained in prison until she died. The same fate might have befallen Mary Watkins had she not asked the jailer to find her a new master, which he did, from Virginia. Tituba, with whom

Parris would have nothing more to do, and who had been incarcerated the longest, was sold to a new owner, but his name and her fate thereafter are unknown.[59]

Poor Margaret Jacobs, as a final example, who had had the courage to recant her confession on the eve of her grandfather's execution, seemed destined to remain in prison. Old George Jacobs had remembered Margaret in his will, but the will of a condemned witch, especially where it bequeathed to another condemned witch, was not a valid contract. Margaret's father had fled and had not yet returned, and her mother, although acquitted in early January and released, remained distracted and penniless, her other children having been taken in by neighbors. One day, however, the story goes, after eleven months in jail, a stranger heard of Margaret Jacob's plight and he—a person named Gammon, believed to be a fisherman—paid her fees, setting her free.[60]

Even being released did not solve the problems of some of the accused. Elizabeth Proctor, for example, had been found guilty and was sentenced to be executed, but never hanged. Her escape from the gallows, however, and even her pardon did not change her legal status. In the eyes of the law, she was a convicted felon and attainted, or "corrupted in blood," as it was often said. She had no existence in the eyes of the law, and therefore she could claim none of John Proctor's property, not even her dower. It would take more than a decade for Elizabeth Proctor and many others like her, as we shall see in the next chapter, to resolve such legal problems.[61]

THE MAGISTRATES AND THE COURT OF OYER AND TERMINER, GUILTY AS CHARGED?

Before concluding this chapter, a final brief assessment should be offered about the Salem magistrates and the Court of Oyer and Terminer, which condemned every individual that came before it and executed nineteen of those so condemned, twenty if Giles Corey is counted. In reviewing the proceedings as best we can—given the loss of the actual trial transcripts—it is difficult to argue against the commonly held proposition that the actions of both the magistrates and judges were anything less than a miscarriage of justice. It might perhaps be argued that the final decision in each case was left to a jury of peers, but the magistrates and judges established the rules of procedure and the admissibility of evidence and instructed the jury regarding its duty, even to the point, as we have seen, of sending a jury back to reconsider its initial innocent verdict.

Although it was standard procedure for the magistrates and judges to personally examine defendants, even in a prosecutorial fashion, it would seem that they were uncommonly zealous in their questioning. By all reports, leading and ensnaring questions and even a browbeating deportment were ever-present. Assumption of guilt was clearly the unofficial rule, and confessions were vigorously pressed. Although offensive to our sense of justice today, however, these were not uncommon procedures and at what point the Court crossed over the line of acceptable behavior, if indeed it ever did, is unclear. It may well be, as Cotton Mather later reported, that the judges "consulted the precedents of former times, and precepts laid down by learned writers about witchcraft" and acted accordingly.[62]

Among the specific procedural points often questioned by historians is the marshall's being encouraged to watch the every move of the defendants and to report on those who might be seen as causing the afflictions of the young girls—the wringing of one's hands, for example—thereby lending credence to the girls' courtroom antics. It has been noted that accusers continually made private communications to the judges both before and throughout the trials, which were in turn used to put the defendants, who were unrepresented by counsel and unprepared in the law, at a disadvantage. In some cases, as we have seen, false testimony was detected yet unpunished, and the witnesses were allowed to continue to testify, while recanted confessions had no effect on verdicts already rendered.

Although beyond the magistrates' and judges' control to an extent, the atmosphere of the hearings and trials was clearly prejudicial. The number and nature of witnesses and depositions placed before the Court was alarming, and as a whole they both reflected and exacerbated the intense fear that had come to seize the people in and around Salem village. And that intense fear—indeed, near panic—spilled over into the courtroom.

As should be now clear, however, the most egregious miscarriage of justice, intended or not, was the use, or abuse, of spectral evidence. The repeated warnings of those who feared that the magistrates and judges were misusing spectral evidence have already been treated at some length. So too we have seen Hathorne and Corwin state publicly on more than one occasion during the preliminary hearings that, contrary to what others had said, they did not believe the Devil could assume the shape of an innocent person. The evidence suggests that at least most of the judges of the Court of Oyer and Terminer concurred.

Neither the magistrates nor judges, however, admitted to having violated the rules of procedure on the use of spectral evidence. They pointed to the overwhelming amount of evidence, including the dozens of confessions, that to their and their jury's way of thinking served to corroborate spectral evidence. To be fair, it is not always clear how much emphasis the judges and jury placed on one or the other. Further, as we have seen, neither civil nor clerical authorities ever actually charged the Court with the improper use of spectral evidence, but merely warned of its possible abuse in an almost theoretical manner. They continually praised the Court for its handling of the cases it had heard.

In the end, however, a fair and dispassionate reading of the evidence—albeit more than 300 years after the fact—leads to the inevitable conclusion that the magistrates and judges of the Court of Oyer and Terminer were guilty as charged. As Charles Upham has put it, in its use of spectral evidence, "innocent persons were slaughtered by a dogma in the mind of an obstinate judge."[63] Nowhere is that made more evident than in the dramatic reversal of fortune of those who faced the Superior Court, as compared to those who were tried by the Court of Oyer and Terminer.

As it was explained earlier, conviction for the practice of witchcraft under Massachusetts law depended not on proof of harm, or maleficia, but also on evidence of diabolical pact or of the accused's having entered into a covenant with the Devil to secure those powers he or she employed in that act of doing harm. As it has also been noted, the difficulty of establishing such a case in a court of law where spectral evidence was limited, as it was in Massachusetts prior to 1692, resulted in the low and declining rate of conviction that marked the seventeenth century. Witnesses other than the afflicted could testify to occurrences that pointed to the possibility of such diabolical collusion, but only the girls could provide any special and direct knowledge of it, provided, of course, that their spectral sightings were allowed, as they were in the Court of Oyer and Terminer. Once that was eliminated, the trials collapsed.[64]

It is important to note that none of the judges, or likely even their most severe critics, questioned the reality of witchcraft or that something demonic was happening in 1692. What changed was the confidence of both, but especially the latter, in the possibility of determining who was responsible for what had transpired. Increasingly, people were coming to believe that the detection of such supernatural malevolence lay beyond human comprehension. As Samuel Willard came to conclude, the Court should not accept any evidence provided "by extraordinary revelations from God, or by the insinuation of the Devil." Testimony should be based on "that which one man can know concerning another by his senses, and that according to the true nature, and use of them."[65] Historian Richard Godbeer has suggested that in reaching that conclusion, given that charges of witchcraft necessarily dealt with matters that were intrinsically supernatural, the courts of New England were anticipating the position that "legal prosecution for witchcraft was inherently impracticable."[66]

And, finally, we must remind ourselves, lest we judge others too harshly in hindsight, that the Salem magistrates and judges of the Court of Oyer and Terminer were, like those they condemned, the products, if not also the victims, of their time. Much as events of the closing decades of the seventeenth century shook New England, Puritans' confidence in the fundamental aspect of their faith—their federal covenant with God—the crisis of 1692 convinced them that they were a people under siege. Many had come to agree with those such as Samuel Parris, who pictured God's chosen people as being engaged in a great cosmic battle with the Devil to see whose will would prevail and what would be the fate of their "Bible Commonwealth."

If in 1692, New England Puritans, including the Salem magistrates and judges of the Court of Oyer and Teminer, were zealous in their defense or relentless and unforgiving in their prosecution of those they saw as the enemy, it was because they believed that they were observing God's will in an attempt to reincur God's blessing on his errant people. Moreover, to listen to Cotton Mather, they were doing so belatedly, thereby giving their actions an added, if not desperate, sense of urgency. Mather had warned them that the end was near, that the Second Coming was upon them and, as all God-fearing Puritans knew, prior to Christ's Second Coming the Devil would come to destroy Christ's church and in the process seduce even some of Christ's people into his service.

Perhaps U. S. Supreme Court Justice Joseph Story struck the appropriate note of caution one should keep in mind when judging those who condemned the Salem witches to death. On September 18, 1828, in recalling the tragic incident for the people of Salem, he explained:

> We may lament, then, the errors of the times, which led to these prosecutions. But surely our ancestors had no special reason for shame in a belief which had the universal sanction of their own and all former ages; which consulted in its train philosophers, as well as enthusiasts; which was graced by the learning of prelates, as well as by the countenance of kings; which the law supported by its mandates, and the purest judges felt no compunctions in enforcing. Witch Hill remains forever memorable by this sad catastrophe, not to perpetuate our dishonor, but as an affecting, enduring proof of human infirmity; a proof that perfect justice belongs to one judgment-seat only—that which is linked to the throne of God.[67]

10

"Ruined in the Mistaken Management of the Terrible Affair Called Witchcraft"

The trials were over, but Salem's ordeal was not. In his February letter to the Crown, Governor William Phips reported that by his actions "the black cloud that [had] threatened this province with destruction" had dissipated.[1] In some ways it had. Miraculously, the accusing girls had fallen silent, even after the accused were released from jail. Logically, the release of so many witches should have led to an onslaught of affliction, the likes of which the girls had never experienced. Instead, they seemed to rest easy. The people of Massachusetts had not ceased to believe in witches, and some wanted the trials to continue.[2] But even they were no doubt confused by just what had been accomplished during those horrendous months of 1692. Even if at one point they believed that in hunting witches they were observing God's will, many had begun to fear that the hunt had gone awry.

Cotton Mather was one of the first to begin the process of reassessment with his *The Wonders of the Invisible World*. On an unknown date prior to September 20, 1692, Mather, Stephen Sewall, John Higginson, John Hathorne, and William Stoughton met at Samuel Sewall's house in Boston. Governor Phips had asked Mather to prepare a report on the trials, and he had convened the meeting to decide whether to include, and thus make even more widely known to the public, the evidence presented in the several witch trials.[3]

Although the hearings and trials had been open to the public, nothing of any substance had appeared in print about them since Deodat Lawson published his *Brief and True Narrative* the previous spring, which had appeared before the Court of Oyer and Terminer convened. Since then, rumors had abounded, many of them ill-informed, and the time was right for an official report on what the Court had accomplished. It was to be an interim report, as the judges expected to go forward with the trials in October, and although there were some signs of protest among those who met in Boston that September, there was little doubt that the Court was adequately performing its judicial duties.[4]

COTTON MATHER and His "WONDERS OF THE INVISIBLE WORLD"

Cotton Mather, who had been gathering information about the Salem witch trials for some time, agreed to prepare the text. On September 20, he wrote to Stephen Sewall of Salem, seeking further information and in the process making his intentions clear. He explained that "with all sorts of objections" having been raised concerning the trials, he felt obliged to prepare a report whereby he might be able "to assist in lifting up a standard against the infernal enemy." In particular, Mather asked that Sewall "intimate over again" what he had previously told Mather "of the awe which is upon the hearts of your juries . . . unto the validity of the spectral evidences." He requested Sewall's observations concerning "the confessions and the credibility of what they [the girls] assert," "things evidently preternatural in the witchcrafts," and whatever else he might recommend as "entertainment for an inquisitive person, that entirely loves you and Salem."[5]

Promising not to use what Sewall might write in any way prejudicial to the "designs" of "those two excellent persons, Mr. Hale and Mr. Noyes," Mather urged Sewall in his writing to imagine him "as obstinate a Sadducee and witch-advocate as any among us":

> Address me as one that believed nothing reasonable; and when you have so knocked me down, in a specter so unlike me, you will enable me to box it about among my neighbors, till it come—I know not where at last.

Mather closed by noting that "His Excellency the Governor" had commanded him to ask the favor of Sewall.[6]

Photograph of a portrait of Cotton Mather (1663–1728), an important figure in the Salem witch trials. Engraving by H. B. Hall's Sons, New York. From the Library of Congress.

By early October, when Governor Phips returned to Boston, the manuscript had been completed and was circulating among the learned and powerful. William Stoughton thought so much of it that he provided a laudatory preface. Phips borrowed entire sections for his report to England, but he nevertheless discouraged its publication. Brattle had just published his attack on the trials, and Phips did not want to encourage any further public discord over the subject. He would not approve of its publication until the new year, when the trials had been resumed on a new and different basis and the "general jail delivery" had begun. By then, attitudes had changed considerably, and Mather's defense of the Court of Oyer and Terminer was received quite differently from how it might have been the previous October.[7]

Mather's narrative was as detailed an account of the trials as would appear for decades to come. It included a wide range of information, including sermons, extracts of other works on witchcraft, Mather's own thoughts on events, a narrative overview of the trials, and a full and accurate account of the examinations and trials of five witches he deemed representative: George Burroughs, Bridget Bishop, Susannah Martin, Elizabeth How, and Martha Carrier. Few could quarrel with the accuracy of his report, at least regarding what he chose to include; by the time it was published, however, many found fault with what he chose to leave out, and with its tone.[8]

Mather avoided what his readers would come to see as embarrassing aspects of the trials—Rebecca Nurse's initial acquittal, John Proctor's public stance, and the troubling case of Mary Easty, for example. He brooked no criticism of the Court, not even for its use of spectral evidence, though by the time *Wonders* appeared many important figures had spoken out against it. That Mather himself had gone on record as urging caution in its use did not enter significantly into his account. If he had gained any sympathy for the accused, if he had had any doubts about their wholesale condemnation, he showed no evidence of it.[9]

Unfortunately for Mather the timing of his *The Wonders of the Invisible World* was critical. As we have seen, the tide was turning against the witch trials, and critiques were appearing at the highest levels. At about the same time Cotton was completing his *Wonders,* for example, Increase Mather was preparing *Cases of Conscience.* When it appeared, Cotton made his fears plain; he warned that people would say that "I run against my own father and all the ministers in the country." Further, he feared his father's account would be used by opponents to the trials—"witch advocates" he called them—to condemn the Court of Oyer and Terminer.[10] Increase's response to those who saw him as repudiating his son's defense of the judges, however, was to add the following postscript to his work: "I perused and approved of that book before it was printed. And nothing but my relation to him hindered me from recommending it to the world."[11]

Although the bringing of charges in the Salem witch trials had ended, they continued to be brought elsewhere, and Cotton Mather was prominently involved in three of them. The first involved Mercy Short, the seventeen-year-old servant-maid of Boston. Short had recently returned from captivity among the Indians, and during the spring of 1692 she had visited and mocked Sarah Good in her Boston prison, only to be afflicted ever since. Whereas the others of the accusing girls had been relieved of their afflictions, and even though Good had been hanged, Short's trauma continued.[12]

In December 1692, Mather began to study Mercy Short. From her he learned that the Devil was "a short and black man—a wretch no taller than an ordinary walking staff." The Devil was not black, however, Mather recorded, but rather one with the complexion of an Indian. He wore a high-crowned hat, wore his hair long and straight, had one cloven foot, and possessed eyes that glowed like the flames of a lantern. On a more personal level, Mather even learned that Short's specters had injured his wife and child, who died shortly after its birth.[13]

At times, Short's affliction took the form of long fasts. At other times, Mather reported, she was seared by flames and her visitors reported smelling brimstone and seeing the burns on her flesh, although they soon disappeared. And she was not beyond name-calling. She cried out against several individuals, especially those with whom she had recently quarreled or who dared question her behavior. She even named Mather at one point. Mather's reaction, however, was quite different from what it had been months earlier. He treated his being charged as a compliment, attesting to the high regard in which the Devil clearly held him! And he resolved, and urged all others present to resolve, to keep the other names to themselves. Short's name-calling, Mather concluded, was the result of delusions caused by the Devil, or, to put it another way, of her being possessed by the Devil rather than her being afflicted by witches. The difference was crucial.[14]

Mercy finally came out of her trance in March 1693, whereupon Mather completed his account of the affair under the title "A Brand Plucked Out of the Burning." He never published it, however, perhaps sensing that the timing was wrong. Or maybe he was embarrassed by the fate to which Short fell upon the completion of his study. As one account put it, "The sad truth was that when the Devil was cast out of her, seven others took its place, these being devils of the more common and carnal sort." Mercy would not make a very good example of those martyred on the Devil's altar after all.[15]

The second post-Salem trials case of possession to involve Cotton Mather occurred several months later, but closer to home. In September 1693, Mather visited Salem to gather information for the completion of his magnus opus *Magnalia Christi Americana* (1702). His purpose was to provide a history of God's divine will made manifest in New England, but the Devil's presence was not to be ignored. While visiting Salem, Mather became interested in the case of a Mrs. Carver. Carver was in direct communication with "shining spirits," who told her that "a new storm of witchcraft" was about to befall the region in chastisement for "the iniquity that was used in the willful smothering and covering of the last," and in order to change the minds of those who had been so fiercely opposed "to the discovery of that witchcraft." As the last "storm of witchcraft" had been smothered, in the minds of many, Carver was not without her supporters.[16]

Perhaps Mather, although clearly not a pro-Carver person, was less than convinced that she was entirely wrong. Had not his own wife, who had once had to smother a laugh at the sight of the afflictions of Martha Goodwin, at the very time the judges were dismissing the witches of Salem had a diabolic vision while sitting on her porch and in consequence given birth to a malformed short-lived child? While Mather was in Salem, had not the Devil interfered directly in his attempt to deliver two sermons by stealing their written texts?[17] Still Mather kept his thoughts on the Carver affair to himself.

Finally, there was the case of seventeen-year-old Margaret Rule, who lived in Mather's own Boston neighborhood. Perhaps most intriguing to Mather in this case was that Margaret Rule, although living in Boston, was able to explain what had happened to him in Salem. The eight specters that had tormented her, Rule explained, told her they had stolen the sermons Mather had lost! And in October the missing manuscripts were found scattered along the streets of Lynn, perfectly preserved. It seems, quipped one source, that "it was not given creatures covenanted to the Devil to keep a hold on a thing so holy."[18]

Margaret Rule's powers were too much for Mather to ignore. Her physical tortures had been preceded by a spiritual phase in which she believed she was damned. Now she was the victim of witches who urged her to sign the Devil's book. She was resisting, as witnesses to her heroic struggles attested, in a struggle so dramatic that she became the theatrical event of Boston. When he treated Rule, Mather usually cleared the room of all spectators, who upon occasion numbered nearly thirty or more, including his father. Occasionally, he did not, and that led to his undoing.[19]

Rule's behavior mimicked that of the girls of Salem village. Early on, the Devil held her mouth closed for nine days, except for brief periods during which her caretakers could administer a sip of rum. Later, witnesses reported that upon occasion Rule was stuck full of pins, and six men signed affidavits that they had seen her pulled to the ceiling by invisible hands, whereupon it had taken all of their combined strength to pull her back to bed. Mather himself once grabbed for something stirring on Rule's pillow, only to feel an imp in his hand that remained invisible. He was so startled by the incident that he let it get away.[20]

Rule had visions from which she was able to forecast the drowning of a young man, almost exactly as it had happened. It seems the young man was persuaded by "devils" to jump into the water, from which he was saved. Rule witnessed the theft of an old man's will, and she saw the faces of some of her tormentors, which included an unnamed old woman who had been arrested during the Salem trials but who had been freed, untried, when the entire matter collapsed. The rest, she reported, had learned from the earlier trials to go about veiled so they could not be identified.[21]

Mather prevailed upon Rule not to publicly proclaim the names of her afflicters, "lest any good person come to suffer any blast of reputation." Name them privately she would, however, and Mather agreed that they were suspicious. He wrote of those named that they were "the sort of wretches who for these many years have given over as violent presumption of witchcraft as perhaps any creatures yet living on the earth." Still, Mather did not report them, nor did he publish his report on the Rule case, titled "Another Brand Pluck'd Out of the Burning."[22]

Rather than receiving praise for his treatment of Margaret Rule, however, Mather was much maligned. As noted earlier, Mather had not always cleared the room of prying eyes when he treated Rule, and not all of those who observed were either as well-informed as he in the diabolical arts or were as sympathetic to the cause. One observer of the second type was Robert Calef, the Boston merchant-turned-critic. In the particular case of Margaret Rule, where Mather saw possession, Calef saw a woman's need for male attention. Rule seems to have liked having Mather stroke her face and naked breast and belly, Calef observed. It was a kind of laying on of hands as far as Mather was concerned, but not to Calef. Let a women do the same, he commented, and Rule would cry out, "Don't you meddle with me." And when Mather withdrew, Calef added, Rule insisted that the women in attendance leave as well, keeping by her side for the night the young man she considered her "sweetheart."[23]

What Calef really resented, even feared, was that by his presence and serious attention, Mather might dignify Rule's actions—or Short's or Carver's, for that matter—and rekindle that "bigoted zeal" that had once served to stir up "a blind and most bloody rage" against innocent people. So Calef acted. He circulated his firsthand observations and commentary about the Rule affair in which he treated Mather brutally, including a description of Mather's stroking of the half-naked Margaret Rule. Mather responded with a letter, in which he described Calef's account as containing nothing "fairly or truly represented" and with a lawsuit for "scandalous libel." When the case went to court, however, Mather did not appear, perhaps fearing the continued unfavorable publicity it would cause, and the case was dismissed.[24]

In 1700, the quarrel surfaced again, or perhaps climaxed, when Calef published his observations on Mather's behavior not only in the Rule affair but also during the Salem witch trials. The title, *More Wonders of the Invisible World,* was clearly a play on the title of Mather's earlier work about the Salem witch trials, and it is due to Calef's book more than any other one that the name of Cotton Mather has been ever since inextricably linked to the tragedy at Salem. As historian Samuel Eliot Morison put it, Calef "tied a tin can to him [Mather] after the frenzy was over; and it has rattled and banged through the pages of superficial and popular histories."[25] Increase Mather clearly saw what was happening. When he received a copy of Calef's *More Wonders,* he had it burned in Harvard Yard.[26]

As later historians would show, Cotton Mather's role in the Salem witch trials was more complex than Robert Calef suggested. On the one hand, Mather believed that the Court, the clergy, and others had uncovered a diabolical plot against Christianity in Massachusetts, and as a result he informed Chief Justice William Stoughton of his "zeal to assist" the judges in their quest to destroy "as wonderful a piece of devilism as has been seen in the world."[27]

On the other hand, Mather had repeatedly advised the judges of the Court of Oyer and Terminer to use caution in their deliberation, especially in handling spectral evidence by which the judges condemned so many people. On January 15, 1697, he noted in the privacy of his diary that he was "afflicted" the night before "with discouraging thoughts, as if unavoidable marks of the Divine displeasure might overtake my family for not appearing with vigor to stop the proceedings of the judges when the inexplicable storm from the invisible world assaulted the country."[28]

Mather kept such sentiments to himself, and he soon gained God's assurance that "marks of His indignation" would not follow his family, and that "having the righteousness of the Lord Jesus Christ" pleading for them, God's "goodness and mercy" and salvation would be theirs.[29] Posterity on earth, however, would not be so kind. It would judge him only by his public statements and actions, and those made him mete for the barbed criticism of the likes of Robert Calef.

SALEM IN RUINS

Returning to Salem, we find the village struggling to heal itself, to pull itself together after its trying and divisive ordeal. Contemporaries made note of the houses left uncared for and the fields untended. Breaking out in mid-to-late winter, the Salem witch trials interrupted the planting season; lasting through the fall and into the next winter, they caused many of the fields that had been planted not to be properly cultivated or harvested. Moreover, as previously noted, the accused or their relatives were occasionally forced to mortgage or sell their farms in order to meet expenses, while a few left the village altogether. The Cloyces, the Bishops, and the descendants of Thomas and Edward Putnam, for example, moved elsewhere.[30]

Over 170 years later, Charles Upham would observe that "one locality in the village, which was the scene of this wild and tragic fanaticism," continued to bear "the marks of the blight then brought upon it." It was the previously thriving old meetinghouse road near the center of Salem village, which, Upham noted, continued to be dilapidated and marked by "old, gray, moss-covered stone walls," the remains of cellars that suggested a once-considerable population, and only one house, still occupied by the descendants of Rebecca Nurse.[31]

Those who have surveyed the wreckage of the Salem witch trials have mostly spoken of the "broken charity" that marked the event and its devastating effect on the community. To paraphrase one historian, husband had "broken charity" with wife and wife with husband, mother with child and child with mother, and neighbor had been pitted against neighbor. Moreover, as it had been building for years, it took years to disappear.[32]

One of the first to feel the "broken charity" the Devil, or man, had wrought in Salem village was the Reverend Samuel Parris. Parris had played a crucial role in the Salem witch trials. Perhaps he did not deliberately provoke them, nor was he responsible for the factionalism that underscored them. Given his position of authority and his active involvement in the trials, however, as well as his having given voice and form to the fears among his people of "a pattern overwhelming in its scope, a universal drama in which Christ and Satan, Heaven and Hell, struggled for supremacy," he would pay a dear price.[33]

As early as mid-August 1692, Peter Cloyce, Samuel Nurse and his wife, and John Tarbell and his wife, in response to Parris's conduct during the trials, absented themselves from the Salem village church. Cloyce's wife Sarah was in prison, while Rebecca Nurse, Samuel Nurse's and Mary Tarbell's mother, had been hanged, and they all held Parris responsible. Parris attempted to persuade them to return, but he failed. Perhaps in response, on October 23, Parris delivered a sermon for which he chose as his text the Song of Solomon 1:2: "Oh that you would kiss me with the kisses of your mouth." Parris pleaded for an end to the village's factionalism. "Oh, be reconciled to me," he exhorted the congregation, "and give me a kiss of reconciliation." "[L]et me sense and feel thy love. . . . Kisses are very sweet among friends after some jars and differences, whereby they testify to true reconciliation." By virtue of their covenant relation, Parris reasoned, he could "sue for kisses," but the dissidents in his midst felt no obligation to submit.[34]

In December 1692, church elders complained to the Essex County Court that the village committee had been negligent in providing for the care of the church and minister. It explained that as a result of the distractions caused by the witch trials, there had been no village meetings to relieve their minister. As a result, not only had Parris gone unpaid but the meetinghouse had fallen into disrepair for want of funds. "By reason of broken windows, stopped up, some of them by boards or otherwise, and others wide open," the elders reported, it was sometimes so cold that it was uncomfortable and sometimes so dark that it was almost unusable. The anti-Parris village committee had not merely neglected the Reverend Parris, however; it had demanded an investigation of what it had all along deemed the fraudulent conveyance of the parsonage and ministry lands to Parris in 1689.[35]

On January 15, 1693, the Essex County Court declared the village committee derelict in its duties and ordered village residents to elect a new one. On January 17, perhaps in an attempt to make himself appear more humane and to influence the election, Samuel Parris wrote to Jonathan Corwin that he was willing to forego six pounds of the salary owed to him for the previous year, as well as the same amount for the present year. He explained that he was acting from the realization that some families in the village had of late suffered some impairment in their estates. His family too had suffered, he hastened to add, but he was nevertheless moved to offer the abatement to "gratify" his neighbors and gain whatever "amity" his action might merit.[36]

Parris's magnanimous, if calculated, gesture notwithstanding, on January 25 the village residents elected a new committee that proved to be as anti-Parris as its predecessor. Soon the church elders brought suit against the new committee—in March, it too was found guilty, and its members were fined forty shillings each, but the committee still took no action to raise the funds necessary for Parris and the meetinghouse. Instead, in July 1693, the anti-Parris faction petitioned Governor Phips and the General Court to appoint outside arbitrators and urged area ministers to press Parris to call for a council of ministers to resolve the impasse.[37]

On August 6, in a sermon about the death of Christ, Parris once again called for reconciliation. As if of himself, he spoke of Jesus as "a dear friend torn and wounded" with "blood streaming down his face and body." Even more affecting than the sight of those wounds, he continued, was the realization that they were "the vile actors" responsible for those injuries. When the harm is done by others, he explained, such a sight should affect all hearts not "more flinty than the rocks." But "when our consciences tell us that we, our cruel hands, have made those wounds, and the bloody instruments by which our dearest friend was gored were of our own forging," it is even more painful.[38] But once again, Parris's plea fell upon deaf ears.

In October 1693, John Higginson and Nicholas Noyes, the minister and assistant minister of the Salem town church, and the Reverend John Hale of Beverly called on Parris to convene a council of Massachusetts ministers to arbitrate the dispute. Parris responded by condemning the irregular methods his opponents were using against him, including their appealing to outsiders. He recognized that he had little choice but to comply with his brethren's request, but he nevertheless managed to postpone the convening of such a council for over a year.[39] In the meantime, he fought back.

In November, Parris drew up a statement of his grievances against the dissenters. He denounced their "precipitate, schismatical, and total withdrawing from the church," as well as "their withdrawing their purses." He charged them with having attacked him with a "factious and seditious libel" and carried their "impetuous pursuit" to the extent of having disturbed him in his own home late at night. They were guilty, he explained, of "extremely disturbing the peace of this church and many other good people amongst us, sadly exposing all to ruin." Formal charges in hand, in December 1693, Parris secured a court order forcing village residents to pay his salary or stand suit, but still none was forthcoming.[40]

In early March 1694, perhaps successfully appealing to the populace for an opportunity to end the discord that had plagued the village, a pro-Parris faction managed to be elected in the majority to the village committee. Nevertheless, in June, Salem town ministers Higginson and Noyes, this time joined by Boston ministers James Allen, Samuel Willard, Samuel Cheever, and Joseph Gerrish, again pressed Samuel Parris to convene a council of ministers to arbitrate the matter. They were acting, they reported, because they had been approached by "some persons of Salem village," but there is no record of Parris's response.[41]

In September, the village committee called a meeting of village residents to see if they could come "together in peace and unity," but no record of the meeting, if it was even held, has survived. Instead, at about the same time the above-mentioned ministers repeated their call to Parris for a council of ministers, in that letter adding, "[W]e . . . find it to be our duty to express our minds more plainly and particularly, that we may be the more clearly understood without mistake."[42]

Instead of accepting the ministers' suggestions, Parris opted once again to deal directly with his opponents. He may have been provided the opportunity to do so when in November 1694 Samuel Nurse and Thomas Wilkins publicly explained why they were reluctant to attend Parris's church. Their antipathy toward Parris had begun, they explained, when the "distractions and disturbing tumults and noises made by the persons under diabolical power and delusion" prevented "sometimes our hearing and understanding and profiting of the word preached." They had been afraid to stay in such a society because they feared that they too would be charged, having heard persons "better than ourselves" accused. Further, they found Parris's preaching "dark and dismal," his dwelling on "mysteries of iniquity . . . offensive," and his observations on events too often different from "the generality of the orthodox ministers of the whole country." They could not in conscience join in his prayers, Nurse and Wilkins continued, because he had been too quick to take the side of the afflicted and because they could find no charity in him, that quality without which a preacher's eloquence is "as a sounding brass and tinkling cymbal."[43]

On November 26, Parris answered his critics with a sermon on the "late horrid calamity," which he called "Meditations for Peace." It was "a very sore rebuke and humbling providence" that the witchcraft had come first into his own family, he began, and that unlawful and diabolical means had been exercised there to raise spirits and create apparitions, though all was done without his knowledge. As a result, he continued, "God has been righteously spitting in my face."[44]

Parris owned any errors he might have made in conducting the witchcraft crisis. He acknowledged that he had given too much weight to spectral evidence, explaining that God might suffer the Devil to take the shape of the innocent after all, and that it was wrong to ask the afflicted who tormented another. Parris told the congregation that in that "sore hour of distress and darkness," he had "always intended but due justice." But "through weakness or sore exercise," he admitted, he and others equally deluded by the "evil angels" might have sometimes, "yea possibly sundry times, unadvisedly expressed" themselves.[45]

Parris offered his sympathy to those who had suffered "through the clouds of human weakness and Satan's wiles and sophistry." He asked pardon of God and prayed that all might "be covered with the mantle of love" and "forgive each other heartily":

> Let all bitterness and wrath and anger and clamor and evil-speaking be put away from you, with all malice; and be ye kind to one another, tender hearted, forgiving one another, even as God, for Christ's sake, hath forgiven you.[46]

Forgive one another they might, but not Samuel Parris. His confession might have been well-intended, but it was too little, too late. As John Tarbell, Rebecca Nurse's son-in-law, commented, "If half so much had been said formerly, it would never have come to this." When the dissenters asked for a copy of "Meditations for Peace" in order "to consider it," Parris refused, likely distrusting what use they would make of it.[47]

On January 18, 1695, the village committee voted a tax for Parris's salary, but dissidents persisted in refusing to pay, and local constables refused to take action against them.[48] Parris, perhaps having by that point realized that an impasse had been reached, agreed to convene the long-sought council of churches. On April 3 and 4, 1695, seven ministers and ten elders from the North Shore assembled in Salem village, with Increase Mather serving as the moderator.

Members of the council listened to both sides and issued their recommendations. The council agreed with the dissidents, that "unwarranted and uncomfortable steps" had been taken by Parris during the "dark time of confusion." But they also recognized that he had been "brought into a better sense of things" and that he had acknowledged his errors. Therefore, as he had otherwise acquitted himself well in the job, the council continued, "Christian charity might and should receive satisfaction." Similarly, Parris and his supporters were to treat the dissenters with "much compassion for the infirmities discovered . . . on such a heartbreaking day." The council concluded, however, that if it were the case that the rupture between the dissidents and the Reverend Parris was incurable, and if Parris, "which God forbid," should find that he cannot "with any comfort and service, continue in his present station," his leaving would not "expose him unto any hard character" with members of the ministerial council nor, they hoped, with anyone else.[49]

The dissidents would not be reconciled, and in late April they sent a petition to Increase Mather bearing the signatures of some eighty-four residents begging him and the Boston clergy "to advise Mr. Parris . . . that he cannot [any longer] with comfort or profit to himself or others abide in the work of the ministry among us." They asked Mather to at least reconvene the council of ministers and reconsider the evidence. After consulting with his colleagues, on May 6, Mather wrote to Parris explaining that such opposition made his removal necessary.[50]

On May 20, 105 of Parris's supporters rallied to his cause with a counter-petition, asking that he be retained. They took the position that Parris's removal would not reunite the congregation. Three ministers had already been removed, they reminded the ministers, and with each leaving their differences had only grown worse. "Therefore, we justly fear that the removing of the fourth may rather prove the ruining of their interests of Christ amongst us, and leave us as sheep without a shepherd."[51]

Perhaps at the Boston ministers' bidding, in late May or early June the Suffield town church inquired about Parris's availability to fill their pulpit, but the Salem village church elders urged Parris not to leave, and "seeing they would not let me go," Parris wrote, he agreed to stay. In April 1696, Parris finally consented to move, provided that the congregation would settle his salary arrears and the matter of his ownership of the parsonage. Parris agreed to leave by July 1, but when no settlement was reached by March of the following year and the anti-Parris faction once again gained control of the village committee, the committee initiated a lawsuit against him. The committee lost the case, however, whereupon Parris brought and won a counter-suit for a back salary of 125 pounds.[52]

The village committee appealed the County Court decision, and both sides agreed to submit the matter to a panel of arbitrators, which included Samuel Sewall and Wait Winthrop, both of whom had served on the Court of Oyer and Terminer, and Elisha Cook, all of Boston. In

July 1697, the panel found that the village should pay Parris seventy-nine pounds, nine shillings, and six pence, in return for which Parris would relinquish the deed to the parsonage. That being settled, Parris left for Stowe, Massachusetts, taking with him his daughter Betty and his son Noyes. Parris's wife had died in mid-July 1696. Other than her marrying Benjamin Barron in 1710, Betty's fate is not known; Noyes, however, grew to manhood, only to die insane. And Samuel Parris succeeded in promptly getting embroiled in another salary dispute, whereupon he left the pulpit and moved to Sudbury as a schoolmaster, landlord, and merchant.[53]

Parris's successor, Joseph Green, was only twenty-two years old when he arrived in Salem. Green, a Harvard graduate of the class of 1695, had not seriously, as an undergraduate, considered the ministry. While teaching in the Roxbury Grammar School and after reading one of Cotton Mather's published sermons, he later explained, he became not only a convert but an evangelist. In this regard, Green may have been somewhat like Parris; unlike his predecessor, and even his mentor, however, he did not dwell on matters of damnation. By all reports, Green was demonstrably cheerful, outgoing, and perhaps most importantly, politically astute when it came to the warring factions of Salem.[54]

Green soon realized that the true devils of Salem village were those forces that had caused such animosity among its residents. Two weeks after his ordination, Green took steps toward reconciliation between the feuding factions within his flock. In November 1698, he announced to the congregation that the family of Rebecca Nurse—John Tarbell, Samuel Nurse, and Thomas Wilkins (Peter and Sarah Cloyce had moved to Marlborough, Massachusetts)—wished to rejoin the congregation. They were unanimously welcomed, but when they returned Green took another bold step. He reworked the seating plan of his church, intentionally mixing the antagonists. He put Samuel Nurse in the same pew with Thomas Putnam, father of Ann; Rebecca Nurse's daughter, the Widow Preston, in the pew of the Widow Walcott, mother of Mary, and so on. The participants accepted the arrangement! If the residents of Salem village were incapable of extending charity toward the Reverend Parris, they were able to forgive their neighbors, thereby lifting the burden that had nearly destroyed their community.[55]

In 1703, Green asked the congregation to consider revoking the excommunication of Martha Corey, and on February 14 they passed a motion to that effect, explaining, "We were at that dark day under the power of those errors which then prevailed in the land; and we are sensible that we had not sufficient grounds to think her guilty of that crime for which she was condemned and executed; and that her excommunication was not according to the mind of God." Six or seven unnamed members dissented from the resolution, and the church's motion was blocked in a town meeting so bitter that Green vowed never to attend town meetings again, but in 1707 the motion was finally adopted.[56]

The families of Rebecca Nurse and Giles Corey also had the satisfaction of having Rebecca's and Giles's excommunication revoked on March 6, 1712, by the First Church of Salem town. In Nurse's case, the church stated that although the congregation had voted unanimously to excommunicate her, she having been convicted of witchcraft by the Court of Oyer and Terminer, the testimony offered against her was no longer "so satisfactory . . . as it was generally in that hour of darkness and temptation." Moreover, it continued, the General Court had since reversed her attainder. They, therefore, voted that Nurse's excommunication be "erased and blotted out" so that it might "no longer be a reproach to her memory, and an occasion of grief to her children."[57]

Corey, the church records continued, had been excommunicated because after being "indicted for the sin of witchcraft . . . he had obstinately refused to plead, and so threw himself on certain death." The church, "having now testimony on his behalf, that, before his death, he did bitterly repent of his obstinate refusal to plead in defense of his life," consented to have his excommunication "erased and blotted out." Although we will never know what exactly happened during Corey's ordeal, there is no evidence to support the contention that Corey had in the end repented of his refusal to enter a plea. It may well have been fabricated by the church to justify its lifting Corey's excommunication.[58]

THE REPENTING BEGINS

In August 1706, a woman stood before the Salem village church while the Reverend Joseph Green read her confession. The twenty-seven-year-old woman sought fellowship with the congregation. Her name was Ann Putnam—the same Ann Putnam who as a child had named some twenty-one people as witches. Ann had led a good life since 1692, by all reports. Her mother and father had died some seven years before, and most tended to hold Ann Sr. responsible for her child's actions. Nevertheless, it was an involvement that even the young girl had to expiate before those whom she had wronged, if she wished to be fully accepted in their midst.[59]

"I desire to be humbled before God," Green read for Ann Putnam, "for the sad and humbling providence that befell my father's family in the year about '92." They were her sentiments, although the minister quite likely helped her choose the words by which to express them. "It was a great delusion of Satan that deceived me in that sad time," Putnam's statement continued, "I did it not out of any anger, malice, or ill will."[60]

Putnam acknowledged that she had been "an instrument for the accusing of several persons of a grievous crime, whereby their lives were taken from them," but that she now believed them innocent. In particular, she admitted that she "was a chief instrument of accusing Goodwife Nurse and her two sisters," the relatives of whom sat before her, and that she wished "to lie in the dust and be humbled for it." She proceeded to "earnestly beg forgiveness of God" and of "all those unto whom I have given cause of sorrow and offence, whose relations were taken away and accused." It was as complete a confession as any could reasonably expect of her, and although the pain must have been great still in the hearts of many whom Ann had wronged, they forgave her. Putnam never married, but she stayed in Salem village her entire life. Much like her mother, Ann Jr. suffered from frequent ill health, and she died at the age of thirty-seven.[61]

Ann Putnam appears to have been the only one of the accusing girls to repent. Elizabeth Booth, Sarah Churchill, and Mary Walcott married, as did Mercy Lewis, after having given birth it seems, and all save Booth left Salem village. It is possible, however it is only speculation, that Abigail Williams was the person to whom John Hale referred when he commented that among the original accusers one was "followed with diabolical molestations to her death."[62] But of the rest we know nothing, except for one line in a subsequent act of the Massachusetts Legislature, which noted that some of "the principal accusers and witnesses in those dark and severe prosecutions" have since "discovered themselves to be persons of profligate and vicious conversations."[63]

Others did confess, and their public statements followed the Salem witch trials by only a few years. Some were quite dramatic. On Christmas Eve 1696, for example, the day after the death of his two-year-old daughter Sarah, Judge Samuel Sewall's son Sam read from Matthew 12:7: "But if you had known what this means, 'I will have mercy, and not sacrifice,' you would not have condemned the guiltless." Sewall, who had prayed with his friend John Alden, stood by the dissident Judge Saltonstall, and defended the Reverend Samuel Willard, had nevertheless concluded that he had done too little to save the innocent of 1692.[64]

Largely through Samuel Willard's efforts, January 14, 1697, was declared a day of repentance for "the late tragedy raised among us by Satan and his instruments." In the words of Provincial Secretary Isaac Addington, the day was to be set aside so that:

> all God's people may offer up fervent supplications unto him, that all iniquity may be put away, which hath stirred God's holy jealousy against this land; that He would show us what we know not, and help us, wherein we have done amiss, to do so no more.

Provincial leaders hoped that by praying and fasting the actions of those who had erred would be forgiven, and that God "would remove the rod of wickedness from off the lot of the righteous."[65]

Samuel Sewall chose January 14 to stand before his fellow congregants of Boston's Old South Church to make his confession. He wished to assume "the blame and shame" of not having more forcefully approved the Salem witch trials. He asked for the pardon of those before him, and he prayed that God, "who has an unlimited authority," would pardon his sins and the sins of others and not visit those sins on the innocent or upon the land. For the rest of his life, he observed annually a private day of humiliation and prayer to keep fresh in his mind a sense of repentance and sorrow for the part he bore in the trials. On April 23, 1720, nearly thirty years after the trials, after reading a recently published account of the affair, he wrote in his diary: "The good and gracious God be pleased to save New England and me, and my family."[66]

Also on January 14, twelve individuals who had served as jurors for the Court of Oyer and Terminer offered their plea for forgiveness:

> We confess that we ourselves were not capable to understand nor able to withstand, the mysterious delusion of the power of darkness and prince of the air, but were, for want of knowledge in ourselves and better information from others, persuaded with to take up with such evidence against the accused as, on further consideration and better information, we justly fear was insufficient for the touching the lives of any.

They feared they had been "instrumental" along with others in bringing upon themselves and "this people of the Lord," though ignorantly and unwillingly, "the guilt of innocent blood." To the survivors of their victims they expressed their deep sense of sorrow and humbly begged forgiveness:

We do therefore hereby signify to all in general, and to the surviving sufferers in special, our deep sense of, and sorrow for, our errors in acting on such evidence to the condemning of any person; and do hereby declare that we justly fear that we were sadly deluded and mistaken . . . and do therefore humbly beg forgiveness, first of God . . . [and then] of living sufferers.[67]

Although admitting their errors, nearly all of the confessions were qualified. They admitted making mistakes and even causing considerable suffering, but they insisted their motives had been beyond reproach. They had acted as they had out of a sense of duty, or ignorance, or weakness. As in the case of Ann Putnam and the jurors, they insisted that they had had no control over their actions because they had been deluded—God had permitted the Devil to use them as instruments to wreak havoc on the province. As Larry Gragg has pointed out, those confessions supplied a framework for the colony to make sense of what happened in 1692. For years to come, the witchcraft crisis was seen as "a dark time of delusion, a time when good people were led astray and shed innocent blood." It was variously termed: "This delusion of the Devil"; "the dark and doleful times"; "that hour of darkness and temptation"; "the hour of sore tribulation and temptation"; and "the dark time of the confusions."[68]

Perhaps the most revealing confession of all came in the form of an explanation of the entire affair. It came from the pen of the Reverend John Hale in the same year of Sewall's confession, 1697, but it was not published until 1702, two years after his death. Hale's account appeared under the title *A Modest Inquiry into the Nature of Witchcraft,* to which the Reverend John Higginson of Salem's First Church added a preface. Higginson found it an essential and a timely work, and he wrote that he hoped it would serve as a "warning and caution to those that come after us, that they may not fall into the like."[69]

Although he blamed himself for "unwittingly encouraging . . . the sufferings of the innocent," Hale saw no human villains in this tragedy, only people who made flawed decisions. The justices, judges, and others concerned, Hale wrote, conscientiously endeavored to do the right thing, but their actions led to the shedding of innocent blood. The judges had followed accepted legal and theological principles of the day, he explained, if not entirely correctly, and chief among those was that "the Devil could not assume the shape of an innocent person in doing mischief unto mankind." Further, that they believed they were right was understandable, given the number of accusations and confessions.[70]

Hale had come to question the Court's reliance on spectral evidence and to realize that convictions should not be based on such evidence, but instead arrived at "in the same way that murder, theft, and such crimes are provable." He posited four acceptable grounds for conviction: confession; the testimony of two witnesses that the accused had committed an act unquestionably dependent on diabolical assistance; the testimony of partners in the crime; or "circumstances antecedent to, concomitant with, or suddenly consequent upon such acts of sorcery" that had "like force to fasten a suspicion of this crime upon this or that person."[71] Such grounds, Hale admitted, were very difficult to establish, which may have pleased critics of the trials but not its supporters, who would conclude that if Hale's recommendations were to be implemented some of the guilty would almost certainly elude punishment, along with the innocent. But, then, all Hale was really suggesting was that rules of evidence already employed de facto, if not by law, prior to the Salem witch trials be reinstated, which would in fact come to pass.

Hale described how the multiplication of confessors had first stilled doubts, regarding the veracity of the girls, and then deepened them. "You are one that brings this man to death," he reported himself as having said to one of the girls who accused George Burroughs. "If you have charged anything upon him that is not true, recall it before it be too late, while he is yet alive." But the confessor did not recant what she had said, and Burroughs was executed. At the time, Hale found the verdict against Burroughs just, but he was nonetheless troubled by it. He could not understand how a man trained in the ministry and in the gospel could go to his death unconfessed, when given every opportunity to repent. He did not trust the procedure whereby the Court allowed those who confessed to continue to live as long as they accused others of similar crimes. He pointed to the fact that nearly all who confessed eventually renounced their confessions, claiming they had been forced into them, and he allowed that he was concerned with the dramatic increase in the number of the afflicted. As the number of the accused grew, so too, contrary to what he might have expected, did the number of the afflicted, he noted, but when the accused were released from jail, nothing happened.[72]

Hale was deeply troubled by all of those inconsistencies, and when he informed Samuel Sewall about his pending publication in November 1697, Sewall was troubled as well. Sewall, whose confession was limited to his own culpability in the trials, feared Hale would "go too far the other way" and damage the reputation of the judges. Hale did not deny their responsibility, but he wished the judges to be treated fairly. "I am abundantly satisfied that those who were most concerned to act and judge in these matters," he wrote, "did not willingly depart from the rules of righteousness." It was "the darkness of that day, the tortures and lamentations of the afflicted and the power of former precedents" that misled them, and in the end, "we walked in clouds, and could not see our way."[73]

Finally, Hale, like so many of his fellow Puritan divines, saw the tragedy of Salem as God's punishment for a profligate people. Thus, all were guilty to some extent for what had happened:

> The errand of our fathers into this wilderness, was to sacrifice to the Lord; that is, to worship God in purity of heart and life, and to wait upon the Lord, walking in the faith and order of the gospel in church fellowship; that they might enjoy Christ in all his ordinances. But these things have been greatly neglected and despised by many born, or bred upon the land. We have much forgotten what our fathers came in the wilderness to see. The sealing ordinances of the covenant of grace and church communion have been much slighted and neglected; and the fury of the storm raised by Satan hath fallen very heavily upon many that lived under these neglects. The Lord sent evil angels to awaken and punish our negligence.[74]

Only a minority of those responsible for the events of 1692 confessed. The most prominent among those who did not were the accusing girls, other than Ann Putnam, and Judge William Stoughton. As acting governor, he had authorized the day of fasting, but until the end he was convinced that as presiding judge for both the Court of Oyer and Terminer and the Superior Court he had done his best to do what seemed just at the time. But even in not confessing, Stoughton's retrospective assessment differed little from that of those who had. Upon hearing of Samuel Sewall's confession, he is reported to have responded, as Thomas Hutchinson put it, that "when he sat in judgment he had the fear of God before his eyes and gave opinion according to the best of his understanding; and although it may appear afterwards, that he had been in an error, yet he saw no necessity of a public acknowledgment of it."[75]

By and large, Stoughton and the other judges of both courts rose above the pall cast on the witch-hunt of 1692. All remained members of the Governor's Council after the trials ended, although upon Phips's death in 1695 English officials passed over Deputy Governor Stoughton to appoint Joseph Dudley the new royal governor![76]

SETTLING UP

Finally, there was the matter of "settling up," both legally and monetarily. Those whose legal records remained tainted and who had suffered considerable financial loss during the Salem witch trials launched an offensive to expunge the court records and recoup their losses.

The dilemma faced by those convicted or who had escaped and been condemned in the process first surfaced when Elizabeth Proctor petitioned the Massachusetts General Court in 1696. She explained that her husband John had signed a will shortly before his execution that excluded her from any of his estate, despite a contract he had made in writing with her before their marriage.[77] Rather than slighting her, John Proctor likely expected Elizabeth to be hanged at some point, and even if she were not, as she had been condemned, he feared she would not be able to receive his estate. As fate would have it, Elizabeth was spared execution, but although pardoned she remained guilty and therefore "dead in the law." As such, John Proctor's eldest sons, her stepsons, became his beneficiaries, and Elizabeth was denied her fair share of her husband's estate, including her dower to which she would otherwise have been entitled. Elizabeth Proctor petitioned the Legislature to place her, as she put it, "into a capacity to make use of the law to recover that which of right by law I ought to have for my necessary supply and support."[78]

In 1696, the General Court was not ready to act on Elizabeth Proctor's motion, but the litany of confessions and the increased number of petitions on behalf of the condemned no doubt moved the Legislature in that direction. On June 13, 1700, Abigail Faulkner wrote to the General Court explaining that her pardon had spared her execution, but that she continued to live "as a malefactor convict upon record of the most heinous crimes that mankind can be supposed guilty of." She asked for "the defacing of the record" as a simple act of justice. The evidence used against her, she explained, was limited to the afflicted who "pretended" to see her "by their spectral sight, and not with their bodily eyes." Moreover, the jury that had convicted her, she continued, had since decided that such testimony was of no value. The House of Representatives voted to grant Faulkner's request, but for some undisclosed reason, the Council did not concur.[79]

In 1702, John Hale, in his *A Modest Inquiry into the Nature of Witchcraft,* called "for clearing the good name and reputation of some that have suffered."[80] On the second day of March of the following year, twenty-one of the survivors and family members of some of the others from Andover, Salem village, and Topsfield petitioned the General

Court. They too asked the Legislature to remove the "infamy from the names and memory" of those who had suffered, so that "none of their surviving relations nor their posterity might suffer on that account." They were supported by another petition subscribed to by several Essex County ministers.[81]

The General Court responded. On July 20, the House of Representatives formally forbade some of the procedures that had been employed in the Salem witch trials. It ordered that spectral evidence no longer "be accounted valid or sufficient to take away the life or good name of any person or persons within this province." It also ruled "that the infamy and reproach cast on the names and posterity of said accused and condemned persons may in some measure be rolled away." This time, the Council concurred and added an additional clause, whereby all the condemned persons were to be acquitted of the penalties to which they were liable upon their convictions and "estate[d] . . . in their just credit and reputation, as if no such judgment had been had." In effect, some have argued, the General Court's ruling reversed the attainders of the condemned, but their convictions stood. Moreover, the Legislature did nothing for those who had not been included in the petition.[82]

On May 25, 1709, seventeen of the condemned or their relatives, in this instance apparently led by Philip English, demanded that the General Court not only restore the good names of those who had been condemned, but also remunerate them for what they had been "damnified in their estates thereby."[83] Other survivors added their petition in the following years, including Isaac Easty, who claimed that Mary's estate had been "damnified by reason of such hellish molestation"; Benjamin Proctor, who as John's eldest son had helped raise all of his father's children; the daughters of Elizabeth How; the son of Sarah Wildes; and all five children of George Burroughs, who opposed as well the making of any award to their stepmother, who had left them "to shift for themselves without anything for so much as a remembrance of their father." Rallying to their support, urging in a letter addressed to the General Court that the petition be honored, was none other than Cotton Mather![84]

Before proceeding, however, perhaps some further explanation of this aspect of the petitions may be necessary. As explained earlier in the case of Giles Corey, in seventeenth-century England penalties for felony convictions could include forfeiture of goods. Moreover, descendants of the convicted could be blocked from inheriting property. English law exempted the felony of witchcraft from the forfeiture penalty, however, and the 1641 Massachusetts Body of Liberties went so far as to forbid the forfeiture of property for convictions of any felony, a situation continued under the new colonial charter of 1692. The provision of the General Court's act of December 14, 1692, that provided for forfeiture in witchcraft cases was disallowed by the British Privy Council.[85]

Nevertheless, seizures of property occurred during the Salem witch trials, and they were presumed to be legal by most governmental authorities. Following the conviction or execution of a family member, several families had their property confiscated by local sheriffs "in their majesty's name." The families of William Barker, Dorcas Hoar, George Jacobs Sr., Samuel Wardwell, John Proctor, Giles Corey, and Mary Parker either had property taken or they were threatened with the action. In Salem, Sheriff George Corwin was responsible for the confiscations, and Robert Calef has recorded what happened after John and Elizabeth Proctor were found guilty:

> The sheriff [Corwin] came to his [Proctor's] house and seized all the goods, provisions, and cattle that he could come at, and sold some cattle at half price, and killed others, and put them up for the West Indies; threw out the beer out of a barrel, and carried away the barrel; emptied a pot of broth, and took away the pot, and left nothing in the house for the support of the children.[86]

In 1710, the Proctor children valued the loss for the General Court at 150 pounds.[87]

Upon George Jacob Sr.'s execution, his son George Jr. later reported, Corwin seized from his estate five cows, eight loads of hay, enough apples to make twelve barrels of cider, sixty bushels of Indian corn, a mare, two feather beds, furniture, rugs, blankets, sheets, bolsters, pillows, two brass kettles, twelve shillings in cash, five swine, "a quantity of pewter," an "abundance of small things" (e.g., meat, fowl, chairs), and "a large gold thumb ring," that according to Robert Calef was the Widow Jacob's wedding ring! The entire loss was valued at just under eighty pounds.[88]

Finally, there was the case of Mary Parker. Following her execution, Corwin sent an officer to seize her estate. When her sons John and Joseph pointed out that she had left none, he seized their cattle, corn, and hay, pending resolution of the case. The Parkers seem to have actually checked the law, if only after the fact, because in their later petition to the governor they wrote, "We know not of any law in force in this province, by which it should be forfeited upon her [their mother's] condemnation; much less can we understand that there is any justice or reason for the sheriff to seize upon our estate." Not knowing the law earlier, however, they had not attempted to block Corwin's action.[89]

Among those who had escaped, Elizabeth Cary, Edward and Sarah Bishop, and Philip and Mary English had their belongings seized, and in their cases the seizures may have been legal. English law did permit seizures of the property of those who fled from justice, and so ruled the Massachusetts Superior Court in 1694, when Philip English sued Sheriff George Corwin. Corwin, the Court explained, had followed William Stoughton's order, and Stoughton was enforcing the statute penalizing those attempting to avoid prosecution.[90]

Nathaniel Cary left some of his personal property with a friend, but the sheriff seized it as well.[91] Following the Bishops' escape, Essex County Sheriff George Corwin seized the family's forty-six sheep, six cows, and an undetermined number of swine, as well as various household items. When their son Samuel Bishop paid Corwin ten pounds, the sheriff returned the household items, but that was all.[92] The largest forfeiture, however, was that of Philip and Mary English. When they fled to New York, Philip English posted a 4,000-pound security bond in Boston to protect his property. Sheriff Corwin nevertheless seized English's property from four warehouses, a Salem wharf, and his home. English listed as being among his losses several hundred bushels of grain; an undetermined number of hogsheads of molasses, sugar, and wine; thousands of boards, staves, and shingles; and several hundred yards of cloth, all of which he valued at over 1,183 pounds. He was no doubt further embittered by the death of his wife soon after their return to Salem, which he attributed to her ordeal of trial, imprisonment, and flight from almost certain execution.[93]

Philip English sought revenge on a number of different fronts. In March 1693, he petitioned Governor William Phips for the return of the property Corwin had seized, insisting that it had been taken illegally. Phips did not specifically agree that Corwin had acted illegally, but he did order the property returned. Corwin, however, did not comply. In 1694, English challenged Sheriff Corwin's confiscations in court, but lost. The Court, presided over by William Stoughton, exempted Corwin and his heirs from any liability resulting from his actions as sheriff. When Corwin died in 1697, however, English seized his body, holding it until a debt of some sixty pounds, three shillings was paid.[94]

It should be noted that victims could buy back whatever they could afford. English refused on principle to take such action, and others did not do so because they could not afford it. They were of modest circumstances and it had taken years for them to accumulate what they had. A few, however, did avail themselves of the opportunity. After Giles Corey's death—a manner of death likely intended by Corey to protect his property—for example, Corwin told Corey's sons-in-law John Moulton and William Cleaves that he would seize Corey's estate. Corey had willed all of his property to his sons-in-law, but they believed Corwin was acting within the law, so they paid him eleven pounds, six shillings to desist, and he did.[95]

To be fair, the reader should keep in mind that there is little evidence that Sheriff Corwin profited or sought to profit personally from the seizures. And as it has already been noted, in the case brought by Philip English against George Corwin in 1694, the Massachusetts Superior Court ruled that Corwin had acted under orders from Deputy Governor Stoughton, and within the law. Nevertheless, it is curious that he does not appear to have seized the property of all of those convicted within his jurisdiction, and it is not clear why he selected the families he did. Some were wealthy, to be sure, but most were relatively poor, with the value of forfeitures later determined to be as little as two pounds, ten shillings, in the case of William Barker.[96]

On September 15, 1710, a special committee of the General Court reported that it had received requests for reversals of attainders from twenty-two of those condemned in 1692, and petitions for compensation in those and other cases totaling over 578 pounds. By September 28, 1711, the latter figure had risen to over 796 pounds, "besides," as the report reads, "Mr. English and his demands," that had been "left to the court's consideration and determination."[97]

On October 17, the General Court ruled, this time explicitly, that "the several convictions, judgments, and attainders" of the convicted petitioners be "reversed, and declared to be null and void." The Legislature explained the Province's behavior by noting that it had been "infested with a horrible witchcraft or possession of devils," and referring to "some of the principal accusers and witnesses in those dark days and severe prosecutions" as "having since discovered themselves to be persons of profligate and vicious conversation." The General Court appointed a committee to evaluate the claims, which included compensation for court costs, jail expenses, travel costs to attend court sessions, and confiscated property, but it also made it clear that "no sheriff, constable, jailer or other officer of the law [would] be liable to any prosecution in the law for anything they then legally did in the execution of their respective offices."[98]

On December 17, upon the recommendation of the General Court, Governor Joseph Dudley ordered payment of some 578 pounds, twelve shillings. Distribution was made through a committee headed by Stephen Sewall. John and Elizabeth Proctor received the most, 150 pounds, while George Jacobs was given seventy-nine pounds, and George Burroughs fifty pounds. At the opposite end, Martha Carrier's survivors were given seven pounds, six shillings, while Mary Parker received eight pounds. Abigail Hobbs, who had been a victim, confessor, and accuser, received ten pounds. The family of Giles and Martha Corey was awarded twenty-one pounds, but the survivors of Sarah Good received thirty pounds, a sum perhaps made greater by the harm done to her daughter Dorcas, who still suffered psychologically from her ordeal.[99]

Left disgruntled was Philip English, who had demanded nearly 1,200 pounds, but received nothing. The estimate of his losses was probably reasonable, but it seemed excessive to the General Court, especially when the total amount of money it was prepared to make available to those who made claims against it totaled only one-half of what English alone demanded. Upon receipt of another petition from Philip English, the General Court appointed another committee to consider his claim, and in November 1718, it recommended payment of 200 pounds to him. English refused the payment, so the matter dragged on.[100]

English lived out the rest of his years without payment, angry and increasingly deranged. In 1722, Salem town minister Nicholas Noyes sued English for having called him a murderer, in reference to his role in the Salem witch trials. In the meantime, English stopped attending Noyes's church and instead exercised his right under the new colonial charter to contribute to the founding of St. Peter's Church, the first Anglican house of worship in Salem.[101]

On his deathbed, the family would later report, English was asked to forgive magistrate John Hathorne. English agreed, reluctantly, but quickly added, "If I get well, I'll be damned it I forgive him!" Philip English did not know that two of his granddaughters would marry grandsons of John Hathorne, and that one of those unions would initiate the lineage of his great-great-grandson, Nathaniel Hawthorne (he added a *w* to his name), who would make his ancestors' quarrel a subject of his writing. Upon Philip English's death, by the way, the colony awarded English's heirs the 200 pounds.[102]

On December 8, 1738, nearly half a century after the fact, the issue of recompense for the Salem witch trials was once more before the Massachusetts Legislature. On that date, Samuel Sewall, the judge's son, introduced a bill whereby a committee would be appointed to secure information relating to "the circumstances of the persons and families who suffered in the calamity of the times in and about the year

1692." The measure was adopted, and Sewall was charged with chairing the committee, but there is no mention in the records of its having taken any immediate action.

In an address before both houses of the Legislature on November 22, 1740, Governor Jonathan Belcher encouraged the committee's work toward easing the "sufferings" of those families "ruined in the mistaken management of the terrible affair called witchcraft," but once again the record grows silent. And finally on May 31, 1749, the heirs of George Burroughs petitioned the Governor and the General Court for "some recompense" for their losses. It was referred to the committee, but there is no evidence that any further action was taken.[103]

Technically, the reversal of attainders of 1711 was imperfect, because, as historians later discovered, Governor Dudley never actually signed the reversals, but no one at the time noticed or at least raised any objections. Moreover, the following individuals were not included in the petition and thus were not covered by the act: Bridget Bishop, Elizabeth Johnson, Susannah Martin, Alice Parker, Ann Pudeator, Wilmot Reed, and Margaret Scott.[104] In 1946, the Massachusetts Legislature considered a bill to clear their names, but it failed to pass, as was the case in 1950, 1953, and 1954. Finally, on August 28, 1957, the measure was adopted, but only after the original bill was modified to absolve Massachusetts of any legal obligations to the descendants of the victims. The Massachusetts General Court concluded that those who had been condemned by the Court of Oyer and Terminer "may" have been prosecuted illegally and according to a "shocking law" of the period, and it resolved that their descendants should be absolved from all resulting "guilt and shame." The act still did not overturn any of the remaining convictions or reverse any of the attainders. But there the matter rests.[105]

Epilogue

The Salem witch trials came near the end of a tragic era. The number of witch trials had begun to decline precipitously throughout the West, until by the mid-eighteenth century they practically disappeared. In the Netherlands, the decline actually began earlier in the century; in Poland, it did not occur until after 1725. The last legal execution in Europe occurred in Glarus, Switzerland, in 1782, but in 1793, two women were extralegally put to death for witchcraft in the Polish city of Pose. Such vigilante actions were not uncommon in Europe, after recourse to the law was blocked for those who were convinced that others were witches and doing them harm.[1]

Large hunts disappeared first, perhaps because of the social dysfunction they had caused, then individual cases, especially after the laws were changed, making conviction more difficult, if not impossible. There were no large hunts in England after the mid-seventeenth century, and one of the last cases in England for which we have any information occurred in Hertfordshire. In 1751, two "superannuated witches, crazed with age and overwhelmed with infirmities," were seized on suspicion of witchcraft and subjected to the water, or swimming, test. Both women were acquitted, the records reveal, but they drowned in the process.[2]

The decline in the number of witch trials was as rapid in New England. In 1693, after attempting suicide, Mary Watkins of Massachusetts accused herself of being a witch, but the jury would not even indict her, finding her instead unfit to stand trial. And, in 1697, the Winifred Benhams, mother and daughter, of Connecticut, appeared in court on charges of witchcraft but were acquitted. Thereafter, witch trial records vanish.[3] The people of New England had come to realize that it was beyond their ability to find witches and to convict them in a court of law, but they did not cease so quickly to believe in their existence.

In 1720, in Littleton, Massachusetts, in a case that paralleled Salem in its early stages, eleven-year-old Elizabeth Blanchard fell into fits, experienced trances and visions, physically attacked herself and others, and complained of "wounds and pinches and prickings, which she said she had received by invisible hands." Soon, her two younger sisters were stricken and all three accused a local woman of afflicting them. The community was divided over the diagnoses, variously believing that the girls were "underwitted," wicked, or "under an evil hand." As a "general cry" to take action against the accused intensified, the woman died, whereupon the children returned to normal, leading most to believe the case had been solved. Years later, however, Elizabeth Blanchard, then a grown woman, confessed to her pastor that out of "folly and pride" she and her sisters had concocted the whole affair.[4]

In 1746, charges of occult practices circulated once again in Salem village. The Reverend Peter Clark reported that he had received information that several people in his parish had "resorted to a woman of very ill reputation, pretending to the art of divination and fortune-telling." Clark's congregation, whose predecessors had been so quick to bring suit only half a century earlier, merely issued a statement condemning such practices. The statement read that it was "highly impious and scandalous . . . for Christians, especially church members, to seek and consult reputed witches or fortune-tellers." The congregation did not recommend any legal action, agreeing instead that such practice rendered "the persons guilty of it subject to the just censure of the church." Similarly, the Reverend Clark admonished everyone against the "infamous and ungodly practice of consulting witches or fortune-tellers, or any that are reputed such," and he exhorted those guilty of such actions "to repent and return to God, earnestly seeking forgiveness."[5]

Writing in the middle of the eighteenth century, one clergyman observed that few towns in New England had failed to experience at least one suspicion of witchcraft, and that some inhabitants "were well-versed in that occupation." In 1800, another minister on a missionary tour of eastern Maine found that in the town of Fayette there was "witchcraft in plenty," including inexplicable physical and mental tortures of one man and mysterious interferences with the production of cheese from milk in the house of the town minister. From 1800 to 1810, a young girl in Bristol, Connecticut, charged her aunt with bewitching her, an accusation that occurred in the midst of a number of mysterious events, while some seventy years later two women of Hopkinton, New Hampshire, were suspected of witchcraft. In this last instance, when asked by the townspeople how they might proceed, the Reverend Timothy Walker of nearby Concord told them that "the most they had to fear from witches was from talking about them; that if they would cease talking about them and let them alone they would soon disappear."[6] Times had changed!

Belief in the supernatural continued, even in intellectual circles, into the eighteenth century. It coexisted with ideas of Lockean psychology and Newtonian science, and the English jurist William Blackstone continued to insist that "to deny the possibility, nay, the actual existence, of witchcraft and sorcery, is at once flatly to contradict the revealed Word of God . . . [and] a truth to which every nation in the world hath . . . borne testimony."[7] By the middle of the century, however, the degree of skepticism concerning the practice of witchcraft brought about an end to belief among the better-educated. Exemplified by the Scientific Revolution, people no longer saw the operation of the universe as quite so mysterious, but rather knowable, orderly, and functioning according to fixed laws beyond the influence of men. The resulting mechanical philosophy denied the existence of occult powers, insisting instead that there were natural explanations for apparently supernatural phenomena.[8] As Richard Godbeer has explained:

> As the realm of natural causation encroached onto territory formerly designated as supernatural, commentators began to explain seemingly occult phenomena in rationalist terms; [and] a growing number of educated people became less willing to categorize particular incidents as supernatural.[9]

Those individuals—the educated, in positions of authority—took the steps necessary, largely revising the law, to stop the prosecutions. In Europe they adopted stricter rules concerning the use of torture, and in England and New England they insisted on more conclusive proof of diabolical pact than spectral evidence. If the masses of people continued to accuse their neighbors of witchcraft, as indeed they did, they were forced to seek regress through extralegal, if not illegal, means, including white magic and vigilantism.[10]

Belief in the supernatural among the more common folk, in fact, did not disappear as quickly. As they had for centuries, the people continued to view the world as an enchanted place, filled with occult forces that could be harnessed for good or evil purposes. For them, the decline in what the better-educated now called a superstition constituted a gradual shift in belief rather than a sudden transformation, and that lasted for a goodly portion of the population, well into the nineteenth century.[11]

By the nineteenth century, even the masses of people were better-educated about the workings of the universe. Further, at least for some, economic conditions had improved, ameliorating the dislocations brought about by the first stages of modernization, and a more tolerant religious climate had evolved, wherein although wars continued to be fought they were more often launched for nationalistic rather than religious reasons. As one historian has concluded:

> In such an environment individuals and communities have less reason to lash out at their helpless neighbors to relieve their general fears, and even less reason to engage in a massive witch-hunt to eradicate an imaginary horde of Devil-worshippers who were threatening to turn the entire world and the social order upside down.[12]

Until the end, those suspected of being witches continued to be women of at least middle age, and incidents of conflict and discordant personalities constituted the most common cause of suspicion. The image of the witch, however, was transferred to that of victim and hag. In his investigation of incidents involving witches in the nineteenth century, John Demos has found several references to witches as victims: In Exeter, Rhode Island, a cat scampered across the road in front of a farmer, startling his horse team. The farmer, suspecting that a local woman had assumed the cat's shape, shot the cat with a silver bullet (believed most effective in such matters), and elsewhere the suspected witch simultaneously fell and broke her hip. A resident of Salem, New Hampshire, attributing his cow's illness to sorcery, cut off its ears and tail, whereupon a suspected witch soon died in a house fire. And a woman of Wentworth, New Hampshire, frustrated in her efforts to churn a store of butter, thrust a hot poker into the churn, at which point the butter came but only after a loud scream was heard in the distance and a long-suspected neighbor suffered a bad burn on her legs![13]

Demos found that whereas descriptions of seventeenth-century witches portrayed a powerful, formidable, and dangerous adversary, by the nineteenth century she had become a "hag-witch," characteristically old and decrepit. As portrayed in the literature of the time, she was ugly, often disorganized, confused, and a trifle "dotty," to use Demos's word. She was an isolate, lived alone, and enjoyed no human contact. Representative is the poet John Greenleaf Whittier's description of Moll Pitcher, a well-known witch of eighteenth-century Lynn, Massachusetts:

> *She stood upon a bare, tall crag*
> *Which overlooked her rugged cot—*
> *A wasted, gray, and meager hag,*
> *In features evil as her lot.*
> *She had the crooked nose of a witch,*
> *And a crooked back and chin;*
> *And in her gait she had a hitch,*
> *And in her hand she carried a switch,*
> *To aid her work of sin.*[14]

The once-powerful witch might still have inspired some fear, but mostly she had become a target for contempt, ridicule, and mockery. And the image stuck, as witnessed through figures in more recent popular culture, such as the Wicked Witch of the West in the film version of *The Wizard of Oz* (1939).

In recent years, there has been a revival of interest in the practice of witchcraft, better known as Wicca. But although misunderstood and even viewed with concern in some quarters, this latter-day neopagan form of nature worship coexists peacefully with its dominantly Christian neighbors. At long last, we can proclaim that we no longer believe in witches. That is to say, our belief in witches as it developed in the West, beginning in the fifteenth century, as so threatening to church and state that they should not be suffered to live, is dead. But perhaps not all forms of "the great fear" have passed.

Andrew Delbanco, in his recent book, provocatively titled *The Death of Satan,* points to the Salem witch trials as the turning point, not only in the belief in witches but in the influence of the Devil. After centuries of cultural development of his diabolical persona, Delbanco argues, in a few short years the Devil became like an old actor whose declaratory story style had become comic and who was losing his audience.[15] But this might be overstating the case a bit for many Americans.

In 1990, a Gallup Poll found that only 14 percent of Americans believed in witches, but fifty-five percent continued to believe in the Devil, and by 1994 the latter figure had risen to 65 percent.[16] Another study has shown that 86 percent of Texans continue to view Satanism as either a serious or very serious problem in our society.[17] One could argue that the attitudes of Texans on such matters do not reflect those of the nation as a whole, but other evidence would belie that. Movies such as *Rosemary's Baby* (1968) and *The Exorcist* (1974), to name just two, were wildly successful, as have been Satanist-related programs on television talk shows—by Oprah Winfrey, Phil Donahue, and Geraldo Rivera, for example. Rivera's two-hour special, "Devil Worship: Exposing Satan's Secret Underground," topped the Nielsen talk show ratings in 1988.[18]

Perhaps these can be dismissed as mere entertainment, and the occasional furor raised over suggestive lyrics embedded in heavy metal music and in response to Anton La Vey's Church of Satan, which is far more hedonistic than diabolical, as the rantings of the uninformed few. Not so easily dismissed, however, are the cover of the June 19, 1972, issue of *Time* magazine, headlined "The Occult Revival," which featured the hooded head of a supposed Satanist and the subtitle "Satan Returns"; and the considerable fear, kept in check only by the lack of any real evidence, generated by criminal cases that appear to bear the marks of ritualistic abuse, which many believe are linked to an organized widespread satanic conspiracy.

It is as difficult to plumb the remaining depths of our fears of the unknown as it is to guard against our inappropriate or disproportionate and often tragic response to it. But therein lies yet another explanation for our continued fascination with the Salem witch trials, now over 300 years old! As Bernard Rosenthal has recently put it, the Salem witch trials have become "the vehicle for countless metaphors of oppression and persecution." For that reason alone, he argues, that which by any other standard would be relatively minor in its magnitude has achieved archetypal status.[19]

Symbolic of this status is that in 1991, when a monument was unveiled in Salem to the victims of the witch trials, Arthur Miller was the guest of honor, and when, the following year, the monument was dedicated, Elie Wiesel officiated. Miller's presence—as author of *The Crucible* (1952), set in Salem in 1692 but written in the midst of the anticommunist "witch-hunt" of the 1950s—was not only appropriate but it also made clear that what had been erected in Salem would not only mark a historical event but also serve as "the validation of truth over superstition and bigotry." And for his life long testimonial to the destruction of European Jewry during World War II, for which he earned the Nobel Prize for Peace in 1986, Wiesel's presence assured the continued association of the Salem witch trials with persecution and suffering.[20]

The Salem witch trials remind us of a barbaric period in American history long past, that might be easily forgotten or at least dismissed except for its entertainment value. We do not hang witches, anymore, after all! We nevertheless continue to remember, because we persist in harboring fears that not only could it happen again, but that it has, repeatedly, if in different forms. That is to say, we still tend to single out innocent victims, or scapegoats, in order to put a human face on our otherwise nebulous and unidentifiable enemies.

Charles Upham, in his nineteenth-century study of the Salem witch trials, was among the first to raise such a specter. He pointed to the colony of New York, where in 1741 a "witch-hunt" occurred in response to a rumor that had been spread of "a conspiracy . . . among the colored portions of the inhabitants to murder whites." The result, he pointed out, much like in Salem, was a "universal panic, like a conflagration," resulting in the imprisonment of over 100, the hanging of twenty-two, the burning at the stake of eleven, and the transporting into slavery of another fifty—nearly all blacks. The moral, he concluded, reflecting on what he had just found in the Salem witch trials, was "that any people given over to the power of contagious passion, may be swept by desolation, and plunged into ruin."[21]

Perhaps the best-known use of the Salem metaphor has been in the history of the anticommunist purges of the late 1940s and early 1950s. Arthur Miller made sure that that would be the case when in his introduction to his dramatization of the Salem witch trials, written at the peak of the anticommunist witch-hunt, he explained that the play was not a history "in the sense in which the word is used by the academic historian." Rather, it was intended to present "the essential nature of one of the strangest and most awful chapters in human history," the application of which, though quite clear by implication, he left to his audience's imagination.[22]

The number of alleged witch-hunts in the United States is far larger, however, including groups long forgotten, except by academic historians and others added from our more recent past. It includes the Illuminati, Masons, Roman Catholics, Jews, Japanese-Americans, child care workers, and feminists, to name just a few. That they were the source of considerable public and even governmental harassment is clear; whether or not the reaction to them constituted a witch-hunt, or even deserves to be mentioned in the same breath as the Salem witch trials, however, is beyond the scope of this book and left to the reader's further investigation. The fear that they do, however, continues to haunt us, returning us once again to Charles Upham's concluding assessment of over a century ago:

> In its general outlines and minuter details, Salem witchcraft is an illustration of the fatal effects of allowing the imagination influenced by passion to take the place of common sense, and of pushing the curiosity and credence of the human mind in this stage of our being, while in these corporeal embodiments, beyond the boundaries that ought to limit their exercise.[23]

Notes

Preface

1. John Demos, "Underlying Themes in the Witchcraft of Seventeenth Century New England," *American Historical Review,* 75 (June 1970): 1311.
2. Larry Gragg, *The Salem Witch Crisis* (New York: Praeger, 1992), 213.
3. Richard Weisman, *Witchcraft, Magic, and Religion in 17th–Century Massachusetts* (Amherst: The University of Massachusetts Press, 1984), 62, 66.
4. David Harley, "Explaining Salem: Calvinist Psychology and the Diagnosis of Possession," *The American Historical Review,* 101 (April 1996): 327.

Chapter One

1. George Lyman Kittredge, *Witchcraft in Old and New England* (Cambridge: Harvard University Press, 1929), 329.

2. Carlo Ginsburg, *The Night Battles: Witchcraft and Agrarian Cults in the Sixteenth and Seventeenth Centuries,* trans. John and Anne Tedeschi (Baltimore: Johns Hopkins University Press, 1983), 438.

3. Jeffrey B. Russell, *A History of Witchcraft: Sorcerers, Heretics, and Pagans* (London: Thames & Hudson, 1980), 29; Brian P. Levack, *The Witch-Hunt in Early Modern Europe,* Second Edition (London: Longman, 1995), 4–7.

4. Russell, *A History of Witchcraft,* 31–33; Ginsburg, *The Night Battles,* 42–50; Norman Cohn, *Europe's Inner Demons* (New York: Basic Books, 1975), 210–219.

5. Elaine Pagels, "The Social History of Satan, The 'Intimate Enemy': A Preliminary Sketch," *Harvard Theological Review,* 84 (April 1991): 105.

6. Pagels, "The Social History of Satan," 111, 115.

7. Russell, *A History of Witchcraft,* 35; Joseph Klaits, *Servants of Satan: The Age of the Witch Hunts* (Bloomington: Indiana University Press, 1985), 22–23; Elaine Pagels, "The Social History of Satan, Part II: Satan in the New Testament Gospels," *Journal of the American Academy of Religion,* 62 (Spring 1994): 17–58; Pagels, "The Social History of Satan, The 'Intimate Enemy,' " 114.

8. Klaits, *Servants of Satan,* 20–21.

9. Levack, *The Witch-Hunt,* 28.

10. Russell, *A History of Witchcraft,* 39–40.

11. Russell, *A History of Witchcraft,* 52–53.

12. Russell, *A History of Witchcraft,* 53–54; Klaits, *Servants of Satan,* 39.

13. Klaits, *Servants of Satan,* 114; Jeffrey Burton Russell, *Witchcraft in the Middle Ages* (Ithaca, NY: Cornell University Press, 1972), 84–95; Russell, *A History of Witchcraft,* 55; E. William Monter, *Witchcraft in France and Switzerland: The Borderlands of the Reformation* (Ithaca, NY: Cornell University Press, 1976), 159–166.

14. Russell, *A History of Witchcraft,* 60.

15. William Shumaker, *The Occult Sciences in the Renaissance* (Berkeley: University of California Press, 1972), 108–159; Cohn, *Europe's Inner Demons,* 176; Levack, *The Witch-Hunt,* 62–63.

16. Levack, *The Witch-Hunt,* 8; Russell, *A History of Witchcraft,* 70.

17. Klaits, *Servants of Satan,* 37.

18. Klaits, *Servants of Satan,* 42.

19. Kramer also developed a reputation for corruption. The Dominicans condemned him in 1490 for embezzlement and for other forms of misbehavior. Sprenger later repented his role in the witch-hunt and condemned Kramer as well. Russell, *A History of Witchcraft,* 79. Although not entirely accurate, the name *Germany* will be used herein, because it is the least cumbersome and the most common reference to that area to become a nation in 1871.

20. They also included an at least partially forged endorsement from the University of Cologne theology faculty.

21. For some discussion of other manuals, see Russell, *A History of Witchcraft*, 79; Levack, *The Witch-Hunt*, 56–57; Klaits, *Servants of Satan*, 44, 141; Geoffrey Parker, "The European Witchcraze Revisited," *History Today*, 30 (November 1980): 24.

22. Russell, *A History of Witchcraft*, 79.

23. Russell, *A History of Witchcraft*, 79; Levack, *The Witch-Hunt*, 92.

24. Russell, *A History of Witchcraft*, 80–81.

25. Klaits, *Servants of Satan*, 38; John H. Langbein, *Prosecuting Crime in the Renaissance* (Cambridge, MA: Harvard University Press, 1974), 130–139.

26. Levack, *The Witch-Hunt*, 79.

27. Klaits, *Servants of Satan*, 141, 144–145; Russell, *A History of Witchcraft*, 79–80.

28. Levack, *The Witch-Hunt*, 93.

29. See Henry A. Kamen, *European Society, 1500–1700* (London: Hutchinson, 1984); Perez Zagorin, *Rebels and Rulers, 1500–1600* (Cambridge: Cambridge University Press, 1983).

30. Richard Weisman, *Witchcraft, Magic, and Religion in 17th–Century Massachusetts* (Amherst: The University of Massachusetts Press, 1984), 54, 61, 69; Alan Macfarlane, *Witchcraft in Tudor and Stuart England* (New York: Harper and Row, 1970), 192–199.

31. Russell, *A History of Witchcraft*, 82; Levack, *The Witch-Hunt*, 22.

32. Macfarlane, *Witchcraft in Tudor*, 161; Keith Thomas, *Religion and the Decline of Magic* (London: Weidenfeld & Nicholson, 1971), 562.

33. Levack, *The Witch-Hunt*, 158–159.

34. Levack, *The Witch-Hunt*, 157–158.

35. Levack, *The Witch-Hunt*, 173.

36. John Tedeschi, "Preliminary Observations on Writing History of the Roman Inquisition," in *Continuity and Discontinuity in Church History*, ed. F. Forrester Church & Timothy George (Leiden: Brill, 1979), 318, 515.

37. Klaits, *Servants of Satan*, 1, 41; Levack, *The Witch-Hunt*, 25.

38. Klaits, *Servants of Satan*, 141; Levack, *The Witch-Hunt*, 21–24; H. C. Eric Midelfort, *Witch Hunting in Southwestern Germany, 1562–1684* (Stanford: Stanford University Press, 1992), 147; Monter, *Witchcraft in France and Switzerland*, 49, 105; E. William Monter, "French and Italian Witchcraft," *History Today*, 30 (November 1980): 31–32.

39. Russell, *A History of Witchcraft*, 82; Levack, *The Witch-Hunt*, 193, 222, 223.

40. Levack, *The Witch-Hunt*, 226; Tedeschi, "Preliminary Observations," 42, 242–243.

41. Gustav Henningsen, "The Greatest Witch Trial of All: Navarre, 1609–1614," *History Today,* 30 (November 1980): 36–38; Henry A. Kamen, *The Spanish Inquisition* (London: Weidenfeld & Nicolson, 1965), 145; Levack, *The Witch-Hunt,* 229; see Benzion Netanyahu, *The Origins of the Inquisition in Fifteenth Century Spain* (New York: Random House, 1995).

42. Levack, *The Witch-Hunt,* 26; Russell, *A History of Witchcraft,* 86.

43. Levack, *The Witch-Hunt,* 151; Mary Douglas, ed., *Witchcraft Confessions and Accusations* (London: Tavistock Publications, 1970), xxi.

44. Although as a whole approximately 80 percent of those accused of being witches during the Great European Witch-hunt were women, in certain areas, mostly on the periphery, the number varied significantly. In the Scandinavian countries, for example, the male-female ratio was close to even. In Russia and Estonia, men outnumbered women. Levack, *The Witch-Hunt,* 134–135; Midelfort, *Witch Hunting,* 281; Klaits, *Servants of Satan,* 5; David Nicolls, "The Devil in Renaissance France," *History Today* 30 (November 1980): 27; see also Anne Llewellyn Barstow, *Witchcraze: A New History of the European Witch Hunts* (New York: HarperCollins, 1994).

45. Jacob Sprenger and Heinrich Kramer, *Malleus Maleficarum,* trans. Montague Summers (1484; reprint, New York: Benjamin Blom, 1970), 47.

46. Klaits, *Servants of Satan,* 51, 53, 66–71, 99; Ronald C. Sawyer, "'Strangely Handled in All Her Lyms': Witchcraft and Healing in Jacobean England," *Journal of Social History,* 22 (Spring 1989): 461–485.

47. Levack, *The Witch-Hunt,* 145–146.

48. Levack, *The Witch-Hunt,* 145–146.

49. Levack, *The Witch-Hunt,* 146–148.

50. Thomas, *Religion and the Decline,* 530; Macfarlane, *Witchcraft,* 158–160; Monter, *Witchcraft in France,* 136–137; Gregory Zilboorg, *The Medical Man and the Witch during the Renaissance* (New York: W. W. Norton, 1941), 204–230; Levack, *The Witch–Hunt,* 155–156; Siegfried Brauer, "Martin Luther on Witchcraft: A True Reformer?" in *The Politics of Gender in Early Modern Europe,* ed. J. R. Brink et al (Kirksville, MO: Sixteenth Century Journal Publishers, 1989), 29–42; Allison Coudert, "The Myth of the Improved Status of Protestant Women: The Case of the Witchcraze," in *The Politics of Gender in Early Modern Europe,* ed. J. R. Brink et al (Kirksville, MO: Sixteenth Century Journal Publishers, 1989), 61–94.

51. Leonard W. Levy, "Accusatorial and Inquisitorial Systems of Criminal Procedure in the Beginnings," in *Freedom and Reform,* ed. Harold Hyman and Leonard Levy (New York: Oxford University Press, 1967), 16–54; Cohn, *Europe's Inner Demons,* 12.

52. Russell, *A History of Witchcraft,* 92; Kittredge, *Witchcraft in Old and New England,* 25.

53. Macfarlane, *Witchcraft in Tudor and Stuart England,* 85, 87, 89–91.

54. Russell, *A History of Witchcraft,* 92; Levack, *The Witch-Hunt,* 10; Cohn, *Europe's Inner Demons,* 12–13; Macfarlane, *Witchcraft in Tudor and Stuart England,* 84; Klaits, *Servants of Satan,* 10.

55. Macfarlane, *Witchcraft in Tudor and Stuart England,* 87–88, 92–94.

56. Kittredge, *Witchcraft in Old and New England,* 27–29, 32.

57. Weisman, *Witchcraft, Magic, and Religion,* 12.

58. Kittredge, *Witchcraft in Old and New England,* 282; Weisman, *Witchcraft, Magic, and Religion,* 12; Russell, *A History of Witchcraft,* 92.

59. Russell, *A History of Witchcraft,* 92–94.

60. Russell, *A History of Witchcraft,* 93–94.

61. Karen Armstrong, "Introduction," to Frances Hill, *A Delusion of Satan: The Full Story of the Salem Witch Trials* (New York: Doubleday, 1995), 82–84; Kittredge, *Witchcraft in Old and New England,* 285; Russell, *A History of Witchcraft,* 96.

62. Kittredge, *Witchcraft in Old and New England,* 278.

63. Kittredge, *Witchcraft in Old and New England,* 278; Russell, *A History of Witchcraft,* 97.

64. Richard Weisman, *Witchcraft, Magic, and Religion,* 12; Levy, "Accusatorial and Inquisitorial Systems," 102.

65. Russell, *A History of Witchcraft,* 97–98.

66. Kittredge, *Witchcraft in Old and New England,* 331, 334.

67. Russell, *A History of Witchcraft,* 100.

68. Russell, *A History of Witchcraft,* 100, 102–103; Levack, *The Witch-Hunt,* 3–4. See also Hugh Trevor-Roper, "The European Witch-Craze," in *Witchcraft and Sorcery* (London: Penguin Books, 1972).

CHAPTER TWO

1. David D. Hall, "Magic and Witchcraft," *Encyclopedia of the North American Colonies* (1993), III, 657.

2. John Eccles, *France in America,* Revised Edition (Markham, Ontario: Fitzhenry and Whiteside, 1990), 144–145; Hall, "Magic and Witchcraft," 657–658.

3. Hervé Gagnon, "Witchcraft in Montreal and Quebec during the French Regime, 1600–1760: An Essay on the Survival of French Mentalité in Colonial Canada," in *Wonders of the Invisible World, 1600–1900,* ed. Peter Benes (Boston: Boston University Scholarly Publications, 1995), 78–79, 83.

4. Irene Silverblatt, *Moon, Sun, and Witches: Gender Ideologies and Class in Inca and Colonial Peru* (Princeton, NJ: Princeton University

Press, 1987), 169–181; Richard E. Greenleaf, *The Mexican Inquisition of the Sixteenth Century* (Albuquerque: University of New Mexico Press, 1969), 172–173; Richard E. Greenleaf, *Zumarraga and the Mexican Inquisition, 1536–1543* (Washington, DC: Academy of American Franciscan History, 1961), 111–117; Hall, "Magic and Witchcraft," 657; Ruth Behar, "Sexual Witchcraft, Colonialism, and Women's Powers: Views from the Mexican Inquisition," in *Sexuality and Marriage in Colonial Latin America,* ed. Asunción Lavrin (Lincoln: University of Nebraska Press, 1989), 179, 183, 200.

5. J. H. Le Froy, *Memorial of the Discovery and Early Settlement of the Bermudas or Somers Island* (London: Longman, Green, and Co., 1879), II, 601–633; Hall, "Magic and Witchcraft," 658.

6. Hall, "Magic and Witchcraft," 658.

7. Francis Neal Parke, "Witchcraft in Maryland," *Maryland Historical Magazine,* 31 (December 1936): 284, 289–290.

8. David S. Lovejoy, "Satanizing the American Indian," *New England Quarterly,* 67 (December 1994): 606, 620.

9. Karen Armstrong, "Introduction" to Frances Hill, *A Delusion of Satan: The Full Story of the Salem Witch Trials* (New York: Doubleday, 1995), ix–x.

10. Richard Weisman, *Witchcraft, Magic, and Religion in 17th–Century Massachusetts* (Amherst: The University of Massachusetts Press, 1984), 23, 96–97; George Lyman Kittredge, *Witchcraft in Old and New England* (Cambridge: Harvard University Press, 1929), 330; John Demos, *Entertaining Satan: Witchcraft and the Culture of Early New England* (New York: Oxford University Press, 1982), vii.

11. Kittredge, *Witchcraft in Old and New England,* 362–363.

12. Richard Godbeer, *The Devil's Dominion: Magic and Religion in Early New England* (Cambridge: Cambridge University Press, 1992), 5, 15, 19, 24; David D. Hall, *Worlds of Wonder, Days of Judgment: Popular Religious Belief in Early New England* (New York: Alfred A. Knopf, 1989), 5–7.

13. Godbeer, *The Devil's Dominion,* 6; W. R. Jones, "'Hill-Diggers' and 'Hell-Raisers': Treasure Hunting and the Supernatural in Old and New England," in *Wonders of the Invisible World: 1600–1900,* ed. Peter Benes (Boston: Boston University Scholarly Publications, 1995), 107–108.

14. David D. Hall, ed., *Witch-Hunting in Seventeenth-Century New England: A Documentary History, 1638–1692* (Boston: Northeastern University Press, 1991), 9; Weisman, *Witchcraft, Magic, and Religion,* 53; Godbeer, *The Devil's Dominion,* 18.

15. Hall, ed., *Witch-Hunting in Seventeenth-Century,* 5.

16. Demos, *Entertaining Satan,* 13, 279, 298; See Keith Thomas, *Religion and the Decline of Magic* (London: Weidenfeld & Nicholson, 1971); and Alan Macfarlane, *Witchcraft in Tudor and Stuart England* (New York: Harper and Row, 1970).
17. Demos, *Entertaining Satan,* 298–299; Macfarlane, *Witchcraft in Tudor and Stuart England,* 197; Weisman, *Witchcraft, Magic, and Religion,* 80–88.
18. Demos, *Entertaining Satan,* 84–86.
19. Godbeer, *The Devil's Dominion,* 21, 68; Hall, ed., *Witch-Hunting in Seventeenth-Century,* 6; Demos, *Entertaining Satan,* 60–61.
20. Demos, *Entertaining Satan,* 66–68, 72–73.
21. Carol F. Karlsen, *The Devil in the Shape of a Woman, Witchcraft in Colonial New England* (New York: W. W. Norton, 1987), 217.
22. Demos, *Entertaining Satan,* 75–76.
23. Demos, *Entertaining Satan,* 77; Jane Kamensky, "Words, Witches, and Woman Trouble: Witchcraft, Disorderly Speech, and Gender Boundaries in Puritan New England," *Essex Institute Historical Collections,* 128 (October 1992): 286–307.
24. Demos, *Entertaining Satan,* 93–94.
25. Demos, *Entertaining Satan,* 97, 154.
26. Demos, *Entertaining Satan,* 155–157.
27. Demos, *Entertaining Satan,* 157–165, 168.
28. Weisman, *Witchcraft, Magic, and Religion,* 44–47.
29. Weisman, *Witchcraft, Magic, and Religion,* 44–47, 50–51.
30. Weisman, *Witchcraft, Magic, and Religion,* 50–51.
31. Hall, ed., *Witch-Hunting in Seventeenth-Century,* 11; Demos, *Entertaining Satan,* 10; Weisman, *Witchcraft, Magic, and Religion,* 13; Godbeer, *The Devil's Dominion,* 158.
32. Hall, ed., *Witch-Hunting in Seventeenth-Century,* 11; Weisman, *Witchcraft, Magic, and Religion,* 15.
33. Hall, ed., *Witch-Hunting in Seventeenth-Century,* 10–11; Demos, *Entertaining Satan,* 297; Weisman, *Witchcraft, Magic, and Religion,* 98, 103, 109–110.
34. Weisman, *Witchcraft, Magic, and Religion,* 103–104.
35. Demos, *Entertaining Satan,* 11.
36. Weisman, *Witchcraft, Magic, and Religion,* 18.
37. John Demos has calculated the annual rate of indictments and executions per 100,000 people in New England and England at 6.69 and 1.03, versus 0.26 and 0.13, respectively. Demos, *Entertaining Satan,* 12.
38. Hall, ed., *Witch-Hunting in Seventeenth-Century,* 19–20.
39. Hall, ed., *Witch-Hunting in Seventeenth-Century,* 21.
40. Hall, ed., *Witch-Hunting in Seventeenth-Century,* 22.
41. Hall, ed., *Witch-Hunting in Seventeenth-Century,* 22.
42. Hall, ed., *Witch-Hunting in Seventeenth-Century,* 23–24.

43. Hall, ed., *Witch-Hunting in Seventeenth-Century,* 95; Charles Upham, *Salem Witchcraft* (Boston: Wiggin and Lunt, 1867), I, 62.

44. Demos, *Entertaining Satan,* chap. 2; Hall, ed., *Witch-Hunting in Seventeenth-Century,* 213.

45. Hall, ed., *Witch-Hunting in Seventeenth-Century,* 25–29.

46. Hall, ed., *Witch-Hunting in Seventeenth-Century,* 30–60; Demos, *Entertaining Satan,* 280–290.

47. Hall, ed., *Witch-Hunting in Seventeenth-Century,* 89.

48. Hall, ed., *Witch-Hunting in Seventeenth-Century,* 147.

49. Hall, ed., *Witch-Hunting in Seventeenth-Century,* 147–148.

50. John Jr. was the son of the previously mentioned Massachusetts Governor John Winthrop. Hall, ed., *Witch-Hunting in Seventeenth-Century,* 147–148.

51. Hall, ed., *Witch-Hunting in Seventeenth-Century,* 197; Demos, *Entertaining Satan,* 99, 106.

52. Hall, ed., *Witch-Hunting in Seventeenth-Century,* 196–198.

53. Hall, ed., *Witch-Hunting in Seventeenth-Century,* 198; Demos, *Entertaining Satan,* 100–101.

54. Hall, ed., *Witch-Hunting in Seventeenth-Century,* 198–199; Demos, *Entertaining Satan,* 101–103.

55. Hall, ed., *Witch-Hunting in Seventeenth-Century,* 200; Demos, *Entertaining Satan,* 103.

56. Hall, ed., *Witch-Hunting in Seventeenth-Century,* 211–212; Demos, *Entertaining Satan,* 101–105.

57. Demos, *Entertaining Satan,* 114.

58. John Hale, *A Modest Inquiry into the Nature of Witchcraft* (1702), in George Lincoln Burr, ed., *Narratives of the Witchcraft Cases: 1648–1706* (New York: Charles Scribner's Sons, 1914), 413–414.

59. Thomas Hutchinson, *The History of the Colony and Province of Massachusetts Bay* (1764), ed. Lawrence Shaw Mayo (Cambridge, MA: Harvard University Press, 1936), II, 17–18.

60. Hall, ed., *Witch-Hunting in Seventeenth-Century,* 265.

61. Hall, ed., *Witch-Hunting in Seventeenth-Century,* 264.

62. Hall, ed., *Witch-Hunting in Seventeenth-Century,* 265–266, 271.

63. Hall, ed., *Witch-Hunting in Seventeenth-Century,* 266, 269.

64. Hall, ed., *Witch-Hunting in Seventeenth-Century,* 266; Demos, *Entertaining Satan,* 171–175; Kenneth Silverman, *The Life and Times of Cotton Mather* (New York: Harper & Row, 1984), 86–87.

65. Hall, ed., *Witch-Hunting in Seventeenth-Century,* 267–269.

66. Demos, *Entertaining Satan,* 7; Hall, ed., *Witch-Hunting in Seventeenth-Century,* 268–269.

67. Hall, ed., *Witch-Hunting in Seventeenth-Century,* 270–271.

68. Hall, ed., *Witch-Hunting in Seventeenth-Century,* 271; Demos, *Entertaining Satan,* 8.

69. Hall, ed., *Witch-Hunting in Seventeenth-Century,* 272–273.

70. Demos, *Entertaining Satan,* 373, 376.

71. Godbeer, *The Devil's Dominion,* 177.

72. Robert G. Pope, *The Half-way Covenant: Church Membership in Puritan New England* (Princeton, NJ: Princeton University Press, 1969).

73. Demos, *Entertaining Satan,* 383.

74. Demos, *Entertaining Satan,* 144.

75. Demos, *Entertaining Satan,* 144; see Francis Jennings, *The Invasion of America: Indians, Colonialism, and the Cant of Conquest* (Chapel Hill: University of North Carolina Press, 1975); Douglas E. Leach, *Flintlock and Tomahawk: New England in King Philip's War* (New York: W. W. Norton, 1959).

76. Silverman, *The Life and Times,* 88; Demos, *Entertaining Satan,* 384.

77. Godbeer, *The Devil's Dominion,* 185.

78. Paul Boyer and Stephen Nissenbaum, eds., *The Salem Witchcraft Papers: Verbatim Transcripts of the Legal Documents of the Salem Witchcraft Outbreak of 1692* (New York: De Capo Press, 1977), I, 13.

79. John Winthrop, "A Model of Christian Charity" (1630), in *Winthrop Papers* (Boston: Massachusetts Historical Society, 1929–1944), II, 294.

80. Alan Heimert and Andrew Delbanco, eds., *The Puritans in America, A Narrative Anthology* (Cambridge: Harvard University Press, 1985), 233–234.

81. For additional titles and information, see Harry S. Stout, *The New England Soul, Preaching and Religious Culture in Colonial New England* (New York: Oxford University Press, 1986), and Perry Miller, *The New England Mind, From Colony to Province* (Cambridge, MA: Harvard University Press, 1953).

82. Miller, *The New England Mind,* 33–37; Godbeer, *The Devil's Dominion,* 75.

83. Larry Gragg, *The Salem Witch Crisis* (New York: Praeger, 1992), 143.

84. Godbeer, *The Devil's Dominion,* 64, 73.

85. Godbeer, *The Devil's Dominion,* 92, 224.

86. Gragg, *The Salem Witch Crisis,* 144–145.

87. Gragg, *The Salem Witch Crisis,* 145.

88. See Sacvan Bercovitch, *The American Jeremiad* (Madison: University of Wisconsin Press, 1978).

89. Godbeer, *The Devil's Dominion,* 155, 178.

Chapter Three

1. Paul Boyer and Stephen Nissenbaum, eds., *The Salem Witchcraft Papers: Verbatim Transcripts of the Legal Documents of the Salem Witchcraft Outbreak of 1692* (New York: De Capo Press, 1977), I, 5.
2. Paul Boyer and Stephen Nissenbaum, *Salem Possessed, The Social Origins of Witchcraft* (Cambridge, MA: Harvard University Press, 1974), 39; Richard Gildrie, *Salem, Massachusetts, 1626–1683: A Covenant Community* (Charlottesville: University of Virginia Press, 1975), 122.
3. Donald W. Koch, "Income Distribution and Political Structure in Seventeenth-Century Salem, Massachusetts," *Essex Institute Historical Collections* 105 (January 1969), 53–56, 59, 61; Koch, "Income Distribution," 53–56; Boyer and Nissenbaum, *Salem Possessed,* 87.
4. Boyer and Nissenbaum, *Salem Possessed,* 39, 41–42; Boyer and Nissenbaum, eds., *The Salem Witchcraft Papers,* I, 6; Koch, "Income Distribution," 30.
5. Boyer and Nissenbaum, *Salem Possessed,* 111.
6. Boyer and Nissenbaum, *Salem Possessed,* 124–126.
7. Boyer and Nissenbaum, *Salem Possessed,* 119–120.
8. Boyer and Nissenbaum, *Salem Possessed,* 129.
9. Boyer and Nissenbaum, *Salem Possessed,* 137–139.
10. Boyer and Nissenbaum, *Salem Possessed,* 46–47.
11. Larry Gragg, *The Salem Witch Crisis* (New York: Praeger, 1992), 31.
12. Boyer and Nissenbaum, *Salem Possessed,* 54–55.
13. Charles Upham, *Salem Witchcraft* (Boston: Wiggin and Lunt, 1867), I, 258–259; Boyer and Nissenbaum, *Salem Possessed,* 56.
14. Gragg, *Crisis,* 30–33.
15. Gragg, *Crisis,* 30–33.
16. Gragg, *Crisis,* 34.
17. Gragg, *Crisis,* 35.
18. Gragg, *Crisis,* 35; Boyer and Nissenbaum, *Salem Possessed,* 62–63.
19. Gragg, *Crisis,* 35; Boyer and Nissenbaum, *Salem Possessed,* 154.
20. Boyer and Nissenbaum, *Salem Possessed,* 44, 63, 131.
21. Gragg, *Crisis,* 36.
22. Gragg, *Crisis,* 37.
23. Gragg, *Crisis,* 37; Boyer and Nissenbaum, *Salem Possessed,* 66.
24. Boyer and Nissenbaum, *Salem Possessed,* 65; Gragg, *Crisis,* 38.
25. Boyer and Nissenbaum, *Salem Possessed,* 169.
26. Boyer and Nissenbaum, *Salem Possessed,* 68.
27. Boyer and Nissenbaum, *Salem Possessed,* 81–83.
28. Boyer and Nissenbaum, *Salem Possessed,* 83.
29. Boyer and Nissenbaum, eds., *The Salem Witchcraft Papers,* I, 15.
30. Boyer and Nissenbaum, eds., *The Salem Witchcraft Papers,* I, 7.

31. Chadwick Hansen, *Witchcraft at Salem* (New York: George Braziller, 1969), 55.

32. Marion L. Starkey, *The Devil in Massachusetts: A Modern Enquiry into the Salem Witch Trials* (New York: Alfred A. Knopf, 1949), 36–38.

33. Boyer and Nissenbaum, *Salem Possessed,* 115.

34. Starkey, *The Devil in Massachusetts,* 39–40.

35. Starkey, *The Devil in Massachusetts,* 40.

36. Starkey, *The Devil in Massachusetts,* 40.

37. John Hale, *A Modest Inquiry into the Nature of Witchcraft* (1702), in George Lincoln Burr, ed., *Narratives of the Witchcraft Cases: 1648–1706* (New York: Charles Scribner's Sons, 1914), 408.

38. Gragg, *Crisis,* 46.

39. Gragg, *Crisis,* 46.

40. Boyer and Nissenbaum, eds., *The Salem Witchcraft Papers,* I, 95–97.

41. Boyer and Nissenbaum, eds., *The Salem Witchcraft Papers,* I, 95–97.

42. Hale, *A Modest Inquiry,* 413.

43. Gragg, *Crisis,* 45, 47–48.

44. Gragg, *Crisis,* 48; Boyer and Nissenbaum, eds., *The Salem Witchcraft Papers,* I, 5.

45. On Tituba, see Elaine G. Breslaw: "The Salem Witch from Barbados: In Search of Tituba's Roots," *Essex Institute Historical Collections,* 128 (October 1992): 217–238; and *Tituba, Reluctant Witch of Salem: Devilish Indians and Puritan Fantasies* (New York: New York University Press, 1996). Kai R. Erikson, *Wayward Puritans: A Study in the Sociology of Deviance* (New York: John Wiley & Sons, 1966), 143–144.

46. Gragg, *Crisis,* 49; Boyer and Nissenbaum, *Salem Possessed,* 203–204.

47. Boyer and Nissenbaum, *Salem Possessed,* 204; W. Elliot Woodward, ed., *Records of Salem Witchcraft Copied from the Original Documents* (1864, reprint, New York: Da Capo Press, 1969), I, 18–19; Gragg, *Crisis,* 49.

48. Gragg, *Crisis,* 51.

49. Upham, *Salem Witchcraft,* II, 17–18; Winfield Nevins, *Witchcraft in Salem Village* (Boston: Lee and Shepard, 1892), 66; Sidney Perley, *The History of Salem, Massachusetts* (Salem: Sidney Perley, 1924), III, 260; Gragg, *Crisis,* 51.

50. Gragg, *Crisis,* 51; Upham, *Salem Witchcraft,* II, 19, 22.

51. Boyer and Nissenbaum, eds., *The Salem Witchcraft Papers,* II, 355; III, 745.

52. Daniel G. Payne, "Defending Against the Indefensible: Spectral Evidence at the Salem Witchcraft Trials," *Essex Institute Historical Collections,* 129 (January 1993): 64.

53. George Lyman Kittredge, *Witchcraft in Old and New England* (Cambridge: Harvard University Press, 1929), 349; Richard Godbeer, *The*

Devil's Dominion: Magic and Religion in Early New England (Cambridge: Cambridge University Press, 1992), 159.

54. Godbeer, *The Devil's Dominion,* 160.
55. Boyer and Nissenbaum, eds., *The Salem Witchcraft Papers,* I, 22.
56. Upham, *Salem Witchcraft,* II, 36.
57. Payne, "Defending Against the Indefensible," 64.
58. Gragg, *Crisis,* 48.
59. Starkey, *The Devil in Massachusetts,* 54–55; Payne, "Defending Against the Indefensible," 63.
60. Starkey, *The Devil in Massachusetts,* 56; Upham, *Salem Witchcraft,* I, 14; II, 30.
61. Boyer and Nissenbaum, eds., *The Salem Witchcraft Papers,* II, 356–357.
62. Boyer and Nissenbaum, eds., *The Salem Witchcraft Papers,* II, 357–360, 363, 372.
63. Boyer and Nissenbaum, eds., *The Salem Witchcraft Papers,* II, 609–611.
64. Boyer and Nissenbaum, eds., *The Salem Witchcraft Papers,* II, 610–611; Upham, *Salem Witchcraft,* II, 21–22; Starkey, *The Devil in Massachusetts,* 57.
65. Boyer and Nissenbaum, eds., *The Salem Witchcraft Papers,* II, 609–610.
66. Gragg, *Crisis,* 48; Upham, *Salem Witchcraft,* II, 23, 32; Robert Calef, *More Wonders of the Invisible World (1700),* in George Lincoln Burr, ed. *Narratives of the Witchcraft Cases: 1648–1706* (New York: Charles Scribner's Sons, 1914), 343; Breslaw, "The Salem Witch from Barbados," 238.
67. Boyer and Nissenbaum, eds., *The Salem Witchcraft Papers,* III, 747–755; Upham, *Salem Witchcraft,* II, 25; Breslaw, *Tituba,* xxiii, 116–117.
68. Boyer and Nissenbaum, eds., *The Salem Witchcraft Papers,* II, 748–749; Upham, *Salem Witchcraft,* II, 23–26.
69. Boyer and Nissenbaum, eds., *The Salem Witchcraft Papers,* III, 748; Upham, *Salem Witchcraft,* II, 25.
70. Boyer and Nissenbaum, eds., *The Salem Witchcraft Papers,* III, 753; Starkey, *The Devil in Massachusetts,* 59; Upham, *Salem Witchcraft,* II, 23.
71. Upham, *Salem Witchcraft,* II, 25; Boyer and Nissenbaum, eds., *The Salem Witchcraft Papers,* II, 747–750; Starkey, *The Devil in Massachusetts,* 60.
72. Starkey, *The Devil in Massachusetts,* 61.
73. Boyer and Nissenbaum, eds., *The Salem Witchcraft Papers,* III, 749.
74. Boyer and Nissenbaum, eds., *The Salem Witchcraft Papers,* II, 369–370, 373, 377.

75. Boyer and Nissenbaum, eds., *The Salem Witchcraft Papers*, II, 371–372.
76. Boyer and Nissenbaum, eds., *The Salem Witchcraft Papers*, II, 365; Hale, *A Modest Inquiry*, 400.

Chapter Four

1. Larry Gragg, *The Salem Witch Crisis* (New York: Praeger, 1992), 56; Paul Boyer and Stephen Nissenbaum, *Salem Possessed, The Social Origins of Witchcraft* (Cambridge, MA: Harvard University Press, 1974), 146.
2. Marion L. Starkey, *The Devil in Massachusetts: A Modern Enquiry into the Salem Witch Trials* (New York: Alfred A. Knopf, 1949), 66; Gragg, *Crisis,* 56.
3. Gragg, *Crisis,* 56; Paul Boyer and Stephen Nissenbaum, eds., *The Salem Witchcraft Papers: Verbatim Transcripts of the Legal Documents of the Salem Witchcraft Outbreak of 1692* (New York: De Capo Press, 1977), I, 260–261.
4. Boyer and Nissenbaum, eds., *The Salem Witchcraft Papers*, I, 261–262.
5. Boyer and Nissenbaum, eds., *The Salem Witchcraft Papers*, I, 247, 258, 264–265.
6. Deodat Lawson, *A Brief and True Narrative of Witchcraft at Salem Village* (1692), in George Lincoln Burr, ed. *Narratives of the Witchcraft Cases: 1648–1706* (New York: Charles Scribner's Sons, 1914), 153; Starkey, *The Devil in Massachusetts,* 69.
7. Starkey, *The Devil in Massachusetts,* 69; Lawson, *A Brief and True Narrative,* 154.
8. Starkey, *The Devil in Massachusetts,* 70.
9. Lawson, *A Brief and True Narrative,* 154; Gragg, *Crisis,* 59.
10. Lawson, *A Brief and True Narrative,* 154; Gragg, *Crisis,* 59.
11. Boyer and Nissenbaum, eds., *The Salem Witchcraft Papers*, I, 248; Charles Upham, *Salem Witchcraft* (Boston: Wiggin and Lunt, 1867), II, 38.
12. Boyer and Nissenbaum, eds., *The Salem Witchcraft Papers*, I, 248–250.
13. Boyer and Nissenbaum, eds., *The Salem Witchcraft Papers*, I, 250–251.
14. Boyer and Nissenbaum, eds., *The Salem Witchcraft Papers*, I, 252–253.
15. Lawson, *A Brief and True Narrative,* 156; Upham, *Salem Witchcraft,* II, 45, 65; Boyer and Nissenbaum, eds., *The Salem Witchcraft Papers,* I, 250; Starkey, *The Devil in Massachusetts,* 74.

16. Boyer and Nissenbaum, eds., *The Salem Witchcraft Papers,* I, 259–260; Upham, *Salem Witchcraft,* II, 39.
17. Boyer and Nissenbaum, eds., *The Salem Witchcraft Papers,* I, 253; Gragg, *Crisis,* 62.
18. Boyer and Nissenbaum, eds., *The Salem Witchcraft Papers,* I, 239.
19. Gragg, *Crisis,* 82–83.
20. Gragg, *Crisis,* 83–84; Boyer and Nissenbaum, eds., *The Salem Witchcraft Papers,* I, 246.
21. Gragg, *Crisis,* 84.
22. Upham, *Salem Witchcraft,* II, 122–123; Starkey, *The Devil in Massachusetts,* 106.
23. Upham, *Salem Witchcraft,* II, 124.
24. Boyer and Nissenbaum, eds., *The Salem Witchcraft Papers,* II, 351–353; Lawson, *A Brief and True Narrative,* 159–160; Starkey, *The Devil in Massachusetts,* 75.
25. Starkey, *The Devil in Massachusetts,* 78.
26. Starkey, *The Devil in Massachusetts,* 76–77; Boyer and Nissenbaum, *Salem Possessed,* 149, 199–200.
27. Starkey, *The Devil in Massachusetts,* 77.
28. Upham, *Salem Witchcraft,* II, 57.
29. Starkey, *The Devil in Massachusetts,* 78.
30. Upham, *Salem Witchcraft,* II, 57; Boyer and Nissenbaum, *Salem Possessed,* 149.
31. Boyer and Nissenbaum, eds., *The Salem Witchcraft Papers,* II, 604; Gragg, *Crisis,* 63.
32. Lawson, *A Brief and True Narrative,* 157–158; Gragg, *Crisis,* 63.
33. Boyer and Nissenbaum, eds., *The Salem Witchcraft Papers,* II, 583; Upham, *Salem Witchcraft,* II, 59.
34. Upham, *Salem Witchcraft,* II, 58.
35. Upham, *Salem Witchcraft,* II, 58–59; Boyer and Nissenbaum, eds., *The Salem Witchcraft Papers,* II, 593–594.
36. Boyer and Nissenbaum, eds., *The Salem Witchcraft Papers,* II, 584.
37. Boyer and Nissenbaum, eds., *The Salem Witchcraft Papers,* II, 584–586.
38. Boyer and Nissenbaum, eds., *The Salem Witchcraft Papers,* II, 585, 604–605; Upham, *Salem Witchcraft,* II, 68–70; Lawson, *A Brief and True Narrative,* 158–159.
39. Boyer and Nissenbaum, eds., *The Salem Witchcraft Papers,* II, 585–587.
40. Boyer and Nissenbaum, eds., *The Salem Witchcraft Papers,* II, 586–587.
41. Gragg, *Crisis,* 66.
42. Extensive excerpts from Lawson's text are included in Upham, *Salem Witchcraft,* II, 77–87.

43. Upham, *Salem Witchcraft*, II, 77–78.
44. Upham, *Salem Witchcraft*, II, 81.
45. Upham, *Salem Witchcraft*, II, 86–87.
46. Upham, *Salem Witchcraft*, II, 78–79.
47. Upham, *Salem Witchcraft*, II, 78–79.
48. Upham, *Salem Witchcraft*, II, 80, 82, 85.
49. Upham, *Salem Witchcraft*, II, 91.
50. Upham, *Salem Witchcraft*, II, 89.
51. Upham, *Salem Witchcraft*, II, 94; Starkey, *The Devil in Massachusetts*, 89.
52. Gragg, *Crisis*, 68, 146; Boyer and Nissenbaum, *Salem Possessed*, 172.
53. Boyer and Nissenbaum, *Salem Possessed*, 172. Parris's sermon is reprinted in Paul Boyer and Stephen Nissenbaum, eds., *Salem-Village Witchcraft: A Documentary Record of Local Conflict in Colonial New England* (Boston: Boston University Press, 1993), 129–131.
54. Gragg, *Crisis*, 68–69; Boyer and Nissenbaum, eds., *Salem Village Witchcraft*, 278–279; Upham, *Salem Witchcraft*, II, 95–96.
55. Gragg, *Crisis*, 76; Boyer and Nissenbaum, *Salem Possessed*, 182.
56. Upham, *Salem Witchcraft*, II, 99–100; Starkey, *The Devil in Massachusetts*, 90–91.
57. Boyer and Nissenbaum, eds., *The Salem Witchcraft Papers*, II, 658–659; Upham, *Salem Witchcraft*, II, 102–103.
58. Boyer and Nissenbaum, eds., *The Salem Witchcraft Papers*, II, 659.
59. Boyer and Nissenbaum, eds., *The Salem Witchcraft Papers*, II, 658–661; Upham, *Salem Witchcraft*, II, 105–106.
60. Starkey, *The Devil in Massachusetts*, 90.
61. Upham, *Salem Witchcraft*, II, 138.
62. Starkey, *The Devil in Massachusetts*, 111.
63. Boyer and Nissenbaum, eds., *The Salem Witchcraft Papers*, II, 288–289.
64. Boyer and Nissenbaum, eds., *The Salem Witchcraft Papers*, I, 289.
65. Starkey, *The Devil in Massachusetts*, 112–113; Upham, *Salem Witchcraft*, II, 201.
66. Upham, *Salem Witchcraft*, II, 200–201.
67. Starkey, *The Devil in Massachusetts*, 115; Upham, *Salem Witchcraft*, II, 201.
68. Upham, *Salem Witchcraft*, 202–204, Boyer and Nissenbaum, eds., *The Salem Witchcraft Papers*, I, 287–288.
69. Gragg, *Crisis*, 82; Boyer and Nissenbaum, eds., *The Salem Witchcraft Papers*, I, 10.
70. Bernard Rosenthal, *Salem Story: Reading the Witch Trials of 1692* (Cambridge: Cambridge University Press, 1993), 205–206.
71. Quoted in Boyer and Nissenbaum, *Salem Possessed*, 32.
72. Rosenthal, *Salem Story*, 151.

73. Boyer and Nissenbaum, eds., *The Salem Witchcraft Papers,* III, 1016.

74. Upham, *Salem Witchcraft,* II, 2.

75. See, for example, Linnda Caporael, "Ergotism: The Satan Loosed in Salem?" *Science,* 192 (April 2, 1976): 21–26, and its rebuttal, Nicholas P. Spanos and Jack Gottlieb, "Ergotism and the Salem Village Witch Trials," *Science,* 194 (December 24, 1976): 1390–1394.

76. Ernest Caulfield, "Pediatric Aspects of the Salem Witchcraft Tragedy," *American Journal of Diseases of Children,* 65 (May 1943): 788–802.

77. Chadwick Hansen, *Witchcraft at Salem* (New York: George Braziller, 1969), x.

78. Rosenthal, *Salem Story,* 41.

CHAPTER FIVE

1. Marion L. Starkey, *The Devil in Massachusetts: A Modern Enquiry into the Salem Witch Trials* (New York: Alfred A. Knopf, 1949), 63.

2. Starkey, *The Devil in Massachusetts,* 63.

3. Sidney Perley, *The History of Salem, Massachusetts* (Salem: Sidney Perley, 1924), 200; Paul Boyer and Stephen Nissenbaum, *Salem Possessed, The Social Origins of Witchcraft* (Cambridge, MA: Harvard University Press, 1974), 201.

4. Boyer and Nissenbaum, *Salem Possessed,* 201; Charles Upham, *Salem Witchcraft* (Boston: Wiggin and Lunt, 1867), II, 305–306.

5. Starkey, *The Devil in Massachusetts,* 63; Paul Boyer and Stephen Nissenbaum, eds., *The Salem Witchcraft Papers: Verbatim Transcripts of the Legal Documents of the Salem Witchcraft Outbreak of 1692* (New York: De Capo Press, 1977), II, 683–684.

6. Starkey, *The Devil in Massachusetts,* 87.

7. Larry Gragg, *The Salem Witch Crisis* (New York: Praeger, 1992), 76.

8. Starkey, *The Devil in Massachusetts,* 93.

9. Boyer and Nissenbaum, eds., *The Salem Witchcraft Papers,* II, 657–658, 674–675; Gragg, *Crisis,* 78.

10. The reader will recall that on April 11 the deputy governor and members of the General Court attended the Salem town hearings. Upham, *Salem Witchcraft,* II, 107; Boyer and Nissenbaum, eds., *The Salem Witchcraft Papers,* II, 659–660.

11. Boyer and Nissenbaum, eds., *The Salem Witchcraft Papers,* II, 660; Starkey, *The Devil in Massachusetts,* 93; Upham, *Salem Witchcraft,* II, 107–109.

12. Robert Calef, *More Wonders of the Invisible World (1700),* in George Lincoln Burr, ed., *Narratives of the Witchcraft Cases: 1648–1706* (New York: Charles Scribner's Sons, 1914), 347.

13. Boyer and Nissenbaum, eds., *The Salem Witchcraft Papers,* II, 660; Upham, *Salem Witchcraft,* II, 109.
14. Boyer and Nissenbaum, eds., *The Salem Witchcraft Papers,* II, 660–661; Upham, *Salem Witchcraft,* II, 109–110.
15. Boyer and Nissenbaum, eds., *The Salem Witchcraft Papers,* II, 482, 655–656, 691–699; Upham, *Salem Witchcraft,* II, 207–208.
16. Boyer and Nissenbaum, eds., *The Salem Witchcraft Papers,* II, 688–690; Upham, *Salem Witchcraft,* II, 310–311.
17. Boyer and Nissenbaum, eds., *The Salem Witchcraft Papers,* II, 689–690; Upham, *Salem Witchcraft,* II, 311.
18. Upham, *Salem Witchcraft,* II, 111–112.
19. Starkey, *The Devil in Massachusetts,* 97.
20. Upham, *Salem Witchcraft,* II, 114.
21. Boyer and Nissenbaum, eds., *The Salem Witchcraft Papers,* III, 793; Upham, *Salem Witchcraft,* II, 116.
22. Starkey, *The Devil in Massachusetts,* 99; Upham, *Salem Witchcraft,* II, 118.
23. Boyer and Nissenbaum, eds., *The Salem Witchcraft Papers,* III, 794; Starkey, *The Devil in Massachusetts,* 99; Upham, *Salem Witchcraft,* II, 118–119.
24. Starkey, *The Devil in Massachusetts,* 99–100; Upham, *Salem Witchcraft,* II, 118–119; Boyer and Nissenbaum, eds., *The Salem Witchcraft Papers,* III, 802–803.
25. Boyer and Nissenbaum, eds., *The Salem Witchcraft Papers,* III, 796.
26. Boyer and Nissenbaum, eds., *The Salem Witchcraft Papers,* III, 797.
27. Boyer and Nissenbaum, eds., *The Salem Witchcraft Papers,* III, 800.
28. Boyer and Nissenbaum, eds., *The Salem Witchcraft Papers,* III, 797.
29. Boyer and Nissenbaum, eds., *The Salem Witchcraft Papers,* III, 802.
30. Starkey, *The Devil in Massachusetts,* 101.
31. Starkey, *The Devil in Massachusetts,* 153.
32. David L. Greene, "Salem Witches I: Bridget Bishop," *American Genealogist,* 57 (July 1981): 129–138; David L. Greene, "Bridget Bishop Conviction," *American Genealogist,* 58 (July 1982): 163.
33. Greene, "Salem Witches I," 129–130.
34. Greene, "Salem Witches I," 100, 129–130.
35. Paul Boyer and Stephen Nissenbaum, eds., *Salem-Village Witchcraft: A Documentary Record of Local Conflict in Colonial New England* (Boston: Boston University Press, 1993), 157–158.
36. Boyer and Nissenbaum, eds., *Salem Village Witchcraft,* 162.
37. Boyer and Nissenbaum, eds., *The Salem Witchcraft Papers,* I, 83, 85; Upham, *Salem Witchcraft,* II, 124–125.
38. Boyer and Nissenbaum, eds., *The Salem Witchcraft Papers,* I, 83; Upham, *Salem Witchcraft,* II, 126.

39. Boyer and Nissenbaum, eds., *The Salem Witchcraft Papers,* I, 83–84, 86; Upham, *Salem Witchcraft,* II, 127.

40. Starkey, *The Devil in Massachusetts,* 108; Upham, *Salem Witchcraft,* II, 124.

41. Upham, *Salem Witchcraft,* II, 124–125; Boyer and Nissenbaum, eds., *The Salem Witchcraft Papers,* II, 405–413.

42. Upham, *Salem Witchcraft,* II, 128–129.

43. Boyer and Nissenbaum, eds., *The Salem Witchcraft Papers,* II, 409–412; Upham, *Salem Witchcraft,* II, 129–130; Starkey, *The Devil in Massachusetts,* 109.

44. Starkey, *The Devil in Massachusetts,* 109.

45. Upham, *Salem Witchcraft,* II, 135–136; Starkey, *The Devil in Massachusetts,* 109.

46. Boyer and Nissenbaum, eds., *The Salem Witchcraft Papers,* I, 95–96.

47. Boyer and Nissenbaum, eds., *The Salem Witchcraft Papers,* I, 96–97.

48. Boyer and Nissenbaum, eds., *The Salem Witchcraft Papers,* II, 419–420; Starkey, *The Devil in Massachusetts,* 110.

49. Boyer and Nissenbaum, eds., *The Salem Witchcraft Papers,* II, 423; Upham, *Salem Witchcraft,* II, 162–163.

50. Boyer and Nissenbaum, eds., *The Salem Witchcraft Papers,* II, 423; Upham, *Salem Witchcraft,* II, 163.

51. Boyer and Nissenbaum, eds., *The Salem Witchcraft Papers,* II, 425–426; Upham, *Salem Witchcraft,* II, 131–132.

52. Boyer and Nissenbaum, eds., *The Salem Witchcraft Papers,* II, 246–248; Upham, *Salem Witchcraft,* II, 132–133

53. See Boyer and Nissenbaum, eds., *The Salem Witchcraft Papers,* III, 806–807; Upham, *Salem Witchcraft,* II, 135.

54. Boyer and Nissenbaum, eds., *The Salem Witchcraft Papers,* I, 113.

55. Boyer and Nissenbaum, eds., *The Salem Witchcraft Papers,* I, 112–114; Upham, *Salem Witchcraft,* II, 136–137; Candy, another slave from Barbados owned by Margaret Hawkes of Salem, was later charged. On July 4, she confessed and named others. Boyer and Nissenbaum, eds., *The Salem Witchcraft Papers,* I, 179; Upham, *Salem Witchcraft,* II, 208, 215.

56. Gragg, *Crisis,* 121, note 40; Boyer and Nissenbaum, eds., *The Salem Witchcraft Papers,* I, 49; Upham, *Salem Witchcraft,* II, 134.

57. Boyer and Nissenbaum, eds., *The Salem Witchcraft Papers,* I, 49; Upham, *Salem Witchcraft,* II, 135.

58. Boyer and Nissenbaum, eds., *The Salem Witchcraft Papers,* I, 140; Gragg, *Crisis,* 121, notes 40, 42; Upham, *Salem Witchcraft,* II, 133–134.

59. Bryan F. Le Beau, "Philip English and the Witchcraft Hysteria," *Historical Journal of Massachusetts,* 15 (January 1987): 1; Boyer and Nissenbaum, eds., *The Salem Witchcraft Papers,* I, 16.

60. Le Beau, "Philip English," 1.

61. Le Beau, "Philip English," 11; William Bentley, *The Diary of William Bentley* (reprint, Gloucester, MA: Peter Smith, 1962), II, 23, 82; Perley, *The History of Salem,* II, 90.
62. Boyer and Nissenbaum, eds., *The Salem Witchcraft Papers,* III, 805–806; Bentley, *The Diary,* II, 22–26.
63. Boyer and Nissenbaum, eds., *The Salem Witchcraft Papers,* I, 313.
64. Le Beau, "Philip English," 1; Bentley, *The Diary,* I, 248; II, 26; Perley, *The History of Salem,* II, 355; III, 70; Upham, *Salem Witchcraft,* II, 142.
65. Le Beau, "Philip English," 11; Upham, *Salem Witchcraft,* II, 143.
66. Le Beau, "Philip English," 13; David T. Konig, *Law and Society in Puritan Massachusetts: Essex County, 1629–1692* (Chapel Hill: University of North Carolina Press, 1979), xi, 154–156.
67. David T. Konig, "A New Look at the Essex 'French': Ethnic Frictions and Community Tensions in Seventeenth Century Essex County, Massachusetts," *Essex Institute Historical Collections,* 110 (July 1974): 169–174, 177; Le Beau, "Philip English," 12.
68. Konig, "A New Look," 178–180.
69. Le Beau, "Philip English," 14.
70. Le Beau, "Philip English," 10–11.
71. Le Beau, "Philip English," 1–2; Boyer and Nissenbaum, *Salem Possessed,* 132.
72. Boyer and Nissenbaum, eds., *The Salem Witchcraft Papers,* I, 320; Le Beau, "Philip English," 2–3; W. Elliot Woodward, ed., *Records of Salem Witchcraft Copied from the Original Documents,* (1864, reprint, New York: Da Capo Press, 1969), I, 189, 191–192.
73. Boyer and Nissenbaum, eds., *The Salem Witchcraft Papers,* II, 313–315.
74. Boyer and Nissenbaum, eds., *The Salem Witchcraft Papers,* II, 474, 693.
75. Woodward, ed., *Records of Salem,* I, 168–169.
76. Boyer and Nissenbaum, eds., *The Salem Witchcraft Papers,* I, 317–318; Le Beau, "Philip English," 4.
77. Boyer and Nissenbaum, eds., *The Salem Witchcraft Papers,* I, 318–319; Le Beau, "Philip English," 4.
78. Upham, *Salem Witchcraft,* II, 309; Le Beau, "Philip English," 5.
79. Upham, *Salem Witchcraft,* I, 242; Le Beau, "Philip English," 5; Bentley, *The Diary,* II, 24.
80. Starkey, *The Devil in Massachusetts,* 116.
81. Boyer and Nissenbaum, eds., *The Salem Witchcraft Papers,* I, 164.
82. Boyer and Nissenbaum, eds., *The Salem Witchcraft Papers,* I, 164; Upham, *Salem Witchcraft,* II, 153–154.
83. Starkey, *The Devil in Massachusetts,* 125; Boyer and Nissenbaum, eds., *The Salem Witchcraft Papers,* I, 176.

84. Boyer and Nissenbaum, eds., *The Salem Witchcraft Papers,* I, 165; Upham, *Salem Witchcraft,* II, 139–140.

85. Boyer and Nissenbaum, eds., *The Salem Witchcraft Papers,* I, 171; Upham, *Salem Witchcraft,* I, 151.

86. Starkey, *The Devil in Massachusetts,* 119; Upham, *Salem Witchcraft,* II, 151–152; Boyer and Nissenbaum, eds., *The Salem Witchcraft Papers,* I, 172.

87. Boyer and Nissenbaum, eds., *The Salem Witchcraft Papers,* I, 172–173; II, 423.

88. Boyer and Nissenbaum, eds., *The Salem Witchcraft Papers,* I, 152; Upham, *Salem Witchcraft,* II, 50.

89. Starkey, *The Devil in Massachusetts,* 122.

90. Boyer and Nissenbaum, eds., *The Salem Witchcraft Papers,* I, 176–177.

91. Boyer and Nissenbaum, eds., *The Salem Witchcraft Papers,* I, 166; Upham, *Salem Witchcraft,* II, 154–155.

92. Boyer and Nissenbaum, eds., *The Salem Witchcraft Papers,* I, 166–167; Upham, *Salem Witchcraft,* II, 155.

93. Boyer and Nissenbaum, eds., *The Salem Witchcraft Papers,* I, 153; Upham, *Salem Witchcraft,* II, 157–158.

94. Boyer and Nissenbaum, eds., *The Salem Witchcraft Papers,* I, 153, 159; Starkey, *The Devil in Massachusetts,* 116.

95. Boyer and Nissenbaum, eds., *The Salem Witchcraft Papers,* I, 162–163.

96. Boyer and Nissenbaum, eds., *The Salem Witchcraft Papers,* I, 160–161, 166–167, 171; Upham, *Salem Witchcraft,* II, 159.

97. Boyer and Nissenbaum, eds., *The Salem Witchcraft Papers,* I, 162–163, 169.

98. Boyer and Nissenbaum, eds., *The Salem Witchcraft Papers,* I, 164, 169, 171, 174.

99. Boyer and Nissenbaum, eds., *The Salem Witchcraft Papers,* I, 172–173; II, 423; Upham, *Salem Witchcraft,* II, 160.

100. Boyer and Nissenbaum, eds., *The Salem Witchcraft Papers,* II, 389; Upham, *Salem Witchcraft,* II, 144.

101. Boyer and Nissenbaum, eds., *The Salem Witchcraft Papers,* II, 390; Upham, *Salem Witchcraft,* II, 144–145.

CHAPTER SIX

1. Charles Upham, *Salem Witchcraft* (Boston: Wiggin and Lunt, 1867), 166.

2. Larry Gragg, *The Salem Witch Crisis* (New York: Praeger, 1992), 162.

3. Paul Boyer and Stephen Nissenbaum, eds., *The Salem Witchcraft Papers: Verbatim Transcripts of the Legal Documents of the Salem*

Witchcraft Outbreak of 1692 (New York: De Capo Press, 1977), II, 473, 480.

4. Boyer and Nissenbaum, eds., *The Salem Witchcraft Papers,* II, 474–475; Upham, *Salem Witchcraft,* II, 166.
5. Boyer and Nissenbaum, eds., *The Salem Witchcraft Papers,* II, 475; Upham, *Salem Witchcraft,* II, 167.
6. Boyer and Nissenbaum, eds., *The Salem Witchcraft Papers,* II, 475–476; Upham, *Salem Witchcraft,* II, 167.
7. Boyer and Nissenbaum, eds., *The Salem Witchcraft Papers,* II, 476; Upham, *Salem Witchcraft,* II, 168.
8. Boyer and Nissenbaum, eds., *The Salem Witchcraft Papers,* II, 477.
9. Upham, *Salem Witchcraft,* II, 169.
10. Upham, *Salem Witchcraft,* II, 169–170.
11. Boyer and Nissenbaum, eds., *The Salem Witchcraft Papers,* II, 490–492; Upham, *Salem Witchcraft,* II, 316–317.
12. Boyer and Nissenbaum, eds., *The Salem Witchcraft Papers,* II, 491–492; Robert Calef, *More Wonders of the Invisible World (1700),* in George Lincoln Burr, ed. *Narratives of the Witchcraft Cases: 1648–1706* (New York: Charles Scribner's Sons, 1914), 364–365; George Malcom Yool, *1692 Witch Hunt* (Bowie, MD: Heritage Books, 1992), 110.
13. Boyer and Nissenbaum, eds., *The Salem Witchcraft Papers,* II, 490–491; Upham, *Salem Witchcraft,* II, 318.
14. Boyer and Nissenbaum, eds., *The Salem Witchcraft Papers,* II, 487, 496; Yool, *1692 Witch Hunt,* 70–71.
15. Boyer and Nissenbaum, eds., *The Salem Witchcraft Papers,* II, 496; Upham, *Salem Witchcraft,* II, 188–190; Yool, *1692 Witch Hunt,* 70–71.
16. Paul Boyer and Stephen Nissenbaum, *Salem Possessed, The Social Origins of Witchcraft* (Cambridge, MA: Harvard University Press, 1974), 195; Sidney Perley, *The History of Salem, Massachusetts* (Salem: Sidney Perley, 1924), II, 294–295.
17. Boyer and Nissenbaum, *Salem Possessed,* 195–197; Perley, *The History of Salem,* II, 294–295, 394.
18. Boyer and Nissenbaum, *Salem Possessed,* 197.
19. Boyer and Nissenbaum, *Salem Possessed,* 197–198; W. Elliot Woodward, ed., *Records of Salem Witchcraft Copied from the Original Documents,* (1864, reprint, New York: Da Capo Press, 1969), I, 275–276; II, 7–10; Boyer and Nissenbaum, eds., *The Salem Witchcraft Papers,* III, 819–820.
20. Upham, *Salem Witchcraft,* II, 173.
21. Boyer and Nissenbaum, eds., *The Salem Witchcraft Papers,* III, 847; Upham, *Salem Witchcraft,* II, 174.
22. Boyer and Nissenbaum, eds., *The Salem Witchcraft Papers,* III, 847; Upham, *Salem Witchcraft,* II, 175.

23. Sarah Buckley was later arrested. Boyer and Nissenbaum, eds., *The Salem Witchcraft Papers,* III, 848; Upham, *Salem Witchcraft,* II, 175–177, 187, 192.

24. Upham, *Salem Witchcraft,* II, 179, 198.

25. Boyer and Nissenbaum, eds., *The Salem Witchcraft Papers,* III, 819–820; Upham, *Salem Witchcraft,* II, 172–174; Marion L. Starkey, *The Devil in Massachusetts: A Modern Enquiry into the Salem Witch Trials* (New York: Alfred A. Knopf, 1949), 148.

26. Boyer and Nissenbaum, eds., *The Salem Witchcraft Papers,* III, 823–824.

27. Boyer and Nissenbaum, eds., *The Salem Witchcraft Papers,* III, 837.

28. Boyer and Nissenbaum, eds., *The Salem Witchcraft Papers,* III, 851.

29. Boyer and Nissenbaum, eds., *The Salem Witchcraft Papers,* III, 824.

30. Boyer and Nissenbaum, eds., *The Salem Witchcraft Papers,* III, 825.

31. Perley, *The History of Salem,* II, 92, 307; III, 42, 71; Boyer and Nissenbaum, *Salem Possessed,* 120–122.

32. Chadwick Hansen, "Andover Witchcraft and the Causes of the Salem Witchcraft Trials," in *The Occult in America: New Historical Perspectives,* ed. Howard Kerr and Charles L. Crow (Urbana: University of Illinois Press, 1983), 121–122; Gragg, *Crisis,* 113; Boyer and Nissenbaum, eds., *Salem Village Witchcraft,* 353–355; Boyer and Nissenbaum, *Salem Possessed,* 57, 65, 121–122, 130.

33. Upham, *Salem Witchcraft,* II, 187–188.

34. Gragg, *Crisis,* 135.

35. Upham, *Salem Witchcraft,* II, 239–240; Boyer and Nissenbaum, eds., *The Salem Witchcraft Papers,* I, 207–208.

36. Boyer and Nissenbaum, eds., *The Salem Witchcraft Papers,* I, 208–209; Upham, *Salem Witchcraft,* II, 240.

37. Boyer and Nissenbaum, eds., *The Salem Witchcraft Papers,* I, 209; Upham, *Salem Witchcraft,* II, 240–241.

38. Upham, *Salem Witchcraft,* II, 241.

39. Boyer and Nissenbaum, eds., *The Salem Witchcraft Papers,* I, 209; Upham, *Salem Witchcraft,* II, 242.

40. Boyer and Nissenbaum, eds., *The Salem Witchcraft Papers,* I, 209–210; Upham, *Salem Witchcraft,* II, 242.

41. Boyer and Nissenbaum, eds., *The Salem Witchcraft Papers,* I, 210; Upham, *Salem Witchcraft,* II, 242.

42. Upham, *Salem Witchcraft,* II, 247; Starkey, *The Devil in Massachusetts,* 143; Gragg, *Crisis,* 112.

43. Boyer and Nissenbaum, eds., *The Salem Witchcraft Papers,* I, 52; Starkey, *The Devil in Massachusetts,* 143.

44. Starkey, *The Devil in Massachusetts,* 144; Gragg, *Crisis,* 112; Boyer and Nissenbaum, eds., *The Salem Witchcraft Papers,* I, 52.

45. Boyer and Nissenbaum, eds., *The Salem Witchcraft Papers*, I, 52; Starkey, *The Devil in Massachusetts*, 144.
46. Boyer and Nissenbaum, eds., *The Salem Witchcraft Papers*, I, 53.
47. Starkey, *The Devil in Massachusetts*, 145; Gragg, *Crisis*, 135.
48. Boyer and Nissenbaum, eds., *The Salem Witchcraft Papers*, I, 54.
49. Boyer and Nissenbaum, eds., *The Salem Witchcraft Papers*, I, 54; Upham, *Salem Witchcraft*, II, 246.
50. Boyer and Nissenbaum, eds., *The Salem Witchcraft Papers*, I, 183; Upham, *Salem Witchcraft*, II, 208; Johnson and Toothaker were later charged as well. Boyer and Nissenbaum, eds., *The Salem Witchcraft Papers*, I, 201–202; Upham, *Salem Witchcraft*, II, 209.
51. Boyer and Nissenbaum, eds., *The Salem Witchcraft Papers*, I, 202; Upham, *Salem Witchcraft*, II, 209.
52. Mary Bradbury would later be charged. Boyer and Nissenbaum, eds., *The Salem Witchcraft Papers*, I, 197–198; Upham, *Salem Witchcraft*, II, 210–211.
53. Boyer and Nissenbaum, eds., *The Salem Witchcraft Papers*, I, 203.
54. Upham, *Salem Witchcraft*, II, 211–212; Boyer and Nissenbaum, eds., *The Salem Witchcraft Papers*, I, 185.
55. Boyer and Nissenbaum, eds., *The Salem Witchcraft Papers*, I, 185; Upham, *Salem Witchcraft*, II, 212.
56. Boyer and Nissenbaum, eds., *The Salem Witchcraft Papers*, I, 185–186; Upham, *Salem Witchcraft*, I, 185, II, 213.
57. Starkey, *The Devil in Massachusetts*, 181; Gragg, *Crisis*, 141.
58. Starkey, *The Devil in Massachusetts*, 181–182.
59. Starkey, *The Devil in Massachusetts*, 182; Gragg, *Crisis*, 141–142.
60. Starkey, *The Devil in Massachusetts*, 182.
61. Starkey, *The Devil in Massachusetts*, 183.
62. Upham, *Salem Witchcraft*, II, 403.
63. Gragg has found reference to forty warrants, Hansen to forty-three, and Weisman to at least fifty. Gragg, *Crisis*, 142; Hansen, "Andover Witchcraft," 46; Richard Weisman, *Witchcraft, Magic, and Religion in 17th-Century Massachusetts* (Amherst: The University of Massachusetts Press, 1984), 143; Starkey, *The Devil in Massachusetts*, 184; Upham, *Salem Witchcraft*, II, 403.
64. Boyer and Nissenbaum, eds., *The Salem Witchcraft Papers*, II, 615, 617.
65. Boyer and Nissenbaum, eds., *The Salem Witchcraft Papers*, II, 616.
66. Boyer and Nissenbaum, eds., *The Salem Witchcraft Papers*, III, 783–784.
67. Boyer and Nissenbaum, eds., *The Salem Witchcraft Papers*, I, 65–67.
68. Boyer and Nissenbaum, eds., *The Salem Witchcraft Papers*, I, 66–67.

69. Boyer and Nissenbaum, eds., *The Salem Witchcraft Papers,* I, 66, 69. Four days before Barker's testimony, on August 25, Susannah Post, also of Andover, reported in her confession that she had attended a meeting with 200 witches and heard that there were 500 witches "in the country." The previous July 30, Mary Toothaker of Billerica told the magistrates that she had heard talk of 305. Boyer and Nissenbaum, eds., *The Salem Witchcraft Papers,* I, 647–648; III, 769.

70. Boyer and Nissenbaum, eds., *The Salem Witchcraft Papers,* II, 342.

71. Boyer and Nissenbaum, eds., *The Salem Witchcraft Papers,* II, 342–343.

72. Boyer and Nissenbaum, eds., *The Salem Witchcraft Papers,* II, 342–343.

73. Boyer and Nissenbaum, eds., *The Salem Witchcraft Papers,* II, 514.

74. Boyer and Nissenbaum, eds., *The Salem Witchcraft Papers,* II, 514.

75. Boyer and Nissenbaum, eds., *The Salem Witchcraft Papers,* II, 524.

76. Boyer and Nissenbaum, eds., *The Salem Witchcraft Papers,* II, 525.

77. Upham, *Salem Witchcraft,* II, 404–405; Boyer and Nissenbaum, eds., *The Salem Witchcraft Papers,* III, 777–778.

78. Boyer and Nissenbaum, eds., *The Salem Witchcraft Papers,* III, 778.

79. Boyer and Nissenbaum, eds., *The Salem Witchcraft Papers,* III, 783–784; Starkey, *The Devil in Massachusetts,* 186.

80. Upham, *Salem Witchcraft,* II, 248; Starkey, *The Devil in Massachusetts,* 187.

81. Starkey, *The Devil in Massachusetts,* 187.

82. Hansen, "Andover Witchcraft," 40; Gragg, *Crisis,* 142.

CHAPTER SEVEN

1. Marion L. Starkey, *The Devil in Massachusetts: A Modern Enquiry into the Salem Witch Trials* (New York: Alfred A. Knopf, 1949), 130.

2. Starkey, *The Devil in Massachusetts,* 131.

3. Starkey, *The Devil in Massachusetts,* 132.

4. Larry Gragg, *The Salem Witch Crisis* (New York: Praeger, 1992), 84.

5. Gragg, *Crisis,* 85.

6. Quoted in Starkey, *The Devil in Massachusetts,* 134.

7. Gragg, *Crisis,* 85.

8. Starkey, *The Devil in Massachusetts,* 135.

9. See Bernard Rosenthal, *Salem Story: Reading the Witch Trials of 1692* (Cambridge: Cambridge University Press, 1993), 3.

10. Gragg, *Crisis,* 84.

11. Paul Boyer and Stephen Nissenbaum, eds., *The Salem Witchcraft Papers: Verbatim Transcripts of the Legal Documents of the Salem Witchcraft Outbreak of 1692* (New York: De Capo Press, 1977), III, 861.

12. Starkey, *The Devil in Massachusetts,* 137; Boyer and Nissenbaum, eds., *The Salem Witchcraft Papers,* III, 861; Robert Calef, *More Wonders of the Invisible World (1700),* in George Lincoln Burr, ed. *Narratives of the Witchcraft Cases: 1648–1706* (New York: Charles Scribner's Sons, 1914), 349.

13. Quoted in Chadwick Hansen, *Witchcraft at Salem* (New York: George Braziller, 1969), 122; Gragg, *Crisis,* 86; Charles Upham, *Salem Witchcraft* (Boston: Wiggin and Lunt, 1867), II, 256.

14. Boyer and Nissenbaum, eds., *The Salem Witchcraft Papers,* III, 861; Gragg, *Crisis,* 86–87.

15. Gragg, *Crisis,* 86–87.

16. Thomas Hutchinson, *The History of the Colony and Province of Massachusetts Bay* (1764), Lawrence Shaw Mayo, ed. (Cambridge, MA: Harvard University Press, 1936), 32; Hansen, *Witchcraft at Salem,* 122.

17. Upham, *Salem Witchcraft,* II, 251.

18. Cotton Mather, *Selected Letters of Cotton Mather,* ed. Kenneth Silverman (Baton Rouge: University of Louisiana Press, 1971), 36–39.

19. Boyer and Nissenbaum, eds., *The Salem Witchcraft Papers,* III, 867.

20. Upham, *Salem Witchcraft,* II, 255.

21. David T. Konig, *Law and Society in Puritan Massachusetts: Essex County, 1629–1692* (Chapel Hill: University of North Carolina Press, 1979), 172; Gragg, *Crisis,* 88–89.

22. Boyer and Nissenbaum, eds., *The Salem Witchcraft Papers,* I, 83; Starkey, *The Devil in Massachusetts,* 153.

23. Boyer and Nissenbaum, eds., *The Salem Witchcraft Papers,* I, 83; Cotton Mather, *The Wonders of the Invisible World (1693)* in George Lincoln Burr, ed., *Narratives of the Witchcraft Cases: 1648–1706* (New York: Charles Scribner's Sons, 1914), 229; Upham, *Salem Witchcraft,* II, 257.

24. Boyer and Nissenbaum, eds., *The Salem Witchcraft Papers,* I, 92.

25. Boyer and Nissenbaum, eds., *The Salem Witchcraft Papers,* I, 93–94.

26. Boyer and Nissenbaum, eds., *The Salem Witchcraft Papers,* I, 92–94.

27. Boyer and Nissenbaum, eds., *The Salem Witchcraft Papers,* I, 104.

28. Boyer and Nissenbaum, eds., *The Salem Witchcraft Papers,* I, 101–102.

29. Starkey, *The Devil in Massachusetts,* 154; Boyer and Nissenbaum, eds., *The Salem Witchcraft Papers,* I, 94–95.

30. Boyer and Nissenbaum, eds., *The Salem Witchcraft Papers,* I, 99–100.

31. Boyer and Nissenbaum, eds., *The Salem Witchcraft Papers,* I, 100; Upham, *Salem Witchcraft,* II, 265.

32. Boyer and Nissenbaum, eds., *The Salem Witchcraft Papers,* I, 97–98; Upham, *Salem Witchcraft,* II, 259–260.

33. Boyer and Nissenbaum, eds., *The Salem Witchcraft Papers,* I, 98–99.

34. Boyer and Nissenbaum, eds., *The Salem Witchcraft Papers,* I, 91–92, 103–106.
35. Boyer and Nissenbaum, eds., *The Salem Witchcraft Papers,* I, 101, 107–108.
36. Starkey, *The Devil in Massachusetts,* 155.
37. Calef, *More Wonders,* 187–188.
38. Starkey, *The Devil in Massachusetts,* 156.
39. Boyer and Nissenbaum, eds., *The Salem Witchcraft Papers,* I, 24; Starkey, *The Devil in Massachusetts,* 156; Upham, *Salem Witchcraft,* II, 267.
40. Starkey, *The Devil in Massachusetts,* 153.
41. Starkey, *The Devil in Massachusetts,* 157.
42. Starkey, *The Devil in Massachusetts,* 157; Paul Boyer and Stephen Nissenbaum, eds., *Salem–Village Witchcraft: A Documentary Record of Local Conflict in Colonial New England* (Boston: Boston University Press, 1993), 118.
43. Boyer and Nissenbaum, eds., *Salem Village Witchcraft,* 118.
44. Boyer and Nissenbaum, eds., *Salem Village Witchcraft,* 118.
45. Starkey, *The Devil in Massachusetts,* 158.
46. Starkey, *The Devil in Massachusetts,* 158; Gragg, *Crisis,* 87, 191.
47. Upham, *Salem Witchcraft,* II, 268–269.
48. Starkey, *The Devil in Massachusetts,* 169.
49. Starkey, *The Devil in Massachusetts,* 170.
50. Starkey, *The Devil in Massachusetts,* 170–171; Boyer and Nissenbaum, eds., *The Salem Witchcraft Papers,* II, 551–552.
51. Boyer and Nissenbaum, eds., *The Salem Witchcraft Papers,* II, 551–552.
52. Boyer and Nissenbaum, eds., *The Salem Witchcraft Papers,* II, 551–552; Cotton Mather, *The Wonders,* 236.
53. Boyer and Nissenbaum, eds., *The Salem Witchcraft Papers,* II, 600–601.
54. Boyer and Nissenbaum, eds., *The Salem Witchcraft Papers,* II, 596–597, 600; Upham, *Salem Witchcraft,* II, 275, 281–282.
55. Boyer and Nissenbaum, eds., *The Salem Witchcraft Papers,* II, 606–607; Upham, *Salem Witchcraft,* II, 275–276.
56. Boyer and Nissenbaum, eds., *The Salem Witchcraft Papers,* II, 592–593; Upham, *Salem Witchcraft,* II, 271–272.
57. Boyer and Nissenbaum, eds., *The Salem Witchcraft Papers,* II, 593; Upham, *Salem Witchcraft,* II, 271–272.
58. Starkey, *The Devil in Massachusetts,* 160.
59. Starkey, *The Devil in Massachusetts,* 160; Upham, *Salem Witchcraft,* II, 283–284.
60. Boyer and Nissenbaum, eds., *The Salem Witchcraft Papers,* II, 607–608; Upham, *Salem Witchcraft,* II, 284.

61. Boyer and Nissenbaum, eds., *The Salem Witchcraft Papers*, II, 607–608; Upham, *Salem Witchcraft*, II, 284–285.
62. Upham, *Salem Witchcraft*, II, 29.
63. Starkey, *The Devil in Massachusetts*, 163–164.
64. Starkey, *The Devil in Massachusetts*, 164.
65. Starkey, *The Devil in Massachusetts*, 175.
66. Starkey, *The Devil in Massachusetts*, 175; Upham, *Salem Witchcraft*, II, 269–270.
67. Starkey, *The Devil in Massachusetts*, 176.
68. Paul Boyer and Stephen Nissenbaum, *Salem Possessed, The Social Origins of Witchcraft* (Cambridge, MA: Harvard University Press, 1974), 132.
69. Gragg, *Crisis*, 137.
70. Gragg, *Crisis*, 137.
71. Starkey, *The Devil in Massachusetts*, 180.

CHAPTER EIGHT

1. Paul Boyer and Stephen Nissenbaum, eds., *The Salem Witchcraft Papers: Verbatim Transcripts of the Legal Documents of the Salem Witchcraft Outbreak of 1692* (New York: De Capo Press, 1977), I, 161–162; Charles Upham, *Salem Witchcraft* (Boston: Wiggin and Lunt, 1867), II, 296–297.
2. Boyer and Nissenbaum, eds., *The Salem Witchcraft Papers*, I, 162–164.
3. Upham, *Salem Witchcraft*, II, 297.
4. Upham, *Salem Witchcraft*, II, 302.
5. Marion L. Starkey, *The Devil in Massachusetts: A Modern Enquiry into the Salem Witch Trials* (New York: Alfred A. Knopf, 1949), 194.
6. Starkey, *The Devil in Massachusetts*, 194.
7. Boyer and Nissenbaum, eds., *The Salem Witchcraft Papers*, II, 689–690; Upham, *Salem Witchcraft*, II, 310–311.
8. Starkey, *The Devil in Massachusetts*, 190–191.
9. Starkey, *The Devil in Massachusetts*, 190.
10. Upham lists thirty–two residents as signatories of the first petition: Upham, *Salem Witchcraft*, II, 305–306; Boyer and Nissenbaum, eds., *The Salem Witchcraft Papers*, II, 682.
11. Boyer and Nissenbaum, eds., *The Salem Witchcraft Papers*, II, 664.
12. Starkey, *The Devil in Massachusetts*, 193
13. Boyer and Nissenbaum, eds., *The Salem Witchcraft Papers*, III, 837; Upham, *Salem Witchcraft*, II, 322.
14. Boyer and Nissenbaum, eds., *The Salem Witchcraft Papers*, III, 837–838; Upham, *Salem Witchcraft*, II, 323.

15. Starkey, *The Devil in Massachusetts,* 194–195; Boyer and Nissenbaum, eds., *The Salem Witchcraft Papers,* I, 189.

16. Boyer and Nissenbaum, eds., *The Salem Witchcraft Papers,* I, 189.

17. Boyer and Nissenbaum, eds., *The Salem Witchcraft Papers,* I, 190–191.

18. Boyer and Nissenbaum, eds., *The Salem Witchcraft Papers,* I, 191–192.

19. Thomas Brattle, *Letter of Thomas Brattle* (1692), in George Lincoln Burr, ed., *Narratives of the Witchcraft Cases: 1648–1706* (New York: Charles Scribner's Sons, 1914), 177.

20. Upham, *Salem Witchcraft,* II, 300–301; Robert Calef, *More Wonders of the Invisible World (1700),* in George Lincoln Burr, ed. *Narratives of the Witchcraft Cases: 1648–1706* (New York: Charles Scribner's Sons, 1914), 360–361.

21. Calef, *More Wonders,* 360–361; Starkey, *The Devil in Massachusetts,* 198.

22. Quoted in Bernard Rosenthal, *Salem Story: Reading the Witch Trials of 1692* (Cambridge: Cambridge University Press, 1993), 145.

23. Upham, *Salem Witchcraft,* II, 299.

24. Upham, *Salem Witchcraft,* II, 299.

25. Upham, *Salem Witchcraft,* II, 301.

26. Upham, *Salem Witchcraft,* II, 320–321.

27. Boyer and Nissenbaum, eds., *The Salem Witchcraft Papers,* I, 119–120; Starkey, *The Devil in Massachusetts,* 199–200.

28. Boyer and Nissenbaum, eds., *The Salem Witchcraft Papers,* I, 260–262.

29. Boyer and Nissenbaum, eds., *The Salem Witchcraft Papers,* I, 263.

30. Upham, *Salem Witchcraft,* II, 324–325.

31. Boyer and Nissenbaum, eds., *The Salem Witchcraft Papers,* I, 302; Upham, *Salem Witchcraft,* II, 326.

32. Upham, *Salem Witchcraft,* II, 326.

33. Boyer and Nissenbaum, eds., *The Salem Witchcraft Papers,* I, 304.

34. Starkey, *The Devil in Massachusetts,* 104–105.

35. Larry Gragg, *The Salem Witch Crisis* (New York: Praeger, 1992), 84.

36. David C. Brown, "The Case of Giles Corey," *Essex Institute Historical Collections,* 121 (October 1985), 282; Upham, *Salem Witchcraft,* II, 338.

37. Brown, "Giles Corey," 285–286, 288.

38. Upham, *Salem Witchcraft,* II, 337; Brown, "Giles Corey," 283.

39. Brown, "Giles Corey," 289–290, 293–294.

40. Brown, "Giles Corey," 294–295, 297.

41. Brown, "Giles Corey," 293, 295, 293.

42. Starkey, *The Devil in Massachusetts,* 205; Gragg, *Crisis,* 151–152; Boyer and Nissenbaum list Corey's date of death as September 16:

Boyer and Nissenbaum, eds., *The Salem Witchcraft Papers,* I, 239, III, 985.
43. Brown, "Giles Corey," 298–299.
44. Boyer and Nissenbaum, eds., *The Salem Witchcraft Papers,* I, 246; Upham, *Salem Witchcraft,* II, 341.
45. Boyer and Nissenbaum, eds., *The Salem Witchcraft Papers,* I, 246; Upham, *Salem Witchcraft,* II, 341.
46. Upham, *Salem Witchcraft,* II, 344.
47. Frances Hill, *A Delusion of Satan: The Full Story of the Salem Witch Trials* (New York: Doubleday, 1995), 185–186.
48. Quoted in Gragg, *Crisis,* 147.
49. Upham, *Salem Witchcraft,* II, 486–487.
50. Quoted in Gragg, *Crisis,* 146.
51. Quoted in Paul Boyer and Stephen Nissenbaum, *Salem Possessed, The Social Origins of Witchcraft* (Cambridge, MA: Harvard University Press, 1974), 178.
52. Quoted in Gragg, *Crisis,* 146–147.
53. Quoted in Boyer and Nissenbaum, *Salem Possessed,* 175.
54. Richard Godbeer, *The Devil's Dominion: Magic and Religion in Early New England* (Cambridge: Cambridge University Press, 1992), 55.
55. Upham, *Salem Witchcraft,* II, 397.
56. John Hale, *A Modest Inquiry into the Nature of Witchcraft* (1702), in George Lincoln Burr, ed., *Narratives of the Witchcraft Cases: 1648–1706* (New York: Charles Scribner's Sons, 1914), 416.
57. Brattle, *Letter,* 189.
58. The only person executed after confessing was Samuel Wardwell, but he recanted his confession at his trial. Calef, *More Wonders,* 376.
59. Boyer and Nissenbaum, eds., *The Salem Witchcraft Papers,* I, 23.
60. Calef, *More Wonders,* 375.
61. Gragg, *Crisis,* 147–148.
62. Gragg, *Crisis,* 148.
63. Gragg, *Crisis,* 149.
64. Gragg, *Crisis,* 149.
65. Gragg, *Crisis,* 149–150.
66. Godbeer, *The Devil's Dominion,* 53.
67. Boyer and Nissenbaum, eds., *The Salem Witchcraft Papers,* I, 112, 280–281.
68. Carol F. Karlsen, *The Devil in the Shape of a Woman: Witchcraft in Colonial New England* (New York: W. W. Norton, 1987), 138.
69. Boyer and Nissenbaum, eds., *The Salem Witchcraft Papers,* II, 562.
70. Godbeer, *The Devil's Dominion,* 54, 61.
71. Quoted in Godbeer, *The Devil's Dominion,* 62, 65.
72. Godbeer, *The Devil's Dominion,* 67–68.
73. Gragg, *Crisis,* 150.

74. Quoted in Gragg, *Crisis,* 151.
75. Brattle, *Letter,* 174.

Chapter Nine

1. Marion L. Starkey, *The Devil in Massachusetts: A Modern Enquiry into the Salem Witch Trials* (New York: Alfred A. Knopf, 1949), 210.
2. Starkey, *The Devil in Massachusetts,* 211.
3. Starkey, *The Devil in Massachusetts,* 211.
4. Starkey, *The Devil in Massachusetts,* 212.
5. Robert Calef, *More Wonders of the Invisible World* (1700), in George Lincoln Burr, ed., *Narratives of the Witchcraft Cases: 1648–1706* (New York: Charles Scribners Sons, 1914), 343; Elaine G. Breslaw, *Tituba, Recluctant Witch of Salem: Devilish Indians and Puritan Fantasies* (New York: New York University Press, 1996), 172–173.
6. Charles Upham, *Salem Witchcraft* (Boston: Wiggin and Lunt, 1867), 189.
7. Paul Boyer and Stephen Nissenbaum, eds., *The Salem Witchcraft Papers: Verbatim Transcripts of the Legal Documents of the Salem Witchcraft Outbreak of 1692* (New York: De Capo Press, 1977), II, 490–492; Upham, *Salem Witchcraft,* II, 408.
8. Larry Gragg, *The Salem Witch Crisis* (New York: Praeger, 1992), 265; Starkey, *The Devil in Massachusetts,* 214.
9. Thomas Brattle, *Letter of Thomas Brattle* (1692), in George Lincoln Burr, ed., *Narratives of the Witchcraft Cases: 1648–1706* (New York: Charles Scribner's Sons, 1914), 178–179; Upham, *Salem Witchcraft,* II, 453.
10. Upham, *Salem Witchcraft,* II, 451–452.
11. Starkey, *The Devil in Massachusetts,* 218; Upham, *Salem Witchcraft,* II, 452; Brattle, *Letter,* 182.
12. Starkey, *The Devil in Massachusetts,* 217–218.
13. Upham, *Salem Witchcraft,* II, 452.
14. Upham, *Salem Witchcraft,* II, 363; Starkey, *The Devil in Massachusetts,* 213–214.
15. Upham, *Salem Witchcraft,* II, 447–449; Starkey, *The Devil in Massachusetts,* 216; Boyer and Nissenbaum, eds., *The Salem Witchcraft Papers,* I, 119–121.
16. Upham, *Salem Witchcraft,* II, 538.
17. Upham, *Salem Witchcraft,* II, 538.
18. Samuel Willard, *Some Miscellany Observations on Our Present Debates Respecting Witchcraft in a Dialogue Between S and B* (Philadelphia: William Bradford, 1692), 6–9.
19. David C. Brown, "The Salem Witchcraft Trials: Samuel Willards' *Some Miscellany Observations,*" *Essex Institute Historical Collections,* 122 (July 1986): 215; Starkey, *The Devil in Massachusetts,* 213.

20. Starkey, *The Devil in Massachusetts,* 214.
21. Boyer and Nissenbaum, eds., *The Salem Witchcraft Papers,* III, 875–876.
22. Boyer and Nissenbaum, eds., *The Salem Witchcraft Papers,* III, 877.
23. Boyer and Nissenbaum, eds., *The Salem Witchcraft Papers,* III, 877.
24. Boyer and Nissenbaum, eds., *The Salem Witchcraft Papers,* III, 876–877.
25. Brattle, *Letter,* 184–185.
26. Boyer and Nissenbaum, eds., *The Salem Witchcraft Papers,* III, 861.
27. Boyer and Nissenbaum, eds., *The Salem Witchcraft Papers,* III, 861–862.
28. Boyer and Nissenbaum, eds., *The Salem Witchcraft Papers,* III, 862; Gragg, *Crisis,* 176.
29. Starkey, *The Devil in Massachusetts,* 220.
30. Increase Mather, *Cases of Conscience Concerning Evil Spirits Personating Men* (Boston: Benjamin Harris, 1693), 17–20, 23–24, 40.
31. Mather, *Cases of Conscience,* 1, 2, 7, 33.
32. Mather, *Cases of Conscience,* 34, 45–46, 51.
33. Mather, *Cases of Conscience,* 34.
34. Starkey, *The Devil in Massachusetts,* 214; Mather, *Cases of Conscience,* 32, 66.
35. Starkey, *The Devil in Massachusetts,* 224; Gragg, *Crisis,* 168.
36. Starkey, *The Devil in Massachusetts,* 225; Gragg, *Crisis,* 168.
37. Discussed in Gragg, *Crisis,* 172.
38. Starkey, *The Devil in Massachusetts,* 225–226; Gragg, *Crisis,* 168.
39. Starkey, *The Devil in Massachusetts,* 226.
40. Starkey, *The Devil in Massachusetts,* 220.
41. Starkey, *The Devil in Massachusetts,* 222–223; Bernard Rosenthal, *Salem Story: Reading the Witch Trials of 1692* (Cambridge: Cambridge University Press, 1993), 183.
42. Boyer and Nissenbaum, eds., *The Salem Witchcraft Papers,* I, 24; Carol F. Karlsen, *The Devil in the Shape of a Woman: Witchcraft in Colonial New England* (New York: W. W. Norton, 1987), 278, note 125.
43. Gragg, *Crisis,* 132–133.
44. Starkey, *The Devil in Massachusetts,* 221; Gragg, *Crisis,* 126, 134.
45. Starkey, *The Devil in Massachusetts,* 221; Gragg, *Crisis,* 181.
46. Boyer and Nissenbaum, eds., *The Salem Witchcraft Papers,* III, 864.
47. Thomas Brattle estimated that there were about fifty confessors alone in jail. Brattle, *Letter,* 173.
48. Boyer and Nissenbaum, eds., *The Salem Witchcraft Papers,* III, 864–865.
49. Boyer and Nissenbaum, eds., *The Salem Witchcraft Papers,* III, 885–886.
50. Second offenses in the latter category could result in death. Boyer and Nissenbaum, eds., *The Salem Witchcraft Papers,* III, 885–886.

51. Starkey, *The Devil in Massachusetts,* 227.
52. Boyer and Nissenbaum, eds., *The Salem Witchcraft Papers,* III, 864.
53. Starkey, *The Devil in Massachusetts,* 228; Boyer and Nissenbaum, eds., *The Salem Witchcraft Papers,* III, 903–930.
54. Boyer and Nissenbaum, eds., *The Salem Witchcraft Papers,* III, 865.
55. Boyer and Nissenbaum, eds., *The Salem Witchcraft Papers,* III, 861, 865; Starkey, *The Devil in Massachusetts,* 228–229.
56. Calef, *More Wonders,* 382–383; Starkey, *The Devil in Massachusetts,* 229.
57. Starkey, *The Devil in Massachusetts,* 229; Boyer and Nissenbaum, eds., *The Salem Witchcraft Papers,* III, 932–944.
58. Starkey, *The Devil in Massachusetts,* 230; Gragg, *Crisis,* 126–127; Breslaw, *Tituba,* 175.
59. Breslaw, *Tituba,* 175.
60. Starkey, *The Devil in Massachusetts,* 231; Upham, *Salem Witchcraft,* II, 353–354.
61. Starkey, *The Devil in Massachusetts,* 231.
62. Upham, *Salem Witchcraft,* II, 361.
63. Upham, *Salem Witchcraft,* II, 357.
64. Richard Godbeer, *The Devil's Dominion: Magic and Religion in Early New England* (Cambridge: Cambridge University Press, 1992), 216.
65. Willard, *Miscellany Observations,* 7.
66. Godbeer, *The Devil's Dominion,* 221.
67. Upham, *Salem Witchcraft,* II, 441.

Chapter Ten

1. Paul Boyer and Stephen Nissenbaum, eds., *The Salem Witchcraft Papers: Verbatim Transcripts of the Legal Documents of the Salem Witchcraft Outbreak of 1692* (New York: De Capo Press, 1977), III, 865.
2. Richard Godbeer, *The Devil's Dominion: Magic and Religion in Early New England* (Cambridge: Cambridge University Press, 1992), 222.
3. Marion L. Starkey, *The Devil in Massachusetts: A Modern Enquiry into the Salem Witch Trials* (New York: Alfred A. Knopf, 1949), 237.
4. Starkey, *The Devil in Massachusetts,* 237.
5. Charles Upham, *Salem Witchcraft* (Boston: Wiggin and Lunt, 1867), II, 488.
6. Upham, *Salem Witchcraft,* II, 488.
7. Starkey, *The Devil in Massachusetts,* 237–238.
8. Starkey, *The Devil in Massachusetts,* 238; Larry Gragg, *The Salem Witch Crisis* (New York: Praeger, 1992), 192.
9. Starkey, *The Devil in Massachusetts,* 239.

10. Cotton Mather, *Selected Letters of Cotton Mather,* ed. Kenneth Silverman (Baton Rouge: University of Louisiana Press, 1971), 45.

11. Increase Mather, *Cases of Conscience Concerning Evil Spirits Personating Men* (Boston: Benjamin Harris, 1693), postscript.

12. Starkey, *The Devil in Massachusetts,* 240.

13. Cotton Mather, "A Brand Plucked Out of the Burning" (1693), in George Lincoln Burr, ed., *Narratives of the Witchcraft Cases: 1648–1706* (New York: Charles Scribner's Sons, 1914), 259–260; David Harley, "Explaining Salem: Calvinist Psychology and the Diagnosis of Possession," *The American Historical Review*, 101 (April 1996): 323.

14. Starkey, *The Devil in Massachusetts,* 241; Harley, "Explaining Salem," 323.

15. Starkey, *The Devil in Massachusetts,* 241.

16. Starkey, *The Devil in Massachusetts,* 242; Cotton Mather, *The Diary of Cotton Mather* (reprint, New York: Frederick Ungar, 1957), I, 171–172.

17. Mather, *The Diary,* I, 171–172; Starkey, *The Devil in Massachusetts,* 242–243.

18. Starkey, *The Devil in Massachusetts,* 243.

19. Starkey, *The Devil in Massachusetts,* 243.

20. Starkey, *The Devil in Massachusetts,* 243–244; Mather, "A Brand Plucked Out," 259–287.

21. Starkey, *The Devil in Massachusetts,* 244.

22. Starkey, *The Devil in Massachusetts,* 245.

23. Robert Calef, *More Wonders of the Invisible World (1700),* in George Lincoln Burr, ed. *Narratives of the Witchcraft Cases: 1648–1706* (New York: Charles Scribner's Sons, 1914), 299, 325; Kenneth Silverman, *The Life and Times of Cotton Mather* (New York: Harper & Row, 1984), 130; Starkey, *The Devil in Massachusetts,* 245.

24. Mather, *Selected Letters,* 50–51; Starkey, *The Devil in Massachusetts,* 245–246.

25. Samuel Eliot Morison, *The Intellectual Life of Colonial New England* (Ithaca, NY: Cornell University Press, 1970), 259.

26. Calef, *More Wonders,* 293.

27. Silverman, *The Life and Times,* 87–88; Mather, *Selected Letters,* 44.

28. Starkey, *The Devil in Massachusetts,* 265.

29. Mather, *The Diary,* I, 216.

30. Upham, *Salem Witchcraft,* II, 381, 465–466.

31. Upham, *Salem Witchcraft,* II, 381.

32. Starkey, *The Devil in Massachusetts,* 248.

33. Paul Boyer and Stephen Nissenbaum, *Salem Possessed, The Social Origins of Witchcraft* (Cambridge, MA: Harvard University Press, 1974), 177.

34. Gragg, *Crisis,* 195; Boyer and Nissenbaum, *Salem Possessed,* 176.
35. Boyer and Nissenbaum, *Salem Possessed,* 69.
36. Quoted in Bernard Rosenthal, *Salem Story: Reading the Witch Trials of 1692* (Cambridge: Cambridge University Press, 1993), 201.
37. Boyer and Nissenbaum, *Salem Possessed,* 69–71.
38. Quoted in Boyer and Nissenbaum, *Salem Possessed,* 177.
39. Boyer and Nissenbaum, *Salem Possessed,* 71.
40. Boyer and Nissenbaum, *Salem Possessed,* 71–72; Mather, *Selected Letters,* 250.
41. Boyer and Nissenbaum, *Salem Possessed,* 72.
42. Boyer and Nissenbaum, *Salem Possessed,* 72.
43. Paul Boyer and Stephen Nissenbaum, eds., *Salem-Village Witchcraft: A Documentary Record of Local Conflict in Colonial New England* (Boston: Boston University Press, 1993), 296–297; Starkey, *The Devil in Massachusetts,* 252.
44. Starkey, *The Devil in Massachusetts,* 251.
45. Boyer and Nissenbaum, eds., *Salem Village Witchcraft,* 297–299.
46. Boyer and Nissenbaum, eds., *Salem Village Witchcraft,* 297–299.
47. Boyer and Nissenbaum, eds., *Salem Village Witchcraft,* 295; Starkey, *The Devil in Massachusetts,* 251; Boyer and Nissenbaum, *Salem Possessed,* 74.
48. Boyer and Nissenbaum, *Salem Possessed,* 76.
49. Boyer and Nissenbaum, eds., *Salem Village Witchcraft,* 306–308; Starkey, *The Devil in Massachusetts,* 252.
50. Boyer and Nissenbaum, eds., *Salem Village Witchcraft,* 260–262, 308.
51. Boyer and Nissenbaum, eds., *Salem Village Witchcraft,* 262–263. Boyer and Nissenbaum have studied both petitions and found that supporters of the Salem witch trials generally continued to support Parris in 1695, while opponents were overwhelmingly against him. Boyer and Nissenbaum, *Salem Possessed,* 76, 185.
52. Boyer and Nissenbaum, *Salem Possessed,* 76, 78.
53. Boyer and Nissenbaum, eds., *Salem Village Witchcraft,* 311; Larry Gragg, *Quest for Security: The Life of Samuel Parris, 1653–1720* (New York Greenwood Press, 1990), 177–180.
54. Starkey, *The Devil in Massachusetts,* 253; Boyer and Nissenbaum, *Salem Possessed,* 218.
55. Upham, *Salem Witchcraft,* II, 506–507; Boyer and Nissenbaum, *Salem Possessed,* 218–219; Starkey, *The Devil in Massachusetts,* 254–255.
56. Starkey, *The Devil in Massachusetts,* 255; Upham, *Salem Witchcraft,* II, 506–507.
57. Gragg, *Crisis,* 191; Upham, *Salem Witchcraft,* II, 483.
58. Upham, *Salem Witchcraft,* II, 483.
59. Starkey, *The Devil in Massachusetts,* 258.

60. Upham, *Salem Witchcraft,* II, 510.
61. Starkey, *The Devil in Massachusetts,* 260; Upham, *Salem Witchcraft,* II, 510; Frances Hill, *A Delusion of Satan: The Full Story of the Salem Witch Trials* (New York: Doubleday, 1995), 215.
62. Hill, *A Delusion of Satan,* 214–215.
63. Upham, *Salem Witchcraft,* II, 465.
64. Samuel Sewall, *Samuel Sewall's Diary,* ed. Mark Van Doren (reprint, New York: Russell and Russell, 1963), 137–138.
65. Upham, *Salem Witchcraft,* II, 473–474.
66. Starkey, *The Devil in Massachusetts,* 262; Sewall, *Diary,* 140; Upham, *Salem Witchcraft,* II, 442.
67. Upham, *Salem Witchcraft,* II, 475.
68. Gragg, *Crisis,* 188.
69. John Hale, *A Modest Inquiry into the Nature of Witchcraft* (1702), in George Lincoln Burr, ed., *Narratives of the Witchcraft Cases: 1648–1706* (New York: Charles Scribner's Sons, 1914), 401–402; Starkey, *The Devil in Massachusetts,* 264.
70. Hale, *A Modest Inquiry,* 415, 421; Gragg, *Crisis,* 200.
71. John Hale, *A Modest Inquiry into the Nature of Witchcraft* (1702, reprint, Bainbridge, NY: York Mail-Print, 1973), 162–164.
72. Hale, *A Modest Inquiry,* 412, 423–424; Starkey, *The Devil in Massachusetts,* 264–265.
73. Sewall, *Diary,* 146; Hale, *A Modest Inquiry,* 427.
74. Hale, *A Modest Inquiry,* 427.
75. Thomas Hutchinson, *The History of the Colony and Province of Massachusetts Bay* (1764), ed. Lawrence Shaw Mayo (Cambridge, MA: Harvard University Press, 1936), II, 46.
76. Starkey, *The Devil in Massachusetts,* 263; Godbeer, *The Devil's Dominion,* 222.
77. Boyer and Nissenbaum, eds., *The Salem Witchcraft Papers,* III, 963.
78. Boyer and Nissenbaum, eds., *The Salem Witchcraft Papers,* III, 963–964.
79. Boyer and Nissenbaum, eds., *The Salem Witchcraft Papers,* III, 967–968; Upham, *Salem Witchcraft,* II, 476.
80. Hale, *A Modest Inquiry,* 427.
81. Boyer and Nissenbaum, eds., *The Salem Witchcraft Papers,* III, 966–967.
82. Upham, *Salem Witchcraft,* II, 477; Boyer and Nissenbaum, eds., *The Salem Witchcraft Papers,* III, 966, 970.
83. Boyer and Nissenbaum, eds., *The Salem Witchcraft Papers,* III, 972.
84. Boyer and Nissenbaum, eds., *The Salem Witchcraft Papers,* III, 973, 1032, 1027, 1007, 1040–1041; Gragg, *Crisis,* 190.
85. David C. Brown, "The Case of Giles Corey," *Essex Institute Historical Collections,* 121 (October 1985): 284, 289–290, 293, 295, 297.

86. Gragg, *Crisis,* 129; Boyer and Nissenbaum, eds., *The Salem Witch-craft Papers,* III, 997–998; Calef, *More Wonders,* 361.
87. David T. Konig, *Law and Society in Puritan Massachusetts: Essex County, 1629–1692* (Chapel Hill: University of North Carolina Press, 1979), 174; Boyer and Nissenbaum, eds., *The Salem Witch-craft Papers,* III, 963.
88. Calef, *More Wonders,* 364; Upham, *Salem Witchcraft,* II, 383.
89. Boyer and Nissenbaum, eds., *The Salem Witchcraft Papers,* III, 636–637.
90. Bryan F. Le Beau, "Philip English and the Witchcraft Hysteria," *Historical Journal of Massachusetts,* 15 (January 1987): 6.
91. Boyer and Nissenbaum, eds., *The Salem Witchcraft Papers,* I, 210.
92. Boyer and Nissenbaum, eds., *The Salem Witchcraft Papers,* III, 979; Calef, *More Wonders,* 370.
93. Boyer and Nissenbaum, eds., *The Salem Witchcraft Papers,* III, 989–991; Le Beau, "Philip English," 6.
94. Rosenthal, *Salem Story,* 219–220; Le Beau, "Philip English," 6, 17 note 35.
95. Boyer and Nissenbaum, eds., *The Salem Witchcraft Papers,* III, 985; Gragg, *Crisis,* 129–130.
96. Boyer and Nissenbaum, eds., *The Salem Witchcraft Papers,* III, 978, 995–996.
97. Boyer and Nissenbaum, eds., *The Salem Witchcraft Papers,* III, 1010–1013.
98. Boyer and Nissenbaum, eds., *The Salem Witchcraft Papers,* III, 1016–1017.
99. Boyer and Nissenbaum, eds., *The Salem Witchcraft Papers,* III, 1017–1018.
100. Boyer and Nissenbaum, eds., *The Salem Witchcraft Papers,* III, 1043–1045; Le Beau, "Philip English," 7–8.
101. Le Beau, "Philip English," 8.
102. Le Beau, "Philip English," 8, 10.
103. Upham, *Salem Witchcraft,* II, 481–482.
104. Gragg, *Crisis,* 190. Not surprisingly, no one ever petitioned for Tituba, either. Elaine G. Breslaw, *Tituba, Reluctant Witch of Salem: Devilish Indians and Puritan Fantasies* (New York: New York University Press, 1996), 177.
105. George Malcom Yool, *1692 Witch Hunt* (Bowie, MD: Heritage Books, 1992), 144; Rosenthal, *Salem Story,* 219.

EPILOGUE

1. Brian P. Levack, *The Witch-Hunt in Early Modern Europe,* 2nd ed. (London: Longman, 1995), 251–252.

2. Levack, *The Witch-Hunt,* 233; Charles Upham, *Salem Witchcraft* (Boston: Wiggin and Lunt, 1867), II, 517.
3. Richard Godbeer, *The Devil's Dominion: Magic and Religion in Early New England* (Cambridge: Cambridge University Press, 1992), 225.
4. John Demos, *Entertaining Satan: Witchcraft and the Culture of Early New England* (New York: Oxford University Press, 1982), 389.
5. Upham, *Salem Witchcraft,* II, 513.
6. Demos, *Entertaining Satan,* 387–388.
7. Upham, *Salem Witchcraft,* II, 517.
8. Levack, *The Witch-Hunt,* 240.
9. Godbeer, *The Devil's Dominion,* 226.
10. Levack, *The Witch-Hunt,* 236; Joseph Klaits, *Servants of Satan: The Age of the Witch Hunts* (Bloomington: Indiana University Press, 1985), 160.
11. Godbeer, *The Devil's Dominion,* 227, 229.
12. Klaits, *Servants of Satan,* 246–250.
13. Demos, *Entertaining Satan,* 290, 388.
14. Demos, *Entertaining Satan,* 391.
15. See Andrew Delbanco, *The Death of Satan* (New York: Farrar, Straus, and Giroux, 1995).
16. Bernard Rosenthal, *Salem Story: Reading the Witch Trials of 1692* (Cambridge: Cambridge University Press, 1993), 209; George H. Gallup Jr., *Religion in America 1996* (Princeton, NJ: Princeton Religion Research Center, 1996), 20. This might be compared to figures released in a 1988 Gallup Poll, wherein it was reported that 30 percent or less of the people living in France, Great Britain, Italy, Norway, or Sweden believed in the Devil. For a brief discussion of this, see John Updike, "Elusive Evil: An Idea Whose Time Keeps Coming," *The New Yorker,* July 22, 1966, 62–70.
17. William W. Zellner, *Countercultures: A Sociological Analysis* (New York: St. Martin's Press, 1994), 77.
18. Zellner, *Countercultures,* 78.
19. Rosenthal, *Salem Story,* 1.
20. Rosenthal, *Salem Story,* 208.
21. Upham, *Salem Witchcraft,* II, 437–438.
22. Arthur Miller, *The Crucible* (1952, reprint, New York: Bantam Books, 1959), xvii.
23. Upham, *Salem Witchcraft,* II, 430.

A Select Bibliography

BARSTOW, ANNE LLEWELLYN. *Witchcraze: A New History of the European Witch Hunts.* New York: HarperCollins, 1994.

BECKER, HOWARD S. *Outsiders: Studies in the Sociology of Deviance.* New York: Free Press, 1963.

BEHAR, RUTH. "Sexual Witchcraft, Colonialism, and Women's Powers: Views from the Mexican Inquisition," in *Sexuality and Marriage in Colonial Latin America,* ed. Asunción Lavrin. Lincoln: University of Nebraska Press, 1989.

BENTLEY, WILLIAM. *The Diary of William Bentley.* Gloucester, MA: Peter Smith, 1962.

BERCOVITCH, SACVAN. *The American Jeremiad.* Madison: University of Wisconsin Press, 1978.

BOYER, PAUL, AND STEPHEN NISSENBAUM. *Salem Possessed, The Social Origins of Witchcraft.* Cambridge, MA: Harvard University Press, 1974.

———, EDS. *Salem-Village Witchcraft: A Documentary Record of Local Conflict in Colonial New England.* Boston: Boston University Press, 1993.

————, Eds. *The Salem Witchcraft Papers: Verbatim Transcripts of the Legal Documents of the Salem Witchcraft Outbreak of 1692.* New York: De Capo Press, 1977.

BRATTLE, THOMAS. *Letter of Thomas Brattle* (1692), in George Lincoln Burr, ed., *Narratives of the Witchcraft Cases: 1648–1706.* New York: Charles Scribner's Sons, 1914.

BRAUER, SIEGFRIED. "Martin Luther on Witchcraft: A True Reformer?" in *The Politics of Gender in Early Modern Europe,* ed. J. R. Brink et al. Kirksville, MO: Sixteenth Century Journal Publishers, 1989.

BRESLAW, ELAINE G. "The Salem Witch from Barbados: In Search of Tituba's Roots," *Essex Institute Historical Collections,* 128 (October 1992), 217–238.

————. *Tituba, Reluctant Witch of Salem: Devilish Indians and Puritan Fantasies.* New York: New York University Press, 1996.

BROWN, DAVID C. "The Case of Giles Corey," *Essex Institute Historical Collections,* 121 (October 1985): 282–299.

————. "The Forfeitures at Salem, 1692." *The William and Mary Quarterly,* 3rd Series, 50 (January 1993): 85–111.

————. "The Salem Witchcraft Trials: Samuel Willards' *Some Miscellany Observations,*" *Essex Institute Historical Collections,* 122 (July 1986): 207–236.

CALEF, ROBERT. *More Wonders of the Invisible World* (1700), in George Lincoln Burr, ed. *Narratives of the Witchcraft Cases: 1648–1706.* New York: Charles Scribner's Sons, 1914.

CAPORAEL, LINNDA. "Ergotism: The Satan Loosed in Salem?" *Science,* 192 (April 2, 1976): 21–26.

CAULFIELD, ERNEST. "Pediatric Aspects of the Salem Witchcraft Tragedy," *American Journal of Diseases of Children,* 65 (May 1943): 788–802.

CERVANTES, FERNANDO. *The Devil in the New World: The Impact of Diabolism in New Spain.* New Haven: Yale University Press, 1994.

COHN, NORMAN. *Europe's Inner Demons.* New York: Basic Books, 1975.

COUDERT, ALLISON. "The Myth of the Improved Status of Protestant Women: The Case of the Witchcraze," in *The Politics of Gender in Early Modern Europe,* ed. J. R. Brink et al. Kirksville, MO: Sixteenth Century Journal Publishers, 1989.

DELBANCO, ANDREW. *The Death of Satan.* New York: Farrar, Straus, and Giroux, 1995.

DEMOS, JOHN. *Entertaining Satan: Witchcraft and the Culture of Early New England.* New York: Oxford University Press, 1982.

————. "Underlying Themes in the Witchcraft of Seventeenth Century New England," *American Historical Review,* 75 (June 1970): 1311–1326.

DOUGLAS, MARY, ED. *Witchcraft Confessions and Accusations.* London: Tavistock Publications, 1970.

DRAKE, SAMUEL G. *Witchcraft Delusion in New England.* Roxbury, MA: W.E. Woodward, 1866.

ECCLES, JOHN. *France in America,* rev. ed. Markham, Ontario: Fitzhenry and Whiteside, 1990.

ERIKSON, KAI R. *Wayward Puritans: A Study in the Sociology of Deviance.* New York: John Wiley & Sons, 1966.

GAGNON, HERVÉ. "Witchcraft in Montreal and Quebec during the French Regime, 1600–1760: An Essay on the Survival of French Mentalité in Colonial Canada," in *Wonders of the Invisible World, 1600–1900,* ed. Peter Benes. Boston: Boston University Scholarly Publications, 1995.

GILDRIE, RICHARD. *Salem, Massachusetts, 1626–1683: A Covenant Community.* Charlottesville: University of Virginia Press, 1975.

GINSBURG, CARLO. *The Night Battles: Witchcraft and Agrarian Cults in the Sixteenth and Seventeenth Centuries,* trans. John and Anne Tedeschi. Baltimore: Johns Hopkins University Press, 1983.

GODBEER, RICHARD. *The Devil's Dominion: Magic and Religion in Early New England.* Cambridge: Cambridge University Press, 1992.

GRAGG, LARRY. *Quest for Security: The Life of Samuel Parris, 1653–1720.* New York Greenwood Press, 1990.

————. *The Salem Witch Crisis.* New York: Praeger, 1992.

GREENE, DAVID L. "Bridget Bishop Conviction," *American Genealogist,* 58 (July 1982): 163.

————. "Salem Witches I: Bridget Bishop," *American Genealogist,* 57 (July 1981): 129–138.

GREENLEAF, RICHARD E. *The Mexican Inquisition of the Sixteenth Century.* Albuquerque: University of New Mexico Press, 1969.

————. *Zumarraga and the Mexican Inquisition, 1536–1543.* Washington, DC: Academy of American Franciscan History, 1961.

HALE, JOHN. *A Modest Inquiry into the Nature of Witchcraft* (1702), in George Lincoln Burr, ed., *Narratives of the Witchcraft Cases: 1648–1706.* New York: Charles Scribner's Sons, 1914.

HALL, DAVID D. "Magic and Witchcraft," in *Encyclopedia of the North American Colonies,* III, 653–664.

———. *Worlds of Wonder, Days of Judgment: Popular Religious Belief in Early New England*. New York: Alfred A. Knopf, 1989.

———. ED. *Witch–Hunting in Seventeenth-Century New England: A Documentary History, 1638–1692*. Boston: Northeastern University Press, 1991.

HANSEN, CHADWICK. "Andover Witchcraft and the Causes of the Salem Witchcraft Trials," in *The Occult in America: New Historical Perspectives*, eds. Howard Kerr and Charles L. Crow. Urbana: University of Illinois Press, 1983.

———. *Witchcraft at Salem*. New York: George Braziller, 1969.

HARLEY, DAVID. "Explaining Salem: Calvinist Psychology and the Diagnosis of Possession," *The American Historical Review*, 101 (April 1996): 307–330.

HEIMERT, ALAN, AND ANDREW DELBANCO, EDS. *The Puritans in America, A Narrative Anthology*. Cambridge: Harvard University Press, 1985.

HENNINGSEN, GUSTAV. "The Greatest Witch Trial of All: Navarre, 1609–1614," *History Today*, 30 (November 1980): 36–39.

———. *The Witches' Advocate: Basque Witchcraft and the Spanish Inquisition (1609–1614)*. trans. Ann Born. Reno: University of Nevada Press, 1980.

HILL, FRANCES. *A Delusion of Satan: The Full Story of the Salem Witch Trials*. New York: Doubleday, 1995.

HOFFER, PETER CHARLES. *The Devil's Disciples: Makers of the Salem Witchcraft Trials*. Baltimore, MD: The Johns Hopkins University Press, 1996.

———. *Law and People in Colonial America*. Baltimore, MD: The Johns Hopkins University Press, 1992.

HUTCHINSON, THOMAS. *The History of the Colony and Province of Massachusetts Bay* (1764), ed. Lawrence Shaw Mayo. Cambridge, MA: Harvard University Press, 1936.

JENNINGS, FRANCIS. *The Invasion of America: Indians, Colonialism, and the Cant of Conquest*. Chapel Hill: University of North Carolina Press, 1975.

JONES, W. R. "'Hill–Diggers' and 'Hell–Raisers': Treasure Hunting and the Supernatural in Old and New England," in *Wonders of the Invisible World: 1600–1900*, ed. Peter Benes. Boston: Boston University Scholarly Publications, 1995.

KAMEN, HENRY A. *European Society, 1500–1700*. London: Hutchinson, 1984.

————. *The Spanish Inquisition.* London: Weidenfeld & Nicolson, 1965.

KAMENSKY, JANE. "Words, Witches, and Woman Trouble: Witchcraft, Disorderly Speech, and Gender Boundaries in Puritan New England," *Essex Institute Historical Collections,* 128 (October 1992): 286–307.

KARLSEN, CAROL F. *The Devil in the Shape of a Woman: Witchcraft in Colonial New England.* New York: W. W. Norton, 1987.

KERN, LOUIS J. "Eros, the Devil, and the Cunning Woman: Sexuality and the Supernatural in European Antecedents and in the Seventeenth–Century Salem Witchcraft Cases," *Essex Institute Historical Collections,* 129 (January 1993): 3–38.

KITTREDGE, GEORGE LYMAN. *Witchcraft in Old and New England.* Cambridge: Harvard University Press, 1929.

KLAITS, JOSEPH. *Servants of Satan: The Age of the Witch Hunts.* Bloomington: Indiana University Press, 1985.

KOCH, DONALD W. "Income Distribution and Political Structure in Seventeenth–Century Salem, Massachusetts," *Essex Institute Historical Collections,* 105 (January 1969): 50–69.

KOEHLER, LYLE. *A Search for Power, The "Weaker Sex" in Seventeenth Century New England.* Urbana: University of Illinois Press, 1980.

KONIG, DAVID T. *Law and Society in Puritan Massachusetts: Essex County, 1629–1692.* Chapel Hill: University of North Carolina Press, 1979.

————. "A New Look at the Essex 'French': Ethnic Frictions and Community Tensions in Seventeenth Century Essex County, Massachusetts," *Essex Institute Historical Collections,* 110 (July 1974): 167–180.

KORS, ALAN C., AND EDWARD PETERS, EDS. *Witchcraft in Europe, 1100–1700: A Documentary History.* Philadelphia: University of Pennsylvania Press, 1972.

LANGBEIN, JOHN H. *Prosecuting Crime in the Renaissance.* Cambridge, MA: Harvard University Press, 1974.

LARNERM, CHRISTINA. *Enemies of God: The Witch-hunt in Scotland.* Baltimore, MD: The Johns Hopkins University Press, 1981.

LAWSON, DEODAT. *A Brief and True Narrative of Witchcraft at Salem Village* (1692), in George Lincoln Burr, ed. *Narratives of the Witchcraft Cases: 1648–1706.* New York: Charles Scribner's Sons, 1914.

LE BEAU, BRYAN F. "Philip English and the Witchcraft Hysteria," *Historical Journal of Massachusetts,* 15 (January 1987): 1–20.

LE FROY, J. H. *Memorial of the Discovery and Early Settlement of the Bermudas or Somers Island.* London: Longman, Green, and Co., 1879.

LEACH, DOUGLAS E. *Flintlock and Tomahawk: New England in King Philip's War.* New York: W. W. Norton, 1959.

LEVACK, BRIAN P. *The Witch-Hunt in Early Modern Europe,* 2nd ed. London: Longman, 1995.

LEVY, LEONARD W. "Accusatorial and Inquisitorial Systems of Criminal Procedure in the Beginnings," in *Freedom and Reform,* eds. Harold Hyman and Leonard Levy. New York: Oxford University Press, 1967.

LOVEJOY, DAVID S. "Satanizing the American Indian," *New England Quarterly,* 67 (December 1994): 603–621.

MACFARLANE, ALAN. *Witchcraft in Tudor and Stuart England.* New York: Harper and Row, 1970.

MAPPEN, MARC, ED. *Witches and Historians: Interpretations of Salem.* Malabar, Florida: Kreiger Publishing Company, 1980.

MATHER, COTTON. "A Brand Plucked Out of the Burning" (1693), in George Lincoln Burr, ed., *Narratives of the Witchcraft Cases: 1648–1706.* New York: Charles Scribner's Sons, 1914.

———. "Another Brand Plucked Out of the Burning" (1693), in George Lincoln Burr, ed., *Narratives of the Witchcraft Cases: 1648–1706.* New York: Charles Scribner's Sons, 1914.

———. *The Diary of Cotton Mather.* reprint, New York: Frederick Ungar, 1957.

———. *Selected Letters of Cotton Mather,* ed. Kenneth Silverman. Baton Rouge: University of Louisiana Press, 1971.

———. *The Wonders of the Invisible World* (1693) in George Lincoln Burr, ed., *Narratives of the Witchcraft Cases: 1648–1706.* New York: Charles Scribner's Sons, 1914.

MATHER, INCREASE. *Cases of Conscience Concerning Evil Spirits Personating Men.* Boston: Benjamin Harris, 1693.

MIDELFORT, H. C. ERIC. *Witch Hunting in Southwestern Germany, 1562–1684.* Stanford: Stanford University Press, 1992.

MILLER, ARTHUR. *The Crucible.* 1952, reprint, New York: Bantam Books, 1959.

MILLER, PERRY. *The New England Mind, From Colony to Province.* Cambridge, MA: Harvard University Press, 1953.

MONTER, E. WILLIAM. *Witchcraft in France and Switzerland: The Borderlands of the Reformation.* Ithaca, NY: Cornell University Press, 1976.

————. "French and Italian Witchcraft," *History Today,* 30 (November 1980): 31–35.

MORISON, SAMUEL ELIOT. *The Intellectual Life of Colonial New England.* Ithaca, NY: Cornell University Press, 1970.

NELSON, MARY. "Why Witches Were Women," in *Women: A Feminist Perspective,* ed. J. Freeman. Palo Alto, CA: Marsfield Publishing, 1979.

NETANYAHU, BENZION. *The Origins of the Inquisition in Fifteenth Century Spain.* New York: Random House, 1995.

NEVINS, WINFIELD. *Witchcraft in Salem Village.* Boston: Lee and Shepard, 1892.

NICOLLS, DAVID. "The Devil in Renaissance France," *History Today*, 30 (November 1980): 25–30.

PAGELS, ELAINE. H. *The Origin of Satan.* New York: Random House, 1995.

————. "The Social History of Satan, The 'Intimate Enemy': A Preliminary Sketch," *Harvard Theological Review,* 84 (April 1991): 105–128.

————. "The Social History of Satan, Part II: Satan in the New Testament Gospels," *Journal of the American Academy of Religion,* 62 (Spring 1994): 17–58.

PARKE, FRANCIS NEAL. "Witchcraft in Maryland," *Maryland Historical Magazine,* 31 (December 1936): 271–298.

PARKER, GEOFFREY. "The European Witchcraze Revisited," *History Today,* 30 (November 1980): 23–24.

PAYNE, DANIEL G. "Defending against the Indefensible: Spectral Evidence at the Salem Witchcraft Trials," *Essex Institute Historical Collections,* 129 (January 1993): 62–83.

PERLEY, SIDNEY. *The History of Salem, Massachusetts.* Salem: Sidney Perley, 1924.

PETERS, EDWARD. *The Magician, the Witch and the Law.* Philadelphia: University of Pennsylvania Press, 1978.

POPE, ROBERT G. *The Half–way Covenant: Church Membership in Puritan New England.* Princeton, NJ: Princeton University Press, 1969.

QUAIFE, G. R. *Godly Zeal and Furious Rage: The Witch in Early Modern Europe.* New York: St. Martin's Press, 1987.

ROSENTHAL, BERNARD. *Salem Story: Reading the Witch Trials of 1692.* Cambridge: Cambridge University Press, 1993.

RUSSELL, JEFFREY B. *A History of Witchcraft: Sorcerers, Heretics, and Pagans.* London: Thames & Hudson, 1980.

———. *Witchcraft in the Middle Ages.* Ithaca, NY: Cornell University Press, 1972.

SAWYER, RONALD C. "'Strangely Handled in All Her Lyms': Witchcraft and Healing in Jacobean England," *Journal of Social History,* 22 (Spring 1989): 461–485.

SEWALL, SAMUEL. *Samuel Sewall's Diary,* ed. Mark Van Doren. reprint, New York: Russell and Russell, 1963.

SHUMAKER, WILLIAM. *The Occult Sciences in the Renaissance.* Berkeley: University of California Press, 1972.

SILVERBLATT, IRENE. *Moon, Sun, and Witches: Gender Ideologies and Class in Inca and Colonial Peru.* Princeton, NJ: Princeton University Press, 1987.

SILVERMAN, KENNETH. *The Life and Times of Cotton Mather.* New York: Harper & Row, 1984.

SPANOS, NICHOLAS P., AND JACK GOTTLIEB. "Ergotism and the Salem Village Witch Trials," *Science,* 194 (December 24, 1976): 1390–1394.

SPRENGER, JACOB, AND HEINRICH KRAMER. *Malleus Maleficarum,* trans. Montague Summers. 1484, reprint, New York: Benjamin Blom, 1970.

STARKEY, MARION L. *The Devil in Massachusetts: A Modern Enquiry into the Salem Witch Trials.* New York: Alfred A. Knopf, 1949.

STOUT, HARRY S. *The New England Soul, Preaching and Religious Culture in Colonial New England.* New York: Oxford University Press, 1986.

TEDESCHI, JOHN. "Preliminary Observations on Writing History of the Roman Inquisition," in *Continuity and Discontinuity in Church History,* ed. F. Forrester Church and Timothy George. Leiden: Brill, 1979.

THOMAS, KEITH. *Religion and the Decline of Magic.* London: Weidenfeld & Nicholson, 1971.

TREVOR-ROPER, HUGH. "The European Witch-Craze," in *Witchcraft and Sorcery.* London: Penguin Books, 1972.

———. *The European Witch-Craze of the Sixteenth and Seventeenth Centuries and Other Essays.* New York: Harper and Row, 1969.

UPHAM, CHARLES. *Salem Witchcraft.* Boston: Wiggin and Lunt, 1867.

WEISMAN, RICHARD. *Witchcraft, Magic, and Religion in 17th-Century Massachusetts.* Amherst: The University of Massachusetts Press, 1984.

WILLARD, SAMUEL. *Some Miscellany Observations on Our Present Debates Respecting Witchcraft in a Dialogue Between S and B.* Philadelphia: William Bradford, 1692.

WINTHROP, JOHN. "A Model of Christian Charity" (1630), in *Winthrop Papers*. Boston: Massachusetts Historical Society, 1929–1944.

WOODWARD, W. ELLIOT, ED. *Records of Salem Witchcraft Copied from the Original Documents*. 1864, reprint, New York: Da Capo Press, 1969.

YOOL, GEORGE MALCOM. *1692 Witch Hunt*. Bowie, MD: Heritage Books, 1992.

ZAGORIN, PEREZ. *Rebels and Rulers, 1500–1600*. Cambridge: Cambridge University Press, 1983.

ZELLNER, WILLIAM W. *Countercultures: A Sociological Analysis*. New York: St. Martin's Press, 1994.

ZILBOORG, GREGORY. *The Medical Man and the Witch during the Renaissance*. New York: W. W. Norton, 1941.

Appendix[1]

The list includes only persons against whom legal actions were initiated during the Salem prosecutions of 1692. Many others were accused informally.

For those of the accused not given a separate case entry in *The Salem Witchcraft Papers,* the page citation for the complaint, warrant, or other reference to the accused is given after the defendant's name in parentheses. All towns and villages cited were in Massachusetts unless stated otherwise.

---

[1]   This appendix is reprinted with permission from Richard Godbeer, *The Devil's Dominion: Magic and Religion in Early New England* (NY: Cambridge University Press, 1992). Appendix B. "Persons accused during the Salem Witch Hunt." Godbeer gathered the information from Paul Boyer and Stephen Nissenbaum, eds., *The Salem Witchcraft Papers: Verbatim Transcripts of the Legal Documents of the Salem Witchcraft Outbreak,* 3 vols. (NY: Da Capo Press, 1977). It is also reprinted with permission by Cambridge University press.

Name	Town or Village	Verdict of Special Court (if any)
Arthur Abbot (I, 183)	?	
Nehemiah Abbot, Jr.	Topsfield	released[a]
John Alden	Boston	escaped
Daniel Andrew (II, 493)	Salem Village	escaped
Abigail Barker	Andover	*2
Mary Barker	Andover	*
William Barker, Sr.	Andover	*
William Barker, Jr.	Andover	*
Sarah Bassett	Lynn	
Sarah Bibber	Wenham	
Bridget Bishop	Salem Village	convicted E[3]
Edward Bishop, Jr. (III, 805)	Salem Village	escaped
Sarah Bishop	Salem Village	escaped
Mary Black	Salem Village	
Mary Bradbury	Salisbury	convicted[b]
Mary Bridges, Sr.	Andover	*
Mary Bridges, Jr.	Andover	*
Sarah Bridges	Andover	*
Hannah Bromage	Andover	
Sarah Buckley	Salem Village	
George Burroughs	Wells, Maine	convicted E
Candy (slave)	Salem Town	*
Andrew Carrier (I, 197)	Andover	*
Martha Carrier	Andover	convicted E
Richard Carrier	Andover	*
Sarah Carrier	Andover	*
Thomas Carrier, Jr.	Andover	*
Hannah Carroll (I, 235)	Salem Town	
Bethia Carter, Sr.	Woburn	
Bethia Carter, Jr. (III, 729)	Woburn	
Elizabeth Cary	Salem Town	escaped
Sarah Churchill	Charlestown	
Mary Clarke	Haverhill	
Rachel Clenton	Ipswich	
Sarah Cloyse	Salem Village	

2   * = confession
3   E = executed

(Name, continued)	*(Town or Village, continued)*	*(Verdict of Special Court, continued)*
Sarah Cole	Lynn	
Sarah Cole	Salem Town	
Elizabeth Colson	Reading	escaped?
Mary Colson (II, 539)	?	
Giles Corey	Salem Village	
Martha Corey	Salem Village	convicted E
Deliverance Dane	Andover	*
Sarah Davis (III, 956)	Wenham	
Day (f)(III, 880-881)	?	
Mary DeRich	Salem Village	
Elizabeth Dicer (II, 651)	Piscataqua, Maine	
Rebecca Dike (I, 305)	Gloucester	
Ann Dolliver	Gloucester	
Mehitabel Downing (III, 880-881)	?	
Joseph Draper (II, 335)	Andover	*
Lydia Dustin	Reading	
Sarah Dustin	Reading	
Rebecca Eames	Andover	convicted *c
Mary Easty	Salem Village	convicted E
Esther Elwell	Gloucester	
Martha Emerson	Haverhill	*
Joseph Emons	Manchester	
Mary English (III, 805)	Salem Town	escaped
Philip English	Salem Town	escaped
Thomas Farrer	Lynn	
Edward Farrington	Andover	
Abigail Faulkner, Sr.	Andover	convicted*d*
Abigail Faulkner, Jr. (II, 335)	Andover	*
Dorothy Faulkner	Andover	*
John Flood (I, 183)	Rowley	
Elizabeth Fosdick	Malden	
Ann Foster	Andover	convicted *c
Nicholas Frost	Manchester	
Eunice Frye	Andover	
Dorcas Good	Salem Village	
Sarah Good	Salem Village	convicted E
Mary Green	Haverhill	
Thomas Hardy (II, 565)	Piscataqua, Maine	

(Name, continued)	*(Town or Village, continued)*	*(Verdict of Special Court, continued)*
Elizabeth Hart	Lynn	
Rachel Hatfield (III, 880-881)	?	
Margaret Hawks	Salem Town	
Sarah Hawkes	Andover	*
Dorcas Hoar	Beverly	convicted* c
Abigail Hobbs	Topsfield	convicted e
Deliverance Hobbs	Topsfield	*
William Hobbs	Topsfield	
Elizabeth How	Topsfield	convicted E
John Howard (II, 465)	Rowley	
Elizabeth Hubbard	Salem Village	
Francis Hutchens	Haverhill	
Mary Ireson	Lynn	
John Jackson, Sr.	Rowley	
John Jackson, Jr.	Rowley	*
George Jacobs, Sr.	Salem Town	convicted E
George Jacobs, Jr.	Salem Village	escaped
Margaret Jacobs	Salem Town	*
Rebecca Jacobs	Salem Village	
Abigail Johnson (II, 499)	Andover	
Elizabeth Johnson, Sr.	?	*
Elizabeth Johnson, Jr.	?	*f
Rebecca Johnson	Andover	
Stephen Johnson	Andover	*
Mary Lacey, Sr.	Andover	convicted *c
Mary Lacey, Jr.	Andover	*
John Lee	?	
Mercy Lewis	Salem Village	
Jane Lilly	Malden	
Mary Marston	Andover	*
Susannah Martin	Amesbury	convicted E
Sarah Morey	Beverly	
Rebecca Nurse	Salem Village	convicted E
Sarah Osborne	Salem Village	
Mary Osgood	Andover	*
Elizabeth Paine (II, 339)	Charlestown	
Alice Parker	Salem Town	convicted E
Mary Parker	Andover	convicted E

(Name, continued)	(Town or Village, continued)	(Verdict of Special Court, continued)
Sarah Parker (III, 1021)	Andover	
Sarah Pease	Salem Town	
Joan Penny	Gloucester	
Hannah Post	Rowley	*
Mary Post	Rowley	f
Susannah Post	Andover	*
Margaret Prince	Gloucester	
Benjamin Proctor	Salem Village	
Elizabeth Proctor	Salem Village	convicted[d]
John Proctor	Salem Village	convicted E
Sarah Proctor	Salem Village	
William Proctor	Salem Village	*
Ann Pudeator	Salem Town	convicted E
Wilmot Reed	Marblehead	convicted E
Sarah Rice	Reading	
Abigail Roc (I, 305)	Gloucester	
Susannah Roots	Beverly	
Henry Salter	Andover	
John Sawdy	Andover	
Margaret Scott	?	convicted E
Ann Sears	Woburn	
Susannah Sheldon	?	
Abigail Somes	Salem Town	
Martha Sparks	Chelmsford	
Mary Taylor	Reading	
Tituba (slave)	Salem Village	*
Job Tookey	Beverly	
Jerson Toothaker	Billerica	
Mary Toothaker	?	*
Toothaker (f)(I, 183) (daughter of Mary)	?	
Roger Toothaker	Billerica	
Johanna Tyler	Andover	*
Martha Tyler	Andover	*
Vincent (f)(III, 880-881)	?	
Mercy Wardwell	Andover	*
Samuel Wardwell	Andover	convicted E*g
Sarah Wardwell	Andover	*f

(Name, continued)	*(Town or Village, continued)*	*(Verdict of Special Court, continued)*
Mary Warren	Salem Village	*
Sarah Wilds	Topsfield	convicted E
Ruth Wilford (II, 459)	Haverhill	
John Willard	Salem Village	convicted E
Abigail Williams	Salem Village	
Sarah Wilson, Sr.	Andover	*
Sarah Wilson, Jr. (I, 335)	Andover	*
Mary Withridge (II, 493)	Salem Village	
156	24 Different Communities	30 Convictions 44 Confessions 19 Executions

[In addition to the 19 executions, Giles Corey was pressed to death during interrogation. Lydia Dustin, Ann Foster, Sarah Osborne, and Roger Toothaker died in prison.]

a   accusation withdraw
b   escaped from prison
c   reprieved after confession
d   reprieved because pregnant
e   may have saved her life by confessing, although no record of her doing so survives
f   convicted by Superior Court of Judicature in Jan. 1693; reprieved by governor
g   withdrew his confession and so was executed

Index